The pastoral ministry of Bishop James Doyle

To Sister Helen Wynne
with gratitude for your help
and with best wishes from

Thomas McGrath

29 XI 1998

By the same author

Politics, Interdenominational Relations and Education in the Public Ministry of Bishop James Doyle of Kildare and Leighlin, 1786–1834

Religious Renewal
and Reform

in the Pastoral Ministry of
BISHOP JAMES DOYLE
of Kildare and Leighlin, 1786–1834

THOMAS McGRATH

FOUR COURTS PRESS

Set in 10.5 on 12.5 point Ehrhardt for
FOUR COURTS PRESS LTD
Fumbally Lane, Dublin 8, Ireland
e-mail: info@four-courts-press.ie
and in North America for
FOUR COURTS PRESS
c/o ISBS, 5804 N.E. Hassalo Street, Portland, OR 97213.

A catalogue record for this title
is available from the British Library.

ISBN 1-85182-371-9

Printed in England by
MPG Books, Bodmin, Cornwall

Do mo mháthair is do m'athair,
Máire agus Donncha Mac Craith

CONTENTS

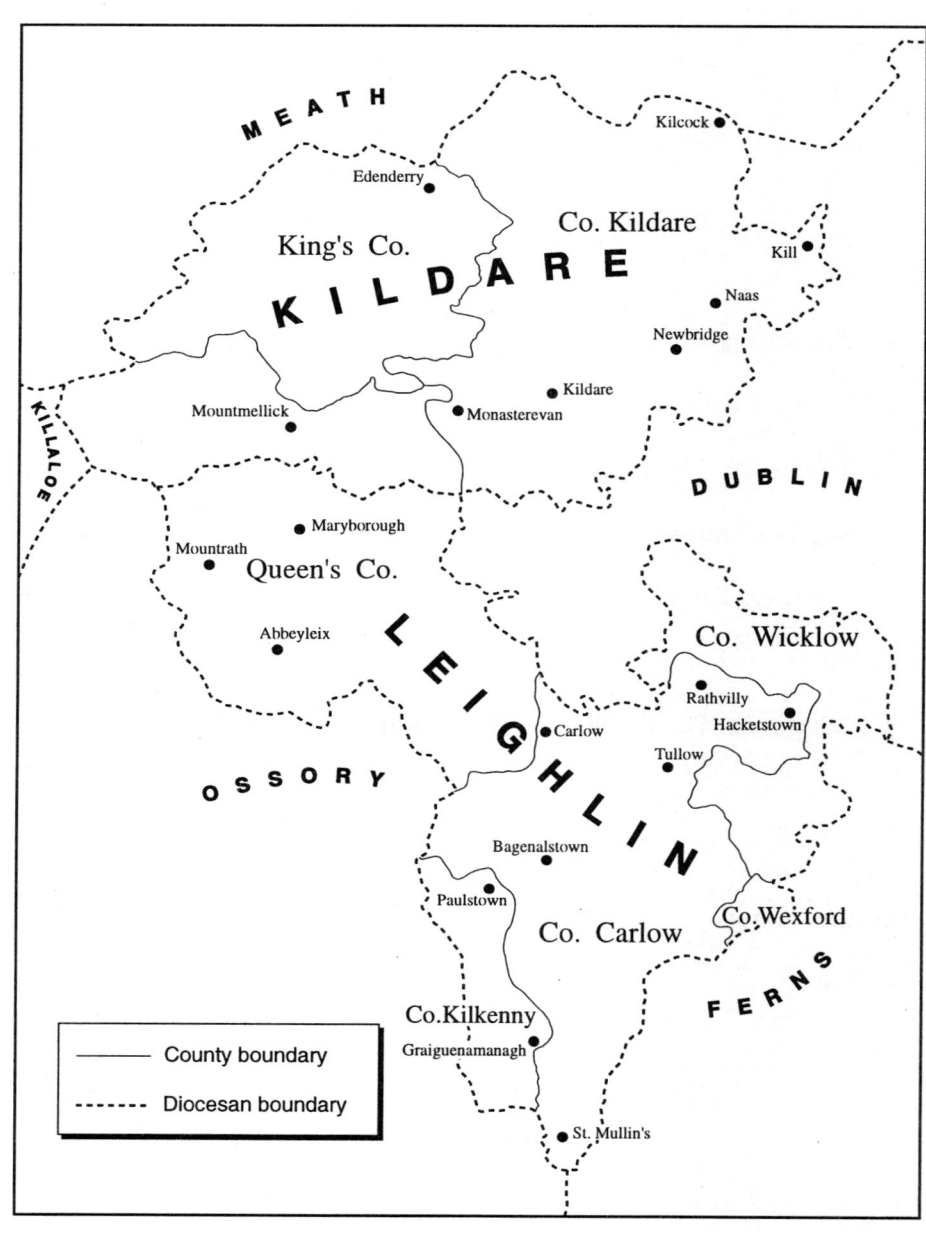

Diocese of Kildare and Leighlin, county and diocesan boundaries

Diocese of Kildare and Leighlin, parochial structure, c.1829

PREFACE

Bishop James Doyle of Kildare and Leighlin (J.K.L.), enjoyed an international reputation as an outstanding bishop in his own time and he continues to enjoy a very high historiographical reputation down to the present day. However, the last account of his life and work was published in the nineteenth century. Consequently, Doyle stands in need of a complete modern critical re-assessment. This book sets out on that process by examining Doyle's administration of his diocese and his role in the pastoral affairs of the Catholic Church at national level.

In outline this book begins with an account of Doyle's pre-episcopal career: his family background, education and early years as an Augustinian priest and Carlow College professor. The second chapter of this work analyses the context of Doyle's episcopacy: the pastoral performance and legacy of his predecessors in the See of Kildare and Leighlin. The main focus is on the Tridentine foundation underlying Doyle's renewal and reform programmes. The Tridentine framework is seen in such systems of management as the holding of synods, diocesan visitations, and the promulgation of pastorals. This chapter concludes with a survey of church building – the impressive expansionism and renewal of the physical fabric of Irish Catholicism best exemplified in the erection of Carlow Cathedral during Doyle's episcopacy. It is worth noting that Doyle's reforming episcopacy fits well into a pattern of Catholic recovery in Europe. A powerful revival of the Catholic Church took place after the trauma of the French Revolution and Napoleonic wars. This was especially evident in restoration France and in Italy.

Perhaps Bishop Doyle's renewal and reform initiatives were nowhere more evident than in his government of the secular clergy. The formation, education and conduct of his priests was always of fundamental concern to him. Chapter three examines how the Kildare and Leighlin diocesan priest was educated, how throughout his clerical life his learning was repeatedly revised and refreshed through retreats and preaching. The reforms instituted by Doyle in ecclesiastical dress, decorum and public presentation are examined as are the strictures imposed on farmer-priests and undisciplined clerics. The support of the clergy and the means by which Doyle regulated clerical incomes are analysed. The fourth chapter on regulars, brothers and nuns considers seriatim Doyle's dealings with strolling friars who were mainly Franciscans and with the Carmelites, Jesuits, Dominicans and Patricians before turning attention to the Presentation and Brigidine nuns in the diocese.

Chapter five focusses on the measures taken by Doyle to improve the faith and morals of the laity. It begins with an assessment of his drive for an educated knowledge of Catholicism among the young, especially his concentration on Sunday school catechesis and the development of confraternities. His extension of this policy through his advocacy of chapel libraries in the diocese and his inspiration and support for the Catholic Book Society at national level is also delineated. An attempt has been made to profile religious observance and the frequency of participation in the sacraments of penance and the eucharist and the levels of attendance at mass and Easter duty. Marriage-related issues and the difficulty posed by clandestine marriages are discussed in the context of Doyle's endeavour to secure the implementation of the Tridentine decree, *Tametsi*, in the province of Dublin, the diocese of Meath and the wardenship of Galway. Chapter five concludes with a survey of three superficially disparate but closely related topics: the practice of popular religion as suggested by patterns and wakes, the drink problem and Doyle's reform of holy days.

The problems faced by the church in maintaining public peace are examined in the penultimate chapter. Doyle adopted a tough, vigorously pro-active policy towards putting down non-constitutional agrarian and political activity in his diocese and his priests acted accordingly. The problems Doyle had to deal with in terms of preserving the public peace were not unique to Kildare and Leighlin but were common to adjoining dioceses such as Killaloe and Ossory. What was perhaps unusual about Doyle's response was the unrelenting nature of his opposition to illegal societies and the harshness of the measures he was prepared to countenance to defeat them. A final chapter, after recounting the end of Doyle's episcopacy in his last illness and death, discusses Doyle's impact on the diocese and assesses his estimate of the state of religion in Kildare and Leighlin juxtaposed against the findings of this work.

Kildare and Leighlin is an extensive Catholic diocese in the south-east midlands of Ireland encompassing almost the whole or parts of no less than seven counties: Carlow, Kildare, Kilkenny, Laois, Offaly, Wexford and Wicklow.

Throughout this book I have generally adopted the nomenclature used in the early nineteenth century; thus, for instance, King's County in preference to Offaly, Queen's County (Laois), Maryborough (Portlaoise), Philipstown (Daingean) etc. Kildare and Leighlin were separate dioceses until 1678 when the administration of Leighlin was granted to the bishop of Kildare, Mark Forestal, O.S.A. By a decree of Propaganda, Leighlin was united to Kildare in 1694 although in the early eighteenth century bishops of Kildare still received a separate provision to Leighlin. This may help to explain why Doyle referred to his jurisdiction as his 'diocess', 'dioceses' and 'united dioceses'. I have treated the whole unit of Kildare and Leighlin as one diocese. To avoid confusion I have preferred to refer to priests mentioned in the text as 'Rev.' rather than the contemporary 'Mr' or 'Rev. Mr'. Abbreviations follow the guidelines laid down by *Irish Historical Studies*.

I am indebted to the bishop of Kildare and Leighlin, Dr Laurence Ryan, for his interest in, and support for, my research on his predecessor. The late Bishop Patrick Lennon of Kildare and Leighlin was also most supportive of this project. I would like especially to thank Professor Donal McCartney who first encouraged the work. Professor Donal Kerr was also helpful from the outset. I wish to thank Monsignor Dermot Farrell, Professor Seamus Smyth and colleagues in Maynooth for providing a pleasant work environment.

I owe a debt of gratitude to former presidents of Carlow College, Rev. Matthew Kelly, Monsignor John McDonald, and the current president, Rev. Kevin O'Neill, for their welcome and kindness in Ireland's oldest third-level Catholic college. When the eminent French Catholic, Montalembert, visited Carlow College in 1830 and passed a day with 'the celebrated Bishop Doyle, the most eminent of Irish prelates' and several of the college professors, he described the hospitality of his reception as altogether Homeric. If Montalembert were to return to Carlow College he would find that the hospitality is still Homeric. I am sincerely grateful to Rev. Kevin O'Neill, who has been an enthusiastic supporter of this project since its inception. The vice-president of Carlow College, Rev. John McEvoy, and the chancellor of the diocese, Rev. Thomas McDonnell, have also been most helpful over many years.

I am also very grateful to Rev. Pádraig Ó Máille and John Cullen who both read and commented on this work. I am particularly grateful to my eagle-eyed copy-editor, Sr Helen Wynne, who made many valuable suggestions. The following all helped in one way or another over several years: Rev. Carlos Alonso, Jack Burtchaell, the late Monsignor P.J. Brophy, Rev. Brendan Byrne, Rev. Gerald Byrne, Archbishop Dermot Clifford, Dr Niall Coll, Professor R.V. Comerford, Monsignor Thomas Coonan, Professor Patrick J. Corish, Professor L.M. Cullen, Rev. James Dollard, Dr Hugh Fenning, Sheila Foley, Sr Anne Holton, John Joyce, James Keenan, Rev. Gerald Kennedy, Dr Noel Kissane, Helen Litton, Gerard Lyne, Professor V.A. McClelland, Rev. John McCullagh, the late Dr Fergal McGrath, Rev. Henry MacNamara, Dr Ambrose Macaulay, Martin Maher, Canon Eoin Mangan, Dr John Mannion, Professor F.X. Martin, Rev. Michael Melvin, Rev. Con Moloney, Dr Thomas Morrissey, the late Monsignor Ignatius Murphy, Professor John A. Murphy, Martin Murphy, Seamus Murphy, Dr William Nolan, Brendan Ó Cathaoir, Eva Ó Cathaoir, Dr Liam Ó Caithnia, Liam Ó Duibhir, Rev. Christopher O'Dwyer, Dr Peter O'Dwyer, Dr Fergus Ó Fearghail, Michael O'Hanrahan, Dr Mary O'Riordan, Sr Teresa O'Shea, Michael Purcell, Professor J.V. Rice, David Sheehy, Mary Sheehy, the late Monsignor Sean Swayne, Dom Mark Tierney, James Townsend, Rev. Finbarr Tracey, Brother Linus H. Walker, Dr Kevin Whelan, Penelope Woods, and Dr C.M. Woolgar.

I wish to express my appreciation of the staff of the many libraries and archives where I have worked. The following institutions wherein much of this work was researched were particularly helpful: the National Library of Ireland, the Royal Irish Academy and the National Archives. I am also indebted to my publisher Dr Michael Adams and his colleagues Martin Healy, Ronan Gallagher and Martin Fanning in the Four Courts Press.

Finally I wish to thank the McGraths of The Park, Ballingarry, Co. Tipperary: my brothers, Seamus and Denis and my sisters, Marie, Clare, Carmel and Philomena. My greatest debt of gratitude is expressed in the dedication.

THE MAKING OF A BISHOP

The family background of Bishop James Doyle has proved to date exceptionally difficult to recover and the available information is still lamentably thin. About 1770 James Doyle, father of Bishop Doyle, became a tenant of the lands of Mullinderry, on the Leslie estate, alongside the Owenduff river in Clongeen parish in the barony of Shelmaliere West in south Wexford. Though evidently of respectable origins, his strong-willed but erratic disposition led to a decline in his fortunes. He and his family resided in one of the out-offices (which still exists under the name of the 'old barn') of the roofless ruin of Mullinderry Castle.[1]

It was probably in the early 1750s that his first marriage took place to Miss Mary Downes of Burkestown in County Wexford. This was an important kinship link as she was a scion of one of Wexford's old Irish Catholic families which had been dispossessed in the seventeenth century but which still (along with similarly disadvantaged old Norman Catholic families) constituted a significant landed middle class who regarded themselves as natural leaders of the community though their avenues to prominence and power lay not so such in politics as in commerce and religion. Mary Downes was a sister of Bryan Downes, P.P. of the parishes of Tintern, Clongeen and Inch and dean of the diocese of Ferns. Five children, three boys and two girls, resulted from her marriage to James Doyle. The social status of the family can be gauged from their occupations and marriage alliances. The eldest, James, born in 1755, was educated in France and became a medical doctor; he married Mary Rossiter of the distinguished old Norman family.[2] His brother Peter was also educated in France, recipient of B.A. and M.A. degrees from Douay.[3] He succeeded his uncle as parish priest of Tintern, Clongeen and Inch and was named a rural dean of Ferns. Thomas became a ship's captain and was possibly among those members of the family who saw service with the East India Company.[4] Both daughters married comfortably: Catherine, to Martin Howlett whose family became the leading mercantile and shipping family in New Ross in the nineteenth century; Alicia, to a farmer named Pierce of Piercestown, also in County Wexford.

James Doyle, senior, was impulsive and idiosyncratic by nature. He speculated in land and made improvements beyond his means to his farm with the consequence that he fell into debt and was unable to retain possession of Mullinderry.[5] About 1780 he moved from Mullinderry to a small farm at

Ballygalvert, between Ballinvegga and Donard, about six miles from New Ross in the direction of Enniscorthy. When his fortunes were at this low ebb his first wife died and he contracted a second marriage to Anne Warren of Loughnageer. She was a Catholic of Quaker extraction[6] who has been delineated as a woman of 'almost masculine strength of judgement'.[7]

Four children, three boys and one girl, came of this union. Little is known of George who appears to have been rather dissolute and who died young in 1815. Patrick was a sizar in T.C.D. from which he graduated B.A. in 1807; he was called to the Irish Bar in 1811.[8] At the outset of a legal and political career which promised much he died in 1814 of tuberculosis, which ran in the family.[9] The only daughter of the second marriage, Mary, married a neighbouring farmer, Dillon of Knockstown. The last child of James Doyle and Anne Warren, the future bishop, was born in September 1786, three weeks after his father's death. The exact date of birth is unknown.[10] Fitzpatrick stated[11] that the child was christened James Warren Doyle but nowhere in his correspondence or published work did James Doyle use the Warren name.

Our subject received his earliest education, probably until the age of twelve, from his capable mother who taught in an elementary school at Clonleigh, near Ballygalvert.[12] As a twelve-year-old Doyle was a witness to the 1798 rebellion which convulsed County Wexford. By early June of that year the insurgents, nominally United Irishmen, had captured most of the county with the exception of the walled town of New Ross which was of strategic importance as it guarded the southern-most crossing of the Barrow and contained the rebels in the south-eastern corner of Ireland. On 5 June 1798 the insurgents under their reluctant leader Bagenal Harvey attacked New Ross in one of the most ferocious battles of the entire rebellion. A laconic entry in the mass book of the Augustinian priory in New Ross recorded the grim outcome: 'hodie repulsus est hostis rebellis ab obsidione oppidi cum magna caede, puta 3,000'.[13] Ballygalvert was on an important approach route to New Ross travelled by the rebels. At some stage during the progress of the rebellion young Doyle was incautiously sauntering along the banks of the Barrow river with his cousin Martin Doyle when they found themselves caught in the middle of a conflict between crown and rebel forces. They escaped from this dangerous predicament by hiding in a clump of furze.[14] A relation of Doyle fell on the rebel side at the battle of Oulart,[15] while his brother James was surgeon to a yeomanry corps.[16] There is an oral tradition that the Warrens of south Wexford fought with the rebels. After the rebellion Doyle saw the spiked heads of its leaders, Harvey, Keogh, and Colclough in Wexford town.[17] Between 1798 and 1800 Doyle attended a school under the management of a Mr Grace, at Rathgarogue, in which Catholics and Protestants were educated together, though they remained conscious of their religious differences.[18] He attended an Augustinian school in New Ross between 1800 and 1804.[19]

The Augustinians could date their arrival in New Ross from the early fourteenth century. The Austin friars first settled there before 1320. They had been turned out of their monastery at the dissolution in 1539. From then until the third decade of the eighteenth century their presence in New Ross, though always tentative and dependent on the prevailing level of anti-Catholic hostility, was rarely extinguished for long. In 1725 Joseph Rossiter, O.S.A., began building a priory, and three years later erected a public church. His nephew, also Joseph Rossiter, was prior from 1760 until his death in 1803.[20] The house books which date from 1783 indicate that the community was very small. In 1800 the detailed monthly accounts of income and expenditure were signed by only three friars: Rossiter the prior, and the brothers Philip and John Crane.[21] The income of the priory derived from collections received at masses said in their own church, from not insubstantial bequests for masses for the dead which were adhered to carefully, and from the traditional quest.[22] In 1796 the community secured a lease of five acres known as the Bowling Green.[23] Land was also rented in Irishtown for the upkeep of horses and a couple of cows and pigs, but a house book entry for 13 December 1802 recorded the payment of nineteen shillings 'to Perry Bryan to defray the expenses of an ejectment although we had regularly payed our rent of meadow in Irishtown'.[24]

From the 1780s the Augustinians maintained a small classical school in the town. John Rice, brother of Edmund Rice, tutored there in 1792 before being sent to Rome to pursue his studies.[25] Hopes of opening a more ambitious undertaking were clouded by the 1798 rebellion. However, shortly after the rising, John Crane opened a 'classical academy' which continued in existence until 1804. As we have mentioned, Doyle attended here from his fourteenth to eighteenth year. The academy was well conducted, but its curriculum may have been rather limited with most emphasis being placed on the classics and English.[26] John Furlong, an elderly novice, was an usher in the academy in 1802 when he taught Doyle classics for three months. He later contended that the academy was not of the highest class and that there were large gaps in Doyle's learning as a result.[27] Given Doyle's assessment of Furlong, namely that his notions of right and wrong were not such as could be acted upon in ordinary society, the latter's testimony must be approached with some caution. In these years a strong relationship of mutual esteem and affection grew up between the conductor of the school, John Crane, who became prior in 1803, and Doyle whom the former called his child.[28] It seems more than likely that Crane's fatherly influence encouraged Doyle's vocation and that a decision was made in his eighteenth year.[29] On 28 September 1804 his mother, Anne Doyle, died.[30] In January 1805 he entered the Augustinian order and undertook his novitiate year at the Grantstown house on the south Wexford coast where the prior, William Doyle, no relation, held a doctorate in theology.[31]

The transition from layman to intending cleric was probably not all that difficult for Doyle. He came of a family familiar with the milieu of priests. If we look at the 1704 registration of the clergy, we find that two Doyles were returned as parish priests in the diocese of Ferns. So indeed also were two Downes.[32] Doyle would have known Dean Downes and his brother who was also a parish priest in Ferns. More influential however would have been the example of his own half-brother Peter who was already a parish priest in Ferns.[33] There was also the example of his cousin and childhood friend, Martin Doyle, who had entered Carlow College and become a priest of the diocese of Kildare and Leighlin.[34]

Why Doyle entered the regular rather than the secular clergy admits of no simple answer. One may presume that his school experiences of the small Augustinian community in New Ross impressed him favourably. A more fundamental factor was Doyle's anxiety to cut himself off from the cares of the world and to indulge his deep love of solitude.[35] His disposition was quiet and studious and he felt himself more suited, more attuned to the lifestyle of a regular than to the vicissitudes of the secular mission. Later a dichotomy inevitably developed between his contemplative disposition and his public pursuits. This curious duality of his episcopal career was a source of stress and tension but was also perhaps the forge of his creativity. Another consideration, more amenable perhaps to historical analysis, influencing Doyle's choice of the regulars is found in his *Essay on the Catholic Claims* where he observed that 'as a clergyman, I feel sensibly the evils which arise from a kind of eleemosynary support – it was one of the motives which, disposed me at an early period, to prefer a collegiate to a missionary life'.[36] In so far as reliance on public support or charity, as exemplified in the quest, was practised in his own order it was repugnant to him. He characterised the ostiatim or door-to-door begging of the Discalced Augustinians in Ireland as a 'degradation', contending that it lowered the dignity of these clergymen per se and in the eyes of the public.[37] But the die was cast and on the successful completion of his novitiate year Doyle took the vows of voluntary poverty, obedience and chastity and was professed on 16 January 1806 for the New Ross priory.[38]

In spring 1806 Doyle and three fellow seminarians – Nicholas Clayton, James Hanlon and Augustine McDermott[39] – were sent by the order to further their education on the continent at the grandiose[40] Augustinian College de Graca in the university city of Coimbra in central Portugal. Doyle was received gratis into the Augustinian house where he attended lectures and, after more than a year's serious application, was prepared for matriculation as a student of the university at the beginning of the 1807–8 academic year. He registered to study rational and moral philosophy on 26 October 1807.[41]

The rationalist philosophy of the Enlightenment posed serious difficulties for European seminaries. Doyle's account of the crisis of faith which he underwent in Coimbra, written retrospectively in 1825, is the only documentary source for this turning point in his life. The passage exemplifies his typically stylish prose:

I had scarcely finished my classical studies and had entered college when

I found myself surrounded by the disciples or admirers of d'Alembert, Rousseau, and Voltaire; I frequently traversed in company with them, the halls of the Inquisition, and discussed in the area of the Holy Office those arguments or sophisms for the suppression of which this awful tribunal was ostensibly employed. At that time the ardour of youth, the genius of the place, the spirit of the time, as well as the example of my companions, prompted me to inquire into all things, and to deliberate whether I should take my station amongst the infidels, or remain attached to Christianity. I recollect, and always with fear and trembling, the danger to which I rashly exposed the gifts of faith and Christian morality which I had received from a bounteous God; and since I became a man, and was enabled to think like a man, I have not ceased to give thanks to the Father of mercies, who did not deliver me over to the pride and presumption of my own heart. But even then, when all things which could have influence on a youthful mind combined to induce me to shake off the yoke of Christ, I was arrested by the majesty of Religion; her innate dignity, her grandeur and solemnity, as well as her sweet influence upon the heart, filled me with awe and veneration. I found her presiding in every place, glorified by her votaries, and respected or feared by her enemies. I looked into antiquity, and I found her worshipped by Moses; and not only by Moses, but that Numa and Plato, though in darkness and error, were amongst the most ardent of her votaries. I read attentively the history of the ancient philosophers as well as lawgivers, and discovered that all of them paid their homage to her as to the best and purest emanation of the one supreme, invisible and omnipotent God. I concluded that religion sprang from the Author of our being, and that it conducted man to his last end. I examined the systems of religion prevailing in the East; I read the Koran with attention; I perused the Jewish History, and the History of Christ, of his Disciples, and of his Church, with an intense interest, and I did not hesitate to continue attached to the religion of our Redeemer, as alone worthy of God; and being a Christian, I could not fail to be a Catholic.[42]

Doyle had been a student at Coimbra for approximately a year and a half when, in one of the most significant long-term decisions of the Napoleonic wars, a French army under General Junot crossed through Spain and invaded Portugal in November 1807. The Portuguese royal family fled Lisbon for Brazil leaving a short-lived Council of the Regency in their stead. Junot quickly established complete French control over the country. His army, while exacting rigorous levies throughout the countryside, was generally well-behaved, no doubt because the Portuguese made no resistance to their occupation. The French seized church valuables, as Doyle recorded. 'I saw at that time 98 yoke of oxen pass through Coimbra laden with silver and other precious commodities from the province of

Tras os montes and Minho, such were the immense quantities of silver found in churches'.[43] As a British subject Doyle was taken prisoner by the French for possibly a month though then allowed on parole for six months until a popular uprising against the French in Spain in early May 1808 sparked off a similar revolt in Portugal.[44] Coimbra knew nothing of the Portuguese rising until after Oporto had fallen: 'there were only a few French in Coimbra who were surprised a few days after by some Portuguese militia and countrymen (for the regulars had all been disbanded and marched into Spain) and so the revolution spread over the country and gained strength and confidence, from the landing of Sir Arthur Wellesley ... all was confusion until the battle of Vimeiro'.[45]

The students at Coimbra, among whom the Irish were prominent, joined the Portuguese resistance forces. Doyle and his Irish colleagues appear to have been employed as language interpreters (rather than as soldiers) with the relieving British forces.[46] Augustine McDermott attended the British officer, Lord Burghersk, at the battle of Vimeiro where, on 21 August 1808, Sir Arthur Wellesley defeated Junot's army.[47] However, at this important juncture, changes in the hierarchical command structure, of the British army brought about by the arrival of two English generals with higher rank but, as it happened, lesser vision than Wellesley, prevented the latter from following up his success by crushing the remnants of the French army.[48] The British generals in fact sued for peace and the resulting agreement between the British and the French, known as the Convention of Cintra, outraged English public opinion and earned the military commanders, including Wellesley, courts martial. The convention decried by Gash as 'unnecessary and humiliating' was signed on 30 August 1808 on terms most unusually favourable to the French.[49] Junot was allowed to withdraw his army in British transports with its arms intact to France where it was to be free to re-enter the war. Moreover the French army was allowed to carry off the spoils of war it had plundered from the Portuguese. Fitzpatrick has claimed that Doyle and Clayton accompanied the British negotiator Colonel Murray to the convention but this seems unlikely.[50] Doyle was thoroughly dismissive of the outcome of Cintra and he subsequently rather acidly commented with a precisianism that was to become his hallmark that

> it was only then the Portuguese began to reflect for priests and friars who exulted in the opportunity of changing monastic discipline for anarchy kept the minds of the people in a ferment until now, but the idea of the French being permitted to return home loaded with the goods of Portugal made every wise man foresee even then that the interests of England and France were the real cause of the war and those of Portugal the pretext. The disgust and hatred of the English rose to such a degree at this time that I thought it necessary not to leave my room for some days for fear of being publicly insulted as an English subject ... the governor even received

me quite coolly when I ventured abroad tho' before I was caressed by him as an interpreter and confidante ....[51]

Evidently Doyle was well-known in several quarters. He acknowledged in his journal that from the bishop of Coimbra (the three-times rector-reformer of the University, Francisco de Lemos de Faria Pereira Coutinho) he had 'often received the most marked attention ...'.[52] Furthermore in his pastoral letter of June 1823 he stated: 'We have at an early period of our life rejected the favours of the great, and fled even from the smiles of a Court ...'.[53] This was apparently an allusion to an offer of employment in the Portuguese royal household.[54] In 1808 Sir Arthur Wellesley established a foothold for England on the continent and Portugal became a centre of operations against the French in the Peninsula almost until the last year of the war. The agitated state of Portugal led to the recall of the Irish Augustinian students whose studies had been much interrupted by the war. The seminarians including Doyle arrived back in Ireland in December 1808[55] without completing their studies and having spent somewhat more than two and a half years in Portugal. The archives of the University of Coimbra record that Doyle matriculated in the first year of the rational and moral philosophy course on 29 November 1808. Thus ended an eventful period in Doyle's life encompassing not alone the benefits of a continental education but 'imprisonment in a foreign country, and all manner of distress, as well as the most alluring prospects'.[56]

Doyle returned to New Ross. Edward Wakefield who visited the town on 16 July 1809 found four priests and six young men in the Augustinian house. He left an account of the support of the priory of which Doyle was now a member:

> Their establishment is supported by contributions, which they levy on the farmers in the country, and to whom they pay regular visits on horse-back, attended by a servant. On these occasions, they generally give previous notice, and after preaching, a collection is made for them among the hearers. Their principal business is to officiate for any of the priests when prevented from performing their duty through illness or any other cause; but as they are competitors with the priests, for worldly gain, a great jealousy subsists between them. The collections consist of corn, butter, eggs and other articles, as well as money.[57]

Doyle could not be ordained until he reached the canonically required age of twenty-three years and one day. As he did not know the precise date of his birth he waited until 1 October 1809 before entering the priesthood. On that date he and John A. Furlong were ordained in Enniscorthy by Dr Patrick Ryan, coadjutor bishop of Ferns. Subsequently Bishop Ryan, who had a hearty dislike of the regulars, refused to examine Doyle and Furlong for faculties within the diocese of

Ferns. According to Fitzpatrick the difficulty was overcome when the vicar-general granted faculties.[58]

In 1809 the provincial of the Augustinian order in Ireland was the celebrated Dr Philip Crane. From 1788 to 1798 he had been rector of San Matteo, the Irish novitiate house in Rome, until it was razed to the ground during the French occupation of the city. During the revolution in France in 1792 Dr Crane saved Charles Tottenham of New Ross from the guillotine. Tottenham, no friend of Catholicism, repaid the favour in 1808 when he leased the site of the old parish chapel of New Ross to the Augustinians for the very reasonable rent of ten shillings per annum.[59]

On 20 November 1809, less than two months after Doyle's ordination, the provincial opened a college in New Ross for the education of Augustinian seminarians to whom the continent was now completely closed for the duration of the Napoleonic wars. Doyle gave Dr Crane the lion's share of the credit for founding this college though he himself was actively involved. Doyle had charge of finances; subscriptions received for the institution from the houses of the order in Ireland and from individuals were entered in careful detail by him in a housebook.[60]

In this college the provincial himself undertook to teach theology; the newly-ordained Doyle was appointed professor of philosophy while he continued as a student of theology.[61] The student body was ten in number and included Doyle's colleagues from Coimbra whom he had now obviously surpassed academically. Four of these students – Augustine McDermott, Daniel O'Connor, Charles Stuart and Bernard O'Neill – were later to become provincials in turn.[62] This was Doyle's first experience of teaching and that he was not unduly rigorous is perhaps suggested by a remark he made on the death in 1812 of the rather strict Dr James Lanigan, Catholic bishop of Ossory: 'he was very pious but very intolerant and would make a good inquisitor. I hope this kind of mental severity did not injure his soul as who can overcome all the prejudices of education'.[63]

THE AUGUSTINIAN FRIAR

During his residence in the priory at New Ross, James Doyle was a member of board of the Houghton fever hospital and dispensary. The act of foundation (1806) stipulated that twelve Catholics and an equal number of Protestants, including the rector and parish priest of New Ross, should govern the hospital. The hospital, established in 1809, received an annual endowment of £300 from the Houghton estate. Doyle was probably nominated to the board by Dean William Chapman, parish priest of New Ross. The rector of New Ross, Rev. James Morgan, sat on the board with his colleague Rev. George Whitmore Carr. The board breakfasted together (at their own expense) every Monday morning for the purpose of managing the affairs of the hospital. Doyle later attributed the religious harmony which prevailed in New Ross (only ten years after a bloodbath) to the goodwill generated by the work of this interdenominational board for charitable purposes.[64]

Corish has remarked that after 1798 despite fairly savage repression County Wexford returned somewhat mysteriously to its peaceful ways.[65] Cullen has pointed out that the south of the county escaped the destruction of 1798 much more than north Wexford.[66] In New Ross the dinner given annually by the Augustinians at the start of the summer vacation was attended by Protestants. But of course Protestantism, either in its religious beliefs or political attitudes, was not a monolithic entity in Ireland. A clear distinction must be drawn between liberal and ultra-Protestants. However, tensions permeated by confessional politics were never far from the surface after 1798 even if Catholic attitudes were characterised by political quietism. An attempt by the government to muster anti-emancipation petitions from the Irish counties late in 1812 moved Lord Courtown to write to Charles Tottenham, urging him to convene a meeting of New Ross Protestants, if he thought he could thereby obtain a majority against emancipation. Doyle watched and noted this development: 'Tottenham has been able to do so, aided principally by the exertions of ministers of the Established church such as Handcock and Glascott of Sutton's parish and Morgan of Ross, already noted for his cruel exactions of tithes'. But even in Wexford, Doyle added, the number of friendly Protestants was at least equal to those who were hostile.[67]

We are fortunate that a journal which Doyle maintained by monthly entries while in New Ross priory is extant. Entries were made between 28 November 1811 and 25 December 1812. The entry for 12 April 1812 reads: 'I have neglected my journal for more than a month. I know not to what I should attribute such neglect unless to an habitual indolence to which I fear I am subject'.[68] Doyle became his own severest critic and during his later career drove himself almost relentlessly while maintaining that he was doing very little.[69] His journal of 1811–12 is essentially reportage and commentary on contemporary political affairs. It contains hardly any religious reflections or remarks by the author on his circumstances in New Ross, the ecclesiastical and social life of the town, his family or friends. The only reference to a family member is significantly a political one. A resolution pledging Catholics not to give their support to any electoral candidate who supported the prime minister, Perceval (who was hostile to the Catholic claims), had been drawn up by his brother, Counsellor Doyle, at a Waterford meeting and afterwards passed at all such meetings in the country.[70]

The journal was sporadically written in Doyle's twenty-fifth and twenty-sixth years. Its entries have no particular order, there is no paragraphing and no sign of re-writing. Doyle wrote fluently, clearly and with rapidity.[71] The value of the journal thus lies in its spontaneity. When Doyle commented upon the passing events of his time his perspective was international not local: the activities of the Luddites in England; the king's illness and the appointment of the regent; the assassination of the prime minister. He identified understandably with the progress of Wellesley's army in the Peninsula; speculated on whether Napoleon's retreat from Moscow had a parallel in history; noted the succession of Robert Peel as Chief Secretary for Ireland and paid much attention to the Catholic Committee which changed its name in 1812 to the Catholic Board. At its meetings in 1811 a lawyer named O'Connell had become conspicuous: 'he spoke prettily and sensibly, there were many other speakers but generally speakers of nonsense ...'.[72]

In his journal Doyle was always appreciative of a good speech whether it came from the Bar, the Catholic Board or the houses of parliament. Henry Grattan was a great orator in an era which could boast men of the calibre of Pitt and Fox. Doyle's high opinion of Grattan as a liberal Protestant, an orator and an Irishman is very much evidenced. He followed the progress of Grattan's Catholic relief bill attentively. Grattan, he wrote, 'spoke the sense of a vast majority of Irish Protestants'; 'his speech ... comprised every argument within the sphere of reason and every beauty within the reach of fancy, it admitted of no answer and could not be added to, it was Grattan for his country'.[73] Doyle tended to idealise liberal Protestants and there is a distinct tendency to rhetoric in remarks such as those made on the performance of the pro-Catholic Lord Donoughmore in the house of lords: 'he spoke as an Irishman and a Hutchinson whose honour was never tarnished, whose patriotism was never pliant and whose courage was never questioned'.[74] The journal was rarely mundane though sometimes naively idealistic; it was the private work of a young man who had not yet reached full intellectual maturity. It was always committed and enthusiastic, now and again displaying flashes of the penetrating insight allied to vigorous conviction which was to be such a distinctive feature of his subsequent published works.

The importance of Doyle's journal is that it enables us to discern the politics of this very politically conscious individual when he was in his mid-twenties and not yet writing for a public audience. A number of journal entries vividly capture the essence of Doyle's political beliefs at this time. His remarks on William Cobbett indicate that Doyle favoured parliamentary reform:

> he is looked [upon] as the best politician in the empire but seems partial to a Republican form of government yet every person not prejudiced believes he would be content with a thorough reformation in the house of commons as that would give us a real Republic and a nominal monarchy – many are divided in opinion as to the effects of reform but all who are disinterested agree that the experiment of a radical reform should be made as a partial one will only prolong the system and tho the king and lords did become a cypher in the constitution the people would be better off than they are.

Doyle revealed himself to be open-minded, liberal and decidedly patriotic. He was a well-wisher to liberation struggles worldwide:

> The revolution in South-America ... proceeds as every lover of freedom should wish .... In the United States ... the congress which is decidedly in favour of their president, will determine their own independence or submit to British and French tyranny. May the spirit of Washington direct their proceedings and may liberty preserve there a resting place ....[75]

> ... the Irish government has again committed itself with the people who are all its avowed enemies, they are thought by many as endeavouring to excite the country to rebellion that they might secure their despotic sway on the ruins of liberty ... the people will suffer whatever the government may inflict but if their complaints be not redressed providence has disposed that Ireland should suffer ....

> O'Connor ... the lineal descendant of the monarchs of this country ... is a man of great ability and persecuted worth, the Irish nation should often reflect in the present times that such a man exists, the Irish government should fear him, he is powerful in talent and in name. He may one day be of use to his country – Oh that Ireland could possess a constitution and he the executive magistrate he might be a second Washington or certainly a Madison.[76]

The fall of the ministry on 21 May 1812 delighted Doyle and he harboured fond hopes of the succession of a pro-emancipation government perhaps led by Marquis Wellesley, whose previous refusal to take a place in the cabinet had reflected greatly to his credit in Doyle's eyes: 'thus we see that the progress of truth and justice though slow is sure'. However his entry for 17 June 1812 tells a tale: 'When writing the last article my heart beat in unison with the nation, at the resignation of the ministers, how fatally have we been all disappointed, the selfsame ministry which then resigned is now re-appointed'.[77]

His patriotism is the chief characteristic of these journal entries. The welling up of his ardent feelings for Ireland did sometimes result in inconsistencies. When Spencer Perceval was assassinated in May 1812 Doyle reflected that he was, 'a great man in every respect' though he did not approve of all his measures. When parliament dissolved a month early in October 1812 to avoid being forced into a committee on the Catholic claims, Doyle imprecated against 'the parliament that voted a monument to S. Perceval who brought the country to ruin'.[78]

It was almost inevitable that in his journal Doyle should make some reference to the veto issue which sharply divided Irish Catholic opinion. He recorded a very critical and dismissive attitude towards the inconsistency of the Irish hierarchy in their handling of the question:

> the decisions of our Catholic bishops about this time [1799–1808] were truly disgusting; one day they would grant [the veto] another day they would not grant; a few of them would promise for all and when they all

met would disavow their own work. Dr Milner who was their official agent
subscribed to their decisions when disapproving of the veto tho he was
one of the first to recommend it ... he published many pamphlets in defence of himself and his opinions but he has sunk I believe like Lucifer
never more to rise ... as to my part I would grant a limited veto as it would
destroy the present system of nominating bishops and restore in reality
the weight of the second order of the clergy, for the government or rather
the whigs would agree (at least their chief men have said so) to the election
by chapter and metropolitan (as practised long ago in the church) of three
candidates on two of whom the crown would exercise its negative.[79]

Doyle's attitude to the whole question of the appointment of Irish Catholic bishops and the veto evolved in line with Irish Catholic opinion. In 1825 he stated
before parliamentary committees on the state of Ireland that there were absolutely no circumstances whatsoever in which he would consent to the English
monarch having a veto in Irish Catholic episcopal appointments. If the British
managed to secure the approval of the pope for such an arrangement he would
resign his See 'and I hope there is not a bishop in Ireland who would not do the
same'.[80] In 1825 he also stated: '... I have observed since I came to manhood, that
there have been uninterrupted and strong efforts made to injure, and even to
subvert the Catholic religion in Ireland'.[81]

CARLOW COLLEGE PROFESSOR

The year 1813, when he moved to Carlow College, was, in retrospect, one of the
turning points in Doyle's life. Carlow College was then only twenty years in existence as a functioning lay college and seminary. The college was founded by
Bishop James Keefe assisted by his coadjutor Bishop Daniel Delany. The establishment followed upon the removal or relaxation of the penal laws against Catholic
education and was a reaction against the pervasive influence of the Enlightenment in continental seminaries.[82] The earliest known reference to work on the
college, which in appearance has the character more of an eighteenth-century
great house than an institutional building, is to 1785, though it has been strongly
contended that work began as early as 1782.[83] Lack of funds and objections from
the Established church delayed the completion and opening of the college until
1793.[84]

The large college building, chapel and infirmary, enclosed by a ten foot high
wall, was funded by weekly subscriptions at a cost which by 1800 ran to little
short of £6,000. Loss of students to the government founded and funded
Maynooth College and a significant rise in the cost of living seriously threatened
to close the college in 1800.[85] The first president of the college was Dean Henry

Staunton, parish priest of Carlow. He filled the office for twenty-one years without a salary while remaining pastor of Carlow.[86]

The first eight students of Carlow College were already priests when they entered.[87] They studied theology for three years having presumably completed their classical and philosophical studies in academies such as the one managed by Bishop Lanigan in Kilkenny city.[88] These priest-students epitomise the compromises in ecclesiastical training forced on the Irish Catholic church in the seventeenth and eighteenth centuries. They were in the tradition of the young men of the penal era who were ordained priests before they went abroad for their theological education. Once ordained they could secure their livelihood from mass-stipends even though they had no more than a grounding in the classics and a knowledge of the catechism of the Council of Trent. In 1793, with revolutionary France out of bounds for clerical studies, it became essential that these priests receive further education at home.

Among the first Carlow College staff were three French émigrés, Nogier, La Brune and Chabaux, who returned to France when the hierarchy was restored in 1801.[89] Andrew Fitzgerald, O.P. (1763–1843), second president of the college (1814–43), first came to Carlow as a professor in 1800. A native of Ossory diocese he was educated at Kilkenny College and Louvain; he received his M.A. Degree at Lisbon where he taught philosophy in the Irish Dominican college of Santo Corpo for seven years. Although he is credited with having had a doctorate it is unclear where it was attained. He was highly regarded as a teacher.[90] In Carlow he successively taught classics, philosophy, theology and sacred scripture.[91] In 1802 Fitzgerald was joined on the staff of Carlow College by Dr Kyran Marum (1772–1827). A former professor and vice-rector of the Irish College at Salamanca, he filled chairs of philosophy and theology in the college before returning to his home diocese of Ossory in 1810, where he was elevated to the bishopric in 1815.[92]

Clerical students of the college came from within the diocese and especially from counties Cork and Tipperary where there were no established seminaries and where nationalist influences may have deterred students from attending Maynooth which was also less accessible than Carlow. Paul Cullen's father would not allow his son to attend Maynooth College because of the oath of loyalty to the monarch which staff and students were expected to take.[93] During the 1798 rebellion the opening of a gate into the college enabled nearly 600 rebels to escape from crown forces during the bloody battle of Carlow.[94] Michael Collins, who was expelled from Maynooth in 1803 for sympathy with Emmet's rising, became a student and teacher in Carlow College and subsequently bishop of Cloyne and Ross.[95] John England of Cork, one of the founders of the modern Catholic church in America, made his presence felt as a dynamic student of the college from 1803 to 1808.[96] Michael Slattery of Cashel graduated from T.C.D. before pursuing his studies for the priesthood in Carlow, 1805–9; on ordination he was appointed professor of philosophy in the college.[97]

The quite fortuitous circumstances in which Doyle transferred from the clois-
ter of New Ross to the more public domain of Carlow College have been adequately documented elsewhere.[98] Andrew Fitzgerald rather summarily vacated
his chair of theology and sacred scripture to open a new college with three fellow
Dominicans in Dublin on 7 November 1813.[99] Doyle went to Carlow to fill
Fitzgerald's chair sometime in that same month.[100] The college which Fitzgerald
attempted to launch in Dublin was unsuccessful. Dean Staunton may have been
unprepared to welcome Fitzgerald back to Carlow College. However, Staunton
appears to have been faced with a student revolt in favour of Fitzgerald. The
latter was evidently highly popular among the student body who determined on
his return. They took matters into their own hands and in a most unusual action
called for Fitzgerald's re-instatement in a newspaper advertisement:

> our late Professor Doctor Fitzgerald has been to us a guide to direct, a
> light to illuminate and an affectionate friend to soften the austerities of
> College life ... we conceive his return to the seminary absolutely and in-
> dispensably essential to the perfect formation of its subjects for the Catholic
> Mission. And we confidently hope that a conviction of such necessity will
> supersede in every mind all anxieties save those which may be felt for the
> preservation of our Holy Religion.[101]

As a result of this pressure Fitzgerald re-appeared in the college – Doyle made
way for him – and he was re-appointed by Dean Staunton to his old chair. Rather
than lose Doyle the president appointed him to teach a new class of rhetoric
which the seminary still lacked.[102] Less than a year later Doyle would return to
the chair of theology and sacred scripture.

This rhetoric professorship was conditional on Doyle's being able to form it
from among those who would voluntarily join his classes. To this end his inaugural lecture, occupying two days in the delivery, comprised a sweeping survey of
the whole pantheon of celebrated religious and profane orators. Beginning with
the ancient Egyptians and the Greeks – Demosthenes, Pericles, Aristotle – it
progressed to Cicero and St Augustine, then down to Bossuet, Bourdaloue and
Massillon, the great French pulpit orators of the late seventeenth and early eighteenth centuries, continued on to the English politicians Pitt and Fox and finally
concluded with the leading orators of Ireland: Grattan, Curran and O'Connell.[103]

For the public examination Doyle recommended that each student should
make himself thoroughly familiar with a particular chapter of the class textbook,
Blair's *Rhetoric*, and he would ensure that each was examined chiefly in the part
he had prepared. He advised that it was in the interests of all who had reputations
to make as orators that this arrangement should remain secret but he did not
compel secrecy.[104] Doyle was obviously determined to form his rhetoric class at
all costs and his examination stratagem no doubt served to that end, binding his

class to him and perhaps easing the fears of average students who were probably somewhat intimidated by the learning and self-possession of their new professor. Later as bishop, Doyle always attended college examinations and no professor was allowed to assist in the examination of his own pupils.[105] One of the class tasks set by Doyle in 1814 was an essay competition on the subject 'An address of congratulations to Louis XVIII on his restoration to the throne of his ancestors'.[106] It was his way of marking the European counter-revolution achieved by the defeat and abdication of the Emperor Napoleon and the restoration of the Bourbon monarchy in France.

Doyle's rhetoric class proved to be a success; his students were receptive to his teaching and they included subsequently distinguished priests such as John Therry, William Kinsella, James Maher and William Clowry.[107] In Carlow College Doyle taught a large proportion of the priests who were to serve under him when he became bishop. Several of these students, appointed pastors by Doyle in the 1820s and 1830s, were still serving in the diocese in the 1870s; some of his curates were still officiating in the 1880s.[108] Doyle had a sharp eye for discerning talent; in 1816 he expressed particular affection for the thirteen-year-old Paul Cullen 'chiefly on account of the simplicity and innocence of his mind, and the good progress he is making in his studies'.[109]

Observations Doyle made on the role of the professor in the teaching of logic, metaphysics and ethics apply equally to his own teaching of rhetoric, theology and sacred scripture. The teacher was to employ two-thirds of the time allotted to each chapter of the textbook in hearing the lessons of the pupils, interrupting them as seldom as possible, and asking them such questions as would give them a vague idea of the answer expected. The professor was to attend to brevity, clarity and close reasoning. Nothing was to be avoided more than the introduction of extraneous matter not immediately relevant to the subject. The nature of logic required the observance of this rule. The 'unlettered' state of the students' minds demanded it, Doyle contended, for such information would distract them. At the beginning of the academic year one day each week was to be set aside for repetition. Later on scanning or parsing the entire course would serve for revision. Attention was to be paid by the professor to student pronunciation and forms of expression – the use and abuse of words constantly regulated – and English reading often commended. Each student was required to write a monthly dissertation in Latin, usually on a subject in metaphysics – the form, arguments and length of which was to be minutely pointed out beforehand by the professor. In weekly exercises difficult problems were to be proposed to talented boys and somewhat easier questions to less capable minds.[110] Doyle's educational methods were based on solid principles and he had a fundamental insight into the dangers and consequences of failure to study among ecclesiastics:

The ignorant priest is a curse to others and he himself is accursed: 'quia scientiam refutasti repellam te'. He commits faults, becomes vicious, having nothing to entertain the mind he lives amidst his appetites; and whilst he exists they suffer no good thought to approach him. He falls into sin and then his scandals !!! They cannot be enumerated. He is an infidel in practice and profanes sacraments and souls without anxiety or remorse. Hence it follows that you should endeavour to become learned.[111]

'The study of theology', Doyle observed, '... is the study of truth ... It is superior to every other science because of its object'. Besides theology all other pursuits become vain: 'Their pleasure passes away and the human mind is often left behind them like a wreck'. In theology and sacred scripture the mode of study inculcated by Doyle was to commit to memory the texts of scripture, the fathers and the councils (from which he himself – being blessed with a retentive memory – could quote readily) or to have the substance of each in the author's words or their equivalent. He required students to note down whatever of importance the lecturer said during or after the class; to obtain if possible one good work on the subject apart from the class text, and having prepared well for class in theology to turn then to sacred scripture, next to church history, leaving belles-lettres aside during study 'because the pleasures of fancy will supersede the more grave pleasure of the understanding and create a distaste in youth for what is an absolute necessity'. In an undated academic address Doyle manifested great satisfaction with the performance of his students at the previous year's public examination: 'You had not the tinsel show of knowledge but you had the knowledge itself, grave and sound and intelligent. You seemed to me in speculative theology to reason, and in practical divinity to decide questions of morality, on unchangeable principles'. The exceptions to this high water mark of student endeavour 'were but few indeed'.[112]

The textbooks recommended by Doyle for the study of theology were by the French theologians Petavius, Tournely and Bossuet.[113] The Jesuit Dionysius Petavius or Denis Petau (1583–1652) was a chronologist, bitter polemicist, distinguished Greek patristic scholar and an outstanding early seventeenth-century theologian, author of the magnum opus, *Dogma Theologica*.[114] Honoré Tournely (1658–1729), was a doctor of the Sorbonne and like virtually all French theologians of his time he was a Gallican though a determined opponent of Jansenism. His writings were lucid, elegant and learned. His lectures published in a multi-volume work under the general title *Praelectiones Theologica* passed through many editions and were much used in seminaries in abridged form.[115] Jacques-Benigne Bossuet (1627–1704), bishop of Meaux, was one of the most celebrated churchmen of his age: pulpit orator; controversialist against Fénelon and Simon; irenical promoter of the union of the Catholic and Protestant churches; and author of the Gallican declaration of the French clergy in 1682.[116] Doyle was deeply versed in his writings. The works of the eminent French émigré cleric, Louis Delahogue, professor of dogmatic theology at Maynooth College, do not appear to have been on Doyle's theology course in Carlow College although they were studied there during his episcopacy.[117] Four (of the five) volumes of Delahogue's theology which belonged to Doyle are extant and bear critical annotations by him.[118] Doyle also differed in some respects, notably on the often disputed question of usury, from the teaching of Francis Anglade, another émigré Frenchman, who was professor of moral theology in Maynooth.[119] Although Delahogue came under suspicion in Rome;[120] theological Gallicanism was not an issue in the Irish Catholic church during Doyle's teaching or episcopal career.[121] If Doyle's ecclesiology is compared to the quintessential statement of Gallicanism in the 1682 declaration of the French clergy, then he is found to be politically Gallican (articles one and three),[122] and theologically ultramontane (articles two and four).[123] Early nineteenth-century Irish political Gallicanism provided Doyle with a coherent framework in which to expound the distinctions between the allegiance of Irish Catholics to Rome in religion and to London in civil matters. It was not a new departure having been first championed in the 1750s and fully accepted by the Irish hierarchy from the 1780s onwards.[124]

The Carlow College texts in ethics were by Burlimachy and Heinicus, both of whom seem to have been rather minor authors.[125] Doyle's profound respect for John Locke, father of the central philosophical and political tradition of the modern western world, can be clearly seen in his recommendation of set texts for the teaching of logic and metaphysics:

> At commencement each student should procure Locke's Essays – there should be no exception and if the Compendium of Logic which has hitherto been used must be continued, a part of the Essays corresponding to the part of the Compendium should be selected each day and form a part of the entire lesson to be accounted for in the afternoon. This practice should be continued throughout that part of metaphysics which has corresponding places in the Essays. The doctrine of Locke if it anywhere differs from that of the Compendium should be preferred particularly in what regards ideas and the nature and source of knowledge. In general the apparent differences should be reconciled – in all cases it is better to reconcile authors than to mark their opposition to each other.[126]

From 1813 to 1819 Doyle's unchanging routine while in Carlow College was one of teaching, reading, and writing. From five o'clock in the morning until ten o'clock at night he had hardly an hour for leisure.[127] Doyle was not long enough in the chair of theology and sacred scripture to bring to maturity those works on theology which would perhaps have emanated from his pen had he not been elevated to the See and his energies diverted into diocesan pastoral administration as well as the political struggle of Irish Catholics. Doyle, as in much else that he did, brought a legalistic view to the study of theology and he did write some theological essays of an adversarial kind.[128]

Doyle's initial reaction to Carlow College was one of unfeigned pleasure: 'You will scarcely believe how well I like Carlow' he informed a correspondent in February 1814.[129] He was in congenial company – friendly with Dean Staunton and his fellow staff members Andrew Fitzgerald, Michael Slattery, Nicholas O'Connor and Patrick Brennan. On first acquaintance he warmed to the Dominican who had displaced him in the chair of theology and sacred scripture: 'Mr Fitzgerald having been prevailed upon to remain here, adds considerably to the happiness of our society'.[130] On 1 September 1814 the president, Dean Staunton, died and was succeeded by Fitzgerald. Doyle competed against Slattery for Fitzgerald's chair and was successful.[131]

However, it was at this point, with the death of the first president, that Doyle's enthusiasm for Carlow College rapidly faded away. Three years later he wrote: 'I never felt at all happy here since the death of my friend Mr Staunton'.[132] The problem was that Doyle did not see eye to eye with Fitzgerald and had very little regard for, or confidence in, his administration. He considered the president far too easy-going in his handling of students: 'there is no person of whom they [the students] are afraid or ashamed in my absence'.[133] Fitzpatrick has a revealing reference, excised from the second edition of his biography, which stated that Doyle would throw a look of 'concentrated scorn and reproach on Father Andrew Fitzgerald whenever he kept the class unnecessarily waiting, or caused business to be temporarily suspended'.[134] Doyle was also disgusted by Fitzgerald's disregard for his personal appearance, a subject on which he was fastidious, the more so in regard to clergymen.[135] A letter from Doyle to Martin Doyle frankly acknowledges his dissatisfaction with the president's administration: 'I don't like Andrew's system of government. I think it has injured and may eventually ruin the establishment, and though my presence and exertions may prop it up for a time, they cannot support it, and you may entirely conceive how unpleasant it is to be an inmate in a falling establishment'.[136]

Doyle resolved to leave Carlow College. A return to New Ross priory, if considered, was ruled out. Doyle's objective was another collegiate position. As early as December 1814, a year after his arrival in Carlow College, and less than three months after his appointment to the chair of theology and sacred scripture, reports of Doyle's intention to leave for Maynooth College had reached the ears of the bishop-elect of Kildare and Leighlin, Dr Michael Corcoran, who 'got alarmed and entreated of me to remain here – if I pleased in perpetuum and on my own terms, as he considered that my going would be the ruin of the establishment'. Doyle decided to remain for the time being but not to commit himself as to his future plans.[137] He seriously considered going to Maynooth at least twice in the next three years.

In June 1816 he actively planned leaving Carlow College. He informed Bishop

Marum of Ossory that he had deliberated leaving 'for some time' and somewhat more cryptically that 'several little circumstances' had almost determined him to do so as soon as any suitable vacancy arose in another college. The professorship of sacred scripture was only provisionally filled at Maynooth. Doyle advised secrecy on Dr Marum lest Andrew Fitzgerald 'hear and resent it though I am not under any engagement whatsoever to him'.[138] As we have seen Marum was a former colleague of Fitzgerald on the Carlow College staff but he was nonetheless very helpful to Doyle whose acquaintance he had obviously made. He directed Doyle to apply to Archbishop Troy of Dublin, a member of the board of trustees of Maynooth, 'who has, more than once heard my opinions of your qualities and acquirements'.[139] In his letter to Archbishop Troy, Doyle shrewdly enclosed Marum's. Doyle told Dr Troy that he intended to leave Carlow College 'as soon as my absence would not be a great inconvenience'.[140] That time had come he informed the president of Maynooth, Dr Crotty, in a similar letter.[141] Troy replied that there was no vacancy in the Maynooth theological department (where Doyle's fondest hopes lay) nor was there any prospect of one; he had however maintained the secrecy Doyle had enjoined upon him and signed his letter 'with perfect esteem'.[142]

Doyle also used at least one lay contact in his effort to remove from Carlow to Maynooth. This was James Bolger of Ballinabarney, The Rower, Kilkenny, who may have been associated with Doyle through the Houghton fever hospital in New Ross. Bolger was a Catholic with a small estate at Ballinabarney and he seems to have been a patron of Doyle's. Doyle wrote asking 'as a continuation of your kindness to me' for Bolger to 'interfere your good offices for me with Sir E. Bellew as one of the trustees of Maynooth College'. Doyle advised Bolger that 'it is necessary for my interests here that this business should be kept secret even *from my friends*'.[143] Bolger duly obliged and represented Doyle to Bellew 'as one who was a decided enemy to Jacobinism and disaffection and not at all a politician, or supporter of the violent party'.[144] Bellew agreed to exercise his influence on Doyle's behalf but pointed out that Maynooth was inclined to give preference in staff appointments to its own priests. However, he believed that he could secure Doyle a lectureship in English elocution: 'I think I would be sure of a preferment there'.[145] Doyle responded that he was perfectly competent to lecture in English elocution but did not wish to do so in Maynooth 'unless assured of getting the next vacant position in the theological faculty.[146] The following month found Doyle back-tracking: if given the elocution lectureship he did not want a promise of preferment from the trustees, only that his name would not be excluded from their consideration.[147] Obviously his chances of securing the lectureship in elocution had receded, perhaps because he seemed to be laying down conditions for acceptance. However, the chair of rhetoric was now vacant and so he advanced his claims to that position. These were that he had studied rhetoric under an eminent master at the University of Coimbra and taught the subject for two successive years in Carlow College.[148] Nothing came of this.

A doctorate would have greatly facilitated Doyle's entry into Maynooth but as it was he did not even have a primary degree. This might have posed a barrier to his academic advancement, especially in the eyes of those who were not personally acquainted with him. Nonetheless, as these letters show, Doyle was rapidly making himself known to, and he was in friendly correspondence with, the archbishop of Dublin, the bishop of Ossory, the president of Maynooth, and at least one other member of the Maynooth board of trustees. It was not in Doyle's nature to be an obscure friar, and this correspondence demonstrates his ambition and his pragmatic capacity to manoeuvre and shape his own career. In a fashion too it hints at a political skill – Doyle's ability to conduct delicate behind-the-scenes negotiations which, if not handled properly, could have permanently damaged his chances of advancement.

In the winter of 1816 the process started again. On 14 November Doyle wrote to Rev. Martin Doyle: 'I don't much relish the idea of setting down here for life, or of depriving myself by any pledge of the power of taking a good place at Maynooth'. Early in November, Doyle, clearly confident of a staff position at Maynooth and stressing the uncertainty of his present circumstances, informed Bishop Corcoran that he 'intended shortly to go to Maynooth'.[149] Incongruous as it may seem for someone holding vows of poverty and obedience, security of employment was valued very highly by Doyle. He was uncertain of the future of Carlow College under Andrew Fitzgerald and keen to safeguard his own options even though he opined 'I should not be solicitous for tomorrow'.[150] Bishop Corcoran made strenuous efforts to retain Doyle's services in Carlow College and made him 'the most flattering offers in his power'[151] to remain for some time longer, probably the possibility of coadjutorship and succession to the aged bishop whose health was very delicate. Doyle promised to answer Dr Corcoran's plea after he had consulted his brother Peter to whom he said he was accustomed to look 'as to a father'. He subsequently replied to Dr Corcoran:

> the substance of his [Peter's] opinion, in which I concur, is that your Lordship has treated me with great kindness and that I should be glad to place myself under your protection, that I should not enter into any arrangement which would bind me to live always in a place which might become very disagreeable, or to a profession which from being sedentary might destroy my constitution, that if after a lapse of some years and when my successors would be bred up for me, I should wish to remove from the College from either of the above mentioned causes, then that I might expect from your Lordship some living in the diocese that, on this condition alone, I should enter into an engagement which would prescribe me from accepting of any other situation to which I might obtain an appointment or from retiring to a convent if such should be my inclination.[152]

The bishop replied that 'if I pleased to remain I might consider myself as permanently settled there independent of every person'.[153] Doyle was inclined to accept this arrangement as it 'seemed to satisfy the object I had in mind in removing to Maynooth. For as in Maynooth I could be provided for during life so here I would be provided for till the end of my life'.[154] He could not bring himself to ask the bishop if he would get a parish in ten years if he wanted one. Accordingly in mid-November 1816 Doyle reached an understanding with the bishop of Kildare and Leighlin that he would remain in Carlow College and somewhat reluctantly abandoned his application for Maynooth.

But Doyle's exasperation with Fitzgerald's presidency did not diminish. On 3 June 1817 he once more informed his cousin Martin Doyle of his concerns: '… were it not for the kind of promise which you know I made the bishop I believe I would forthwith renew my application at Maynooth'.[155] But his 'promise' to the bishop was no more than that and in mid-1817 we find him complaining: 'my uneasiness here has increased'[156] and again advancing his claims to Bellew and Crotty (though not to the bishops) for a place in Maynooth, but to no avail.

During his years in Carlow College, Doyle was clearly marked by many as an up-and-coming man. His name was mentioned in connection with every ecclesiastical vacancy of consequence in south-east Ireland. Many persons, not least his clerical relations, were concerned about his future advancement, while Doyle attempted to maintain a disinterested though watchful stance.[157] He himself began to take a more mature and philosophical approach to his career. He begged his confidant Martin Doyle to keep silent about his prospects, writing apparently without any sense of irony: 'We should not only be humble but appear so. For it is a maxim of common life as well as of the gospel, he who humbles himself will be exalted and vice versa'.[158]

When Doyle first arrived in Carlow, Bishop Daniel Delany was dying. The deaths of both the bishop and the president of Carlow College in the second half of 1814 caused an 'entire revolution' in the ecclesiastical affairs of the diocese.[159] Doyle kept clear of high running party spirit and succeeded to the position of his choice. In the interval between the death of Delany and the appointment of a successor rumour made him a bishop 'twice over'[160] even though he was still only twenty eight years of age.

Doyle enjoyed the friendship of Delany's successor Bishop Corcoran and as we have seen Dr Corcoran laid great store by Doyle's continued presence in Carlow College. The bishop gave Doyle extensive faculties within the diocese; power of absolution in all cases reserved to the pope and the bishop except the crimen clerici and the contracting or being present at a clandestine marriage.[161] Doyle was in some sense Dr Corcoran's protégé and it is probably fair to state that the bishop hoped he would be his successor. Doyle seems to have become the aged and bed-ridden bishop's personal representative within the diocese, performing delicate tasks which would normally only have been carried out by

the bishop himself. In 1818 for instance Dr Corcoran authorised and requested
Doyle to inform the parish priest of Killeshin, Richard Fitzgerald, that if he
continued to obstruct his curate in the performance of his duties, he would be
suspended from office: 'Assure him that no subterfuge will enable him to escape
out of my hands'.[162]

In Doyle's home diocese of Ferns there may have been some disposition to
name him on the terna for coadjutor but, according to Fitzpatrick, Bishop Ryan's
prejudice against the regulars stifled it.[163] Doyle was acting-president of Carlow
College from late January until at least early April 1818 during Andrew Fitzgerald's
absence through illness. Doyle speculated that, if Fitzgerald died, and he hoped
he would not, he would be induced to accept the presidency, but the prospect did
not attract him and he was determined not to accept the office for more than a
few months or for two years at the very most.[164] When the presidency of St Peter's College, Wexford, was speculatively mentioned Doyle was uninterested.[165]
On Christmas day 1818 he informed a relative that he would have no objection to
the parish of Wexford provided that 'it were not encumbered with too heavy a
pension'.[166] He seems to have been more attracted at this stage to the possibility
of pastoral work than to another academic position.

Doyle's pastoral experience before he became bishop was slight but by no
means negligible. In New Ross he had fulfilled the public duties of the Augustinian priory in the town.[167] In 1812 when his brother, Peter, the parish priest of
Tintern, sustained a broken leg, Doyle undertook his duties for three months
while he recovered. Doyle was struck by the arduousness of life on the mission,
remarking to Martin Doyle, C.C., Clonegal in 1816: 'I think it would be much
easier to suffer martyrdom for Christ, than to do what you are obliged to perform'.[168] In Carlow town (where Dean Staunton's successor as P.P., William
Fitzgerald, suffered from bad health), Doyle celebrated mass in the parochial
church on Sundays and was required to do much preaching which he found
almost as beneficial to himself as to his congregations: 'There is an accession of
character on such occasions which to a person like me is of more real value than
banknotes'.[169] Most Saturdays were spent in the confessional where Doyle won
regard as a spiritual director.[170] Nonetheless his main duties both in New Ross
and in Carlow were much more educational than pastoral.

The inner spiritual life of James Doyle is of course unknown to us and outside
the scope of this work except in so far as documentary evidence allows us an
insight into his motivation as a reforming prelate. His 'Rule of Life' dated 18
February 1817 (when Doyle was in his thirtieth year) gives an important insight
into his interior life which was one or the mainsprings of his profound and in-
elastic sense of the duties of the priest. As the secret 'rule' reveals an integral part
of Doyle's religious life, the private life behind the public figure, it is worth quoting in full here:

I purpose and resolve to observe in future the following rule of life.

Daily Meditation
I shall rise as soon after five o clock as possible at all seasons of the year and during every hour until nine at night, shall spend a few minutes on the sufferings or virtues of our Redeemer. I may anticipate or postpone the duty of one or two of these hours and may supply the defect of forgetfulness at one time, by adding to the meditation at another.

Preparation for mass, office, de Gratia
I shall endeavour to spend at least half an hour, if convenient three quarters, in prayer and meditation, as a preparation for saying or hearing mass, which I shall do every day – I shall pay particular attention to the recital of my office, and shall say the office de Gratia, or five mysteries of the rosary on two days each week, one of them being Friday.

Mortification
I shall perform certain works of mortification on the Wednesdays and Fridays in Lent, four times in Passion week, and on every Friday in the year unless a reasonable impediment should occur.

Self denial and fraternal charity
The spiritual mortification of my will I will constantly attend to, shall be attentive to others, not think or speak of their faults or defects – shall not speak of myself without necessity or utility and whenever I feel self-complacency, shall check it by the recollection of my Saviour's sufferings and my own crimes.

Presence of God – dangerous company
I shall every half hour call to mind the presence of God and adore him. I shall love my neighbour only for the sake of Christ. I will make particular endeavours to prevent or check natural affections and will avoid intimate intercourse with those persons whom I know to be attached to me or to whom I feel a particular inclination. I will endeavour to be disengaged from myself and the things and persons of the world that I may be attached to God and to him alone.

Devotion
I shall endeavour to keep myself in a total abandonment to the will of God in all possible occurrences and will cherish the desire of contempt and the fear of human praise.

Observances of vows and necessary practices
I shall observe my vows in the manner which shall appear to me and to my confessor most agreeable to the will of God, and shall omit no opportunity of practising virtue, giving good example, hearing confessions, relieving the distressed.

Lively faith
I shall never suffer my faith to relax, and resolve to live and die in the C. and Ap. Faith.

Annual confession
I shall make an annual confession each year on or about the first of January and then shall formally renew the resolution of observing these rules.

Mode of diet
In addition to the mortifications of the body alluded to I shall in future eat of not more than two dishes of meat, and hope to reduce it to one, when I can do so unnoticed.

Weekly masses
I shall say the mass each week in honour of my Redeemer's sufferings and for the remission of my sins. And one each month in honour of the Eucharist and in atonement for all the injuries committed by myself and others against that wonderful pledge of the love of Christ and of our immortality – and adoption into the number of the children of God.

Confession and Patron SS
I shall go to confession generally once a week or thereabouts and particularly on the feasts of my patron saints, St Martin of Tours, the conversion of St Paul, St Miliana [?], St Augustine, St Nicholas of Tolentino, St Thomas of V. Nova, St Charles Borromeo and St Francis of Sales on which I shall say mass in their honour and fast on the vigils of their feasts.

Devotion to Blessed Virgin
I shall have a particular devotion to the B.V. Mary, Queen of Heaven, Mother of our Redeemer, and chiefly confide in her intercession to obtain for me grace to keep these resolutions.

Secrecy of this rule and manner of its observance
I shall never communicate these rules to any person being satisfied that they contain nothing improper for me to practise and need no person's approbation, if through inadvertence or necessity I omit any part of these

observances I shall not repute myself blameable, if through sloth or neglect, I will consider myself as having fallen and I confess I shall do so, by
saying I broke a certain resolution.

A prayer
May the God who suffered for my sins grant me the strength and grace in
all things to fulfill his holy will until he takes me hence, which I most
humbly and fervently pray will be soon. I shall pray each day for charity,
humility, meekness and truth.[171]

Even allowing for Doyle's vow of poverty his management of his personal
finances was quite unworldly. Doyle never felt the want of money on his own
account.[172] His remuneration in the chair of rhetoric was £79.12s.6d.; as professor of theology and sacred scripture he received a salary of £113.15s. annually.[173]
In 1816 he lent his entire resources to a needy family.[174] His finances were often
straitened and he was 'plagued' with borrowing though he could not bear to be in
debt[175] and regarded himself as a 'strict economist'.[176] The chaotic state of his
personal finances derived from his wholesale charity to the poor and needy rather
than from budgetary incompetence. His management of public finances entrusted
to his care was always most correct, indeed scrupulous. He maintained very clear
and accurate accounts.[177]

After a long illness Bishop Corcoran died on 22 February 1819. A month later
the bishops of the ecclesiastical province of Dublin and the diocesan clergy gathered in Tullow to celebrate the month's mind for the late bishop and to decide on
their choice of a successor to be proposed to Rome. Thirty-five of the forty-two
parish priests of Kildare and Leighlin assembled to nominate their choice; the
curates did not have a voice in the matter. Six of the seven absentees were from
Kildare[178] which indicates, perhaps, some degree of unconcern about the decision or alternatively a lack of canvassing. While there was no overwhelming consensus among the parish priests that James Doyle, O.S.A., should succeed to the
See he had no serious challenger as votes were fragmented among numerous
candidates. His thirty-eight per cent of the vote represented more than twice
that of his nearest rival, Dr Michael Prendergast, P.P. of Bagenalstown, who sac-
rificed his own claim by urging the gathering not to confine their selection of the
most suitable candidate to their own number or indeed to the secular clergy.[179]
Perhaps it was as a result of this that not one but two regulars figured on the
terna. On the first ballot Doyle received sixteen votes, Dr Prendergast, seven,
and Charles Aylmer, S.J., rector of Clongowes Wood College, three. The remaining nine votes were divided in ones and twos among priests whose names are not
known to us. Doyle was thus, in accordance with customary practice, named
dignissimus on the terna. On the second ballot Dr Prendergast received fourteen

votes and was elected dignior. The Jesuit, Aylmer, with ten suffrages, was declared dignus on the third and final ballot.[180]

Doyle's sixteen votes probably came from a reform party among the priests who felt that a dynamic young man was needed to invigorate the religious life of the diocese after a decade of weak episcopal management owing to or resulting from the infirmity of Delany and Corcoran. In Doyle's favour were the prestige of his key chair of theology and sacred scripture in Carlow College and his public image as a protégé of Bishop Corcoran. The clerical contacts of his relations, Martin Doyle, P.P. Clonegal and Gerald Doyle, P.P. Naas, were no doubt canvassed on his behalf; likewise young curates who had been taught by Doyle spread his name and reputation around the diocese.

Evidently only Doyle's name was seriously considered by the bishops of the Dublin province – Archbishop Troy of Dublin and his coadjutor, Archbishop Murray, Bishop Marum of Ossory, and Bishop Keating of Ferns when they met to recommend their choice for the See of Kildare and Leighlin to Rome. As we have already seen Doyle was a familiar name to Marum, and to Troy who had been prepared to promote his candidacy for a staff position in Maynooth College. The bishops of the province had in fact unanimously decided to adopt Doyle's name for recommendation to Rome before they were informed of the result of the ballot of the second order clergy.[181] Doyle's was apparently the only name forwarded to Rome by the bishops so the Vatican had limited freedom of choice. However, the apostolic internuncio in Lisbon championed the candidacy of one Patrizio O'Brennan Hay, an Irish cleric working in Portugal. While favourably disposed towards O'Brennan Hay, the congregation of Propaganda Fide, at their meeting on 2 August 1819, felt that the postulation of the bishops and second order clergy in Ireland for Doyle could not be overlooked without 'grave inconvenience'.[182] The elevation of Doyle was ratified later in that same month by Pope Pius VII.[183]

It was indeed a singular occurrence, given the prevailing prejudices against the regulars and the disposition to elect elderly experienced priests, that a thirty-two–year-old Augustinian friar who was not a native of the diocese, to which he had come only five and a half years before, should have been the choice submitted to Rome. Doyle himself believed that the 'concurrence of the prelates, clergy and people in their approbation of the choice that has been made is a sign that it was directed by Providence'.[184] He discharged the duties of a bishop-elect while continuing to fill his chair in Carlow College until his election was sanctioned by Rome. He had just entered his thirty-third year and the tenth year of his priesthood when he was consecrated bishop of Kildare and Leighlin in Carlow parish church on 14 November 1819.[185]

BISHOP OF KILDARE AND LEIGHLIN

While the early and medieval church in the diocese does not, per se, form part of this work it would be unwise to overlook the significance of its tangible forms on the landscape. The still visible remains of churches, crosses, holy wells, round towers, etc., and the traditions associated with the local saints of the early Irish church exerted a long influence in the oral tradition.

The churches of Iserninus at Aghade and Auxilius at Killashee in the east and north of the diocese respectively were associated with the very foundations of Irish Christianity over one thousand three hundred and fifty years earlier. The diocese took its names from St Brigid's great church of Kildare and St Laserian's church at Leighlin. Many parish churches in the north of the diocese were dedicated to Brigid, one of the three patron saints of the Irish church. Doyle signed some of his writings 'E.B', that is Episcopus Brigidae and he had the status of her feast day, 1 February, elevated in the diocese in 1821. In Leighlin, Laserian was bishop of one of the important churches of the Barrow valley. Willibrord, the patron saint of Frisia, spent several years in exile in one of these monasteries in the seventh century.

Virtually every parish in the diocese had at least one early Irish church. Parish names such as Kilcock, Kill, Killeigh, Killeshin, Monasterevan and St Mullin's indicate their early church origins. Other parishes emerged from ancient abbacies as in the case of that of St Fintan at Clonenagh and St Abban at Kilabban. We shall have cause to refer to traditions associated with local saints in discussing patterns.

The later European church influence can be seen in parish names such as Abbeyleix and Graiguenamanagh, named after the Cistercians, the first of the continental orders to come to Ireland, followed by the mendicant orders who were established in the towns of the diocese and will also be considered later. The ancient sites of churches and monasteries forfeited during the reformation were a constant reminder of the antiquity of the Irish Catholic experience for early nineteenth century Catholics.

An active bishop can exercise a decisive influence in shaping church organisation, discipline and religious observance within his diocese. Doyle's episcopal inheritance was in large measure that of Bishop Daniel Delany's twenty-six years' administration, 1788–1814. Delany's successor, Michael Corcoran, enjoyed an episcopacy of only four years, 1815–19, and was very much a transitional figure. It is necessary to concentrate especially on Delany's episcopacy because the problems facing Doyle in 1819 were chiefly those created by Delany's historically controversial pastorate. However, for a proper perspective on the context of Doyle's episcopacy it is necessary to go further back in time. The history of the diocese of Kildare and Leighlin in the century preceding Doyle's appointment is one of slow re-emergence from harassment and fear of the penal laws and consequent lack of organisation and church discipline.

   Bishop James Gallagher (1681–1751), author of the popular *Sixteen Irish sermons in an easy and familiar stile* (1736), experienced penal molestation in Raphoe (where he was bishop from 1725), before he was translated to the diocese of Kildare and Leighlin which he ruled from 1737 until his death in 1751. Bishop Gallagher's diocesan statutes of 1748 dealt with the problems of clandestine marriage, wake abuses and non-fulfillment of the Paschal duty.[1] Dr Gallagher resided in primitive conditions in the bog of Allen where he prepared young men for the priesthood. In the 1820s Doyle found that Gallagher's pastoral impact in north Kildare was considerable and that his influence and memory were still alive and revered. On visitation in Allen parish in 1823 he remarked that

> in those remote and uncultivated districts there are found a purity and simplicity of morals truly surprising. From five to six o clock this morning, the roads and fields were crowded with poor people, young and old, healthy and infirm, hurrying to see the bishop, and assist at his mass, and hear his instructions.[2]

This idyllic picture of later Catholic practice should not blind us to the reality that the mission on which Bishop Gallagher served was fraught with pastoral difficulties. For many Catholicism was more a matter of instinct than of learning, of custom than of dogma. The manpower and resources needed to catechise thoroughly could not be provided under the penal laws. Catholicism was not a book learned religion since the vast majority of the population could neither read nor write. Because the usual pathways to prosperity and progress through education were closed to Catholics by the penal laws, medieval ways lingered on in the countryside where there was little to stimulate recognisably modern work practices and modes of living. It would of course be anachronistic to expect modern standards from the Catholic church at that time; moreover the oral traditions that have been transmitted to us from the pre-1750 period of the Catholic faithful meeting at mass rocks, bushes or in pits to hear mass, while a priest at some peril of his life celebrated, have a solid basis in fact and demonstrate the resilience and tenacity of Irish Catholicism under persecution.[3]

As in the case of Gallagher extraordinarily little is known of the career of his successor Bishop James Keefe (1702–87), even though he was a leading and politically controversial figure within the Irish hierarchy. Similarly, what little information is extant on Keefe comes largely from the pen of Doyle who drew pastoral inspiration from his episcopacy.[4] Dr Keefe ruled the diocese in a transitional period between the end of the enactment of the penal laws and the beginning of their removal from the statute book. By a law passed in 1697 all archbishops, bishops and regular clergymen were banished from the country.[5] Letters from Rome to the bishop were addressed to 'Patrick Keefe, shopkeeper, Tullow' and his letters to Rome were signed 'ex loco nostri refugii'.[6] This, despite the fact that the law had fallen into desuetude soon after its enactment; however, it was not rescinded until 1782.[7] The bishop kept a low profile, being wary of local prejudices which, if played upon, could lead to severe intolerance.[8]

Keefe was an active bishop. He resided in Tullow parish at Aghade and frequently visited every part of his extensive diocese. Keefe's correspondence, now presumed lost, was perused by Doyle, who gave a brief account of his pastoral management:

> Finding that his clergy were few, and almost without fixed abodes or regular organisation, he laboured to educate youths of piety and talents, that the number of his fellow labourers might be augmented; he established conferences of the clergy and seldom failed, at whatever personal inconvenience to attend them. He prescribed rules and regulations according to which the clergy were, when it was possible for them, to discharge their duties. He preached the word of God incessantly, often in glens and bogs, for chapels in his time were few and wretched …. Religion seemed to arise at his call from the grave in which she was buried, and the vineyard assigned to him changed from a state of desolation to comparative fruitfulness.[9]

Owing to lack of financial resources the normal physical fabric of Catholicism in late-eighteenth century Ireland was one of mud walls and thatched roofs. Keefe did not live to see the completion of his brainchild, Carlow College, which marked the beginning of the great institutional building phase of the Irish Catholic re-emergence, and which took place mainly in the first half of the nineteenth century.

In 1781 the thirty-five-year-old Propaganda educated Richard O'Reilly, vicar general and parish priest of Kilcock, was named coadjutor to Bishop Keefe. However, only two years later he was transferred to the disturbed archiepiscopal See of Armagh as coadjutor *cum iure successionis*.[10] Daniel Delany (1747–1814), a Tullow curate, was appointed coadjutor bishop of Kildare and Leighlin in 1783, succeeding to full jurisdiction on Keefe's death. The pastoral problems which he

faced in his mensal parishes of Tullow and Mountrath were paralleled throughout the parishes of the diocese.

Tullow was very impoverished, the population, according to Delany, 'the most
wretchedly poor and absolutely of the lowest and meanest condition, with the
exception of a small number of individuals in middling circumstances, of any
throughout the entire diocese of Kildare and Leighlin'.[11] He described Tullow
parish chapel in 1800 as being 'for the greater part reduced almost to a heap of
ruin, without our being able to obtain, hitherto, a lease to rebuild the same',
though the aggregate Sunday mass attendance was 3,000 people.[12]

Delany stated that the inhabitants of Mountrath consisted 'almost entirely in
town and country of persons of a very inferior class, viz., petty manufacturers,
little dealers, cottagers, and families of the lowest degree'.[13] Like Tullow,
Mountrath was dominated by Protestant interests. Its mass house was sited on a
sandbank in a tributary of the river Nore where the congregation were frequently
obliged to worship 'in the midst of water or kneeling on wet sand and mud'.[14]
Mountrath was part of the Castlecoote estate. Every lease on the estate contained
a clause prohibiting ground to be let or sold or bestowed for the purpose of erecting a Catholic chapel.[15] Delany succeeded in securing a 999-year lease for a chapel
in 1795. Work on it had to be suspended during the 1798 rebellion. Planned on
an impressive scale it was half-built in 1800 with the only funds coming from
'brass or halfpenny collections and the bishop's contribution'.[16] After ten years of
effort the chapel was still not quite completed in 1805, though it was possible to
celebrate mass in it in that year. The administrator of the parish, Rev. Thady
Duane, used to accompany the men engaged in drawing building materials for
the chapel armed with a stout blackthorn stick, to ward off the attacks or intimidation of ultra Protestants. In 1808 the home of the administrator was attacked
by Orangemen and his death was an indirect result.[17]

In Tullow, Delany introduced Sunday school catechesis for children and adults
and established the confraternities of the Christian Doctrine and the Eucharist.
In the 1780s his Corpus Christi processions in the town constituted an audacious
public display of popery. There is evidence of confraternities of the Christian
Doctrine in the early 1790s in the parishes of Carlow, Leighlinbridge,
Mountmellick, Rathvilly and Rosenallis.[18] Sunday school catechesis in some form
probably became general though it seems doubtful that there were confraternities,
particularly of the Christian Doctrine, or chapel libraries in much more than a
quarter of the parishes of the diocese.

Delany's posthumous reputation has rested on his foundation of two diocesan congregations (which subsequently expanded overseas) – the Sisters of St
Brigid or Brigidine Sisters and the Brothers of St Patrick or Patrician Brothers –
though their beginnings were unstructured, haphazard and not without grave
difficulties. In 1792 in what has been termed 'the first of a few sporadic attempts
to found the Brigidine Congregation',[19] Dr Delany sent six pious female catechists

from Tullow to Mountrath. It seems probable that these women, members of the confraternity of the Eucharist, had made private vows of celibacy. We may gather from a letter of Bishop Delany to Archbishop Troy, dating from 1793, that Catholic religious practice in Mountrath prior to the sending of these catechists had been very inadequate.

> A dozen priests would hardly suffice to hear between this [early March] and Easter, the general confessions of persons of both sexes that these six poor mistresses have under heaven, been the entire acknowledged cause of reforming since they went up thither, and that in a place where as many clergymen assembled by me not long since to give a general station in the close of the Easter confessions, would not have as many penitents as one priest almost could with ease dispatch. Never was there such a universal and thorough reformation wrought, to my knowledge at least, in any parish almost in as many years, as they have hitherto only spent six months in accomplishing in that town where a regular and proper clergyman in the care of it told me before they went up that he absolutely despaired of ever seeing the people doing any good and yet they attend thrice a week (all aged persons for the most part) in such numbers and with a hunger and thirst for instruction! And on Sundays this chapel was never more crowded by scholars of every denomination .... [20]

However, perhaps because Bishop Delany was unable to establish his catechists permanently in Mountrath, they were withdrawn after only six months.[21]

Six years later, in 1799, Bishop Delany sent a further group of six devout lay women to Clonegal, five miles from Tullow, where they ran a school. These pious women are sometimes associated with the Brigidine Congregation but there does not appear to have been any formal connection between the Clonegal religious and the house established in Tullow in 1807.[22] In Clonegal they were under the patronage of the Spanish-educated James Purcell, P.P., 1758–1810, a capable canonist often relied upon by the bishop.[23] His successor, Thomas Cummins, P.P., 1810–18, was also favourably disposed towards the community. In 1814 we find James Doyle writing from Carlow College to Martin Doyle, then C.C., Clonegal, advising him against allowing the sisters to manifest their consciences to their female superior.[24] A popular account states that Martin Doyle as P.P., 1817–27, did not like the sisters and persuaded Bishop Doyle to disband them in 1824.[25] Perhaps Dr Doyle refused to recognise these devout women as religious unless they followed a regular observance. The school managed by two of the women, Anne Synott and Bridget Kenny, presented a 'wretched appearance' in 1824. They did not claim attachment to any religious institute in that year.[26] Several of the women who taught in this school opened their own pay schools elsewhere. The last of the Clonegal group, Anne Synott, or 'Mother' Synott persevered with her school until her death in 1861 aged seventy-one.[27] The Clonegal 'sisters' are representative of an important stratum of exceptional Catholic piety – lay devouts – which has been but little noticed by historians.

After several false starts and much agonising, Bishop Delany finally realised a twenty-year ambition when he founded the Brigidine congregation on 1 Febru-ary 1807. Six catechists from the Blessed Sacrament confraternity formed the first Brigidine house in Tullow. These were not young women – the average age of five of them was thirty-two years (the age of the sixth is unknown). O'Riordan has written that 'the first six Brigidines were practically illiterate'.[28] Miss Judith Wogan-Browne who was employed by Dr Delany to teach these women com-plained that they seemed incapable of learning. Although a laywoman Miss Wogan-Browne moved into the convent and became one of the conventual household. Then aged fifty-seven she never became a Brigidine but she had an influential voice in the management of Tullow convent for most of the remaining forty-one years of her life. When Bishop Delany was absent from chapter meetings he del-egated her to preside.[29] A second Brigidine convent was founded at Mountrath in 1809. Dr Delany financed both convents from his own resources.

On 2 February 1808 the bishop founded the Patrician community of lay male religious in Tullow. Like the Brigidines, the original Patrician membership was drawn from the ranks of the Tullow chapel catechists. The first brothers, or monks as they were then known, supported themselves by running a small day school, by trades and by day labouring. They suffered financial embarrassment and at one point their prospects for survival seemed so bleak that Dr Delany informed them that they were free to return to their former occupations. On a shoestring budget they survived and in 1810 a filiation was established in Mountrath. One brother, John Clancy, was actually ordained for the sole purpose of being chap-lain to the Tullow comunity.[30]

Bishop Delany's health which had been failing for many years went into defi-nite decline in 1812. In his two remaining years he agonised over the disposition of his substantial finances. He had at his disposal as much as £7,000, apparently acquired from his family. However, the law of charitable bequests was penal; bequests for Catholic religious purposes could be and were often sequestrated. Dr Delany took the advice of the leading Catholic barrister, Denys Scully, and circumvented the problem by willing the vast bulk of his money to sisters in the convents he had founded, on the understanding that it was in trust for these institutions. The names of the sisters were to be kept secret but Miss Wogan-Browne was among them. The Patricians were much less fortunate. They re-ceived only twenty pounds annually and had to rely on their own devices to make ends meet.[31] It was almost as if Delany held out little hope for their future sur-vival. Neither the Brigidines nor the Patricians had a written rule or constitu-tions of their own when Delany died in 1814. The Brigidines had been provision-ally given the Rule of St Augustine together with the Constitution and Directory of St Francis de Sales whom Delany especially venerated. He did give the Brigidines some spiritual letters of guidance though these could hardly be construed as a rule and constitutions. O'Riordan has commented that by comparison with the rigidity of other founders' rules, Dr Delany's instructions were characterised by a mildness which was extraordinary for the time.[32] No member of the Patricians or Brigidines was actually a professed religious at the period of Bishop Delany's demise.

The pastoral administration of Bishop Delany, sharply criticised by Fitzpatrick in his biography of Doyle, has been defended by historians of Delany's congregations such as Margaret Gibbons and Mary O'Riordan. Fitzpatrick's criticisms can be reduced to two charges which will be examined here in turn in the context of some general remarks on his episcopacy. The first of these charges was that Delany 'altogether neglected to hold conferences with his clergy'.[33] It is probably safe to presume that conferences did take place up to 1798 because in that year a conference in Mountrath was dispersed by a party of armed yeomanry during the rebellion.[34] Furthermore in an account of the diocese which he wrote in 1800 Dr Delany stated that he personally attended 'six several conferences' annually in counties Carlow, Kildare and Queen's.[35] It may have been that in the light of the 1798 Mountrath incident Dr Delany deemed it wise to curtail to a minimum the number of conferences to be held yearly. The Corpus Christi processions in Tullow, which were very dear to Delany's heart, were dropped in 1798 and did not take place again until 1805.[36] If this delay of seven years is an accurate barometer of the disruption caused by the rebellion it would suggest that Catholic activities in the diocese were disrupted if not set back for several years. When loyalists seized a Catholic parochial register and construed it as a list of rebels, registers in many parts of Kildare and Leighlin were destroyed as a precautionary measure and some were not maintained until Doyle gave orders that they be recommenced at the beginning of his episcopacy.[37] The year 1798 was not only politically but socially also a traumatic event in the history of this region. Gatherings at some holy wells on pattern days ceased in that year and were never resumed. Church building was temporarily halted in many places. Ancient folk traditions died and in that sense the rebellion had a modernising effect.

Only one priest ministering in the diocese, a friar named Edward Prendergast, was executed in the rebellion.[38] However several priests from outside the diocese were executed by crown forces in the environs of Kildare and Leighlin. In Tullow, Dr Delany's chapel was taken over as stabling for the horses of the military and the rebel leader, Rev. John Murphy of Ferns diocese was tortured and executed in a barbarous manner.[39] From 1798 it would seen that Dr Delany maintained a discreet profile in his diocese. In 1799 he was one of ten bishops prepared to give the government a limited veto in the appointment of Irish Catholic bishops. When state payment of the Catholic clergy was mooted at the same time Dr Delany hoped that a portion of the payment to his diocesan clergy would be directed by the government for the upkeep of Carlow College.[40] It is more than likely that some of his diocesan clergy disapproved of his stance on the veto issue but Delany was interested in politics only in so far as it served the church in his estimation. He did not see any function for the Irish Catholic prelate in politics. In a letter to a fellow bishop he observed: 'The kingdom of our Divine Master ... is ... not ... of this world. Away, away with politics, with committees and their chairmen, with pamphlet and newspaper polemics, with conventions and addresses and petitions, and the plague knows what application and diplomatic negotiations ...'. [41]

The second and more serious charge brought against Dr Delany by Fitzpatrick was that he 'procrastinated to such an extent that years rolled over without any attempt to administer with regularity the sacrament of confirmation'.[42] There is no reason to believe that Dr Delany failed to conduct visitations with some regularity from 1788 to at least 1803. In a letter to Archbishop Troy written shortly after he had taken over full jurisdiction of the diocese he spoke of his return to Tullow after an absence of several weeks spent 'visiting seven or eight parishes in the most distant parts of the County of Kildare, King's and Queen's Counties'.[43] The Mountrath Brigidine annals state that after the foundation of the convent 'the bishop left, to go round the diocese on visitation';[44] this was in 1809 only five years before he died although admittedly these annals were written *c*.1873 and the bishop may not have been visiting the whole diocese. There is strong evidence to suggest that from 1803 onwards Dr Delany failed to visit all the parishes of his diocese with regularity.

In 1820 Bishop Doyle administered confirmation to over 900 adults, only sixty of whom were unmarried, in Portarlington; the following year he conferred the sacrament on 1,100 at Emo – a marquee had to be erected in the chapel yard to accommodate the numbers that attended. The confirmations that took place in 1820 were the first in the parish (Portarlington and Emo) since 1803, a lapse of seventeen years.[45] Even allowing for the final two years of his life when Delany was incapacitated there is still a lacuna of nine years when confirmation was not celebrated in Portarlington and Emo. Delany's successor, Corcoran, was bedridden and probably unable to administer confirmation. However, it was not unusual that Catholics who had not received an elementary education in their youth failed to receive confirmation. In Dublin, in 1838, 800 persons both young and old were discovered in the parish of Howth who had not been confirmed.[46] The Vincentian missioners of the mid-1840s found thousands of people in Kerry who had never received confirmation. For many of these people confirmation was a sacrament associated with childhood or adolescence and they believed that if they had not been confirmed as children they had lost all chance of receiving the sacrament.[47]

Delany had been shaped by his French education. A cultured and dignified ecclesiastic, he was by nature more suited to the role of the collegiate professor than to the rigours of the mission. In a letter dating from 1788 he complained that after he had completed a visitation his spirits were 'harassed and depressed ... after a hungry, solitary, and joyless November ride of about thirty miles, which I was obliged to perform ... without the smallest refreshment or company to beguile in any way the tedious way'.[48] It seems probable that as the years rolled by Dr Delany became less and less enamoured of the visitation round and procrastinated more and more about making it. His pastoral horizon at times did not seem to extend beyond his mensal parishes of Tullow and Mountrath. He spent his time in managing the affairs of his diocesan congregations or in private retreat or in the company of close friends such as Bishop Moylan of Cork and Lord Cloncurry where his Francophile manners and speech found a ready appreciation. All things considered it seems that Fitzpatrick's two criticisms of Delany had some justification.

A more serious criticism still and one not mentioned by Fitzpatrick was Dr Delany's failure to take action against clerics who did not live up to their sacred calling. His disposition was too gentle and he was not temperamentally equipped to deal with unruly priests who took advantage of his good nature. The most notorious case and perhaps the most serious instance of gross moral turpitude encountered by James Doyle during his residence in the diocese was that of Rev. James O'Neill. He was appointed parish priest of Maryborough by Bishop Delany in April 1789[49] and there he remained until 1816 when at Doyle's instigation he was forced by Bishop Corcoran to resign his parish and suspended for life for soliciting in the confessional, which was one of a number of his failings.[50] When this suspended cleric made the mistake of corresponding with Bishop Doyle in 1820 he was told that he had spent his life 'in an almost uninterrupted course of the blackest iniquity that has ever come to my knowledge'. In the language of Trent, Doyle observed that his vices were committed 'at an altar where you ministered covered with sacrileges eating and drinking damnation to yourself'. Doyle's chastisement of this immoral cleric also included an indictment of Bishop Delany:

> to repair the evils occasioned by your ministry, and to restore religion to the good people amongst whom you laboured to extinguish it, would require the unceasing exertions of many. May the Lord not enter into judgement with D. Delany who tolerated you, while he lamented aloud your iniquities ... which I have been hearing of since I became a resident in this diocese and with which I find the Prelates of the province and most of the clergy have been acquainted for years.[51]

Fitzpatrick's portrayal of Dr Delany in his life of Doyle drew the anger of the Patricians and the Brigidines who naturally revered their founder's memory. One aged Brigidine annotated her copy of his biography with the comment 'The biographer seems not to know the saintly character he lowers in order to exalt the hero of his work'.[52] There is a grain of truth in this remark but it applies more to

Fitzpatrick's treatment of Bishop Corcoran than to his characterisation of Dr
Delany. In the second enlarged edition of his *Doyle*, Fitzpatrick was able to bring
James Delany, a kinsman of Bishop Delany, to his own defence. He had been a
curate in Portarlington and Emo in 1820–21 and was parish priest of Ballinakill,
1824–74, and twice on the terna for Kildare and Leighlin. He remarked that 'the
state of discipline that prevailed throughout the diocese in his [Dr Delany's] declining years contrasted strangely with that inaugurated by Dr Doyle, the facts
stated by his biographer were patent'. Rev. Delany did mitigate his criticism somewhat by adding that the 'shortcomings' of Dr Delany's episcopate 'arose as much
from the poverty of his overworked clergy, as from inactivity or want of zeal on
his own part'.[53]

    In 1800 there were eighty-five priests on the mission in the diocese. The Catho-
lic population was an estimated 185,000, giving a ratio of one priest to 2,176
people. Bishop Delany required curates in no less than eleven parishes but there
were no means to support them on the mission, so impoverished was the flock.[54]
Of Dr Delany, Doyle generously commented that the 'tenderness of his heart
caused him often to be too indulgent to others, he imposed restraints only on
himself ... humbly he made himself all to all that he might gain all to Christ'.[55]
But the truth cannot be denied. As a diocesan pastor Bishop Delany was weak
and ineffective. Higher standards, tighter discipline and greater uniformity of
religious observance were expected and exacted by the next generation of bishops to which Doyle belonged.

    When Delany died on 9 July 1814, Arthur Murphy, parish priest of Kilcock,
was elected vicar capitular. He headed the terna for the vacant See and his appointment as bishop was made by Propaganda on 19 September 1814 and ratified by the pope on 29 September.[56] Murphy, however, declined the See, and the
dignior on the terna was elevated in his stead. Michael Corcoran, who was educated in Paris, had been successively parish priest of Balyna and Kildare before
he was consecrated bishop in March 1815.[57] Fitzpatrick was very dismissive of
his credentials for the office:

> For thirty years he had unostentatiously discharged the duties of a simple
> country pastor. Pious and cautious – classically learned, but not polished
> – professionally au fait, without much theological lore. Fr Corcoran was
> selected in default of a more eligible candidate.[58]
>
>   ... weakened by repeated attacks of illness, he could not muster suffi-
> cient energy to be more than casually useful. The discipline of the diocese
> became still more relaxed under the administration of this pious but inac-
> tive prelate.[59]

However, Fitzpatrick's poor opinion of Bishop Corcoran was not shared by Doyle
who observed that the bishop possessed a 'strong and discriminating' mind but

'his health declined from the period of his appointment so that he was unable to realize those wise views for the improvement of ecclesiastical discipline, the education of youth, and the more regular fulfillment of every duty by the clergy and laity, which he had formed'.[60] Corcoran died after less than four years as bishop. Those 'wise views' which Doyle attributed to him became part of the renewal and reform programme of his own episcopacy.

DIOCESAN STRUCTURES AND APPOINTMENTS

The basic unit of the diocese is the parish. Kildare and Leighlin had forty-two parishes in 1819.[61] In church law when a parish priest, competent in the discharge of his duties, was unable to fulfill them on account of the extent of his parish or the number of his parishioners, the bishop had the right to divide the parish and erect a new one in part of it provided there was an adequate support for two priests.[62] Thus when the largest parishes in the diocese became vacant Doyle divided them. These extra large parishes had remunerations of up to £500 which was more than adequate for the support of two priests.[63] In this fashion Doyle created five new parishes. On 24 November 1823 he removed Paulstown from Leighlinbridge and Goresbridge from Graiguenamanagh to create the new parish of Paulstown (Goresbridge), which was originally apparently conceived as two separate parishes.[64] The parish of Leighlinbridge was renamed Leighlin. In 1824 Doyle divided Ballinakill to erect Abbeyleix parish.[65] In 1828, Clonaslee, separated from Rosenallis parish in 1793, and reunited with it in 1811, was once more given its parochial identity.[66] The creation of Raheen and Ballyfin are dealt with below. There were other adjustments such as the detachment of the district of Sletty from Arles and its annexation to Killeshin parish and minor boundary changes in the parishes of Carlow, Tinryland and Portarlington.[67]

It would appear that if there was a deanery system in operation under Bishops Delany and Corcoran, the deaneries did not meet very often.[68] Under Doyle the diocese was divided originally into six rural deaneries – Carlow, Ballon (which was subsumed into the Carlow deanery by 1827), Borris, Maryborough, Mountmellick and Kilcock – over each of which was appointed a rural dean or vicar forane.[69] The jurisdiction of the rural dean was delegated, restricted to a particular area and to certain matters specified by the bishop. He was obliged to hear complaints, adjust disputes, scrutinise the manner and honesty of the clergy and generally look after all matters concerned with religion in his district.[70] His jurisdiction was voluntary rather than coercive. The bishop normally communicated with his clergy through his rural deans. The rural dean was usually though not invariably appointed master of the theological conference in his deanery.[71] Within a month of his elevation to the bishopric Doyle had defined the following deanery structure throughout the diocese: William Fitzgerald, P.P., Carlow, was named rural dean of the Carlow deanery which comprised the parishes of Carlow, Arles, Doonane, Killeshin and Tinryland. The Ballon deanery was headed by James Conran, parish priest of Ballon, whose jurisdiction extended over the parishes of Ballon, Baltinglass, Clonmore, Hacketstown, Rathvilly and Tullow.[72] Dr Michael Prendergast, P.P., Bagenalstown, was rural dean of Borris deanery which contained the parishes of Borris, Bagenalstown, Clonegal, Graiguenamanagh, Leighlinbridge (designated Leighlin from 1823), Myshall, Paulstown (from 1823), and St Mullin's.[73]

Nicholas O'Connor, P.P., Maryborough, was rural dean of the deanery of Maryborough, which comprised Abbeyleix (from 1824), Ballinakill, Ballyadams, Ballyfin (from 1824), Maryborough, Mountrath, Stradbally and Raheen parishes. The deanery of Mountmellick/Portarlington, consisted of the parishes of Clonaslee (from 1828), Clonbullogue, Killeigh, Monasterevan, Mountmellick, Portarlington, Philipstown and Rosenallis. Anthony Duanne, P.P., Mountmellick, was rural dean from 1819 until 1823 when he was succeeded by John Dunne, P.P., Portarlington. The deanery of Kilcock was by far the largest in the diocese comprising the parishes of Allen, Balyna, Caragh, Carbury, Clane, Edenderry, Kilcock, Kildare, Kill, Naas, Newbridge and Suncroft. John Dunne, P.P., Kilcock, was dean until his transfer to Portarlington in 1823. He was succeeded by Michael Flanagan, P.P., Balyna.[74]

The next tier of the diocesan structure is the chapter. In most dioceses chapters survived the penal era in a very weak state. Their main function was to fulfill their contentious right of recommendation to the papacy of suitable candidates for episcopal vacancies.[75] There were no cathedrals and apart from the office of dean – the head of the chapter – other positions such as archdeacon, chancellor, precentor, canon, etc., were often left unfilled. In the late eighteenth century there were only remnants of chapters in both Kildare and Leighlin. In 1780 only the offices of dean and chancellor were filled in the Kildare chapter. In Leighlin the positions of dean and archdeacon were occupied.[76] Apparently neither Dr Delany nor Dr Corcoran filled the chapter offices. Doyle recorded that the Kildare chapter became extinct in 1812 and the chapter of Leighlin shortly before.[77] All chapter offices, except one, were in the nomination of the bishop. Nomination to the office of dean was made by the pope. However, the so-called deans of Kildare and Leighlin do not appear to have been appointed by the papacy. Doyle referred to William Cullen, P.P., Leighlinbridge as only the 'nominal' dean of Leighlin.[78]

During Dr Michael Corcoran's episcopacy, Doyle warned Rev. Martin Doyle to have nothing to do with an application to revive the Leighlin chapter as the bishop was 'averse to all interference of the clergy with regard to elections of bishops or vicars'. Doyle took the view that the chapter was extinct and could only be revived by the pope. He himself was also opposed to chapters commenting: 'I would be sorry to be in Tullow on the day when there will be a question of a chapter, but shall go to see the bishop ... as I don't like the clangour of your noisy priests'.[79]

Doyle perhaps allowed himself to be over influenced by the medieval experience where chapters as corporations were notoriously guilty of simony and the 'diabolical custom' of choosing their own successors. He believed that chapters were bodies liable to be corrupted.[80] Furthermore chapters could threaten to impinge on episcopal rights which all Irish bishops guarded closely. Doyle was familiar with the divisions which bedevilled episcopal succession throughout Ireland and which could in many dioceses be traced in some degree to the squabbling of chapters.

The highest office in the Catholic diocese below that of Ordinary is that of the vicar-general. The power of the vicar-general, by reason of the office and deputation, extended to all causes in the ordinary episcopal jurisdiction, except those which canon law reserved. The vicar-general's acts were considered the acts of the bishop himself. The vicar-general was normally a cleric distinguished for his probity and learning and usually a holder of a licentiate or doctorate in canon law.[81] Bishop Doyle had two vicars-general in the united diocese: Dr Michael Prendergast, P.P., Bagenalstown, and Dr Patrick Dowling, P.P., Stradbally (died, 1826), succeeded by Dr Anthony Duanne (died, 1833), succeeded by Rev. James Maher.[82]

At the apex of the diocesan structure was of course the Ordinary. Historically the seat of the bishop gave its name to the diocese as did the towns of Kildare and Leighlin in the early medieval period. But from the Reformation until Doyle's episcopacy successive bishops had no defined seat or episcopal residence in Kildare or in Leighlin either before or after the dioceses were effectively united in 1678. Delany and Corcoran, Doyle's immediate predecessors, had resided in the town of Tullow and held the parish of that name and Mountrath as their mensal parishes. Mountrath was part of the ancient abbacy of St Fintan which also comprised the parishes of Ballyfin and Raheen and was more generally known as Clonenagh.

Doyle did not hesitate to re-examine the accepted arrangement. Raheen was given its own parochial identity in 1820. He perceived that Carlow town, location of Carlow College, was the focus and centre of ecclesiastical life in the diocese and should determine the site of his episcopal seat. Tullow he described as a 'villaggio situato quasi nell extremita della Diocesi'.[83] Moreover, Tullow and Mountrath were approximately forty miles apart and thus unsuitable for the close personal supervision which characterised Doyle's pastorate. Doyle decided to establish his seat in or near Carlow parish and to centralise his mensal parishes. Immediately on his consecration as bishop he petitioned Rome to allow him to switch his mensal parishes to Carlow and the adjoining parishes of Killeshin and Tinryland.[84] Dr Michael Prendergast, vicar-general, concurred with the proposal but advised the bishop in February 1820 that 'it would be improper to make it public at present' because of the danger of parochial hostility in Tullow.[85] Rome, following normal procedure, referred the proposal to the suffragan bishop's metropolitan, in this case Dr Troy.[86] But for whatever reason, the tardiness of Rome, the archbishop, the difficulty of creating mensal parishes until they became vacant, or Doyle's concentration on more pressing pastoral concerns, the matter was dropped for two years when Doyle eventually settled for only half his original scheme.

From his elevation until mid-1823 he held Tullow and Clonenagh as mensal parishes. In June 1823 the parish priest of Carlow died and Doyle took the opportunity to make the parish mensal; at the same time he erected Mountrath into a parish.[87] In October 1823 he requested Roman sanction for this arrangement.[88] In December, Rome approved the siting of the episcopal seat in Carlow[89] and in February 1824, having consulted Archbishop Murray, it approved the new mensal parish.[90] The dues of Ballyfin, which now also assumed its own parochial identity, were granted by rescript to Doyle on the express condition that they were to be expended for the support of the new Maryborough convent or other charitable purposes.[91] In 1824 the administration of Raheen was annexed by Doyle to Mountrath parish during the lifetime of the incumbent parish priest[92] (who died in 1835).

Doyle never resided in Tullow. From 1819 until 1822 he lived in Carlow College and for some time in Carlow town. He then removed two miles from Carlow to Old Derrig, a three storey house and twelve acres, in Killeshin parish in Queen's County. Here he lived until 1826 when he returned somewhat reluctantly to Carlow parish to occupy Braganza House purchased for his use and that of his successors by the clergy and faithful of the diocese at a cost of nearly £3,000 sterling.[93] Braganza had been named by a former owner, Sir Dudley Hill, who had been in the Portuguese military service. Doyle lived there until his death.

The difficulty of tracing curates renders it impossible to give a precise breakdown of the exact number of priests in each parish of the diocese. The majority of parishes had two priests, a parish priest and a curate; some big parishes such as Graiguenamanagh and Killeigh had two or more curates. In 1825 there were 'several' parish priests who had no curates but by 1829 only three were found to be so.[94] In 1827 Doyle enumerated ninety-five priests in the diocese.[95] In 1832 he estimated that there were more than 100 but less than 110 clerics on the mission.[96] In 1835 there were 108 secular priests in Kildare and Leighlin.[97]

In his 1821 pastoral Doyle lamented the 'small number of our fellow-labourers which the want of a competent support does not permit us to increase'.[98] In 1825 he still had 'not employed upon the mission more than two-thirds of the number, which would be necessary, for the due discharge of the priestly functions among the people' because he did not wish 'to burthen the people, who are too much weighed down with other claims ...'.[99] Yet again in 1827 he reiterated his view that clerical numbers were 'not at all proportioned to the wants of the ministry'.[100] By Doyle's own tally he had one priest to 2,960 people in 1827.[101] This ratio had been reduced despite an increasing population to one priest to 2,685 people in 1834–5[102] but it was nonetheless the highest and worst ratio in the Dublin province. The neighbouring diocese of Ferns had a ratio of one priest to 1,941 people in 1834–5 which was the best in Ireland.[103]

It is commonplace to read that the Catholic church was unable to cope with a dramatically increasing population in the immediate pre-famine period but as Doyle's comments make clear, if such was the case, and it is debatable, it sprang from a pastoral concern not to overburden the poor who constituted an overwhelming proportion of the flock rather than from an actual shortage of priests – readily supplied in this case by Carlow College. Indeed, as Doyle told a colleague, 'it is a sin to oppress the poor for whatever reason however holy'.[104] One should be wary of placing too much reliance on statistics alone. Because the ratio of priests to people in Kildare and Leighlin was not the ideal one it does not follow that there was pastoral negligence, rather a greater work-load befell those priests who were actually on the mission. And it was precisely this point – the quality of priests on the mission rather than their number – that was of most pressing concern to Bishop Doyle.[105]

The socio-economic status of a parish, rather than its size, extent or the arduousness of its pastorate, dictated the qualities of the parish priest appointed to it. A parish containing an urban area required a priest of 'better information' and 'more improved habits' by contrast with a priest of 'less conspicuous character' who ministered in a backward or hill parish. The town priest had to dress in a better fashion than his country colleagues. When a town parish fell vacant, the bishop first looked among his curates for a suitable candidate; if no one was to be found there, he translated a parish priest who had the requisite qualities. On the other hand, Doyle stated, for a parish 'where a person not specially gifted is necessary, we take from amongst the curates some man who has laboured for several years, and whose morals have been good, and who has a capacity for giving instruction in public'. But if a curate was incapable of preaching or had been immoral at any time he remained a curate for life.[106]

The Council of Trent allowed a right of patronage where there had been a foundation or endowment.[107] Presentation to all parishes within the diocese of Kildare and Leighlin lay within the remit of the bishop and this points to the absence of an old Catholic aristocracy or strong gentry class within the diocese. Although in at least two cases, prominent Catholics thought their influence with Doyle would result in their favour, we must distinguish between presentation and representation. There are four recorded cases of lay representation to the bishop to influence his choice of appointment of parish priest.[108]

In 1821 Arthur Kavanagh, Esq., wrote to the bishop in favour of the appointment of Michael Graham, C.C., Ballyadams, as parish priest of Arles, vacant on the death of Jeremiah Lalor.[109] Kavanagh's appeal was unsuccessful. Patrick Hickey,

P.P., Hacketstown (1814–21) was translated to Arles.[110] Graham, who, Comerford stated 'had been for a long time a curate' became parish priest of the new parish of Clonaslee in 1828.[111] More influential perhaps was Dominick O'Reilly of Kildangan Castle who advocated the appointment of the thirty-five-year-old Patrick Murphy, C.C., Monasterevan, to succeed John Robinson, P.P., Monasterevan.[112] O'Reilly had a better case than Kavanagh. He claimed to be expressing the views of more than just himself. It was his contention that the entire parish agreed on Murphy as Robinson's successor. Murphy was appointed[113] although events were to prove that he may have been lacking in resolution.[114]

A democratic influence on the ecclesiastical process can be detected in the interesting Philipstown parish case of 1825. In June of that year William Scully wrote to Doyle on his own behalf and that of the parishioners of Philipstown petitioning the bishop for the appointment of Patrick Rigney, C.C., to replace the deceased parish priest Matthew O'Reilly.[115] In response Doyle praised the 'very proper' manner in which Scully's and the parishioners' sentiments had been conveyed and took 'particular pleasure to know that Mr Rigney has deserved of the Protestant and Catholic people of Philipstown that favourable opinion which they have expressed of him'. He stated that he would consider the wishes of the people of Philipstown when making the appointment.[116]

As a curate of Killeigh parish in 1820, Patrick Rigney had been the subject of a strong and possibly over-enthusiastic complaint from his superior, James Dowling: 'no P. Priest in Ireland *ever* met with such insolence, [and] abuse in my own house before my servants' as he had suffered from Rigney.[117] It was probably in consequence that Rigney was transferred to Philipstown and he was not the bishop's first choice for the new vacancy in 1825; that went to Patrick Brennan, P.P., Kildare and Rathangan. Brennan was preparing to comply with Doyle's wishes when the weight of popular opinion against his removal made him request the bishop for sanction to remain.[118] Doyle permitted this change of mind stating that he 'hoped the voice of the people was supported by the voice of God'.[119] In these circumstances Patrick Rigney became parish priest of Philipstown.[120]

Though the appointment of curates lay fully within his control, Doyle normally took care to ascertain beforehand the views of the parish priests who were to receive them.[121] The curate in the parish and the lay sister in the convent constituted a kind of religious proletariat which did a great deal of the work that history has been inclined to overlook. As will be seen in a later chapter, Doyle, made every effort to ensure that the curate was adequately maintained by his parish priest.[122]

Prior to Doyle's elevation, induction by letter was the only form of induction common in the diocese, as indeed it had long been the custom throughout Ireland.[123] Doyle immediately implemented the practice of requiring the P.P., on appointment, to go before an authorised priest who would receive his profession of faith as found in the Roman pontifical *De Synodo habendo*[124] and to take an oath binding him to observe the canons of the church and the statutes of the diocese.[125]

Doyle forbade clergymen to bequeath property acquired by virtue of their office to relatives or friends.[126] The provincial statutes contain a strong injunction that church property was to be left for church or charitable purposes only.[127] Clergymen were warned against dying intestate. The rural dean was ordered to ensure that the dying priest had made a will.[128] Many parochial houses were lost to their parishes when claimed or seized by relatives of parish priests who had died intestate.[129] Doyle refused to allow the month's mind mass for one priest whose parochial house fell into the hands of relatives on his death.[130] He abhorred the alienation of church property, holding that 'all things derived by a churchman on account of his ministry are a sacred trust, bound by the tie of religion, so that it is a species of sacrilege to alienate it from those purposes'.[131]

ADMINISTRATION: THE TRIDENTINE MODEL

The originality of Doyle's pastorate does not lie in his formulation of new laws but in his implementation of existing laws for he was part of the world-wide church governed by canon law. A recurring theme of this book is the influence of Tridentine legislation on Doyle's episcopacy. The canons and the decrees of the Council of Trent were a constant point of reference for him and he exalted the catechism of the Council of Trent stating that

> next after the Divine Revelation, I have perhaps learned more from it than from all the books I have ever perused. My judgement in religious matters has been cast in it, as it were in a mould – my decisions in matters of controversy and morals have been framed in it, and much of the public instruction I have ever communicated has been little more than the unfolding of its doctrines, its authorities and proofs.[132]

Both Corish[133] and Cullen[134] agree that there was a time lag of several centuries before the full establishment of the Tridentine church model in Ireland, which the former dates to *c*.1875. However, Tridentine forms and practices were instituted in Kildare and Leighlin during Doyle's episcopacy and throughout the Dublin province before his death. The laxity and weaknesses which Doyle endeavoured to reform and repair rarely sprang from widespread religious negligence per se among priests or people; rather they were largely a by-product of the success of the penal laws against normal Catholic religious organisation. The Catholic hierarchy during the penal era was forced to tolerate practices which it would otherwise have rooted out. Indeed, as Bossy[135] has pointed out, an attempt to institute full Tridentine practice in Ireland during that period might well have been disastrous for Catholicism in Ireland. The church under the penal code could not minutely examine the lives of the faithful or even engage in careful preparation of candidates for the priesthood. The fine print of Trent was almost a luxury which could not be invoked where the church was just about tolerated most of the time and its members lived in fear of a return to persecution. This was the situation in which the Irish Catholic church found itself from the time of Trent until the anti-Catholic legislation began to be dismantled in the last quarter of the eighteenth century. The process of re-emergence and recovery may have taken up to a century from then in the more disadvantaged dioceses but in the province of Dublin generally and specifically in Doyle's diocese it was complete within fifty years.

Unlike some of his colleagues on the hierarchical bench, Doyle had his finger on the pulse of his times. In the 1820s he perceived that the penal era was in large measure past (and for him it finally ended with the concession of emancipation in 1829) and in his own person, as the harbinger of religious and political change, he embodied a new era. He was psychologically free of the low profile and submissive mentality which the penal era had engendered. Unlike older bishops, notably Archbishops Curtis and Murray,[136] Doyle looked forward in hope to the future he was helping to create rather than backwards in trepidation at what might be again. In this changing situation the bishops, and none more than Doyle, were concerned to establish uniformity of practice and observance throughout their dioceses and the Irish church.[137] The general spirit of Trent was not good enough for Doyle who demanded strict observance to the letter of its legislation. This was not a goal to be aimed for at some distant date; it was a practice to be instituted from the beginning of his episcopacy.

Trent required that a diocesan synod be held yearly,[138] and accordingly during an annual week-long retreat for his diocesan clergy Doyle devoted one day 'to the revising, amending or enlarging the statutes of the diocese'.[139] Doyle held his first diocesan synod in Carlow College in July 1820 and undoubtedly it confirmed the statutes he had already issued at the beginning of that year.[140] Regulations dealing with masses for the dead, marriage, clandestine marriage, and the stations of confession were enacted at the diocesan synod held on 21 July 1821. Each priest was required to obtain a copy of the statutes and to publish to the faithful those parts which directly concerned them.[141] The complete dearth of information on diocesan synods between 1825 and 1834 inclusive, probably arises from the likelihood that Doyle in the years 1820 to 1824 promulgated the disciplines he wished to inaugurate throughout the diocese and subsequent synods merely oversaw minor alterations and improvements to these statutes.

Even though Trent made a provincial synod mandatory every three years[142] the detailed and comprehensive statutes of 1831 were the first in the province of Dublin since the late seventeenth century. Four Dublin provincial synods were held in the seventeenth century: Kilkenny (1614), Tycrogir (1640), and Dublin

(1685 and 1688) during the brief reign of James II when the public exercise of the Catholic religion was restored. Rev. William Meagher, biographer of Archbishop Murray, writing in 1853, described this seventeenth-century synodal legislation as useful for the insight it gave 'into the origin of so many peculiarities of discipline, that even to the present, in some degree prevail in our national church'.[143]

The decrees of the synod of Kilkenny which were re-enacted by all subsequent seventeenth century synods are legislatively the most important. The prelates who convened at peril of their liberty and even their lives professed their acceptance of the Council of Trent but regretted that owing to the position of the Catholic church in Ireland *vis-à-vis* the state, they could not insist on full publication of Tridentine legislation. Furthermore 'from the mournful condition of the times, it would be dangerous and often impossible to reduce its every ordinance to practice'.[144] The synod denounced clandestine marriages as impious and detestable and excommunicated all participants but notably abstained from declaring such marriages null and void as Trent had done. The synod of 1685 forbade a Catholic to contract marriage before a Protestant clergyman.[145] With parochial clergymen in short supply, the synod of Kilkenny was unable to give effect to the strong recommendation of Trent on promotion to vacant parishes through public examination of suitable candidates.[146] In fact, on account of the shortage of secular priests, bishops were allowed to arrange with the superiors of religious orders for regulars to be assigned to parishes provided it could be accomplished without detriment (and it hardly could) to regular observance.[147] Trent decreed that the bishop should not allow the mass 'to be celebrated, either by any seculars or regulars whatsoever, in private houses; or at all out of church'.[148] This ruling could not of course be complied with where there were no proper churches or even mass houses with perhaps mass celebrated only in the open air on unconsecrated ground. Similarly the ceremonies which accompanied the rites of passage – baptism, matrimony and the funeral service – were most unlikely to be performed in church as Trent required. In the disestablished Catholic church tithes could not be collected in full or at all and it would have been a very foolhardy policy to excommunicate withholders of dues as Trent recomended.[149]

The 1685 synod of Dublin formally accepted the decrees of the Council of Trent except the decree annulling clandestine marriages and that enjoining the conferring of benefices by concursus, the enforcement of the latter being left to the prudence of the Ordinary.[150] In practice, however, the full discipline and rigour of Trent was rarely implemented as is suggested by the 1688 provincial synod which gave each bishop in his respective diocese freedom to dispense, provided there was just cause, from each and every statute enacted at all provincial synods throughout the seventeenth century.[151] The problem for the Irish church was that the statutes of the Council of Trent were framed in the context of established and institutional churches such as those found in Italy, France and Spain. Until the late eighteenth and early nineteenth centuries, Irish Catholicism was unable to re-develop the organisational and institutional structures forfeited during the Reformation. The most striking feature of the Catholic church in Ireland in the intervening centuries was just how non-Tridentine it had become.

The 1831 Dublin provincial statutes are of key significance in the history of the Irish Catholic church in the nineteenth century. The pastoral legislation of the national synod of Thurles in 1850 merely extended to the rest of Ireland what had been laid down for the Dublin province in 1831.[152] In 1832 Doyle stated that 'our church has been in such a state that we could for a long time past have no regular discipline' but this situation had been rectified by the previous year's synod.[153] Its legislation he delineated as

> a collection of the statutes and ordinances of the province of Dublin, col-
> lected and arranged and new modelled and re-enacted by my metropoli-
> tan and his suffragans ... it embodies, arranges and re-enacts the disci-
> pline of the Catholic church in Ireland for centuries, so as to make it ap-
> plicable to the present circumstances of our country.[154]

In July 1831 the bishops of the Dublin province each held synods in his respective diocese to give their clergy an opportunity to express their opinions on the proposed legislation. But if the methods employed by Archbishop Murray were typical, the synods were public relations exercises rather than opportunities for a real input by the second order clergy. His synod got through its agenda in only three days. Dr Murray appointed a Procurator Cleri through whom alone communications were to be channelled from the assembled clergy to the archbishop as 'no debating whatever could be allowed in the synod'. Unlike Doyle, Archbishop Murray found himself burdened with a diocesan chapter. Before synodal decrees could be published they had first to be submitted to the chapter for its 'counsel and advice' otherwise, Dr Murray feared, there was a danger that the enactments might be canonically null and void. Murray held a chapter meeting at which the statutes were read only pro forma. At this meeting, he informed Doyle, with some sarcasm, he had stated 'I should request the Counsel of my Beloved and Venerable Chapter, whose judgement I valued so much'. The chapter requested a 'month!' to deliberate which Murray refused stating that they had proposed no material changes in the statutes. He humoured them in a 'little Latin oration' and closed the synod 'somewhat peremptorily'.[155] However, Murray was no match for Doyle when it came to getting his own way. Among the prelates of the province (and nationally) Doyle's was the dominant voice, and Murray, though his metropolitan, was neither desirous nor capable of competing with him; instead he acknowledged his ability, invariably sought his advice and generally decided to do whatever he suggested, even if he did not like it. The 1831 statutes appear to have been a case in point. At the end of July 1831 Murray complained to Doyle that he had 'not complied with the engagement to consult the bishops on the debated points of the statutes ...'.[156] A good authority has stated that these statutes 'were drawn up by Dr Doyle, with the exception of the sixth chapter, which was written by Dr Kinsella, bishop of Ossory'.[157] This is a statement we have sought to prove conclusively in this work by demonstrating how the disciplines effected by Doyle in Kildare and Leighlin in the 1820s were reflected in the 1831 statutes.

In the discharge of his duty Bishop Doyle was obliged to make regular visitations of his diocese with a view to maintaining faith and morals. The visitation practice had fallen somewhat into desuetude before it was re-established by the Council of Trent:

> bishops shall not fail to visit their respective dioceses, either personally, or, if they be lawfully hindered, by their vicar-general or visitor; if they shall not be able, on account of its extent, to make the visitation of the whole annually, they shall visit at least the greater part thereof, so that the whole shall be completed in two years, either by themselves or their visitors.[158]

A canonical investigation of his diocese was thus incumbent on Doyle every two years. He chose to visit Kildare one year and Leighlin the next.[159] He devoted at least two months – usually February and August or September – each year to an exhaustive visitation[160] made without the assistance of a secretary, registrar, or official which were denied in law to a Catholic bishop.[161]

Doyle subjoined to his first pastoral letter in 1820 extracts from the Roman pontifical, *de visitatione*; from the Bull of Sixtus V *de visitatione liminum Apostolorum*; and from the rules prescribed by Benedict XIV *de relatione fucienda S. Cong. S. Con. Trid.* – an index of those matters which he was obliged to inspect or inquire into at the visitation of each parish, prior to his making a report on the state of the diocese to the Holy See.[162] There is an important account, in note form, of the general objects and subjects of an episcopal visitation in Doyle's commonplace book for 1820. These were the matters he intended to inquire into on visitation and they indicate clearly his priorities at the outset of his episcopacy:

> The lives and manners of the clergy, their age, residence, family, labours and merits.
>
> The mode of instructing the children in the Catechism, to ascertain the plan, and suggest any improvements it may require, with a view of rendering it uniform and general throughout the diocese. If there be no plan to require the immediate establishment of one.
>
> The manner of preaching, its frequency, to reprove at first the neglect of it, to require it afterwards even under pain of censure, to declare to

coadjutors that not one of them will be promoted who does not instruct as frequently as is consistent with their other avocations, the number of times to be determined at the conferences.

The mode of administering the sacraments of penance and the Eucharist at Christmas and Easter, and of collecting the dues at these times, to pronounce unequivocally that it is simoniacal to enforce the payment of them – subtractione Ministerii, St Thomas. To introduce gradually one mode of collecting them through the diocese and if possible to have it done by committee of the laity, but this is only to be recommended, till it is proposed and settled in a synod.

To ascertain the number of absentees from amongst those who received the sacraments at one time – also of those above twelve years of age who have not yet received them, also the number of those who receive communion frequently, or only twice in the year.

The state of the divine worship, first the number and state of the chapels, or chapel houses, the latter to be encouraged by every means but always to be held in trust – The trustees to be two parishioners, the incumbent and the Ordinary.

The state of all the vestments, public and private in the parish, of the chalices, pyxis, oil-stocks and also the library where there is one, and where there is not to recommend its formation.

The state of the choir or confraternity of the Christian Doctrine. If these be not formed let them be earnestly recommended.

The parochial registers of births and marriages – where these are not found to require their immediate formation.

The number of those who may have died without the sacraments and the cause thereof.

The manner of administering the sacraments of baptism and matrimony. Let the practice of bringing the children to the [chapel] houses be encouraged, and baptism never refused on any pretext but above all for want of money.

The fees of marriage to be regulated by a general rule but in no instance to be enforced by a refusal to marry the parties, evil cannot be done for any end. Also if the parties be required to go to confession before the marriage? And this to be regulated by a general rule.

The number of schools in the parish, if endowed, and by whom, if visited by the clergy, the number of children, the plan of education.

Soutanes and additional vestments to be procured by means of small collections on Sundays. There must be a soutane in each chapel.

Before making his visitation Doyle distributed a printed schedule to be filled up and answered by his priests and returned to him.[163] This form contained five large blanks for a statement of the titles on which the chapels and parochial houses (if any) were held, the name of the lessee, the term of years and the rent, the name of the person with whom the lease was deposited; the saint to whom the church was dedicated; the number of chalices, ciboria, or other plate, vestments, albs, copes, altar linen, missals and the number of volumes in the chapel library; the number in the confraternities of the Christian Doctrine and the Blessed Sacrament; the number of adults and monthly communicants and the names of the most obstinate absentees from their Easter duty; of public sinners in the parish with an account of their crimes; of public abuses, such as illegal combinations, drunkenness, quarrelling, violation of the Lord's day, night wakes or public dances, the number of schools, the names of the masters and mistresses, and the average attendance of pupils; the number of masses on each Sunday, and if special dues were paid for any; the time at which the catechism was taught, and also vespers, if celebrated.

Doyle normally began his visitation at ten o clock in the morning and generally spent two days in each parish. The first day was spent in examining the children to be confirmed, in inspecting the altar fabrics and vestments, and in settling 'such private business' of those parishioners who wished to have recourse to him. A public invitation to this effect was to be published by the parochial clergy before his arrival.[164] It would appear that the bishop did not so much have to settle disputes as to adjudicate on 'numberless cases of conscience'[165] which were referred to him – a positive indication that many were taking their religion very seriously indeed. The second day of the visitation was devoted to catechesis of the flock though apparently only the heads of families and schoolteachers were required to attend.[166] The confirmation of children and admission of members into the Confraternity of the Blessed Sacrament were also carried out on the second day. On his first visitation Doyle confirmed not less than 32,000,[167] and there is no mention on his part of dissatisfaction with candidates for the sacrament or the rejection of any because of lack of preparedness, although it seems that both situations obtained. On visitation Doyle also preached almost every day for several successive weeks. The purpose of the visitation was to ascertain exact details which would enable Doyle to achieve a complete investigation into the spiritual and temporal affairs of his diocese. His Relatio Status of 6 November 1820 was received with the warmest thanks by Rome. Cardinal Fontana, prefect of Propaganda Fide, marked his approval by presenting Doyle with a two volume condemnation of the synod of Pistoia.[168]

The visitation ritual provided the bishop with an opportunity for the punishment of those guilty of causing public crimes or scandals among the faithful. The Council of Trent stated that

the sword of excommunication is the very sinews of ecclesiastical discipline, and very salutary for keeping people in their duty, yet it is to be used

with great sobriety and great circumspection; seeing that experience teaches
that if it be rashly or for slight causes wielded, it is more despised than
feared, and produces ruin rather than safety.[169]

There were three types of excommunication: ipso facto, and greater and lesser
episcopal excommunication. In his parliamentary evidence on the state of Ireland in 1825 Doyle stated that ipso facto excommunication was 'extremely rare'
and required 'so many conditions in order that it be incurred, as that no person,
morally speaking, now, unless clergymen whose profession makes them acquainted
with those kind of things, does incur it'. A person who incurred lesser excommunication could not receive the sacraments during the period when he was subject
to it, but it was a censure so light as to be hardly known and its use scarcely ever
incurred. Greater excommunication however was 'the most awful censure the
church can inflict',[170] and it was quite often inflicted by Doyle on visitation.

The ceremony of excommunication, where the candles in the church were
extinguished and the bishop commended the body of the offender to the Devil
and his soul to God, was a solemn, imposing and frightening occasion, designed
to leave an indelible impression on the guilty party and all who witnessed it. One
man excommunicated by Doyle for criminal complicity committed suicide. In
Tullow, Doyle excommunicated a man guilty of incest. He quoted St Paul's first
letter to the Corinthians warning the parishioners not to eat or keep company
with the unclean man and to shun him. The excommunicated party had to leave
the parish as a result.[171] In 1826 the bishop excommunicated several persons who
had entered into communion with proselytisers in Clane parish. The lesser offenders were received back into the fold without too much difficulty; the ringleaders were required to kneel in the chapel yard of Staplestown for three successive Sundays during the celebration of mass – which mandate was fulfilled.[172]
Doyle put down faction fighting in Mountrath in 1825 by excommunicating the
ringleaders who, as public sinners, did public penance and were soon afterwards
received back into the church.[173]

The faithful were not allowed to communicate with the excommunicated 'os
orare, vale, communio, mensa negatur' unless 'utile, lex, humile, res ignorata,
necesse' allowed such communication. In 1825 Doyle stated that it would be
difficult to find a person who would not be entitled to enter into communication
with an excommunicated person. Excommunication only had severe consequences
for the person thus placed when it was accompanied by a public denunciation.
Doyle allowed: 'I have no doubt it would do him [the excommunicated person]
serious injury'. However, a person who had been excommunicated and denounced
might resort to the courts for redress and in consequence the Catholic hierarchy
were generally very careful, for our own safety's sake, even in cases where the
criminal is most obstinate and wicked, and scandalous, not to denounce him so as
to bring upon him any of those temporal evils which would follow from his being

so denounced'.[174] The threat rather than the actual performance of excommunication was sometimes all that was required to bring recalcitrants to heel. Excommunication was threatened in 1822 and 1832 on members of secret societies but it does not appear to have been enforced – it would have been difficult, in any case, to lay hands on the perpetrators of terrorism. Excommunication was a faculty regarded with such horror by the general body of Catholics that the bishop had to be wary of incurring hostility for imposing it[175] except in cases of absolute necessity.

For the duration of Doyle's episcopacy – a period of fifteen years – fourteen diocesan pastorals have been traced. He published two diocesan pastorals in the years 1823, 1829 and 1831. No pastorals have been discovered for 1824, 1827, 1828 and 1830, although it seems likely that Doyle did publish letters to the faithful in those years which have yet to be found.[176] At least four national pastoral letters were written by Doyle though published as the collective work of the Irish hierarchy.[177] The diocesan pastorals are most appropriately treated in the context of Doyle's various ecclesiastical and pastoral reforms rather than collectively.

Doyle's June 1823 pastoral promulgating a miracle through the intercession of the Catholic clergyman, Prince Hohenlohe, is both interesting and significant as it captures the spirit of almost millenarian fervour within resurgent Irish Catholicism in the 1820s and also demonstrates the pastoral platform which was Doyle's springboard on to the national political stage. This pastoral which had important interdenominational and political consequences is discussed at length elsewhere.[178]

The priest chiefly responsible for popularising the merits of Prince Hohenlohe in Ireland was the remarkably ascetic and humble Henry Young – a Dublin diocesan curate. In his own person he epitomised resurgent Catholicism in Ireland. Roman-educated and influenced by the Vincentians, he was a dedicated giver of parochial missions in the 1820s and was also notable for the number of ultramontane devotional practices which he received faculties and licences to introduce into Ireland.[179] Doyle held Young in high regard[180] and he invited him to conduct a mission in at least one Kildare and Leighlin parish – Baltinglass in 1828. Young made a considerable impact,[181] erecting the stations of the cross in the churches, establishing a Purgatorian society, and enrolling parishioners in the devotion of the Brown Scapular of Our Lady of Mount Carmel.[182] His parochial missions or 'spiritual exercises' began with morning prayer and meditations followed by mass and confessions for adults until midday. Meanwhile and on alternate weekdays boys and girls were instructed separately in the chapel (by catechists with only six to a class) from early morning until noon when Rev. Young would 'assemble them round the rails and interrogate them from the altar steps'; after which their confessions were heard until four o'clock in the afternoon. There was instruction for adults in the evening and confessions of the elderly until late. In the fourth week of these exercises the children were admitted in classes to general communion 'which they make with fervour, in neat dress and lighted wax candles in their hands, which they blow out on point of receiving'. This missionary programme, Young informed Doyle, was 'the order of the days, weeks and months and I hope of my whole life'. Young generally devoted seven or eight weeks to each parish which he found 'too little to go thro' a regular course of instruction';[183] he made house-to-house visitations and spent 'some months'[184] in Baltinglass as part of a mission in the Wicklow mountains.

In terms of stimulating Catholic devotion the 1826 Jubilee[185] or 'holy year' was in some ways complementary to the promulgation of miracles by Doyle and Archbishop Murray in 1823. The 'pious excitement which it caused was most vivid, and its results most salutary and lasting'.[186] In our period the benefits of the first jubilee published could only be gained by pilgrims who visited Rome in 1825. The encyclical *Quod hoc ineunte* (25 May 1824)[187] announcing this jubilee was received by the Irish hierarchy but Doyle in particular had grave doubts about the wisdom of its publication.[188] What exactly Doyle objected to in the encyclical is unclear but it may have seemed to him to have struck a note of triumphalism (concerning the European Catholic resurgence after the desolation of the church during the French revolutionary and Napoleonic periods) which he felt would only become a source of controversy and add to interdenominational tension, then very high, in Ireland. Curtis, who agreed that it was a 'thorny subject' informed Murray that Doyle (whom they relied upon in such matters) considered it 'impossible to propose [the Jubilee] in the same victorious manner'[189] as it had been written, to the Irish public. Doyle's opinion prevailed; he stated in 1825 that the Irish hierarchy 'did not think it proper' to publish the Jubilee in Ireland. Nor was he aware of a single individual who had travelled from Ireland to Rome for the Jubilee.[190] Significantly the holy year commenced on Christmas Eve 1824, the same date on which many Irish Protestants feared they were to be slaughtered in a Catholic uprising.[191]

By the encyclical *Charitate Christi* (25 Dec. 1825)[192] the Roman Jubilee of 1825 was extended to the whole world for 1826. This time the hierarchy had apparently no difficulty with its promulgation. The encyclical was translated and published in Ireland together with a pastoral address of the bishops written by Doyle.[193] To obtain the benefits of the Jubilee (a plenary indulgence) the faithful were required to visit designated chapels on any fifteen days within the space of six months. The number of chapels to be visited on those days was, in ordinary cases, four, but in country areas this was reduced to one chapel in each parish.[194] Bishop Doyle reported to Cardinal Somaglia that the Jubilee was received with great devotion and frequentation of churches in Kildare and Leighlin.[195] The 1826 Jubilee has been acknowledged as a very significant catalyst of devotional resurgence in the diocese of Dublin. Archbishop Murray's biographer commented that 'during the entire period of the Jubilee, which had to be extended again and again[196] ... scenes of excited devotion were continually witnessed, in almost every parochial and every conventual church within the city, and in several throughout the rural districts'.[197] He admitted that prior to the Jubilee

> the attachment of the Metropolitan Catholics to the observance of their religious duties had been, in fact, for a long time anything but edifying. In later years owing to several concurrent circumstances consoling progress for the better was discernible, but to the fidelity with which the graces of the 'holy year' were husbanded was due, in a chief degree, the amazingly increased frequentation of the sacraments ....

Uplifted hands, streaming eyes and shouting of responses were features of the behaviour of huge congregations at enthusiastic devotions.[198] The intensity of this religious experience was paralleled by similar happenings within evangelicalism and might be likened to a modern day Charismatic Renewal meeting.

On 2 December 1832 Pope Gregory XVI promulgated a Jubilee limited to three weeks' duration in 1833. In Kildare and Leighlin Doyle announced the Jubilee with a pastoral letter. The Jubilee began on 3 March 1833 in the diocese and continued until Pentecost, both days included. The conditions prescribed for gaining the plenary indulgence were: a penitent confession; devout communion; two visits to any chapel within the individual's parish where prayers were to be offered for the pope's intentions; a fast on Wednesday, Friday and Saturday of one of the three weeks; and finally alms-giving according to devotion.[199]

A major theme of the pastoral letters, usually issued for the beginning of Lent, was the manner of observance of this period of penance within the Catholic church from Ash Wednesday to Easter Sunday. Bishop Doyle's rules for the observance of Lent[200] required the faithful to fast daily on one meal and one collation, and to abstain from flesh meats. The use of eggs was permitted once daily to all, except on Fridays, the three days following Ash Wednesday, and Wednesday and Friday in Holy Week. Excepted from these regulations were tradesmen and others employed in hard labour, the poor whose ordinary diet was not good, persons enfeebled through old age or who were otherwise infirm, those under twenty-one years of age and pregnant or nursing women. These people, though obliged to abstain from flesh-meats, were exempted from the obligations of fasting but were expected to retrench a portion of their meals occasionally when they could do so without prejudice to their health. A further category was permitted to eat flesh meat throughout Lent. In this group were the sick and convalescent, children under the age of seven,[201] mendicants, and servants who could not conveniently get fasting fare. They were not allowed to eat meat more than once daily, or to use it on the same day with eggs or fish. In his 1823 Lenten pastoral Doyle warned that the use of butter or milk-meats at breakfast, by young persons or others not obliged to fast, was an 'abuse gradually creeping in' and was to be prohibited to all except the sick or labouring poor.[202]

Doyle's Lenten regulations serve as an annual crude index of poverty, deprivation and unemployment levels within the diocese. In 1822, 1823,[203] possibly 1827[204] and 1832,[205] and again in 1834[206] Doyle permitted to all the use of flesh meat from the first Sunday of Lent to Palm Sunday inclusive, at dinner only, except on Wednesdays, Fridays and Saturdays. Eggs were allowed on all days except Fridays within this period. It was not lawful under the indulgence to eat flesh meat and fish at the same meal even on Sundays, nor to take two meals on any one day – Sundays excepted.[207] This relaxation derived from the bishop's conviction in these years that he simply could not impose the full discipline of Lent on his near famine-stricken flock.[208] Those who availed of the indulgences but were not impoverished were expected to repair the infringement of church discipline by prayer and active charity to the poor. On days when they had an option of eating meat Doyle exhorted the faithful to eat boiled meat so that the poor might be fed.[209] In his diocese Archbishop Troy recommended the boiling of plain dishes so that nourishing broths might be given to the poor.[210]

The Lenten regulations of the diocese of Dublin were similarly relaxed in 1823,[211] 1824,[212] 1827[213] and possibly 1832.[214] Dr Troy felt compelled to relax the discipline in 1823 on account of the 'almost general unemployment' and agricultural depression on top of 'the ordinary proportion of want and poverty always to be found in the capital'.[215] In 1824 and 1827 Archbishop Murray decided that because of the poverty of the poor it was unsafe for their health to enforce the abstinence laws in all their rigour.[216] In 1827 (the year in which the New Reformation enjoyed most success) Bishop Marum informed Doyle that 'never were the distresses of the lower orders, more heavy, or more universal, than at present, and they are likely to become, every day, more oppressive. The question is, whether the permission of using meat, eggs, etc., would operate in any considerable degree, as a relief'.[217] Dr Marum intended (as usual) to follow Doyle's advice.

In the above-mentioned years of great poverty or near famine the bishops only granted relaxations from Lenten discipline after much heart searching and with extreme reluctance. They were caught on the horns of a dilemma between their concern to uphold church discipline and their solicitude for the distress of their flocks. This dilemma Doyle frankly acknowledged in his 1823 Lenten pastoral:

> Why, dearly beloved, have we resolved to inflict as it were a new wound on the ancient and venerable usage of our holy church .... We have yielded as it were to the tears of the poor .... Pardon us then, dearest brethren, and pray that God may pardon us, if moved by an excessive charity for the poor, we have opened wider the gate, and made broader the way which leads the sinner to perdition.[218]

Dr Murray's 1824 Lenten pastoral referred to the 'humiliating fact' that little remained of the 'wholesome austerity' which their forefathers held necessary for the Christian observance of Lent.[219] Doyle likewise in his 1834 Lenten pastoral referred to church Lenten discipline as only a shadow of what it had once been.[220] Nevertheless both Doyle and Murray felt obliged on several occasions to place their maintenance of strict church discipline second to their anxiety for the health of their flocks.

Personally Doyle did not shirk a rigorous observation of Lenten requirements. His Lenten diet consisted of ling, macaroni and potatoes.[221] But not surprisingly with his delicate health he found Lent unusually trying.[222] In 1823 he acknowledged that he had been rash enough to abstain from meat and as a result had been obliged to eat it in Holy Week. Indeed, he was 'actually at death's door'.[223] In all of Doyle's Lenten pastorals particular stress is laid upon the obligation to practise mortification[224] – 'the mortification of your passions, by the pain, and anguish, and illness of the flesh, this is one of the ends of fasting'.[225] Prayer, penance and most especially alms-giving were expected of the faithful during Lent. Pretences to justify breaking the fast were denounced.[226] Hunger and thirst were inseparable from fast and abstinence yet Doyle urged perseverance unless the fasting was excessively inconvenient.[227]

In his 1820 Lenten pastoral the bishop recommended that the faithful assist at mass as often as possible during Lent and also attend the rosary and pious instructions in the evening at their respective chapels or in their own homes. During Lent Doyle gave talks in Carlow chapel a few evenings in the week to the people who assembled to pray there. The rosary devotion was 'especially recommended to all' in Doyle's 1823 Lenten pastoral.[228] Fathers of families were exhorted to say night-prayers with their children or domestics who did not have the opportunity of attending at chapel. In his 1820 pastoral Doyle hoped it was unnecessary to stress that all entertainments and public amusements were highly unbecoming during Lent.[229]

PLACES OF WORSHIP: CHURCH BUILDING

In 1825 Doyle maintained that 'one of the great obstacles to the instruction of the people in Ireland, is the want of sufficient room in our chapels'.[230] However, the financial pressure upon the Catholic population from a variety of quarters was so great that they could not enlarge their chapels, still less re-build them 'without making sacrifices which are peculiarly oppressive to them'. Doyle admitted that he had

> often ordered a chapel to be enlarged, or said, that otherwise I would not permit mass to be celebrated in it, and yet upon representation of the

priest, as to the distress and extreme poverty of the people, I have withdrawn such order, and suffered them to proceed as well as they could.[231]

The erection of the church of the Holy Cross in Killeshin by Rev. Michael
McDonald under Doyle's keen eye was in some ways a trial run for the building
of Carlow Cathedral by the bishop. The building of Killeshin church provides us
not alone with interesting examples of contemporary Protestant liberality but
also of the difficulties encountered in erecting in this instance a handsome, indeed architecturally distinguished, house of worship. The site was presented by
William Cooper of Cooper Hill who also made a contribution towards the building as did Colonel Bruen of Oak Park and the earl of Portarlington, all of whom
had land in the parish. The foundation stone was laid by William Cooper in early
May 1819. A meal for the gentry in attendance was provided in a tent while the
band of the Carlow Militia staff played several 'loyal, national and patriotic airs'.

Doyle promoted a sacred concert and charity sermon given in Carlow chapel
on 3 October 1819 to raise funds for the building. This 'grand Oratorio and sermon' was under the patronage of Lady Butler, Lady Burgh, Mrs Bruen, Mrs
Rochfort, Mrs Cooper and Mrs Fishbourne. Although the concert performed by
Italian opera singers who were not very familiar with the church music tradition
was less successful than it might have been, a meeting of Killeshin parishioners
on 11 October returned thanks to the Protestants who had attended especially
Sir Ulysses Burgh, W.P. Browne, Esq., Sir Charles Burton, Bart., W. Cooper, N.
Vigors and R.M. Fishbourne, who also acted as collectors. Protestant benefactors and especially Sir Henry Parnell enabled the parishioners to build the walls
and roof of this 'very beautiful' church, as Doyle described it. A few years later,
after the beginning of the New Reformation, Protestants were less likely to take
such a prominent part in a Catholic service. From his own income Doyle subscribed forty to fifty pounds for two or three years. In his Diocesan Book, Doyle
recorded that he had obtained from Pope Pius VII a decree dated 18 May 1821
granting a plenary indulgence for the souls in purgatory to all the faithful who
attended the sacraments of penance and eucharist in Killeshin church and prayed
for the propagation of the faith on the feast of the invocation of the Holy Cross or
on any day during the octave. The feast was marked by a procession of parishioners in Killeshin. Doyle celebrated high mass and preached a sermon to mark the
third anniversary of the laying of the foundation stone of Killeshin church on 6
May 1822. Yet despite significant Protestant aid and support from many families
of prominence in Queen's County and Carlow, indeed much more support than
was usual, after six years the building still remained unfinished and Doyle stated
that 'from the extreme poverty of the parishioners, I have not till lately [1825]
ventured to call upon them for any aid'. Rev. William Clowry preached the sermon in Killeshin on 4 May 1828. Funds collected at the annual procession in that
year were for the benefit of the new church.[232]

Difficult as it may have been, the provision of suitable, respectable, commodious places of worship in all the parishes of his diocese was a priority for Doyle. Church building was a *sine qua non* of his administration. Fitzpatrick claimed that if Doyle witnessed

> a parish priest, through laziness or apathy, deferring year after year to lay the foundation stone of a new chapel on a scale befitting the increased requirements or importance of his flock, the bishop has himself taken the initiative in tearing off the straw-thatch which covered the crumbling edifice, and made such arrangements, there and then, as led to the speedy erection of a suitable place of worship.[233]

By any standards Doyle's achievement in this regard was remarkable. By 1829 he had begun to build a cathedral, twenty-seven new churches had been erected; twenty-two churches had been rebuilt from their foundations and enlarged; forty-three churches had been greatly improved and enlarged and two new churches were planned. Out of a diocesan total of 104 churches only eleven were of a sufficiently satisfactory size and state of repair to lie beyond the scope of this extraordinary surge of church building and renovation.[234]

The significance of these new Catholic churches is that they were the first for several centuries to have been built with a view to permanence. Hence Doyle's concern with church leases. A permanent building demanded a very long lease, fee farm grant or preferably the fee simple of the site, and not simply a grace and favour arrangement. In earlier times, insecurity of tenure of the church site must have been a major factor inhibiting the erection of permanent churches. Even though finances were extremely stretched these new Catholic places of worship were not traditional mud-walled thatched barns but stone and slate structures which rivalled their state funded Protestant counterparts in giving glory to God. The Board of First Fruits heavily subsidised Anglican churches which were erected throughout the country in the early nineteenth century. These buildings no doubt indirectly influenced the Catholic church to match their scale. Most of the churches built during Doyle's episcopacy continued in constant use into the mid-twentieth century before it was found necessary to renovate them. They signify – and Carlow Cathedral is the outstanding example – the new self-confidence which invigorated Irish Catholics from at least the early years of the nineteenth century as they openly proclaimed their faith and threw aside the submissiveness of a ghetto mentality which had been engendered by the penal era. Doyle's achievement in Kildare and Leighlin was mirrored to a lesser extent throughout the other dioceses of the Dublin province.[235]

Each class within the Catholic community contributed to this church building boom according to its means. It has been suggested that the early nineteenth century churches were built by a nascent Catholic bourgeoisie and that the poor were largely irrelevant in their construction.[236] Self-evidently each class could only contribute according to its means and it should not be overlooked that the poor who could not contribute in cash drew building materials and laboured on church sites. Apart from a few notable families little enough is known of Kildare and Leighlin's Catholic bourgeoisie.[237] There is evidence however both from Bishop Delany's experience of church building in Tullow and Mountrath[238] and Bishop Doyle's at Killeshin and Carlow Cathedral (see below) to demonstrate convincingly that the poor were not loathe to contribute. Indeed both of these churchmen were anxious that the poor should not be asked to contribute because of the burden which this would impose.

Protestants of all hues were an important source of financial assistance for Irish Catholic church building. Doyle claimed that he could not draw a distinction in this matter between Protestants who were in favour of and against emancipation; 'they all seem to think it a duty, on their part, to contribute to provide for the people a place of worship'.[239] A number of letters preserved in the diocesan archives, usually in answer to requests for sites for churches, indicate Protestant liberality.[240] The only extant refusal of such a request made by Bishop Doyle, that of Wellesley Pole of Ballyfin, did not affect their good relations.[241]

In response to one request from Doyle for a church site, James Grattan, M.P., promised to check to see if he had any land in the area. He observed that Protestants and Catholics had to travel great distances on Sundays to their places of worship.[242] New churches were erected in densely populated areas usually more than three miles distant from the parochial church. Walter Berwick, agent to James Grattan on his Stradbally estate, pointed out to Doyle in 1825 that Grattan had given half an acre and a subscription for a new church at Vicarstown, Stradbally, but that construction had not proceeded and the poor were inconvenienced by the distance they had to travel to mass. The problem was the difficulty of finding priests free to say mass on Sundays.[243] The parish priest and his curate were engaged on Sundays at the churches of Stradbally and Esker. A 'fine Gothic church' was erected at Timahoe in the parish in 1832. Vicarstown had to wait until 1836 before its Catholic church was completed.[244]

By 1829 some furniture had been provided in nearly all the churches of the diocese.[245] The main aisles of these churches were usually unfurnished and except perhaps for some benches, the poor simply stood or knelt on the paved floor during mass. The new edifices however did contain galleries which provided opportunities for social point scoring.[246] Pews in these galleries were purchased by those who could afford them and they were reserved for the use of their own family only.

Carlow parish church had three galleries: front, north and south. Without exception, according to Doyle, the 'old and respectable' families of the town were subscribers to the prestigious front gallery. The occupants of the north and south galleries were socially superior to the congregation in the main body of the church but not as elevated as the members of the front gallery.

In 1814 the occupants of the front gallery each agreed to subscribe six guineas towards the purchase of an expensive organ. A parochial committee demanded a similar amount in 1822 from new-comers who occupied the front gallery for mass (though not apparently its railed off pews). A qualification of moral character was also required for entry to this gallery, though this was of less importance than capacity to pay. The moral character of subscribers was decided by the parochial committee not by scrutinizing the private life of anyone, but by taking cognizance of their public name. The 'door-keeper' or 'porter' placed on the front gallery was directed to refuse admission to anyone who refused to pay. 'Investigator', in a lengthy letter to the *Carlow Morning Post* published on 25 February 1822, complained on behalf of those who were refused, that six guineas was too much to have to pay as the value of money had increased since 1814. It was apparently Doyle who responded in the Carlow paper on 28 February 1822 under the nom-de-plume 'An impartial observer'. He stated that

> there is no church or chapel in any place that I know, where pews or galleries have not been erected by individuals, or by private subscriptions; the laws of the land, and those of the Church, deem such places private property and who can interfere with private property? No person, of whatsoever rank or office, can or ought to do it, for if such places were wrested by an abuse of power from their rightful owners, who would build them in future and without such places would not all be disorder? The sturdy vagrant and the delicate female might contend in the House of Prayer!

In the *Carlow Morning Post* of 4 March 1822, 'Investigator' contended that in chapels built by indiscriminate public subscription there should be no distinction of places 'except such as might be absolutely necessary to keep the wealthy and the extremely indigent, distinct from each other – the apparel, and want of cleanliness, in the latter, afford sufficiently obvious causes for this separation'. The Carlow gallery dispute assumed such proportions that Doyle found it necessary to hold a public meeting of parishioners in the parish chapel to resolve it on 10 March 1822. It was decided that the parochial committee were to receive not less than two guineas from each subscriber to the front gallery, or to demand more than four guineas, either sum, according to circumstances, being deemed equal to a subscription of six guineas in 1814. Subscribers to the north and south galleries were to give not less than one pound or not more than two pounds.

Many of the charges of poor stewardship brought against the parish committee were sustained by this lively meeting. From the chair, Doyle had to repress an 'attempt to excite disorder'. The meeting ended with Thomas Finn publicly moving a resolution complimenting the bishop for 'subduing the most angry passions' which had prevailed among the parishioners. The Carlow paper declined to publish further letters on the controversy but in April 1822 an anonymous 'friend to true religion' denounced the 'profane practice of seat buying' in an open letter to the archbishop of Dublin. 'The unhallowed crime of simony', he alleged, 'is now becoming general throughout Ireland'. His particular attention was focussed on the diocese of Kildare and Leighlin. Carlow, he stated, was the 'principal theatre where the malady has raged like a plague for the last nine years'. Furthermore seat buying was a form of taxation which also divided rich from poor to the extent that seats were changing hands for 'no less a sum than ten pounds'.[247]

When exactly Doyle introduced his gallery rule is not known, but it was probably at the time of this controversy. He decreed that: 'No person having a right to accommodation in a gallery can sell, bestow, transfer, or alienate such right, because all galleries, pews, etc., which are immovable, become a part of God's house, and cannot be disposed of or held as property by any individual'.[248] The subscribers to the building of a gallery, or a pew, were with their families, though not their collateral relations, entitled to seating therein provided they continued to reside in the parish. The right ceased if the family moved to another parish or ipso facto the line became extinct. The subscribers to the gallery, under the presidency of the parish priest, determined the sum to be paid for the upkeep of the chapel by those who sought admission to accommodation in the gallery, but the parish priest alone admitted such a person to the gallery.[249] Doyle encountered opposition to his gallery rule in the parishes of Tullow[250] and Graiguenamanagh.

We are in a position to state how Doyle coped with this latter case. There had been a recent history of poor relations between the administrator of Graiguenamanagh and his parishioners.[251] Martin Doyle, P.P., Clonegal, was translated to Graiguenamanagh in 1827.[252] Unlike his cousin, the bishop, he was no intellectual, but he was an equally tough and decisive cleric as he demonstrated in this parish during the tithe war. A spirit of opposition to the parish priest lingered in Graiguenamanagh from an earlier dispute between priest and people.

In July 1829 the parish priest informed his bishop that his new church gallery had been completed;[253] there had been a full meeting of subscribers at which 'all things went off very well, church law, custom, the bishop's practice, and the priest's will prevailed'. This latter point was perhaps the most important. He had however to notify Dr Doyle that there was a rumour of powerful opposition to his arrangements for the gallery but he was standing firm: 'I am never stouter than when hard pressed even tho' opposed to a General'.[254] The 'General' was Thomas Cloney, parish resident, descendant of a dispossessed Catholic landed family, rebel commander in 1798 and local politician – a figure of consequence.[255] It seems possible that he was leading the poorer classes of the parish in opposition to the new church gallery – certainly there was opposition to the payment being required by the P.P. for seating but it may be impossible now to decipher the exact

nature of the opposition. In November 1829 Bishop Doyle issued typically reso-
lute instructions to his parish priest:

> Keep the gallery closed until each person who has paid his contribution in
> part, or the vast majority of them, pay the residue and express unequivo-
> cally their assent to your regulation. Then, when it is opened, place at the
> door a man furnished with a list of those entitled to seats, and direct him
> to tell other persons (not a respectable stranger), who would attempt to go
> there, that he had your directions to refuse admittance to any other. If any
> person should attempt to enter by force, let him do so; but as soon as you
> hear of it, call upon him by name to retire; and if he refuse to do so, open
> your most severe rebukes upon him. Not however in a manner unbecom-
> ing your office or the place where you are. If this mode of proceeding
> should not suffice, we will then see what further steps should be taken.[256]

The building of Carlow Cathedral occupied much of Doyle's time between
1828 and 1833. From the outset of his episcopacy he had settled on erecting a
new church in Carlow: 'the only monument in stone I intend to leave after me'.[257]
Carlow parish had only one small chapel for a Catholic population of over 3,000
people.[258] In the late 1820s, mass was celebrated four times in the chapel on Sundays but the building was not big enough to accommodate the size of the congregation, some of whom were forced to remain outside in all weathers. The new
building however was not begun until the ninth year of Doyle's episcopacy. The
initial church building success of Gerald Doyle, P.P., in Naas parish, under difficult circumstances, spurred the bishop to start the work in 1828.[259] On 24 February 1828, Doyle chaired a meeting of the Catholic parishioners in the chapel
whch decided to enlarge the building and to establish a committee for fund-
raising purposes. Initially there was no mention of designating the enlarged building a cathedral.

On Easter Monday, 1828 Doyle laid the foundation stone of what would become Carlow Cathedral on a site lying between Carlow College and the Presentation convent and purchased from the latter.[260] Fitzpatrick has facilely written
that 'this splendid temple shot up almost by magic'[261] but this was far from the
reality of the case. At the outset, Doyle's finances were extremely limited for
such a large undertaking. He had established a weekly collection in Carlow town
and purchased several hundred cart-loads of stone, which, with sixty pounds in
cash, comprised his entire building fund. The religious of the diocese and the
Discalced Carmelite nuns of Ranelagh were requested to offer daily prayers for
the success of the enterprise.[262]

Doyle was severely embarrassed, and almost abandoned the work, when the
foundations were flooded by water from adjacent quarries. Moreover, the plan of
the first architect, Joseph Lynch, was 'too contracted',[263] for Doyle's ambition to

display 'a better style of architecture'[264] and Lynch retired from the project. Doyle obtained ground at either side of his site from Carlow College and the Presentation convent to extend the transepts. He then engaged Thomas A. Cobden, architect of Braganza, Ballykiely House, Killeshin church, and several other notable buildings in the Carlow region,[265] to erect the main structure and finish the building.[266]

Apart from Carlow town collections, Doyle received some support from neighbouring parishes.[267] He also addressed peers of the realm (with whom he was acquainted such as Leinster, Downshire, Mayo, Cloncurry, etc.) and gentry who had estates in the diocese.[268] Under the heading 'New Catholic church, Carlow' the *Carlow Morning Post* of 1 September 1828 reported:

> The work is now proceeded in with rapidity, and the spirit with which the farmers of a neighbouring parish – Dunleckney [Bagenalstown] – supply granite for the walls is truly admirable.
>
> On Friday last, one of the most extraordinary processions ever witnessed here was that of far more than 500 cars laden with blocks of iron-stone, drawn by very good horses and led by nearly as many fine athletic young men, coming from that single parish with unpurchased aid to the chapel – on every hundredth car, a musician. The train covered more than an English mile. The men were regaled on the lawn before the Right Rev. Doctor Doyle's residence, with [an] abundance of bread, cheese and beer – and, hot as the day was, many of them afterwards indulged in the merriest Irish jig dances upon the green turf.

By December 1828 when work stopped for the winter the 'new chapel' stood twenty feet high at a cost of £1,600 sterling. Doyle estimated that a further £3,000 'would be necessary to roof it in, and Providence must be very careful of it, or its advancement will be slow'.[269] The eventual cost was double Doyle's total estimate of £4,500.

By October 1829 Doyle was describing his 'new chapel' of a year before as a 'small cathedral'.[270] He solicited contributions from his diocesan clergy in the second half of 1829. The smallest sum promised by any of his parish priests was ten pounds, and each curate, except six from whom he would not accept money, gave five pounds.[271] This collection brought in £700.[272] In August 1830 Doyle sent Brother Serenus Kelly of the Patrician monastery in Tullow on a fund-raising trip to England. Despite his best efforts, Brother Kelly, who was an accomplished fund raiser, was not very successful. The bishop sent him an address to the English public which contained a brief history of the struggle of the Catholic church during the penal era and outlined the poverty of its places of worship.[273] In November 1830 Doyle sent Kelly a detailed report on the progress of the cathedral:

Our building is in a very advanced and gratifying state; the walls, forty feet high, with a cornice, parapet, and embrasures of seven feet in height, all of cut stone, are now nearly completed. At each end of the transept, as also at the eastern end, which terminates the choir and is opposite to the tower, the walls terminate in a point surmounted by a large stone cross, the summit of which is seventy-five feet from the base, and each of the eight angles which the building forms is ornamented on the outside by a large octagon tower of most beautiful architecture, raised twenty-two feet above the summit of the cornice. The whole front and tower are of cut stone; the latter, when finished, will be 120 feet high. The whole length is about 160 feet; that of the transept 120, and the width throughout is fifty feet. The figure of the building is cruciform. If we had sufficient means we could roof it next year, otherwise we must postpone doing so.[274]

Doyle expected to have finished building the walls by 1 December 1830. Their appearance, he enthused, was 'magnificent and beautiful'.[275]

Baroness Montesquieu gave Brother Kelly a subscription of fifty pounds and settled fifty pounds on Doyle for life or until the cathedral should be completed.[276] Doyle was also presented with a carriage which he sold to raise money for the cathedral.[277] Several absentee Carlow landlords resident in England were approached by Brother Kelly but they refused to contribute because they feared that Doyle favoured the repeal of the union.[278] Serenus collected a total of £500 in England.[279] From within the diocese, Patrick Maher of Kilrush contributed £200 on condition that one mass be celebrated in Carlow Cathedral every week forever for the 'temporal and spiritual good' of Patrick Maher and his descendants whether living or dead.[280]

The annual contributions 'of every class and descriptions of persons',[281] the several donations of peers and gentlemen, but especially those received from the diocesan clergy, had enabled Doyle to build the walls and raise a belfry but he lacked the £2,500 he reckoned was necessary to roof the building and put in the windows and doors. On 24 October 1830 he addressed the prioress of the Discalced Carmelites at Ranelagh:

> I think the prayers of the saints in Heaven and on earth are raising our Church without much human means for it has become even now the admiration of every person. And hitherto money has not failed us, so that though I don't know where to turn or look for money wherewith to roof it I am sure it will come to us.[281]

For the first and only time, Doyle, very reluctantly, appealed to the faithful of the diocese as a whole for funds to complete the cathedral.[282] The gross expenditure he now estimated more accurately at between £8,000 and £9,000.[283] His

January 1831 pastoral on the cathedral claimed that a diocesan collection was the 'only means of completing a building now so much advanced and so justly admired'.[284] A collection was made at all masses in every chapel of the diocese on 23 January 1831. How much the collection raised is not known. A year later, on 2 January 1832, Doyle wrote 'We owe nothing. One thousand pounds or thereabouts are still necessary to complete this work ... The bishop will next week call on the parishioners for their last contribution ...'.[285] Doyle still had to struggle, even selling some of his own 'property' to raise cash.[286] Efforts to raise funds during Doyle's visit to London in February 1832 to give evidence before the parliamentary committees on tithes were unsuccessful: 'The rich people there gave me nothing for our building, which notwithstanding is proceeding prosperously'. He was eventually, through lack of finance, forced to roof the building even though it was recommended that he heighten the walls.[287] The result was a somewhat low-sized Regency Gothic cathedral. On 1 December 1833 the new cathedral was dedicated to the Assumption of the Blessed Virgin Mary.[288] 'After six years of care and toil', Doyle wrote a few days later, 'we saw our task accomplished and our anticipation realised'.[289]

THE SECULAR CLERGY:
RENEWAL AND REFORM

Far superior to the average diocesan seminary,[1] Carlow College's standing was almost on a par with Maynooth College during Doyle's episcopacy. Strict entrance requirements and a thorough training imparted by a capable professorial staff ensured a supply of competent, well-educated priests for the home diocese.

Given Doyle's hostility to Dr Andrew Fitzgerald's populist presidency during his teaching years in Carlow College it is perhaps surprising that the latter remained president throughout Doyle's episcopacy. It is unlikely, however, that he would have remained president unless he had conformed to the bishop's will. Fitzgerald was a formidable figure: between 1828 and 1832 he combined the office of president of Carlow College with that of provincial of the Irish Dominicans, against the wishes of Doyle and the definitors of his own order.[2] On one occasion when Bishop Doyle expressed dissatisfaction with the performance of a student at a college examination, Fitzgerald is said to have muttered 'what is it to him? I wish he'd mind his own business'.[3] Relations between the two clerics may not have been easy but it seems that a *modus vivendi* was reached. In 1824, during the president's absence from Carlow, Doyle was requested to name a student for free admission to the College. He responded: 'I can make no promise ... until the return of the President, as I have made it a rule not to interfere with his office'.[4]

The education of youths prior to their reception into Irish seminaries was 'very various', according to Doyle, but 'much superior' on average in his diocese.[5] Even so an apparent deficiency in learning, indicated by peculiarities of grammar and spelling, is indicated by the correspondence with Doyle of the secular priests, particularly the older parochial clergy.[6] An important 'diocesan seminary' or minor seminary in Tullow, the school of the Patrician brothers, provided Carlow College with many distinguished students.[7] Prospective seminarians attended fee paying hedge schools, so-called classical academies, or were perhaps schooled by their parochial clergy before being sent to Carlow College. Doyle ironed out educational deficiencies by insisting that all intending seminarians attend the Carlow lay college prior to entry into the seminary.[8] The lay college was in the south wing of Carlow College and it was extended in 1817 to accommodate 100 students[9] normally of 'wealthy families'[10] who paid fees of thirty guineas a year. Doyle estimated that the total expense on a lay student was between forty guineas and fifty pounds annually.[11]

Educated public opinion rather than formal examinations determined the status of Ireland's newly emerging lay Catholic secondary schools – the first of which were generally attached to seminaries. Carlow College had its own private examinations which Doyle usually atttended in July and December. However, as there was no widely accepted or state organised examining board at second level until 1878, colleges such as Carlow and Clongowes Wood organised their own well attended public exhibitions known as 'academical exercises'. These allowed their pupils (who had usually been carefully selected) to indicate their educational attainments by a display of learning. Students of Carlow lay college were examined in an impressive range of subjects: French, Italian, Latin, Greek, Hebrew, History, Natural Philosophy, Astronomy, Chemistry, general and British law.[12] In 1818 Doyle described the lay college as 'undoubtedly the best school in Ireland'.[13] The students of the lay college were sometimes from socially superior backgrounds to the seminarians and may have been treated accordingly. Under the headline 'Carlow College' the *Carlow Morning Post* of 24 June 1830 described a day's outing for these students:

> We understand that the venerable President [Dr Fitzgerald] ... entertained the young gentlemen of the Lay College, with a boating party [on the river Barrow] on last Monday. The professors and students left the quay about nine o'clock, and proceeded about twelve miles down the river. The musical band of the College was in attendance. The fineness of the weather, the superior character of the music, with the buoyant spirits of the young gentlemen, doubly joyful with the pleasures of the day and the anticipated happiness of the coming vacation, rendered the whole a very lively and interesting scene.

From its outset, Carlow College had experienced financial difficulties but the success of the lay college ensured economic stability. The funding of Carlow College, derived partly from donations and bequests but primarily from the profits of the lay college, enabled Doyle to put together a 'very considerable' sum of money. The college was maintained by the interest accruing on this money.[14]

Wealth was so unevenly distributed in Ireland that denominational attitudes to class were radically different. Protestant polemicists depicted Irish Catholic seminarians as peasants while Catholics themselves looked on the same clerical students as scions of middle class backgrounds. Kildare and Leighlin seminarians were generally the sons of a 'more opulent'[15] type of farmer than that found in many Irish dioceses. Indeed, Doyle opined that students from the poorer northern dioceses would not be able to afford Carlow College fees; but within his own diocese, he maintained, 'we have a great number of substantial farmers, who are able to pay what is charged for the education of their sons'.[16] However, the annual fee charged in the seminary in the mid-1820s was only twenty-five pounds,[17] a figure which tells us more about the relative impoverishment of Irish Catholic society in general than it does about the affluence of Kildare and Leighlin farmers and shopkeepers.

In 1820 there were forty seminarians in Carlow College.[18] In the mid-1820s the number ranged annually between sixty and eighty.[19] Doyle was very stringent in his scrutiny of candidates for the ecclesiastical state and, as he grew older, his attitude hardened, as is revealed in a letter of 1830: 'the dangers to those engaged in it [the priesthood] are great, and their deficiencies generally so painful, that I look now, as I advance in life, with exceeding dread upon the entry of almost every young person into the Church'.[20] As early as 1814 we find Doyle commenting that some academically poor students had left Carlow College (they appear to have been deficient in Latin) for Birchfield (subsequently St Kieran's), Kilkenny, 'where an examination is merely a matter of form'.[21] A historian of the Ossory diocesan seminary attempted to erase this blot on the college's escutcheon by maintaining that Doyle was 'not a sympathetic examiner, and was more likely to overawe a candidate than to extract information from him'.[22] Doyle's manner may have been unconsciously intimidating but he did raise standards and endeavour to be fair to all seminarians whether capable or weak and to pose questions commensurate with their ability.[23] While bishop-elect in 1819 Doyle informed the president of Maynooth College, Dr Bartholomew Crotty, that none of the fourteen Kildare and Leighlin diocesan students in the college were to be admitted to orders until they had been personally examined by their bishop. One student, Peter Maher of Tullow, was ordered to leave the establishment.[24] In December 1822 Dr Crotty informed Doyle of

> the secession of another of your students from Maynooth ... this change was altogether unexpected by his superiors here, as he had always been a young man of religious and every way unexceptionable conduct. His talents were not of the first order, and perhaps it was an apprehension that they might not come up to your Lordship's standard, that induced him to adopt the resolution he has taken.[25]

While the rather timid may have been frightened by Doyle's bearing and reputation there was no shortage of candidates for the priesthood. Bishop Keating of Ferns had to cope with an 'almost general vocation to the church in the barony of Forth and Bargey'.[26] Many candidates were unsuitable; the uncouth or unintelligent, exemplary moral conduct notwithstanding, could not hope to succeed in Carlow College. John Carroll, who became a curate in Ferns, had been refused ordination in Carlow College.[27] In 1824 he attempted a bizarre 'exorcism' on a child who died as a result. Charged with murder he was found not guilty but insane.[28] He was, the *Dublin Evening Post* declared, echoing Doyle's sentiments, 'a melancholy proof of the extreme danger which may arise to society from the appointment of an insufficient person to the exercise of the function of a Christian clergyman'.[29] In 1829 the hierarchy deplored the fact that in many instances proper means were not employed in the selection of candidates for the priesthood.[30]

Before the house of commons' parliamentary inquiry into the state of Ireland in 1825 Doyle stated that a testimonial from Carlow College was equivalent to one from Maynooth College.[31] He considered the seminaries at Kilkenny, Waterford and Tuam to be small and 'insignificant' compared to Carlow.[32] Carlow College provided an ecclesiastical course similar to that of Maynooth except in Moral Theology where Carlow offered a more extensive syllabus.[33] Its science course was similar to that of Maynooth. Pure Mathematics and Experimental Philosophy were taught in the same manner as in Trinity College.[34]

Even before his appointment to the board of trustees of Maynooth, Doyle's influence was felt in that college. When a commission comprising Archbishops Curtis and Murray and the college president Dr Bartholomew Crotty was appointed in summer 1822 to inquire into the Dunboyne institute for higher studies, the coadjutor archbishop of Dublin wrote to Doyle: 'I entreat your Lp. to arrange a plan according to your notions of the business, and I think, I shall not have much difficulty in getting it adopted'.[35]

The episcopal trustees of Maynooth College were appointed by rota from the ecclesiastical provinces. The archbishop of the province whose turn it was to fill a vacancy simply proposed the trustee for his province and the appointment followed as a matter of course. On the death of Archbishop Troy, Dr Murray informed Doyle that his appointment to the board would present no difficulty.[36] But Doyle's colleague and friend, Bishop Marum, had a prior claim to the seat which rested on his seniority. In May 1823 Murray again wrote to Doyle stating 'there can be no further question of delicacy as Dr Marum has declined accepting the office of trustee'.[37] Clearly Marum had waived his right so as to allow Doyle onto the board of trustees. Doyle's appointment followed on 26 June 1823.[38] He was diligent in the improvement of studies and the maintenance and reform of discipline within the college, particularly with reference to the Dunboyne establishment. In 1825 he publicly stated that 'there might be an improvement in the system pursued',[39] in Maynooth, though at a meeting of the trustees on 19 January 1826 he expressed satisfaction with the standards obtaining in the Dunboyne institute.[40] In January 1834, only a few months before his death, Doyle was requested by the trustees to formulate a detailed schema for a report on studies and discipline to be presented at every board meeting.[41] The minutes of the trustees of Maynooth are terse and unrewarding but it would be unwise to doubt Doyle's dominance once on the board. In 1828 Doyle recorded that 'this year the Board at my instance has remodelled the mode of teaching theology by dividing the students into three classes or sections and appointing to each section a professor bound to give one lecture on speculation and one on moral theology each class day.'[42] The college presidents – Bartholomew Crotty and Michael Slattery – during the years of Doyle's episcopacy had reason to be grateful to Doyle for his role in their appointments to subsequent bishoprics.

In 1824 in an effort to improve standards of ecclesiastical training still further Doyle invited the distinguished seminary order, the Society of St Sulpice, of Paris, to take over the management of Carlow College. The superior of the order, Antoine Duclaux, declined, chiefly on account of his small numbers and the nature (unspecified) of the order's rules. He offered to train Kildare and Leighlin seminarians in Paris for the future management of Carlow College.[43] No further correspondence survives on this subject, so for whatever reason it was not pursued by Doyle.[44]

Generally seminarians studied in Carlow College for more than six years although the minimum course was only of five years' duration.[45] Under Doyle Carlow College had a post-ordination or post-graduate school of studies with a strong pastoral emphasis on catechesis and preaching. 'There are', wrote Rev. Henry Young in 1821,

> always in the house from 7 to 10 priests, who having finished their ordinary course of study, apply themselves to their further improvement according to a plan of studies arranged by the bishop, who holds for them quarterly examinations. The destination of these ecclesiastics is to supply the wants of the mission, particularly by catechesis and preaching in the several towns of the diocese during Lent, when they are found sufficiently prepared for so arduous and important a duty.[46]

The overseas mission of Carlow College began when newly ordained clergymen who could not be accommodated on the home mission, volunteered to go abroad. Thomas Walsh, coadjutor to John Milner, Vicar Apostolic of the Midland District in England, expressed that prelate's thanks to Doyle for two priests sent in 1825.[47] In 1826 Doyle offered three priests to Peter Collinridge, Vicar Apostolic of the Western District.[48] When the secretary of state for the colonies requested two Catholic priests to join Rev. John Therry in Australia, Dr Poynter, Vicar Apostolic of London, passed the request to Doyle.[49] Dr Benedict Joseph Flaget, the distinguished Sulpician bishop of the huge Bardstown diocese thanked Doyle for sending a young priest to Kentucky in 1826.[50] Priests for the foreign missions, however, amounted to only a trickle from Carlow College before the famine though their number increased significantly in the second half of the nineteenth century.[51]

For the education of talented candidates for the priesthood Doyle maintained that the challenge of a foreign university was preferable to that of a college in

Ireland.[52] In 1820 Paul Cullen left Carlow College, refused Doyle's offer of a place at Maynooth, and went to Rome as a student.[53] In 1829 Doyle was anxious to have him back in Carlow College as a professor.[54] Doyle gave several individuals leave to pursue their studies in France (though not in the Irish College, Paris, before 1825). When educated they were free to apply to any bishop anywhere in the world to ordain them. Their Ordinary was not bound to receive them.[55]

The fate of the Irish colleges on the continent was a constant source of worry to the Irish hierarchy in the revolutionary period. In 1825 Doyle stated that the hierarchy did not have a college worth noticing for secular priests on the continent.[56] After the French Revolution the Irish College in Paris was re-established by a decree of the first consul and placed under the control of a board appointed by the French government. From 1805 the administration of the college was subject to a 'Bureau de Surveillance' which caused constant difficulties until it was dissolved by King Charles X in 1824. From then on the rector, appointed by nomination of the Irish archbishops, became official administrator of the college, subject to the French minister of the interior.[57] From the period of the French Revolution until 1825, according to Doyle, the Irish hierarchy had no confidence in the 'morals or capacity' of either the students or the administration of the Irish College.[58]

In 1825 Doyle reckoned that burses for Irish students in the college amounted to well over £3,000 sterling.[59] There were three burses for Kildare and Leighlin, respectively the burses granted by Tobias Walsh (1729), worth 150 francs, Philip Rousse (1748), worth 604 francs and Robert McCormack (1748), valued at 1,035 francs. At the close of the revolutionary period these burses were reduced to one third of their original principal. Their combined value in 1819 was 1,106 francs. Doyle permitted the burse fund to accumulate while the Irish College was 'vested generally in the hands of an infidel bureau'.[60] In 1825 he sent M. Nolan of Ballon to Paris to take up the Rousse burse then worth 764 francs annually and the following year he sent a second seminarian, W. Duggan, to avail of the Tobias Walsh burse then worth 300 francs per annum.[61]

In November 1826, Patrick Magrath, an Ossory parish priest, and former president of St. Kieran's College, was appointed rector of the Irish College in Paris.[62] By 31 August 1827, however, he had still not left his parish of Templeorum in south Kilkenny.[63] After only a brief period in Paris he resigned the rectorship in early May 1828 and returned to Kilkenny.[64] The college which had twenty-eight students was in disorder and debt and Magrath did not feel equal to the task of resolving its problems. From the beginning of 1828 most unfavourable reports on the state of the college were received by the Irish hierarchy from the archbishop of Paris (who refused to confer orders on its students) and others.[65]

In September 1828, Archbishop Murray and Bishop Doyle were delegated by the Irish hierarchy to visit Paris to impose order on the discipline, studies and finances of the college.[66] They found the problems of the college to be the result of 'maladministration not vice', framed a code of statutes, obtained the consent of the French government for their new regulations, and held an eight day retreat.[67] Dr Patrick McSweeney (who had succeeded Doyle as professor of theology and sacred scripture in Carlow College) was appointed to the post of rector.[68] The bishops also made representations to the archbishop of Paris about the 'immoral and scandalous' conduct of several Irish ecclesiastics resident in Paris under the pretence of pursuing their studies.[69]

In 1824, Michael Blake, vicar-general of Dublin, went to Rome to re-establish the Irish College there.[70] He had been a student of the college at its dissolution in 1798 during the French occupation.[71] It was not without difficulty that the establishment was finally effected by a brief of Pope Leo XII dated 18 February 1826.[72] The diocese of Kildare and Leighlin was entitled to one of ten free places at Rome. A Doyle confidant, Christopher Boylan, succeeded Blake as rector in March 1828.[73] Boylan had been vicar-general of Meath diocese and a Maynooth College professor. On his arrival in Rome a row broke out between him and Blake over the state of the college finances.[74] Boylan's tenure of office was an unhappy one. In 1831 Propaganda advised Archbishop Murray to accept his resignation which was tendered on health grounds. Discipline had deteriorated within the college to the point where there was constant quarrelling. According to Propaganda someone capable of establishing order was urgently required.[75] In January 1832 Dr Paul Cullen succeeded Boylan as rector and the problem was resolved.[76]

Bishop Doyle sent Brian Delany[77] of Mountmellick parish to St Patrick's College, Lisbon, in 1827. The pension was small and badly paid but the claim of the diocese was founded more on custom than on right. Nonetheless Doyle intended to adhere to it until it was contested.[78]

CONFERENCES

The primary purpose of the clerical deanery conference was to ensure that clergymen on the mission maintained and revised their familiarity with moral and dogmatic theology at regular intervals so that they had a good knowledge of these subjects for catechetical and homiletic purposes.[79] The conference also had other ends: in Bishop Doyle's case it served to instill a uniformity of religious observance ('that uniformity may be preserved in this matter as well as in every other throughout the diocese'[80]), and fostered a sense of an exclusive esprit de corps among the clergy.

In the early Tridentine church Charles Borromeo was the most important proponent of the clerical conference among the secular clergy. In Milan he ordered that conferences be held monthly, presided over by the deans or vicars-forane.[81] Bishops were not obliged to hold clerical conferences[82] although the practice was recommended by Trent[83] and publicised by bishops of the repute of Massillon[84] and several popes including Innocent XIII and Benedict XIV. Deanery clerical conferences were 'firmly established' in Ireland from the mid-eighteenth century.[85]

As we have seen the status of the clerical conference in Kildare and Leighlin prior to Doyle's elevation was somewhat unclear.[86] A uniform conference practice was quickly introduced by Doyle. The conferences were based on the rural deaneries; each rural dean (with the exception of James Conran, V.F., Ballon deanery)[87] was appointed master of conference in his deanery. The conference in each deanery was directed to meet once a month from June to October inclusive.

In 1820 the deanery of Carlow met in Carlow on the first Monday of the month; William Fitzgerald, V.F., P.P., Carlow, presided. Borris deanery met on the first Tuesday of the month; Dr Michael Prendergast, V.G., P.P., Bagenalstown, was master of conference. Nicholas O'Connor, V.F., P.P., Maryborough was master of conference in the deanery of Maryborough which convened in Ballyroan on the first Wednesday of the month. The Mountmellick/Portarlington deanery assembled on the first Thursday of the month; Anthony Duanne, V.F., P.P., presided as master of the conference. Finally the clergymen of the deanery of Kilcock gathered at Robertstown on the second Tuesday of each month under the superintendence of John Dunne, V.F., P.P., Kilcock, as master of conference.[88] All clergymen, both regular and secular were obliged to attend. Doyle invariably attended these conferences – a total of twenty five in all – whenever he could and presided when he did so.[89] This familiarity with his clergy tightened the bonds binding them to their bishop.

Theological conferences in the diocese of Kildare and Leighlin followed a detailed format laid down by Doyle. Subjects to be treated at each conference were the rubrics of the missal, the procedure for administering the sacraments (especially penance[90]) and the diocesan statutes. In accord with Pope Benedict XIV's *Institutiones Ecclesiasticae*,[91] one of the classic texts of the post-Tridentine church, Doyle required each clergyman to furnish himself with a textbook on moral theology. Doyle recommended the work of the moderate rigorist, Dens, although he had grave doubts about that author's treatment of non-Catholics. Doyle's own copy of Dens revealed sharp disagreements with the text annotated by the bishop; for example, where Dens posed the question 'An haeretici recte puniantur morte?' and answered in the affirmative, Doyle wrote: 'shockingly false!'.[92] However, Dens remained in use during his episcopacy perhaps for want of a better text. In Dublin where Archbishop Murray followed Doyle's rules for the conduct of theological conferences[93] Dens was also the standard text in moral theology. The work achieved a great deal of notoriety in the mid-1830s when some of the leading Irish evangelicals attacked Archbishop Murray for permitting its use.[94]

The conference in Kildare and Leighlin opened in chapel or other suitable meeting place at eleven o'clock in the morning of the appointed day. The master of conference took his place at the head of the choir and the clergy ranged along either side of him according to their rank. The assembly then recited the Veni Creator followed by the oration Deus qui Corda. The master delegated a clergyman (chosen at the previous conference) to preach on a printed treatise[95] taken as the theme of the conference and usually from moral theology (cases of conscience) or controversy (dogmatic theology). His sermon, which was not to occupy more than half an hour, then began. When the preacher had finished, the laity, who might have attended, were asked to withdraw. The master of conference then asked two or three of those present to give their opinion on the sermon which they were to do 'briefly and modestly' commending what met with their approval and pointing out whatever was incorrect or unreliable in the sermon or its delivery. The master then concluded this part of the conference by giving his opinion.

Then, two (previously appointed) priests, drawn from the ranks of the curates, regulars or parish priests who had not been five years collated, were required to sustain the printed treatise which was the subject of the conference. Two priests (who might or might not have been forewarned), were called upon to argue the treatise. If an answer was unsatisfactory the master (who was invested with the power of the Ordinary and entitled to an unqualified deference) was to be approached. If the master's decision appeared doubtful an objection could be stated but not urged. He was to be approached after the conference when he would 'not hesitate to correct or confirm his former opinion'.

Doyle decreed that those who disagreed during the conference were to take special care 'to abstain from harsh language or insinuations and to avoid a spirit of contention', mindful of the words of St Paul: 'If any person loves disputes, we have no such custom, nor the Church of God'.[96] Rev. M. Coleman, a Carmelite of the Leighlinbridge house, was ordered not to attend the Borris conference where Dr Michael Prendergast presided so 'that you and he may not be led into temptation, or charity which is the bond of peace, be violated'.[97] No desultory conversation on theological or other subjects was to be allowed by the master. The conference continued in this manner for not less than an hour and not more than two. Every clergyman present was permitted or might be called on by the master to propose questions or doubts to the defendants.

The conference closed at three o'clock with the singing of the antiphon Actiones Nostras. An hour later

> a frugal dinner at which no lay person shall be admitted, shall be prepared ... and at which the conversation should be as becomes the ministers of Christ, should profane conversation be incautiously introduced, the master will mildly remove it, by introducing a more proper subject.

The master was to order 'such wine or spiritous liquor or both' as he deemed sufficient for the company. No person under pain of suspension was to bring or order any more spirits or punch on that day either in that house or in the town where the conference took place.[98] Doyle in 1820 determined on strictly regulating the time for dinner and retiring 'as great excesses have been committed'. Subsequently, to avoid the appearance of luxury and to promote economy, all alcoholic beverages were forbidden on the day of the conference.[99] During the meal, no doubt, problems of the mission were discussed. After two hours at table, precisely at six o'clock, the master was to rise and commence the Te Deum. He then appointed the preacher and defendants for the following month's conference.

Any priest absent from a conference and dinner without 'manifest necessity' (such as severe indisposition) and even with the bishop's written consent, was to be fined: three shillings and four pence if absent from the dinner; five shillings if absent from both conference and dinner; fifteen shillings if absent from two successive conferences; and to be suspended from all offices for a third successive failure to attend (later reduced to just two absences without the written permission of the bishop or vicar-general).[100] The fines were to be levied by the master of the conference and applied as the conference decided. The 1821 diocesan statutes required the rules on fines and the time and circumstances of dinner to be exactly observed.[101]

SPIRITUAL RETREATS AND PREACHING

Throughout his episcopal career Doyle organised spiritual retreats annually for his diocesan clergy. The parish priests attended one year, the other clergy the next. These retreats, usually of six days' duration, were presided over by the bishop, and took place in Carlow College.[102] In one year, 1830, he held separate spiritual retreats for both parish priests and curates, preaching no less than four times daily on the duties of ecclesiastics.[103] The 1831 provincial statutes made a six day retreat every two years obligatory on all priests, on pain of suspension, unless with the permission of the Ordinary. Where possible an annual retreat was recommended.[104]

Doyle valued the retreat as an exercise in contemplation and renewal of the religious life. In preparation for his own elevation to the See he made a ten day retreat.[105] In 1820 he ordered a recalcitrant priest to make a retreat of at least ten days' duration.[106] Fitzpatrick has made a large claim for a retreat conducted by the bishop during the first year of his episcopacy: 'One thousand priests and nearly every prelate in Ireland assembled at Carlow by his invitation'.[107] Doyle conducted this retreat in July 1820 unaided and preached three times a day for ten days.[108] Keenan, following Fitzpatrick, states that 'The magnitude of this enterprise shows that it must have been the common decision of the hierarchy'.[109]

The extant sources do not indicate anything as large – perhaps at most a provincial or Leinster rather than a national retreat. In a letter of mid-July 1820 Doyle stated: 'I am now going to prepare for our two retreats ... Drs Troy, Hamill, Blake, all the most respectable clergy of Dublin, some I believe from Meath, and all our own friends, attend this week. I am left alone to instruct ...'.[110] A year later, in July 1821, Doyle repeated the exercise on a smaller scale. This retreat 'went on exceedingly well' and was again attended by Archbishop Troy accompanied by twenty of his clergy.[111] Doyle conducted at least two retreats for the students of Maynooth College. One held in late November 1823 was remembered by a future president of Maynooth, Dr Laurence Renehan, then a student, for its impressiveness.[112] Another in autumn 1828 deeply moved Charles William Russell (who became Renehan's successor as president). He found that Doyle's 'explanations of the duties, obligations, and responsibilities of the priesthood made him tremble'.[113]

In the early church the office of preaching belonged to the bishop, and priests preached only with his permission. The Council of Trent had pronounced that the primary duty of preaching devolved on bishops, unless they were hindered by a legitimate impediment, and ordered that they were to preach in person in their own churches and through their pastors in their dioceses.[114] Effective preaching was of course of paramount importance to a successful pastoral mission. The standard of preaching in the early nineteenth century Irish church was poor.[115] Doyle asserted in 1820 that, even in Maynooth College, a certain 'bad taste' in eloquence had 'long prevailed'.[116] 'Briefness and plainess of discourse' were recommended by Trent[117] and as far as possible Doyle favoured extempore preaching (from perhaps the outline notes of a sermon) and a simple style. His clergymen, busy with their pastoral duties, did not have time, nor were they encouraged to compose elaborate sermons. Their sermons were in any case more catechetical than homiletic. Trent laid down parameters outside which pastors of ordinary congregations were warned not to stray:

> let the more difficult and subtle questions ... which tend not to edification, and from which for the most part there is no increase in piety, be excluded from popular discourses before the uneducated multitude. In like manner, such things as are uncertain, or which labour under an appearance of error, let them not allow to be made public and treated of. While those things which tend to a certain kind of curiosity or superstition, or which savour of filthy lucre, let them prohibit as scandals and stumbling-blocks to the faithful.[118]

Priests were expected to put some thought into their sermons and to speak sincerely from the heart – this, Doyle felt, had a far more impressive effect on the faithful, and no doubt was better understood, than carefully studied compositions.[119] The provenance of the chapter 'de Verbi Dei Praedicatione' in the provincial statutes, which required a sermon to be preached at each mass, can be attributed to Doyle.[120]

Doyle was acknowledged as the outstanding Irish Catholic preacher of his time.[121] In accordance with Trent he preached on every possible occasion. In Carlow he preached every Sunday when not on visitation. 'We must preach brethren and woe to him who does not preach' were the opening words of a sermon he delivered in Carlow Cathedral while severely ill a few weeks before his death.[122] On visitation he preached daily and even by the wayside.[123] He preached the funeral panegyric of Archbishop Troy extempore.[124] He preached at the dedication of the Pro-Cathedral in Dublin on 14 November 1825 before 3,000 people and virtually the entire Irish hierarchy.[125] As the unrivalled contemporary preacher Doyle was in constant demand for church dedications and charity sermons.

Doyle was always available to preach on Augustinian occasions and at the opening of new Augustinian churches. His sermon at the dedication of St Augustine's church, Limerick, was grandiosely described by Fitzpatrick as 'possessing a majesty of diction with a sublimity of aspiration quite etherealising'.[126] He preached a panegyric on St Augustine in the Augustinian church, John's Lane, Dublin, in August 1823[127] and again at the opening of the new Augustinian church in Cork on 14 October 1827. Protestants as well as Catholics thronged to the latter event which raised £348.[128] On 1 May 1829 Doyle delivered the consecration homily in the new Catholic church in Newry, County Down.[129] He preached on the occasion of the dedication by Archbishop Murray of the new church of SS Mary and Peter, Rathmines, Dublin, on 15 August 1830.[130]

Doyle's reputation as a preacher packed churches and guaranteed exceptional collections. A sermon by him in Westland Row church, Dublin, for Brother Edmund Rice's Hanover Street school brought in £287.[131] When Rev. William Young was building a new chapel at Phibsborough, Dublin, he hoped that Doyle would preach the dedication sermon: 'we could then fix the tickets at almost any price and expect an overflowing attendance'.[132] In 1823 Daniel O'Connell requested Doyle to preach the annual sermon at the Summerhill female orphanage.[133] The proliferation of urban charity institutions in the period under discussion constitutes a little researched and little recognised burden on the strained resources of the unendowed Catholic church in Ireland. The annual charity sermon was of the utmost importance as a fund-raising event for the financial subsistence of these institutions.[134] The appearance of Doyle on such an occasion ensured healthy receipts from a large paying congregation of both Catholics and, perhaps surprisingly given the sectarian tensions of the time, liberal Protestants. Irrespective of the preacher it seems that a genuine religious feeling which transcended denominationalism influenced middle-class attitudes towards the support of the poor and destitute.[135]

DRESS, VESTMENTS AND PUBLIC DECORUM

> And forasmuch as, though the habit does not make the monk, it is never-theless needful that clerics always wear a dress suitable to their proper calling, that by the decency of their outward apparel they may show forth the inward correctness of their morals .... [136]

Doyle determined that his diocesan clergymen should be – and be seen to be, by virtue of their dress – men of God, set apart from the ordinary mass of human-kind. Whether Doyle can be credited, as Fitzpatrick has stated, with being the first to insist on full restoration of clerical dress in Ireland[137] is a moot point but he certainly gave every encouragement. It has been claimed that, before Doyle's episcopacy, priests almost always wore brown, and black was virtually unknown.[138] Martin has asserted that in the first two decades of the nineteenth century the Irish Catholic clergyman dressed in a 'variety of colours, but rarely in clerical black'.[139] Indeed when Doyle first met the parish priest of Kill, Daniel Nolan, he found it difficult to credit that this man was a priest and not a layman as he was wearing a frieze coat.[140] Lay dress was another by-product of the penal era when no sensible cleric advertised his profession by his attire.

The 1820 diocesan statutes specified that black or blackish cloth was to be worn by clergymen.[141] This regulation was written into the provincial statutes where a chapter is devoted to the subject. No formal definition of clerical dress was made but priests were required to distinguish themselves from laymen by their habiliment and they were recommended to wear the Roman collar which proclaimed their status.[142] In his 1820 diocesan statutes Bishop Doyle demanded strict attention from his clergymen to the cleanliness of their sacramental vest-ments and altar cloths: 'praecipimus, ut mappae, seu linteamina altaris sint integra et munda; paramenta similiter tanto ministerio convenientia, non lacerata, neque sordida ...'.[143] The bishop's reputation as a strict disciplinarian derived more per-haps from his attention to liturgical details than from any other aspect of his ecclesiastical administration.

On visitation, whenever clergymen failed to meet his requirements, peremp-tory action was taken to rectify the abuse and if necessary a public rebuke deliv-ered as allowed by Trent.[144] Unsatisfactory or unsuitable vestments, altar cloths, mass books, etc., were burned or destroyed by him.[145] The dirty chasuble of Rev. Maurice Kearney was torn in two by Doyle.[146] In consequence the bishop in-formed Kearney's visitation congregation that their priest would be unable to celebrate mass on that day.[147] Finding a cracked chalice, Doyle crushed it with a paving stone.[148] Doyle felt that no priests were in such straitened circumstances that they could not afford to purchase respectable vestments.[149] Even his vicar-general, Dr Patrick Dowling, P.P., Stradbally, was rebuked for not taking proper care of his vestments.[150]

An episcopal committee which discussed Irish church discipline in 1829 stated that 'It is ... to be feared that some make use of vestments and altar cloths not becoming the Sacred Ministry'. It also noted that the clergy at the stations of confession 'seldom wear a stole or any thing to distinguish them from the laity'. The committee observed that a comparatively small number of priests were supplied with soutanes[151] – a problem which Doyle had set out to remedy in his 1820 statutes, though not without some unfavourable comment. 'Surely you know', he wrote to his friend Dr Jeremiah Donovan in 1824, 'that to leave the track in any usage, if it were only in wearing a soutane at the altar ... is calculated to excite sneers, and censures, and jealousy'.[152] Yet all these clerical dress reforms merely brought Ireland into line with Catholic practice in continental Europe which had been initiated by Trent more than two and a half centuries earlier.

The horse was the basic mode of transport of contemporary society. The tradition of running the turf was very strong on the plains of County Kildare. Fitzpatrick's facile assertion that (at the time of Doyle's accession to the See) the priests of Kildare and Leighlin ejaculated 'Tally Ho' as often as 'Dominus Vobiscum' conjured up an image of a socialising, hunting and race-going clergy, which was to over-state the case though it had perhaps some basis in fact.[153] Not surprisingly his felicitous remark has entered the historiographical literature.[154] Doyle held that to perfect the ecclesiastical character required that it should partake as little as possible of that of the layman.[155] Thus clergymen should positively avoid all associations with public revelries, entertainments and amusements. One pastoral decried 'that endless routine of frivolous amusements in which a portion of society is but too often engaged'.[156] His diocesan statutes in 1820 specifically admonished clergymen to avoid such abuses:

> effugiant (Tred. Ses. 22 cap. 1 de Ref.) caveant consortia publica, ludos, nundinas, cursusque equorum; a venationibus vero clamosis abstineant omnes Clerici nobis subditi, vel intra has Dioceses degentes, sub poena suspensionis ipso facto incurrendae, cujus absolutionem nobismetipsis reservamus.[157]

On visitation in St Mullin's parish, Doyle noticed that the parish priest, Thomas Moore, was about to celebrate mass while wearing spurs. The bishop roundly denounced him before his congregation 'with a caustic severity remembered with terror by many'.[158] Although it is clear that Doyle had an extremely rigid conception of the code of behaviour and duties expected of a priest he never acted without due warning. He endeavoured privately to bring recalcitrant priests into line with church law and the diocesan statutes before delivering public rebukes where such were unavoidable. But when a bishop was forced to reprimand, Doyle believed that it should be done in a most indelible manner[159] so that the chastisement was felt and remembered. Unlike Archbishop Murray[160] Doyle never lacked the courage to rebuke; 'indignation when justly excited is a virtue much to be prized'.[161] That there was another side to Doyle can be seen from his reply to an application from Gerald Doyle, P.P., for permission to attend the Naas races:

> I wish you with all my heart peace and good running during this week, and am happy you will be present on the turf to preserve the one as I am confident you will enjoy the other. Nor do I see why on that occasion you should be deprived of the aid of your coadjutor, who has no slight acquaintance with men and horses.[162]

The hierarchical committee on church discipline in 1829 recommended that clergymen should never appear at theatres, races, public hunts or balls.[163] The 1831 provincial statutes re-affirmed this recommendation but with an interesting modification which perhaps reflected some slight change of attitude on Doyle's part to the issue:

> Praecipimus etiam clericis, ut abstineant ab omni loco ubi ludi publici fiunt, praecipue vero, a venatione clamosa; a cursu publico equorum; a theatrorum publicorum spectaculis; et a publicis choreis. Publicis laicorum conviviis non intersint, nisi aliquod opus charitatis, aut aliqua functio ministerii id requirat .... [164]

This statute was followed by the synod of Thurles for the whole of Ireland.[165]

FARMING CLERGYMEN

During the penal period priests were obliged to supplement their meagre incomes by farming and cattle dealing. Extant sources do not enable us to determine exactly how many priests were tenant farmers in the diocese of Kildare and Leighlin in 1819. Farming priests seem to have been common in pre-famine Tipperary[166] and in his work O'Shea asserts that at least forty of the sixty-four parish priests in the county at mid-century rented farms.[167] No curates farmed.[168] Implying that the practice was widespread in Kildare and Leighlin, Fitzpatrick remarked that 'several' parish priests farmed upwards of 140 acres, speculated in land and made money by it.[169] There is some evidence that, unlike Tipperary, curates farmed as well.[170]

The diocesan clergy were, in the main, the sons of relatively comfortable and respectable tenant farmers, as Doyle stated, and it was but natural that they should retain the closest connections throughout their lives with the social milieu of their origin. Undoubtedly many of these priests would have ploughed the sod had they not entered seminaries. Perhaps inevitably many sought to combine both professions. Richard Lalor Sheil fiercely criticised a priest who refused to collect the Catholic Rent as a 'consecrated grazier' and a 'sacerdotal agricultural-ist'.[171] In a closely knit, class conscious agricultural society priests were not im-mune to the conventional wisdom which decreed that worth and rank and status could be measured by landholding size.

The phenomenon of the farmer priest was opposed by Doyle from the outset of his episcopacy. For both theological and mundane reasons he deprecated large-scale farming contending that God and Mammon could not be served together; that it was impossible for a priest to fulfill his religious duties and also to manage a farm.[172] In 1819–20 Doyle took peremptory measures against the more notori-ous cases of farming clergymen. Parish priests were presented with a stark choice: relinquish their farms or be removed from office. When one agriculturally minded clergyman doubted the bishop's resolve, Doyle arrived with another cleric in the recalcitrant's parish and threatened the immediate appointment of this new priest to the cure if the P.P. did not forthwith forfeit his farm.[173] In his Diocesan Book, 1819–20, Doyle noted that John Lalor, the parish priest of Allen, was a farmer: 'The pastor seems to have many disputes on his hands, he has also two farms and is said to have much money'.

Daniel Nolan is one of the few farming priests in the diocese on whom defi-nite information is available. He was said to be 'much more a pastor of sheep than of souls'.[174] He was appointed parish priest of Kill in 1804.[175] He was so strongly recommended by Bishop Delany to Lord Cloncurry that he was accommodated for two years at Lyons, Cloncurry's home in the parish, while the peer was on the continent.[176] Daniel Nolan concentrated on farming while his brother Thomas, who was his curate, attended to spiritual matters.[177] Cloncurry (who was not a disinterested party as he had had a row with the P.P.) reported to Doyle that in 1806 Nolan 'took a place in Lord Kilwarden's estate in a small farm adjoining Lyons to the great annoyance of my tenants and labourers who were ground down by his avarice and rapacity'.[178] Doyle characterised this priest as 'a most unmanageable sort of being'.[179] By his own proud admission Daniel Nolan had heard an unwilling parishioner's confession at the point of a gun.[180] It was prob-ably in response to a representation from Lord Cloncurry that Nolan was trans-ferred to a parish distant from Lyons in 1823, although Doyle later had cause to write: 'I hoped when I removed him from Lyons he would cease to give trouble'.[181]

James Dowling, P.P., Killeigh, attributed his curate's lack of attention to his share of the parochial duties to his farming proclivities. He complained that Patrick Rigney did not attend the stations – having been absent from eighteen of them at Easter – and was never at home to answer sick calls. The cause of the problem was that 'Rigney has got a farm in co[mpany] with his mother which calls him every day from the duty of my parish except Sunday .... All I ask is, to remove him, and send me some other who will not be so convenient to his farm'.[182]

Bishop Doyle did not rule against the possession of all land. He saw that some land was necessary for the upkeep of the parish priest.[183] When translating parish priests to new parishes he avoided interrupting the farm work of the season in which they might be engaged.[184] Land, however small in acreage, relieved the priest somewhat of that dependence on absolute charitable support which Doyle so abhorred. The problem was how to ensure that parish priests had enough to support themselves decently (to meet their needs for potatoes, vegetables, milk for their own use and corn and hay for their horses, etc.,) without making them too comfortable, wealthy or independent of their flocks. Doyle himself referred to the twelve acres he held at Old Derrig (1822–26) as 'my farm'[185] which it certainly was by prevailing Catholic standards of landholding measurement. On this farm he kept horses, saved hay, and also had two or three milch cows which supplied his household needs.[186] Not more than fifteen acres seemed to Doyle adequate for the maintenance of his parish priests.

This reform measure, which was followed by the synod of Thurles,[187] was not completely effective in the diocese until it was written into the 1831 provincial statutes: '... ne quis Parochus in posterum conducat plusquam quindecim agri jugera, sub poena suspensionis ab officio'.[188] Indeed, up to six parish priests had been allowed 'in particular cases' and for unstated reasons to hold farms up to 100 acres.[189] In 1831 Doyle was spurred to implement the fifteen acre rule by priests who seemingly thought his stricture against farming clerics was a thing of the past. One of these, the bishop's own cousin, Martin Doyle, P.P., took a thirty to forty acre farm at Graiguenamanagh and defended his action from the accusation of self-aggrandisement on the grounds that his parish had a vast number of poor who were constantly applying to him for relief. He claimed that the farm would supply milk and potatoes to the needy.[190] Priests who held farms gave employment. Doyle had a steward on his farm at Old Derrig,[191] and later at Braganza he employed a 'considerable number of labouring people'.[192]

In 1832, before a parliamentary enquiry, Doyle publicly threatened to deprive a Queen's County farming priest of his parish or part of it if he did not 'correct the abuse' and conform to the statute.[193] The provincial statutes of 1831 forbade curates from farming: 'Vicariis vero non licet conducere domum quae annexum quidquid terrae praeter hortum ...'.[194] The synod of Thurles also prohibited curates from farming unless with the consent of the bishop.[195]

DISCIPLINE

Whereas it is properly the office of bishops to reprove the vices of all who are subject to them, this will have to be principally their care - that clerics, especially those appointed to the cure of souls, be blameless; and that they do not, with their connivance, lead a disorderly life .... [196]

The Irish Catholic episcopacy under the penal laws was in large measure unable to exercise that careful vigilance of diocesan clerics which Trent enjoined. Inevitably in a disorganised and disadvantaged church there was indiscipline. Indeed, parish priests came to enjoy such a substantial degree of independence that many became quite wilful and even heedless of all episcopal authority. Furthermore bishops were sometimes forced to risk encountering the civil authorities in order to bring recalcitrants back to the fold. A feature of the penal period was the suspended or degraded priest who purely out of pique and malice reported his Ordinary to the civil authority. In the early nineteenth century there was more than one diocese in Ireland in which the resident bishop had an exceptionally troublesome priest denouncing him to Rome.

It was inevitable too that the penal laws should give rise to a certain laxity of observance in the finer points of the liturgy. This might have been understandable once but it was no longer acceptable as far as Doyle was concerned. Rural pre-famine Catholicism in all regions except the south-east was a curious blend of traditional popular and Tridentine religious models. A people's church often disdained episcopal authority, particularly in the matter of parochial clerical appointments where the choice of the people (usually the curate) was overruled for the position of parish priest. Popular disturbances ensued, sometimes led by the curate, with the chapel doors nailed up against the incoming clergyman who was normally unable to take possession of his church unless by main force. For many rural Catholics the Catholic church was embodied in their parochial clergymen whose attitudes became their attitudes. Perhaps not surprisingly, the priests as power brokers in the community were sometimes more akin to factional leaders than to pastors. The horizons of popular Catholicism thus espoused were quite circumscribed by parochial localisms and blind to the wider world view of the church at Trent.

Under Doyle, Kildare and Leighlin was largely free of such problems. His main concern was to ensure that his clerics measured up precisely to the Tridentine model of an exact, unselfish and hard-working priesthood. Doyle firmly believed that the religious improvement of the laity must depend on the quality of the parochial clergy. Before the commons' select committee on the state of Ireland in 1825 Doyle gave evidence of his detailed knowledge of the character and capacity of every priest in his jurisdiction:

> I had, whilst professor of theology, the care of educating the greater part of the clergymen of the diocese, and I am still obliged to inquire into their theological knowledge, to ascertain the manner in which they discharge their duties; to receive the reports of the rural vicars, as to their morals and conduct; so that I know as intimately the life and habits, and conduct, of every individual of the clergy under me, as a father can be acquainted with the life and habits of his own son.[197]

In his 1821 pastoral Doyle observed that he 'found consolation in the zeal of many of those who share with us the pastoral solicitude'.[198] There were, no doubt, some priests who were lacking in religious zeal,[199] although it may be presumed that, in the majority of such cases, it was simply a matter of pointing out to clerics what exactly was required of them and they readily conformed. Nonetheless there was a fairly small though hardly negligible number of instances where Doyle found clerics on the mission failing to live up to their sacred calling, unsatisfactory in one fashion or another, and moreover unwilling despite repeated exhortations and warnings to reform themselves.[200] These cases are discussed below; the Kearney and Fanning cases are of more than passing interest for the light they shed on relations between priests and people and for Doyle's perhaps unusual exercises in ecclesiastical democracy. Doyle never gave any parishioners cause to claim that he failed to investigate just complaints against their clergymen.

After induction and three years' residence in his parish, a parish priest had tenure and could not be translated to another parish without his consent. The curate had no such title and could be arbitrarily moved to another parish at the will of the bishop. The same applied to the administrators who were the chief priests in the bishop's mensal parishes. A parish priest could not be removed from his parish unless a charge, defined by canon law, were proved against him. He could then be reprimanded, temporarily suspended, or suspended indefinitely.[201]

Doyle's approach to the question of disciplining erring priests is outlined in the Kennedy case, which otherwise is poorly documented.[202] Mark Kennedy was parish priest of Clane from 1810.[203] Doyle found his conduct 'an outrage on the gospel'. His faults, however, were of a temperamental rather than a malicious nature and the bishop confessed that he was at a loss to know how to deal with this priest who was 'unfitted by nature for any office which has charge of souls'.[204] Doyle consulted his rural deans and sought the opinion of his metropolitan, Dr Troy, and Troy's coadjutor, Dr Murray, on the case. Doyle's attitude was conditioned by the need to balance the correction of one individual clergyman against the effect the scandal would have on the diocese:

> to see and know these things, and not to punish them, as they deserve, weakens essentially the pastoral authority throughout the entire diocese, and gives a pretext to the evil-minded to malign the priests and insult religion. May God forgive those who bring such evil upon His Church![205]

The bishop was reluctantly forced to consider suspending Rev. Kennedy, at least temporarily, from office.[206] We do not know what decision was reached, or if a decision was reached in this case, as Kennedy died in 1821. But Bishop Doyle did not shirk decisive disciplinary action where the abuse merited it. He firmly maintained that 'a priest has no greater enemy to his temporal and spiritual good than a Bishop who suffers him to proceed in doing wrong'.[207]

In 1820, a Catholic curate of Arles parish was removed from the mission 'never to be restored'.[208] In 1825, Rev. Hanrick, parish priest of Clonbullogue from 1823, was removed from his parish for habitual drunkenness and other unknown reasons.[209] Bishop Doyle did not confine his reforming zeal to his own diocese. When he reported an erring pastor of the Dublin diocese to Dr Troy, the archbishop expressed his gratitude while admitting 'I am generally the last to hear of the misconduct of a clergyman'.[210] In 1821 Doyle reported a Meath priest to his Ordinary, Dr Plunkett, and in consequence, the priest, an alcoholic, was suspended.[211]

Failure to attend to the religious duties of his parish was the cause of Patrick Moore's removal from his position in Rathvilly parish. In his Diocesan Book, 1819–20, Doyle remarked that Moore must attend at Rathvilly every second Sunday so that all the people might be instructed: 'he seems not to require a knowledge of the mysteries or a confession of the number of sins in his penitents and absolves those who are in the habit of sin'. Doyle's note of 4 October 1819 expressed no confidence in Moore and resolved that if he did not alter his mode of hearing confessions he would be suspended. Rathvilly was one of the biggest and most populous parishes in the Ballon deanery. On visitation in 1820 Doyle discovered that there were 6,000 to 7,000 adults in the parish but not 2,000 annual communicants. This state of affairs was largely unchanged in 1823 when Doyle judged that the adults of Rathvilly were still 'exceedingly negligent' in approaching the altar.[212] The bishop appears to have laid the fault at the door of the parish priest rather than his parishioners. In 1825 Rev. Moore who had been parish priest from 1813 was 'silently removed' from the care of the parish and granted a provision out of its dues.[213] As we have already noted,[214] Richard Fitzgerald, P.P. of Killeshin (from 1787) was a troublesome cleric who had been threatened with suspension by Bishop Corcoran. Comerford states that in his later years Fitzgerald 'was in great measure relieved from the charge of the parish'.[215] In fact, in 1819, Fitzgerald was silently deposed by Doyle, though he continued to enjoy the reputation of parish priest.[216] These silent depositions mark Doyle's anxiety not to give public scandal to the faithful or indeed to Protestants in the diocese.

Fitzpatrick has stated that after Doyle's death his successor, Bishop Edward Nolan, found a manuscript book of the late bishop's 'wherein was recorded, for the guidance of that prelate and his successors, the names of families in the diocese of which no member should be at any time ordained priest. He made this rule in the case of families who had already given to the altar persons not of exemplary conduct'.[217] The extant evidence for this claim relates only to the Goss family. When William Cullen, P.P., Leighlinbridge, died in 1823 Doyle took the opportunity of erecting the new parish of Leighlin. Cullen's nephew and curate, Anthony Goss, who had been in effect administrator of Leighlinbridge, expected to be promoted to P.P. But the bishop knew Rev. Goss 'from several reasons to be scarcely deserving of toleration in the ministry'.[218] Doyle was at this time however greatly indebted to two local notables, Colonel Rochfort of Clogrennan House and Mr John Alexander, mill-owner of Milford, for assistance in building Milford (Ballinabranna) chapel. He laid the foundation stone in mid 1823 (though as it happened the chapel was not completed and consecrated for a further seven years).[219] Doyle was induced by Rochfort and Alexander to 'suffer' Rev. Goss to retain the administration of Leighlin though he had no intention of satisfying the priest's patrons by giving Goss title to the parish. Furthermore, in a note in his Diocesan Book, Doyle recommended to his successors in the See that 'should he, Goss, survive me then to remove him from Leighlin, [here several words have been inked over and are illegible] also to exclude other members of his family from the S[acred] Ministry'.[220] Fitzpatrick may have read too much into this. Doyle's reference to other members of the Goss family may have been to persons whose characters were known to him rather than a binding edict denying orders to descendants of that family at any time. Goss did not in fact survive Doyle's episcopacy. He was removed from the ministry in 1827.[221]

Rev. Maurice Kearney rarely saw eye to eye with his bishop.[222] A difficult and strong-willed priest, Doyle described him to Thomas Spring Rice as an 'obstinate and powerful man, a fierce opponent of those who differ from him'.[223] Kearney had been appointed parish priest of Carbury by Bishop Corcoran in 1816.[224] Doyle transferred him to Suncroft parish as administrator in 1820 or 1821[225] and in October 1821[226] he was moved again to Graiguenamanagh as administrator. In the latter parish he took over from the parish priest, the remarkable Benjamin Joseph Broughall, who suffered from persistent delicate health. Broughall's health problem limited his capacity to carry out his pastoral duties and probably caused ill-feeling among his two overworked curates.[227] When Rev. Kearney took over the management of the parish Broughall was allowed one-third of the income for his support. The following year during the course of a serious illness Broughall made a vow to make a pilgrimage to Jerusalem if he recovered, and later left the diocese ('to atone for the grievous sins of my past life') and went on this pilgrimage without informing the bishop. He thus forfeited his pension although he remained de iure parish priest until 1827.[228]

Graiguenamanagh was a parish where the near-starvation years, 1822–3, leaned particularly heavily on the poor. Ejectments, high rents and excessive tithes on tillage were features of life in this parish according to the new administrator.[229] Rev. Kearney had to support one curate who resided away from him and to account for Rev. Broughall's share of the income, which Bishop Doyle put to charitable purposes within the diocese. Kearney found it difficult to balance his books; he complained that the encumbrances on his income 'will not leave me with the common necessaries of life'.[230] But his parishioners were no doubt in a worse state: 'all are going into debt with us and we cannot prevent it except we make our ministry odious'.[231] That, however, is precisely what he proceeded to do. He advised Doyle that because of non-payment of dues 'it will be necessary to deprive them of [second] mass for some time'.[232] Doyle unwittingly assented. Rev. Kearney also disbanded a parochial committee which was raising subscriptions for a new school, took control of the enterprise himself and insisted that all school funds be channelled through his person. These developments caused opposition within the parish led by the able 'General' Thomas Cloney. Writing to Doyle he accused Kearney of malversation.[233] Doyle tried to get to the root of the matter by arranging a meeting between Kearney and Cloney, to discuss the dissension in his presence. The meeting went off unfavourably for Kearney as he afterwards wrote apologetically to Doyle: 'I regret I had not becoming patience and humility with him in your presence'.[234] The bishop must also have found Kearney's references to 'payment for mass' and 'fixing a salary'[235] for the same more becoming a professional man than a Christian minister.

From then on Kearney's fortunes quickly declined. The bishop did not move directly against this grasping cleric. In an exercise in ecclesiastical democracy which had all the characteristics of a modern day referendum, Doyle looked for a memorial from Cloney expressing the general feelings of the parish. The memorial was carried around Graiguenamanagh by the principal boatmen and shopkeepers of the parish.[236] Kearney (perhaps unaware that the bishop had originated this poll on the merit of his ministry) claimed that Cloney was unable to obtain respectable signatures but was active among tradesmen and the lower classes.[237] The memorial, an understated petition to the bishop, simply noted the discontent between priest and people and called for 'the only remedy now left [to] be speedily adopted'. It bore 152 signatures, twenty-seven by consent.[238] Rev. Kearney counter-attacked with a petition of his own, bearing testimony to his worth. His bore 190 signatures.[239] In his own defence he pointed to the moral reformation he had carried out within the parish (although this either was ineffectual or else Graiguenamanagh needed little reformation). He only posited the decline of cursing and swearing and the regular attendance of children on Sundays in chapel 'which before never was nor could be effected'. He painted himself as the victim of a 'restless and revengeful demagogue'.[240] Although he must have realised that Doyle could hardly ignore the level of public opposition to him in Graiguenamanagh which Cloney's poll had demonstrated, Kearney decided to brazen it out: 'If St Paul that most disinterested apostle preached here, and asked for money they would complain of him'.[241]

In early January 1825 Kearney sought to postpone his transfer to Clane parish until after Lent so that he could put the best gloss on it in Graiguenamanagh.[242] He went to Clane as administrator. Doyle recorded that 'on account of some constitutional errors of his mind and an avaricious disposition which occasions disputes between him and the faithful I would not give him title to the parish, but keep [him] dependent upon my will'.[243] Maurice Kearney was far from pleased with his removal to Clane where he feared a 'vicious peasantry' who were evidently even less malleable than his erstwhile Graiguenamanagh flock. A letter of his to Doyle in February 1825 betrays a considerable capacity for self-pity and an unyielding concern for his own pocket:

> to be the last and one of the most wretched of my contemporaries, to be a butt for the sneers and censures of both clergy and laity with no prospect before me entering a parish where no priest has yet lived with comfort to himself, and advantage to the people and from which every priest for half a century has run away, and the one who died made his exit in absolute misery, this is a view I cannot contemplate with evenness of mind.[244]

Doyle later allowed that, in Clane parish, Kearney 'being very distant from me, may act unknown to me and against my advice',[245] thus perhaps acknowledging the priest's contention that his punishment was the inhospitality of the parish. Unlike previous clergymen in the parish however Rev. Kearney prospered, largely through extensive cattle dealing, and on his death in 1842 he left the munificent sum of £8,000 to Carlow College to initiate a foreign mission fund[246] for which his memory is held in benediction.

In 1815, Matthew Fanning was appointed parish priest of Kildare and Rathangan by Bishop Michael Corcoran, the parish's previous incumbent.[247] The case against this parish priest was brought by Stephen Garry, Esq., 'a very obstinate man whose wealth gave him great influence in Kildare'.[248] In February 1820 Garry issued instructions to an attorney to begin legal action against Fanning for defamation.[249] Doyle deprecated this course and apparently persuaded Garry to have his case determined before the appropriate Catholic ecclesiastical authority, namely the bishop himself.

Garry alleged that Fanning had initiated and maintained a vigorous and vindictive campaign of persecution against him and his family. In the course of his ecclesiastical investigation Doyle took affidavits from witnesses to the affair and heard evidence from two lay persons and the Kildare and Rathangan curate, Rev. Mooney. He then laid the entire case before his metropolitan, Dr Troy, and the bishop of Ossory, Dr Marum. They concurred that the charges against the parish priest were sustained. It was held that Fanning had prevented his curate from attending to the spiritual needs of the Garry family, as authorised by Bishop Corcoran. Moreover, he was held to have grossly abused his office by marrying Garry's son, then under twenty years of age, to his father's elderly maid who was 'of much experience, having served a long time in a public house'. Garry Junior had apparently seduced the servant by means of a promise of marriage and she had become pregnant. Doyle informed Fanning that 'in any circumstances, but particularly in those which then existed, you should have acquainted his parents with the conduct of their son, and referred the parties to the Ordinary'. Doyle seemingly believed that the maid, in consequence of the respective ages of the parties, 'their circumstances and condition of life', was not entitled to the fulfillment of the promise.[250]

It was publicly known that Garry Senior was prepared to oppose any attack made on him for his refusal to contribute to the parochial building fund, and Bishop Corcoran had expressly forbidden Fanning to do so. However, the parish priest had used the interval between the death of Dr Corcoran and the nomination of his successor to launch a stinging public attack on Garry, from the altar of his church, beginning on 21 March 1819. The sixth charge against Fanning is worthy of notice as it illustrates the demagogic and dictatorial capacities of this priest and Doyle's legalistic manner of dealing with the case.

> on the Sunday following ... the 28th of March, 1819, you did resume this subject, and in a long and premeditated discourse, did abuse him, the said Mr Garry and his family, did liken him to his cattle, did compare him with Luther and forbode for him that he would burn in hell as you said, Luther now does, that you did intimate that Garry's vices were natural to him saying 'What could be expected of him'. 'What is bred in the bone cannot be got out of the flesh'. That you called him wicked and ill disposed, and threatened that not a vestige of him or his family would remain in Kildare, that you said he had no principle, no religion, that you called his son a puppy, and a blackguard, and that the female whom he had lately married was better than him or any of his family, that you said, you ought to have raised up your hands and called down the vengeance of heaven on him, that you had the same power to curse him, as to bless the faithful, that you said his conduct was publicly scandalous, and of that description which the late bishop thought might properly be censured in public, that you said, that he nor one of his family had not been at their duty for two years where as you had prevented your curate from attending them, that you predicted that Stephen Garry and his family would be made an example of down to the fourth generation and so forth.[251]

Troy, Marum and Doyle could find no language sufficiently strong to express their indignation at the conduct which was proved against Rev. Fanning. Besides removing him from office as parish priest of Kildare, Doyle required him to undertake a spiritual retreat of at least ten days. He informed Fanning that if he felt satisfied with him then, he would appoint him to the administration or part administration of a parish. In the light of the charges proven against Fanning it is perhaps surprising that his punishment was not more severe. However we are not wholly aware of the circumstances which perhaps stimulated him to attack Garry.

Before leaving Kildare and Rathangan, Fanning made a contentious claim on his former parishioners for the expenses he had incurred in building the parochial house. Doyle's erstwhile colleague on the staff of Carlow College, Rev. Patrick Brennan, was sent by him to Kildare as administrator with instructions to resolve the impasse between Fanning and the parish. At the bishop's instigation, a twelve-man committee of parishioners, under the chairmanship of Arthur Kavanagh, Esq., was established to enquire into the justice of Fanning's claim. This committee expressed their surprise that a clergyman should claim right of title to a parochial house beyond the duration of his jurisdiction in a parish.[252]

Brennan called a public meeting (again at Doyle's request) and it reached agreement to give Fanning almost half of the £130 he claimed. Brennan commented: 'indeed it was not easy to bring them to it. I truly believe only for the hope of a successor they would not do more than they had first done, as it is I fear it will be with no small difficulty it will be made out'.[253] When Fanning vacated the parish, Brennan informed Doyle that he had 'never seen any man leave a place so little regretted. I should say leaving the people so well pleased at his departure'.[254] In 1820 Fanning was appointed administrator of Raheen though he did not cease to cause trouble. In February 1823 the bishop seems to have temporarily suspended him and appointed Rev. John McEvoy in his stead. The latter reported to Doyle that Fanning would not let him say mass in either of his chapels: 'He said he would suffer his head to be cut off before he would submit to your Lordship's regulations'.[255] In March 1823 the Raheen priests jointly informed Doyle that 'when the people were not going to him [Fanning] he came into the chapel and told them he would hear [the confession of] any person who wanted him'. On another occasion he went to the sacristy and 'received the confessions of such persons as presented themselves to him, one of whom is a monthly penitent'.[256] Shortly thereafter Rev. Fanning was relieved from his office as administrator for 'ill conduct'.[257] Fanning was reduced to the rank of curate, receiving for his emolument one-third of the dues of Raheen.[258] Thus through his own lack of judiciousness his descent from parish priest of the relatively prosperous parish of Kildare to curate of the poor parish of Raheen was complete.

Perhaps the most interesting aspect of the Kearney and Fanning cases is Doyle's leniency under the circumstances in dealing with these recalcitrant clerics. These cases also demonstrate that Doyle's was a strict but just administration. Disciplinary decisions were carefully made after all the available information had been collated and consultations carried out with his own rural deans, his metropolitan and the bishop of Ossory. Where public scandal had already been given Doyle was, unusually for the time, not indisposed to seek a democratic solution to parochial complaints against his priests. Although his ecclesiastical rule was rigorous, Doyle, in disciplining troublesome priests did not act unfairly or without justification. In fact, where documentation on these cases survives, it can be seen that Doyle never took disciplinary action without good reason.

THE SUPPORT OF THE CLERGY

In 1825 Doyle estimated his episcopal income at between £450 and £500 per annum and remarked that it was 'not so considerable as that of many other bishops in the kingdom'.[259] In the south, Doyle believed, episcopal incomes were 'very considerably more'.[260] One bishopric in Leinster returned £700 per annum while in the north and west revenues were, as might be expected, lower. The income of the archbishop of Armagh never reached £500, while that of the archbishop of Tuam was above that figure.[261]

Doyle employed an administrator and a curate in each of his mensal parishes. When these priests were paid out of the dues the remaining one-third belonged to the bishop.[262] Doyle, himself, hardly ever accepted offerings for masses which he celebrated sometimes daily, always two or three times a week.[263] He received the cathedraticum annually at Easter. This amounted to three guineas from each parish priest and one guinea from every curate of the diocese.[264] There were numerous claims on the bishop's income. He was expected to contribute to every charity, to support the erection of churches and schools; and he undertook to feed a considerable number of the poor at his own expense. Doyle admitted that without the support of friends he would not be able to maintain a house or servant.[265]

In 1800 the annual income of the Kildare and Leighlin clergy (including the bishop) was an estimated £6,975 – an average of £162 per parish.[266] In 1820 the figure was an estimated £9,200, giving an average annual parochial revenue of nearly £220.[267] Bishop Delany allowed that his parochial clergy were 'tolerably well provided for'.[268] Corish has stated that 'the clergy as a whole had a distinctly 'middle class' standard of living' and that 'where nearly everyone was very poor, the priest stood out as a rich man'.[269] In his pastoral against Ribbonism, Doyle remarked: 'Your clergy have a competency, alike removed from poverty and affluence'.[270] Cullen also adopts this view when he states that 'Irish priests' incomes were modest though secure'.[271] For France the concomitant rise in religious fervour and the material comfort of the parochial clergy under the *ancien régime* has been stressed by Delumeau[272] though Doyle always feared that the opposite might occur in Ireland.[273] In 1820 Kildare and Leighlin contained three parishes which returned annual revenues of £500. Two of these, Leighlinbridge and Ballinakill, were divided by Doyle when they fell vacant. One parish returned £400 and another £300 exactly. Fourteen parishes had revenues of more than £200 yearly. The twenty-three remaining parishes returned between £100 and £200 per annum.[274]

Doyle recommended the abolition of the custom of collecting dues at stations (which perhaps resulted in an association of payment for the sacraments) in favour of a twice-yearly collection at Christmas and Easter. He suggested that one or two men be delegated from each parish to collect the dues. If this was not feasible the bishop allowed the priests to invite the faithful to offer their dues apparently on the altar table at the conclusion of mass.[275] Doyle, however, was fearful that those who were too poor to subscribe to their priests' support would be driven from the church through social embarrassment. In other dioceses the custom pursued down to the twentieth century of reading a list of parishioners' names and their respective subscriptions from the altar gave an inadvertant public witness to the parochial class structure. In Kildare and Leighlin no individual was to be denounced from the altar for non-payment.[276] Doyle also recommended that the custom of priests collecting corn at the doors of the faithful, which he claimed gave 'no small offence' to many non-Catholics, should be abandoned. As a temporary measure he suggested that both regulars and seculars delegate servants to do this work. He hoped to find a suitable means of replacing this long-standing custom.[277] In 1800 Bishop Delany noted not just collections for corn but for offerings of grain, hay, fuel, candles, and 'feeding of cattle'.[278]

Over three-quarters of the parochial income of Kildare and Leighlin derived from the Christmas and Easter collections.[279] On these occasions the small farmer with a large family contributed an English shilling (thirteen Irish pence). The more substantial and wealthier farmer could afford sums ranging up to ten shillings. Very few gave more.[280] The remainder of the parochial revenue – less than a quarter – had its provenance in the rites of passage: offerings for baptism, marriage and burial services.[281] In 1825 Doyle acknowledged that there had been instances of clergymen (though not necessarily in Kildare and Leighlin) withholding ministry because they had not received offerings.[282] In 1829 the hierarchy's sub-committee on church discipline recommended that any clergyman withholding ministry for this reason should be punished by his Ordinary. In Kildare and Leighlin clergymen were prohibited under pain of suspension from withholding their ministry for remunerative reasons. They were obliged to discharge their ministry and then to receive, if offered, the sum fixed by custom or rule. On visitation Doyle enquired closely into this matter. In his Diocesan Book, 1819–20, he carefully and repeatedly noted for each parish that 'no dues were extorted', 'there was no subtraction of the ministry', 'no person died without the sacraments', 'no sacraments [were] withheld on account of dues', etc.[283]

To spare the poor from exacting or avaricious clergymen and to uphold the character of his priests, Doyle regulated 'in some degree' – on a sliding scale relative to affluence, or more correctly poverty – the offerings that might be received for baptisms, marriages and deaths.[284] The stipend for private mass was usually two shillings. The general sum received for baptisms – which were performed in the home – was half a crown.[285] In 'some few parishes' (unnamed but distant from the episcopal residence) it was traditional to hold a collection for the priest at baptisms.[286] Marriage offerings varied from five to ten shillings, 'very often' 16s.3d., and more 'generally' one guinea. Persons in good circumstances often gave more.[287] With the exception of a few parishes the wedding cake custom of the south of Ireland, a very considerable source of emolument (the cake was distributed in small slices – and each recipient made an offering to the priest), did not prevail generally in the diocese.[288] Doyle decreed that where the custom was carried on offerings should be free and spontaneous.[289] Unlike the bishops of the Cashel province and the bishop of neighbouring Ferns, the bishop of Kildare and Leighlin did not receive any contribution from the marriage offerings.[290]

Ten shillings was the accepted sum received by a curate for officiating at a funeral. The parish priest could expect to receive from half-a-guinea to fifteen shillings, often a pound.[291] Even in contemporary times in some of the more traditional parishes of the diocese, once the church service was over the priest's role in the funeral was at an end. He did not attend the actual burial where a lay person generally recited the De Profundis and the prayers for the dead.[292] The office for the repose of the soul of the dead was not apparently said unless six priests were present. The parish priest was entitled to receive one pound and the assistant priests ten shillings each for this service.[293] Again the tradition of making a collection for the officiating priest at funeral services was customary in a few parishes of the diocese.[294]

There are very many parallels between the rules for the collection of dues laid down in the 1831 provincial statutes and what is known of Doyle's regulations for the support of his clergy in Kildare and Leighlin. Indeed it seems clear that the chapter 'De Debitis Colligendis' in the provincial statutes owes its provenance to Doyle. The statutes inaugurated a standard scale for the collection of dues throughout the ecclesiastical province of Dublin. It drew a distinction between well-to-do solvent tenant farmers and the poor – cottiers and labourers – and made sure that if there was to be a burden it would not lie on the latter.

For baptisms a donation of five shillings was expected from farmers and shopkeepers, half that sum from labourers. The well-to-do were expected to give two pounds for the services of a priest at marriage; labourers gave one pound. For a licence to dispense with the banns of marriage they gave ten and five shillings respectively. Two shillings was the expected donation for a private mass. For an ordinary mass for the dead (a corpse mass) the poor gave five shillings, those in better circumstances gave ten shillings. A sung funeral mass was a more expensive business; fifteen shillings for the parish priest, and ten shillings for each assistant priest and five shillings for any priest who was unable to officiate on the day but said the mass for the deceased nonetheless. From those who were too poor to give anything – 'nihil exigatur'.[295]

Doyle's rule for offerings operated on the just basis that each person gave according to his means[296] (thus the pauper ipso facto gave nothing at all) and the priests received an equitable recompense for their services. A parishioner could, if he so desired, withold any offering at all but the contrary seems to have been the case.[297] In 1814 Doyle believed that the public were 'scarcely able or willing to support their parochial clergy' but in 1825 he maintained that offerings 'at present are much higher than they need be, and though they are called voluntary they are not strictly speaking so'[298] – a remark indicative of the very strong social and moral pressure to conform to a certain standard within the Catholic community.

Almost inevitably the diocesan clergy were 'very frequently' unable to collect their dues on account of the poverty of the poorer classes.[299] Doyle, however, observed that the inability of the clergy to collect dues also resulted 'often from an unwillingness on the part of some to contribute'.[300] Giving parliamentary evidence on the Whitefeet disturbances in Queen's County in 1832 – a very difficult year for labourers – the parish priest of Abbeyleix, Michael Keogh, admitted that 'Some of them may complain a little [of clerical dues] at the moment, but I do not think that there is any complaint against the clergy of a serious nature regarding their demands'.[301] Doyle's statement hints at some element of anti-clericalism but the extant evidence to prove his contention is meagre enough. Nevertheless it seems probable that there was a strain of anti-clericalism among a substratum of society which has no voice in history because it left no written evidence. The case of the Nurney parishioners of Monasterevan is exceptional in that it is documented. In 1827 Patrick Murphy, P.P., Monasterevan, sought his bishop's advice:

> What shall I do with regard to the Nurney people concerning the £20 subscription for the labour in officiating there on Sundays and holy days .... From the numbers of poor in the parish and the difficulty there is in collecting dues from the greater portion of the parishioners, I assure your Lordship it's not easy for me to manage.[302]

Three years later this problem was no nearer resolution. Doyle informed Murphy that he would not countenance that 'the altar and the priest of God be, day after day, disgraced by seeking the payment of a just debt'. He advised the cessation of mass in Nurney.

> I have told you repeatedly that you are at liberty to discontinue your attendance, or that of your curates, at chapel in Nurney, should the people who attend that chapel not pay to you regularly £25 sterling a year .... I found that neighbourhood without schools, without a chapel, and all I required in return was £25 a year, which they cheerfully and repeatedly promised to contribute to the support of such clergymen. They have broken faith with me ... and they now compel me to sanction a measure which will entail on themselves no small disgrace, and which in its consequences involves the loss of their chapel, and the removal of that religious worship and instruction from them without which men are little better than the beasts of the field.[303]

Sometime within the next three years, 1830–33, Nurney returned to the fold but the problem continued to a lesser extent. In April 1833 Doyle demanded an explanation from Rev. Hyland, the curate of Monasterevan with responsibility for Nurney, for his absence from the distribution of the holy oil. He responded that he would have great difficulty in offering an explanation if necessity did not compel him to act as he did:

> I have not at present ... clothes fit to appear in anything like a respectable assembly, and from the poverty of my situation, cannot procure better for some time ... my salary is but £45 a year out of which I have to maintain a horse, etc., etc. Considering these things, is it not to be wondered that I would sometimes be inconvenienced.[304]

Bishop Daniel Delany contended that the value of a parish was to be estimated not only by its extent, population and affluence but by the ability of its clergymen to collect their dues:

> the sturdy and importunate beggar ... will not fail to make out ... a tolerably handsome provision in what is called a poor and small parish, while the modest, diffident petitioner, the timid and bashful, or rather silent supplicant, will often fare very ill in the reputed great and rich one.[305]

Bishop Delany's curious writing style may convey a slightly false impression, and probably does not do justice to Kildare and Leighlin clerics who were in the vast majority of cases far more philanthrophic than avaricious. One suspects that Nicholas O'Connor was fairly typical of the priests of the diocese during Doyle's episcopacy and that his modus operandi in the collection and distribution of dues was commonplace. The utmost extent of clerical exaction, he maintained, was that 'if there be a rich person that we think gives us too little, we sometimes complain'. He pointed out that 'it has been published frequently from the altar [to the poor] not to stay away or avoid calling us to do our duty for want of money'. O'Connor fed and clothed the poor and even ground for them the corn which he had for his horses – 'whatever we get beyond a very moderate maintenance we consider ourselves bound to distribute for the good of the people'.[306]

A Kildare and Leighlin diocesan clerical fund was formed by Doyle on 4 September 1820 for the support of 'our poor but deserving brethren'. Each priest employed on the mission made an annual contribution. The bishop generally contributed five guineas, each parish priest gave one guinea and each curate, ten shillings or more. The treasurer (a diocesan priest) paid out on orders issued by the bishop, on application being made to him, by the priest in need of financial assistance.[307]

Doyle considerably raised the status of the Irish Catholic curate. Under Bishop

Delany the established usage of the diocese was that the curate received one-third of the monetary dues of the parish and also one-third of the corn when he lived apart from his parish priest. When he resided with his parish priest (which was generally the case in 1800) he received one fourth of the pecuniary income, plus grass, hay and oats for his horse. But this arrangement did not always prevail. In the 'great' parish of Ballinakill the curate received his board and only £30 per annum in 1800.[308] A parish priest could bargain with his curate for the latter's support and maintenance, on the lowest possible terms, and the possibility existed, because of the dependence of the curate on the parish priest's goodwill, of his being inveigled into an inequitable contract. Fitzpatrick referred to curates as the 'mere hired servitors' of the parish priests, to whom they were subject.[309]

Doyle prohibited private contractual agreements between parish priests and their curates. Under his rule the curate received one-fifth of the parish revenues (an estimated £44) if he resided with his P.P. who was obliged to supply him with board, lodging and support for his horse. If the curate supported himself, that is lived away from his parish priest, he received one-third (an estimated £73) of the parochial income and provided for himself. The curate thus placed was less under the control of the parish priest who no doubt felt the expense of supporting him more than he would a resident curate. The avaricious Maurice Kearney disliked the idea of his curate residing away from him.[310] Bishop Kinsella of Ossory, on completion of his first visitation in 1829, reported to Doyle:

> The curates are not so badly off as I thought. When residing abroad (a great evil) they have £40, and all the Unction money and corpse masses, except where the parish priest is *singularly* penurious. But still the system gives rise to eternal squabbling, and I hope with God's help to alter it.[311]

In larger parishes of Kildare and Leighlin where two curates resided with the parish priest each received one-eighth of the parish revenues. Where one lived away from the parish priest he received one-third of the dues and paid £25 a year to the curate who resided with the P.P., and was supported by the latter without charge.[312] Doyle did not approve of collections being made for curates and he deemed it bad policy to remunerate curates one above the other, so they were paid equally.[313] The guidelines which he laid down for the support of curates in his diocese were incorporated in the provincial statutes of 1831.[314] Corish has called these regulations a 'curates' charter'.[315]

REGULARS, BROTHERS AND NUNS: OBSERVANCE OF THE RULE

... if those things which are the basis and foundation of all regular discipline be not strictly preserved, the whole edifice must needs fall.[1]

AUGUSTINIANS

We now examine Doyle's relations with the religious – the regular clergy, brothers[2] and the conventual sisters or nuns in his diocese. It is appropriate at the outset to examine the bishop's relationship with his own order as this illustrates a number of difficulties facing the regulars in Ireland

The great care taken by Doyle in the examination of candidates for the priesthood has already been seen with regard to his secular clergy. But it would seem that even more stringent conditions were applied to those who wished to enter the religious life. From time to time youths from the diocese applied through their bishop for admission into the Augustinians. Doyle held no official position within the order but he did not shirk from stating his distaste for poorish candidates whom the Augustinian authorities, to his mind, too readily seemed to accept. Not for the first time, Doyle, in 1823, warned his order against a candidate named McEvoy:

> this young man is so deficient in learning and talents, and so advanced in age as to be in my opinion unfit for the religious state except as a lay-brother. It is an odious thing on my part to thwart the views of one of my own people and he a religious youth but I should prefer doing so ... to having the order encumbered with automatons of this sort, through the folly of those Dublin people, who seem to me not the least judges of who would be truly useful to them.[3]

On 22 March 1827, commiserating with his former Coimbra colleague and New Ross student, Augustine McDermott, then rector-provincial, 'on the prevarication of that idiot Murphy' – an Augustinian priest who had publicly read his recantation in one of Dublin's Anglican cathedrals – Doyle commented: 'it is only a just judgment upon our Order, as well as upon other Orders in Ireland, for admitting into their society the stupid and vicious whom every other class had rejected'.[4] As one historian of the regulars in the eighteenth century has rightly observed – and it was true of Doyle's attitude in the early nineteenth century – 'the Augustinians accepted only the most promising candidates, preferring to go out of existence, rather than tarnish the cause of religion in any way'.[5] This attitude is exemplified and reiterated in a letter (again of 22 March 1827) of Doyle to Brother Paul O'Connor on entrants to the Patrician Brothers:

> Our poverty in Tullow and the difficulty of finding suitable subjects of whom we could fully approve, are great obstacles to the increase of those monks who could be truly useful but I should rather see our Institute perish through the divine permission than relax in the rigorous scrutiny of those who are to be fixed in it for life or rather for eternity.[6]

On the other hand Doyle never denied talent when he perceived it. Recommending John Doyle (a relative of his own) to the provincial, the bishop wrote that he was 'the most highly gifted with talents that I have known for many years. His life is also as pure and virtuous as we could almost desire'.[7]

It was only to be expected that Doyle should have retained, throughout his life, a great interest in the affairs of New Ross priory. As bishop he granted faculties in his diocese to all members of the New Ross house which could be enjoyed without application to him.[8] In 1823 he intervened sharply with the provincial, Dr Gibbons, on behalf of his old preceptor, John Crane, who lay under threat of severe ecclesiastical censure.

John Crane was prior or rector of New Ross from 1803 to 1811 and again from 1815 to 1826.[9] As rector he was generous to a fault and over many years the house fell into debt. From 1805 until July 1817 house accounts were signed on a gross monthly basis without a detailed break-down of income and expenditure, as required by general practice. When Thomas Tierney, then provincial, came on visitation, he recorded, on 8 August 1817, that he found it 'absolutely necessary to recommend a strict system of Oeconomy' and warned of bankruptcy.[10] Rather surprisingly this visitation report was signed by John Crane's brother, the ex-provincial Philip,[11] who must have been responsible, at least in part for the situation which had arisen, during his own period (1811–15) not long ended, as rector. There was evidently some friction between the Crane brothers. When Philip died[12] John was not named either an executor or beneficiary of his will. The executors John A. Furlong and James Crane, both New Ross Augustinians, were, as Doyle did not hesitate to inform the provincial, 'two young fools' who had behaved uncharitably towards their prior (John Crane) in this sensitive business. This and other matters came to a head in 1823 when the provincial contemplated John Crane's removal as prior. He was charged with bringing the house into debt and personal empire building although this could largely be ascribed to a somewhat over-ambitious building programme. On Crane's behalf Doyle wrote a rather stiff letter to the provincial Dr Gibbons, stating: 'there is no person now living, with the exception of one brother, to whom I have been so long allied by affection and friendship, or to whom I am under more weighty obligations'. Doyle asserted that Crane's faults arose from the goodness of his heart and that his extravagance was over-rated. He contended that Crane was entitled to retain, by virtue of Augustinian tradition, all that he had been permitted to acquire.

> I saw him building almost with his own hands, and certainly by his own influence, the house in the Bowling Green; he let it for £20 a year as a College to the Order, and of this £20 he gave £10 as his subscription. He did more - he almost supported us there. Why, then, should this house be taken from him in his present distress, and the £50 rent due to him [be] overlooked?

Doyle pleaded for an internal resolution of the dispute: 'let us leave Rome undisturbed; let us not send there the dissensions of our own family'.[13]

Fitzpatrick erred when he stated that Doyle's appeal to the provincial on Crane's behalf was unsuccessful and indeed that a new prior was appointed.[14] Crane continued as prior of New Ross though he remained under a cloud and may have suffered some disciplinary action. In 1824 the definitors of the province, Augustine McDermott and John Augustine Cronin were appointed by the provincial as commissioners to investigate the state of New Ross priory. They reported that 'a misunderstanding had for a long time existed within the community' and recommended that all debts be paid off; the procurator should enter an exact monthly account of receipts and expenses and no entertainment should be given at the expense of the priory without the consent of the community.[15] A year later, on visitation, the provincial's representative greatly deplored the house's indebtedness and the fact that the economy measures recommended by the commissioners had not been fully implemented. In future, he directed, there should not be more than one or two dishes at most for dinner and 'no victuals [were to] be given out [to the poor] from the parlour as seems to be the practice at present' (an old custom in New Ross). The Bowling Green was to be kept for the cows and horses of the community alone and no other pigs or goats were to be allowed on it. The prior was especially admonished to conform to this rule. Further building was prohibited and steps taken to ensure a financial return from the property of the priory. Some satisfaction was taken from Rev. John Crane's assurance that he would be 'amenable' to the rules of the order.[16] John Crane died in 1826 and with him it would seem that the dissensions within the New Ross community, in which Doyle had taken so much interest, were laid to rest.[17]

As has been mentioned, three of Doyle's students in New Ross (1809–13), his Coimbra colleague, Augustine McDermott (1827), Daniel O'Connor (1827–31), and Charles Stuart (1831–5), became provincials of the Irish Augustinian order during his episcopacy.[18] Understandably his influence with these provincials was very great and they in turn relied upon him for advice in difficult matters. In 1830 he urged O'Connor to concentrate the resources of the order on teaching. He was heartened that a new school he had advised the provincial to undertake in New Ross had not failed:

> Take care to extend the system – so only will our order revive and never want good subjects. Go before all the other orders in this, for to it they must all turn in some years or become effete, but if you first acquire for ours the characteristic of a *teaching* order it will continue foremost.[19]

Long before his elevation to the hierarchical bench Doyle had often expressed his desire to be in a position where he could serve the regular orders. He had himself been the victim of intolerance directed against the regulars in the refusal of Bishop Ryan to confer faculties. In a letter to Nicholas Clayton, O.S.A., in 1814, Doyle noticed 'how regularly the Regulars are at war; but in justice to ourselves we appear to have the right in every dispute'. The friars in Cork had 'defeated' Bishop Moylan and Doyle was 'glad of it; he acted cruelly and capriciously'.[20] Religion, Doyle maintained in 1830, had suffered greatly from disputes between bishops and regulars. He observed that he never knew of one difference in fifty which could not be resolved by patience and goodwill.[21] Doyle was invited to intervene to resolve disputes between Augustinian houses and diocesan bishops on several occasions during the provincialships of Daniel O'Connor and Charles Stuart.

Perhaps because he was dealing with provincials who were former students and friends Doyle did not pull his punches when giving advice. On completing a new church in Dungarvan, the Augustinians were not obliged but had rather foolishly applied to Bishop Patrick Kelly for permission to open it. It was refused. Doyle did not mince his words: 'I suppose the application ... was made when some old woman was provincial for it was the most absurd abandonment of right I ever heard of'.[22] Bishop Kelly had nailed up the church doors against the Augustinians and refused all efforts towards a settlement with the order. In 1829 O'Connor appealed to Doyle to mediate. The latter however was in no position to intervene directly. He had 'counteracted' Bishop Kelly's strenuous efforts to have his uncle appointed to the See of Ossory in 1828 when Doyle's nominee (Kinsella) had been appointed. In these circumstances Doyle felt it best not to intervene in any way in Dr Kelly's diocese as 'no person knows better how to resent an injury real or supposed'.[23] But Doyle did offer some advice. The Augustinians had received a rescript from Rome securing their main claim: their right to open their new church but apparently only allowing them to do so with the bishop's consent. Dr Kelly remained recalcitrant; Doyle commented to the provincial that Kelly was 'prone by nature to contradiction. It was entire ignorance of the man's

character which led your friends at Rome to hope that he could be led by reasoning to act rightly'. The dispute affected the provincial's nerves; he began to doubt
his own capacity to manage the province and to worry over the possibility of
disedification to the faithful in Dungarvan. Doyle steadied his nerves and referring to disedification advised, in typical no-nonsense fashion, 'don't speak of
that, for no person minds it when there is a question of interest or right ...'. The
only course open to the order, the bishop counselled, was 'to pester them at Rome'
for a rescript permitting the church to be opened without reference to the bishop.[24]
The problem was resolved when Bishop Kelly died in 1829. Doyle's good relations with, and high opinion of, the vicar capitular of Waterford and Lismore
diocese, Rev. Nicholas Foran, prevented a continuation of the dispute.[25] In 1833
Doyle successfully intervened, at the request of the provincial, Charles Stuart,
with the new bishop of Waterford and Lismore, Dr William Abraham, to resolve
a row that flared again in Dungarvan over the loss of emoluments to the seculars
in the town because the Augustinians had increased the number of masses celebrated in their church.[26]

In 1830, again at the request of O'Connor, Doyle mediated personally with
the bishop of Limerick, Dr John Ryan, with whom the Augustinians in that city
were in dispute over diocesan statutes which had, they claimed, curbed some of
their ancient rights and privileges. Doyle sagaciously remarked to the provincial
that 'a reference to privilege (a thing odious of its nature) is always calculated to
beget opposition. Privilege is like a treasure – it ought to be guarded, but never
spoken of'. Bishop Ryan expressed himself satisfied to abide by Doyle's decision
on the merits of the case. Doyle found that only one rule in the statutes was
contrary to church law and advised O'Connor that there was no difference worth
noticing between the order and the bishop.[27] In 1834 O'Connor was appointed
bishop of Madras through Doyle's influence.[28] During his episcopacy Doyle's
reputation for mediation was well-known and not confined to the regulars alone.[29]

STROLLING FRIARS

In general the regular clergy were low in numbers and poorly organised in the
early years of the nineteenth century. A Roman rescript of 1751 decreeing that all
postulants make their novitiates abroad had brought about a sharp decline in
numbers and perhaps also indirectly in the observance of discipline.[30] Ten regulars served on the mission in the diocese in 1800, three in Kildare and seven in
Leighlin; the majority of these were Franciscans. Under Doyle the number of
regulars who officiated in parishes probably never numbered more than two to
four at most. Neither under Bishop Delany (in 1800) nor Doyle was any regular
a parish priest in the diocese.[31] A regular (possibly a Franciscan though not a
Jesuit) laboured in Clane parish in 1824.[32] A Franciscan named Joyce served as a

curate in Carlow town parish under Doyle.[33] There had been a Franciscan presence in the parish in 1800. In 1822 another Franciscan arrived in Carlow to join Joyce. Doyle had no objection to his residing in the same fashion as Joyce, that of a 'mere missionary', but he felt that the friar would be unable to secure support in Carlow even if the parish priest accepted him. Under these unpropitious circumstances the friar left Carlow. Doyle could not employ him elsewhere in the diocese 'having several men unprovided for at present'.[34]

The bishop determined that in his diocese all friars apart from the few on the mission should lead monastic lifestyles.[35] He was totally opposed for political as well as religious reasons to the strolling friar who begged ostiatim. These friars wandered the countryside seeking support and occasionally settled in parishes which they considered would facilitate their requirements. Politically Doyle foresaw danger to the friars arising from the hostility which prevailed against them in the highest reaches of English public life. Doyle wished to see the regulars free from all accusations of ill-discipline and bad conduct so that he could plead for them without embarrassment 'should a day of danger to them arrive'.[36]

At the beginning of his episcopacy a number of Franciscans were scattered singly throughout the diocese. James Dempsey, O.S.F., lived in Rosenallis parish in 1820.[37] Another Franciscan named Johnson died in Carbury parish in 1824.[38] James O'Donnell, O.S.F., lived in Leighlin parish where he died in 1825 aged seventy-eight.[39]

A friar was often to be found locum tenens in a parish where his order once possessed a medieval religious foundation.[40] This was the case in Killeigh parish where a sole Franciscan, John Joseph Donovan, resided. He was the recipient of a letter from Bishop Doyle disapproving of his presence. Doyle was hostile to the idea of an individual friar wandering about the diocese or residing in a parish on his own. He quite rightly maintained that this 'bad system' led to abuses because the friar had neither a monastic discipline nor a systematic occupation.[41] Doyle ruled that all strolling friars should return to their monasteries by nightfall thus severely restricting their movements. Nor was the strolling friar to partake of poitín in farmers' houses or accept of hospitality for the night. If the friar could not return to his monastery by nightfall he was to seek accommodation overnight in the house of the nearest priest.[42]

The Franciscan in Killeigh parish replied to Doyle that he intended to make his residence at Killuran and was 'in no wise obnoxious to such objections'. He planned to erect a small chapel to facilitate neighbouring parishioners who through 'necessity or circumstances' could not attend the parish church on Sundays and holy days. He also proposed to teach Christian doctrine and he expected to be joined by one or two priests of his order and indeed by 'some devout laics who wish to consecrate themselves to God in religion'.[43]

Such extensive plans inevitably aroused the ire of the seculars. James Dowling, P.P., Killeigh, informed Doyle that a Franciscan had celebrated mass for several months in his parish without consulting any parish clergyman. The friar's excuse was that the houses where he said mass were far from the parish church, although the P.P. claimed they were only three miles distant which he evidently felt was quite within walking distance. The parish priest shrewdly alleged that the Franciscan had planted a couple of acres of potatoes with men 'said to be carders'.[44] John Joseph Donovan's ambitious expansionism did not come to fruition and no more is heard of his project. Wandering Franciscans disappeared from the diocese as Doyle put an end to regulars, outside of their monasteries, ministering in Kildare and Leighlin – a tradition that had persisted at least from the time of the Reformation.

CARMELITES

Historically Kildare and Leighlin had two Calced Carmelite monasteries. The Kildare town foundation, established in 1290, could claim only two members (not, of course, living in the original monastery) in 1800.[45] The house had two members in 1820.[46] In one list two John McCormicks, senior and junior, are given as members of the house in the early 1820s. Michael Hughes was named as prior by the Carmelite chapter in 1823.[47] He left the diocese in the mid-1820s in consequence of 'slight differences' with Doyle, and it may be presumed that the Kildare house was then at least temporarily closed. Hughes however was never under ecclesiastical censure and in 1827 he and Doyle were 'thoroughly reconciled'. Doyle at first did not allow Hughes to return to Kildare town or to serve on the mission in the diocese as there were no vacancies; instead he introduced him to the archbishop of Dublin hoping that Dr Murray would adopt him for his diocese.[48] Nonetheless in 1829 Hughes registered as a regular and gave White Abbey, Kildare as his usual place of residence.[49] During the remaining years of Doyle's episcopacy Hughes was the only Carmelite in Kildare town.[50]

In 1820, Doyle prohibited Rev. W. Murphy, a 'strolling Carmelite' based in Arles parish, from exercising his ministry in the diocese and determined that he was never to be reinstated.[51] The Leighlinbridge Carmelite monastery, founded in 1272 (and strangely not mentioned by Dr Delany in 1800) functioned until 1826 when it was in effect suppressed by Doyle on account of disorders of a somewhat indeterminate nature. Michael Coleman would appear to have been prior in 1820 when the house had only one member.[52] In that year Bishop Doyle, as has been mentioned, endeavoured to keep the peace between Coleman and Dr Michael Prendergast, the vicar-general. By virtue of his 'dealings and disputes' in Graiguenamanagh parish Coleman had made himself unpopular with the diocesan clergy.[53] For 1821 one source records that 'In the district of this [Leighlinbridge] convent live two young men [i.e., friars]. Maguiness is one and the other George Brophy, both about thirty years of age'.[54] Patrick Barry was prior in 1823. The acts of the 1823 chapter also name William Britton and Richard Whelan as conventuals in Leighlin.[55] In the three years, 1823–6, these Carmelites appear to have exacerbated an already poor situation in Leighlin to the point where the house had to be closed.

On 26 February 1826, Rev. Thomas Coleman, provincial of the Irish Carmelites, informed Doyle that he hoped 'to repair the scandal given by the former persons occupying the convent [at Leighlinbridge] as they did in defiance of all order, power and authority'. He could not, the provincial asserted, consistent with the constitutions of his order, act otherwise than to send two members of the order to take charge of the Leighlin convent. If he declined to send new men to Leighlin, the provincial maintained, the chapter would consider his inaction 'grave neglect' and 'tantamount to the suppression of the house' which lay not in his power but in that of the provincial chapter or general of the order. However, if he failed to send two friars, the 'probable result' would be his own 'suspension' from office. He intended to send two exemplary clergymen whose characters were in every way opposed 'to the character of the late unfortunate and unhappy man'.[56] The provincial hoped that Doyle would be swayed by the calamities which threatened his own tenure of office and so would permit the Carmelites to exercise faculties in the diocese.[57] Without faculties the members of the convent at Leighlinbridge could not function pastorally within the diocese. Evidently these faculties were not granted and the demise of Leighlinbridge convent in 1826 can be attributed to Doyle. For whatever reasons, it fell far short of his idea of monastic discipline.[58]

JESUITS

Doyle's relations with the Society of Jesus are extremely interesting in the light of a fascinating controversy which developed. The only Jesuits in Kildare and Leighlin diocese ran an expensive public school in Clane parish. The formidable Dr Peter Kenney, S.J., purchased Castle-Browne for £16,000 and restored the old name of Clongowes Wood to the college he established there in 1814, the year in which the Society of Jesus was restored by Pope Pius VII. Clongowes was one of Ireland's first modern Catholic public schools. In the mid-1820s the establishment maintained fourteen Jesuits who taught at least 150 'very respectable' pupils who paid fifty guineas annually for the privilege.[59] The Jesuits were also active in the neighbouring community: celebrating masses, hearing confessions, visiting the sick, and generally assisting the parish priests of Clane and Kill parishes.[60] On account of his continental training and outlook Doyle was suspicious of Jesuits per se; his stormy relationship with the Clongownian Jesuits reached its nadir in 1824 when he withdrew the community's faculties to hear confessions and to preach to parishioners of the surrounding parishes.[61]

Doyle's attitude to the Jesuits cannot be divorced from the context of the experience of two and a half centuries of European history. From the sixteenth to the nineteenth centuries it was by no means unusual for a well-educated and cultured churchman to harbour grave suspicions about the Society of Jesus. Popes such as Innocent XIII and Benedict XIV, the latter 'the most distinguished canonist of the eighteenth century',[62] were hostile.[63] So too was the leader of the so-called English 'Catholic Enlightenment', Doyle's contemporary, John Lingard.[64]

The Jesuits had been deeply involved in European politico-religious history from their foundation in 1540. Under Ignatius Loyola they had startled Europe and the Catholic world (which they had greatly expanded from the reductions of Paraguay to China) as the 'shock troops' of the Counter-Reformation, sworn by a vow of special obedience to the pope. Their lengthy fifteen year formation, centring on Loyola's 'Spiritual Exercises'; their industry, intelligence and discipline, made them a potent and feared voice in the service of God. They became figures of great influence and latent power in European courts, playing roles such as confessors to monarchs and tutors of royal children. In time their very success brought a backlash against them and they were accused of devious machinations and power-hunger by a variety of European monarchs who had been their erstwhile patrons. Their suppression in 1773 is a useful example of the dangers to the weaker party in church-state relations. Even from within the Catholic religious community the Jesuits were opposed by the Dominicans, Franciscans and secular clergy. They were not helped by the weakness of the papacy which capitulated and suppressed them under pressure from European rulers.

In France the Jesuits had been caught in a cleft stick between Pope Innocent XI and ultramontanism on one side and the Gallicanism of the clergy and King Louis XIV on the other. To their Gallican-Jansenist opponents the Jesuits were grasping, ambitious clerics who lowered standards of morality in order to gain control of consciences. Their success as confessors was ascribed to their allegedly lax moral doctrines; their non-doctrinaire flexibility on the missions resulted in problems such as the Chinese Rites controversy. In Portugal the internal troubles created for the order by Simon Rodriguez, S.J., were very insignificant compared to the persecution of Pombal. Doyle's alma mater had been the home of the Conimbricsences of the early seventeenth century. But at the period of Doyle's brief university education the Jesuits were suppressed and he undoubtedly, and perhaps not unnaturally given the prevailing climate, imbibed Gallican leanings against them.

An early example of Doyle's deep mistrust of the Jesuits is provided by a letter he wrote from Carlow College in 1814 condemning the 'Jesuit' practice of manifesting conscience to a religious superior outside the confessional: 'The constitutions of the Jesuits which prescribe this modified manifestation, like many other of their institutions and opinions, seem to savour more of a political than of a religious nature, and have never been approved by other religious orders'.[65]

Doyle's hostility to the Jesuits was ultimately theological. The Society of Jesus had been very active particularly against the Dominicans in the post-Tridentine controversies on grace. The central question of this vast controversy was the help afforded by grace, while the crucial issue was the reconciliation of the efficacy of grace with human freedom. Catholic teaching holds that efficacious grace given for the performance of an action obtains, infallibly, man's consent and that the action takes place. On the other hand is it certain that, in so acting, man is free? Hence the question arises how can the two things – the infallible result and liberty – be harmonised? In this controversy the most notable writers on the Jesuit side who stressed free will were Lessius and more especially Molina. Naturally Doyle inclined towards the views of St Augustine – the central historical figure of the dispute – who seemed to favour efficacious grace almost at the expense of free will. The more extreme Augustinists founded Jansenism. The Jesuits accused the Dominicans of pre-determination, while the latter, believing that not alone St Augustine but also St Thomas Aquinas had been impugned, accused the former of denying efficacious grace.

In his 1820 Relatio Status Doyle stated that in Clongowes the faith was strictly observed.[66] However, perhaps some misgivings about the Jesuit presence may be inferred from a letter to Doyle from the rector of Clongowes, Dr Kenney, dated 6 March 1823. Kenney asserted that 'the nature of the establishment which we here conduct ... is the occasion of all the jealousies, that are felt, of all the clamour, which is raised against us'. He maintained that the Jesuits had no province or vice-province in Ireland and thus Clongowes was not a corporate body even according to canon law. Moreover his college was 'not an establishment of Jesuits or of the Society of Jesus. It has neither the name nor the object of any one of our houses'.[67] The Irish Jesuits did not enjoy corporate status; they had no wish to provide a focus for their many opponents among Catholics and Protestants (though as Kenney admitted the magnificence of Clongowes itself was target enough). The Jesuits by quietly conducting their school sought to avoid becoming a bugbear of emancipation. (In this they failed, and the Roman Catholic Relief Act, 1829, legislated specifically against the Society of Jesus.) Kenney's letter helps to explain some apparently peculiar answering by Doyle before the lords' select committee in 1825; when questioned on Clongowes Doyle stated: 'I know nothing officially of those at Clongowes being Jesuits'.[68] Similarly he informed the commons' select committee that the Clongownian Jesuits 'do not seem as far as I can understand, to act in any other capacity than that of individual clergymen collected together'.[69]

On visitation in Kildare in 1823 Doyle was struck by the poverty yet religious simplicity of the parish of Allen compared to the grandeur of Clongowes Wood College. He feared that the splendour of the (newly decorated) college would promote voluptuousness and pride unless checked by fasting, prayer and abstinence. The richness of the dinner table repelled him.[70] Ironically it had been laid in honour of the prelate's visit and was not every day fare. It was a maxim of Doyle's episcopacy that poverty was no injury to a monastery.[71] The physical appearance of Clongowes merely helped to confirm Doyle's suspicions that this was an environment in which a lax moral theology could thrive. On Doyle's visit in 1823 conversation at dinner turned on canon law; the bishop expressed himself forcefully of opinions which gave offence to the rector, Dr Kenney, who exclaimed 'I am unused to such language at my table' and walked out.[72]

The *Vindication* published in early October 1823 contained a gratuitously uncomplimentary allusion to the Jesuits which clearly indicated Doyle's hostility to the Society and did not go unnoticed among the secular clergy and laity of the diocese. Indeed it was often thrown in the face of the community. J.K.L. concluded his letter to the Marquis Wellesley by remarking that it was longer than he had intended but 'as Pascal said, when writing one of his provincial letters to the Jesuits, I have not time to make it shorter'.[73] This was a revealing reference. The name of the Jansenist Pascal was anathema to the Society of Jesus. *The Provincial Letters* were a defence of Jansenism published pseudonymously by him in 1657. The first four letters treat of the dogmatic relationship between grace and human liberty which formed the basis of Jansenism. The fifth to sixteenth letters contain a brilliant (if misdirected) censure of the 'Jesuit moral code' or rather Jesuit casuistry. Pascal depicts a naive Jesuit, who, through vanity, revealed to him the pretended secrets of Jesuit policy and continues with a stringent denunciation of 'Jesuit theology' particularly probabilism.

Briefly the central doctrine of probabilism was that in every doubt which concerns merely the lawfulness or unlawfulness of an action it is permissible to follow a solidly probable opinion in favour of liberty, even though the opposing view is more probable. Rigorism or Tutiorism held that the safe opinion should be most probable, if not absolutely certain, before it could be lawfully put into practice, while probabilism, which enemies of 'Jesuit theology' labelled 'Laxism', maintained that, if the less safe opinion were slightly probable it could be followed with a safe conscience.[74] Dens, author of the text in theology recommended for clerical use at theological conferences in Kildare and Leighlin, espoused a moderate rigorist or tutiorist position.

Pascal unjustly blamed the Jesuits, attacking the Society exclusively and attributing to it a desire to weaken the Catholic moral code in pursuit of its own policy objectives. He went further and attacked casuistry itself, thus providing fuel for Enlightenment scorn of Catholicism in eighteenth century Europe. Despite being condemned by Pope Alexander VII in 1657 the *Provincial Letters* enjoyed great success in educated circles; the work was a masterpiece of French prose - eloquent, satirical, passionate and of course extremely damaging to the Society of Jesus. Doyle's reference to Pascal in the *Vindication* was a clear public hint of his worsening relations with the Jesuits.

The secular clergy of Clane parish, despite outward appearances of friendliness, looked on the Jesuit presence with a certain degree of resentment. In itself this was not unusual for there had always been tensions between regulars and seculars over rights and customs which often could be reduced in the last analysis to a question of dues. The Clongownian Jesuits had developed quite a reputation as confessors. They manned their confessionals literally all day long[75] and were, according to themselves, almost overwhelmed by penitents, from surrounding and indeed distant parishes, so great was the demand.[76] This inevitably gave rise to a feeling among the parochial clergy that the Jesuits were crowding them out of their proper spheres of activity and influence; how were the parish clergy to determine who had and who had not fulfilled their Paschal duty if parishioners claimed to have gone to confession to the Jesuits?

The parochial clergy complained about the Jesuits to their bishop. They contended that their rights and functions were being injured and that Jesuit leniency in the confessional was being taken advantage of by all sorts of thugs and reprobates. Such an accusation could not have failed to make an impression on Doyle. Jesuit laxity in the confessional was one of the most often quoted charges against them,[77] virtually a canon of Gallican-Jansenist opposition to the Society. Thus in 1824 Doyle withdrew from the Jesuits their faculties to hear confession and to preach in public. Dr Esmonde of Clongowes had long been a friend of Doyle's.[78] He entered into a private correspondence with the bishop, defending the Society and endeavouring to persuade him to lift his curtailment of faculties. In response to Esmonde, Doyle stated that the withdrawal of faculties 'was the only remedy I could apply with a prospect of success, to evils I was satisfied existed to a considerable extent.' Many representations had been made to him, Doyle commented, 'and it was more than once intimated that, if some such remedy were not applied, the pastor could not be responsible for the observance of any discipline nor for the souls of his flock'. Doyle was reluctant to curb the liberty of the faithful in choosing a confessor but it was maintained that the priest confessors at the college 'were supposed to be deceived or misled by the partial, imperfect or perhaps false statements of the persons resorting to them, sometimes in defiance, often in contempt of the just authority of their pastor'. Such representations impressed themselves on Doyle and made him mindful of 'how necessary it often is for a confessor to have an extrajudicial knowledge of some penitents in order to induce them to take a just view of their own misdeeds'. Doyle was also inclined to believe that a desire to withhold dues to which the parish clergy were properly entitled, was not infrequently a reason why some withdrew from the authority of their parish clergy or induced others to do likewise.

In this letter to Esmonde of 5 April 1824 Doyle professed his lack of enmity towards the Jesuits though acknowledging that 'the conduct of some few of them for some time after the decease of Mr Kennedy wounded my feelings severely'. Doyle however added insult to injury by seeking toleration of the fact that he dissented, he informed Esmonde, 'from many maxims of your institute or theology'.[79]

The withdrawal of faculties was greeted with horror, astonishment and resentment by the Jesuits who claimed to have led 'multitudes',[80] to return to the sacraments from which they had been absent for years. Dr Esmonde, S.J., described this 'extraordinary stigmatising stricture' as 'the most painful wound' which has affected us since the opening of our college'.[81] The Jesuits found the sanction all the more galling because a regular of another order officiated as a curate in Clare parish without any restriction. A prohibition on attendance at Clongowes for religious purposes was proclaimed to the public from the altars of Clane and Kill parishes. The Jesuits, of their own accord, withdrew from all pastoral contact with the parishioners of these parishes.[82] The submission of Dr Kenney, on behalf of his community, to Doyle's mandate, was decidedly double-edged if not actually ambiguous. 'My Lord', he wrote, 'I will accept of no such condition. I have not hitherto heard many penitents – I shall hear fewer for time to come'.[83] Esmonde replied to Doyle by informing him that the Society had no theology peculiar to itself and,

> while she enforces the most perfect submission to the decisions of Rome, she allows her children as much liberty in forming their opinions in unde-clared matters as are enjoyed by the secular priest ... and in fact I frequently find her on this espousing opposite sides of the question, and abused most copiously for opinions which they borrowed from Lotus [?], Navarre, etc. ... and our Society is far from wishing her children to be all 'unius libre'.[84]

Navarre is associated with the doctrine of mental reservation which grew out of Catholic church teaching on lying. Catholics are never allowed to tell a lie even to save human life. They are also under an obligation to keep secrets faithfully. Sometimes the easiest way to comply was to use an equivocal expression. Mental reservation was a theory centring on the permitted use of an equivocal expression put forward to satisfy claims both of justice and veracity. Martin Aspilcueta ('Doctor Navarrus') developed a doctrine of strict mental reservation in which the speaker mentally added some qualification to the words which he uttered; the words together with the silent mental qualification made an assertion in accordance with fact. Navarrus was received as probable by some Jesuit theologians of consequence, though opposed, as Esmonde observed, by others. His theory of strict mental reservation was condemned by Pope Innocent XI in 1679.[85]

Dr Esmonde pointed out to Doyle that the course in moral theology followed internationally by the Jesuits was that of Alphonsus Liguori (1696–1787). We do not know how Doyle viewed the theology of the founder of the Redemptorists. At one time Liguori had been a defender of probabilism but he finally adopted a middle position between rigorism and laxism which he called equiprobabilism. He was close to the Jesuits and attacked by some non-Catholics as a patron of lying. During Doyle's lifetime Liguori's stock was rapidly rising within the Catholic church. Declared venerable in 1796, beatified in 1816, he was canonised in 1839 and declared a Doctor of the Church in 1871. A Roman decree of 22 July 1831 allowed confessors to follow any of Liguori's opinions without weighing the reasons on which they were based. Only moral theologians could appreciate the finer points of the probabilism controversy.[86]

The charge Doyle professed against the Jesuits was "that the decay of morality and consequent defection from religion in latter times may be traced to the relaxed morality of the Society", and this charge was supported by reference to the Jesuit doctrines on probabilism and mental reservation.[87] Esmonde did not offer a refutation of the latter part of this charge. He had already pointed to the freedom of opinion allowed to members of the order on questions which had not been definitively pronounced upon by the church. While not calling Doyle a Jansenist he almost implied as much. He preferred to counter Doyle's charge by claiming correctly that it was the same as the accusations of Pascal and almost all the modern Catholic enemies of the Society. Pascal at Port Royal 'fell with all his forces on the body of the Jesuits, whom the Jansenists had long honoured with their particular hatred'.[88] Neither did Esmonde attempt a refutation of the *Provincial Letters*, confining himself to the observation that Pascal's method tended to undermine lawful authority and to substitute Socinianism and the 'Protestant' principle of private judgement:

> The success of the publication in question was the triumph of a ruinous principle, it showed what could be done by artful appeals in religious matters to the opinions and to the passions of the public, it showed that there was nothing sacred in religion which could not be dressed up into a subject of ridicule. If the laughter had ceased with the extinction of the Society of Jesus the evil might perhaps not be worth your Lordship's notice. But the professors of iniquity availed themselves immediately of the lesson which the success of Pascal taught them, and the evil genius of Voltaire and of his associates seized on all that [was] awful in heaven and hell and presented it as an object of laughter to a Parisian rabble.[89]

Esmonde put forward an argument much favoured by the Jesuits against their detractors. The suppression of the Society was due to the same causes which in further development had brought about the French Revolution. The monarchies which were active in the suppression in France, Italy, Spain and Portugal had all been overthrown during the revolutionary period, a happy coincidence of retrospective historical justification.

Doyle met Esmonde in Clongowes during May 1824 seemingly as part of a

peace making process. Doyle subsequently stated: 'almost every day since I had
the pleasure of seeing you ... I thought of apprizing you of my almost entire
conversion to your opinions; probably after a few interviews more with you I
shall be as dark as the most devoted children of the society'. These encouraging
words were however overturned by an intended compliment to Esmonde:

> Providence has compensated her [the Society of Jesus] generally for the
> overcondescension of her wise men to the frailties of our nature by sup-
> plying to others of her sons those indescribable and invaluable qualities
> which are so conspicuous in the person whom I have the honour of ad-
> dressing.

Doyle had written permissions for 'some pious persons', including a Miss Morris, a convert from Clane, to attend various confessors at Clongowes but found
that some of these had been refused. Indeed Miss Morris had been refused by
the person responsible for her conversion. Doyle had urged on Esmonde that
these confessors 'might be induced to assist not to thwart me in my endeavours
to unite the pastors with their flocks'. Doyle wondered why these priests 'created
and published amongst the poor obstacles which I certainly never contemplated'.
Doyle hoped Esmonde would persuade these priests 'to resume their wonted
charity to the poor and the rich'.[90] The practical issue had now been largely resolved. Nonetheless Esmonde was disappointed to find that Doyle had not abandoned his doubts about the Society. For this reason perhaps Esmonde's reply to
Doyle of 2 June 1824 was more vehement than heretofore. Yet he again failed to
offer a specific answer to Doyle's reservations. He preferred to ridicule the 'comic
Evangelist of Port Royal' and to introduce eminent names in defence of the Society. How could the immortal Pope Pius VII have called forth the Society from
extinction if the Jesuits were guilty of overcondescension to the weaknesses of
human nature? For Doyle's benefit Esmonde added that even Pius VII in his
early years had been unfavourably disposed to the Jesuits.[91]

While apparently retaining his theological doubts, Doyle, at this stage, conceded the main point at issue: he allowed parishioners once again to attend confessions at Clongowes though under a ticket system which was in the control of
the parochial clergy.[92] But in a display of injured pride (now that the presenting
issue had been sorted out) Dr Esmonde wondered whether the Jesuits could ever
again work in harmony with the parochial clergy. It is clear that, when Doyle's
stricture had become publicly known in Clane and Kill, the bishop had received
anonymous petitions from parishioners on behalf of the Jesuits. The Clongowes
community disavowed any knowledge of this proceeding and according to
Esmonde 'were all hurt not a little at receiving a severe lecture from your Lordship in the letter to Miss Morris; it pained me to see it addressed particularly to
[a] foreigner among us thro' the hands of a convert'.[93] Esmonde was now writing

for the record. He foresaw the accusations which might some day be brought against the Clongowes community.

By July 1824 relations between the Jesuits and Doyle had been restored to the extent that Kenney, through Esmonde, was inviting Doyle to the annual academical exercises in Clongowes in early August. In conveying this invitation Esmonde complained to Doyle that many of the clergy in the neighbourhood of Clongowes were strongly impressed with the idea of Doyle's dislike of the Jesuits. Esmonde was particularly annoyed with the attitude of Malachy McMahon, parish priest of Clane, who had made 'uncandid and uncharitable' reflections on a Jesuit of the college who regularly celebrated mass, preached and assisted at vespers in Clane at McMahon's request. Moreover McMahon extended his remarks to the college and to the Jesuits in general and was heard to profess that he quite agreed with Dr Doyle in his dislike of them. Esmonde informed Doyle that there was more than one instance in which the parish priest of Clane had manifested 'his unfriendly disposition towards us'.[94]

In response to Esmonde, Doyle stated that he lost no opportunity of impressing on McMahon's mind 'the necessity and advantage of his cultivating the favourable opinions and good-will of the gentlemen of the college.' McMahon agreed to abide by this reasoning but he, stated Doyle, 'by talking over much commits faults'. Doyle asked what could he do – an unusual complaint from him: 'it is not in my power to govern the tongues of persons who cannot always be themselves guided by their own good sense'. (In his Diocesan Book, 1819–20, Doyle had characterised McMahon as 'zealous, disinterested, pious'.) In this letter Doyle once again clearly indicated his goodwill towards the Jesuits as individuals but his doubts about the society:

> As to your house I have, whenever I could do so with propriety, spoken favourably of it. I have done so of your system of education. I have recommended your school to the parents of children, and I have omitted no opportunity of professing my affectionate esteem for those members of your family with whom I happened to be best acquainted, and if after this, my name be used to do them injuries, I am unable to repair or prevent it.
>
> If I have thought, as you know I have, less favourably of the Society than many others, and that I have sometimes reasoned or spoken on those matters of their history which I could not justify in my own mind, as others have done, I have been at the same time ever careful to commend what I thought commendable in the body at large, but above all in the members of your College, so that, if the priests in the diocese show an unkind disposition to so useful an establishment they are not warranted by my example, and I can only do in future as I have done – hitherto, endeavour to produce gently a better feeling.

Doyle mentioned that he had heard of a 'direct and public attack' made on one of his publications by a Dublin based Jesuit but he had chosen to ignore it.[95] Esmonde could hardly have found this letter satisfactory but at least on the practical rather than the substantive question at issue – the withdrawal of faculties – Doyle had reversed his decision under Esmonde's influence. Doyle was unable to accept the invitation to attend the academical exercises at Clongowes because he was on visitation to several parishes of the diocese but on 7 August 1824 he invited Esmonde to visit him in Old Derrig. Esmonde was absent from Clongowes when the bishop's letter containing this message arrived. Dr Kenney opened it and was 'agreeably surprised', he told Esmonde, 'to find him still desirous of your visit. You must go to him'.[96] Good relations were thus restored and Doyle was afterwards in annual attendance at the academical exercises in the college.[97]

Doyle had a typically Gallican prejudice against the Jesuits which derived from his own education and ecclesiological outlook and was perhaps compounded by ignorance. Under examination before the lords' select committee on the state of Ireland in 1825 Doyle was asked if he was aware of the proper habit of a Jesuit. He answered that he had never seen a Jesuit properly habited, and seemed unaware that the Society had no special habit.[98] Doyle's relations with Clongowes make very manifest the fact that no regular lay outside or could escape his jurisdiction. Before the commons' select committee in 1825 he stated that the Jesuits 'can do nothing in my diocese unless in virtue of authority derived from me; I have over them a full and perfect control in the exercise of their ministry'.[99] The Clongownian Jesuits had good reason to know that Doyle meant exactly what he said.

DOMINICANS

In contrast to his relationship with the Jesuits, Doyle had apparently no complaints about the conduct of the Dominicans in Kildare and Leighlin and in consequence his dealings with them need only be briefly addressed. The Dominicans, like the Jesuits, possessed only one house in the diocese, established at Newbridge in 1756.[100] Dr Patrick Moore, sometime professor of theology in Louvain, became prior and probably the only occupant of the convent in 1796. As befitted a member of his order he was an eloquent preacher. He taught a school in Newbridge where he resided until his death in 1829.[101]

In 1819 the 'large room' of his monastery became too small for his congregation and he began to build a church. Local people contributed enthusiastically in money and labour according to their limited means and the church was completed the same year.[102] In about 1819 Dr Moore was joined by a Rev. Dunne, O.P., of whom it has been claimed that he was known 'when destitute of money, to have taken off his shirt and vest to give alms'.[103]

As far as can be ascertained, the Newbridge Dominicans emerged unscathed from Doyle's reforming administration. Indeed his protection of their right to quest helps to elucidate the context in which his dispute with the Jesuits took place. In August 1823 Doyle wrote to Rev. Dunne apologising for the conduct of Malachy McMahon, P.P., Clane, who would not let the Dominicans quest in his parish.[104] In February 1824 Doyle wrote again on the same subject and gave the Dominicans permission to quest in Clane parish on the first three Sundays of Lent in each year, when alms-giving was highly recommended.[105] Doyle's correspondence with the Dominicans on this topic clearly indicates that the parish priest of Clane was hostile to all regular clergymen, not just the Jesuits.

In July 1826, Doyle requested Dunne's services and two weeks later thanked him for his assistance on the mission in the diocese.[106] In 1829, Nicholas Frayne, O.P., succeeded Dr Moore as prior. In 1831 he demolished the mud-walled monastery built in 1773 and replaced it with a two storey edifice dedicated to St Eustace.[107] The substantial and significant progress made by the Newbridge Dominicans reflected in microcosm the rapid advances made by the Catholic church in Kildare and Leighlin during Doyle's episcopacy.

PATRICIAN BROTHERS

The origins of the Patrician Brothers have been discussed in our treatment of Bishop Daniel Delany's administration.[108] It will be recalled that the Patricians benefited only to a very minor extent, in comparison to their sister congregation, the Brigidines, from Dr Delany's will. They were at a further disadvantage, which they shared with the Brigidines, in that Dr Delany left them no definite rule and constitutions. He bequeathed them only guidelines, believing that time and experience – perhaps as long as twenty years – would enable the community to define its own rule. This could be seen as a remarkably enlightened view for that time.

Doyle inherited this state of affairs and found it highly unsatisfactory. The brothers, however, were able to inform him of Dr Delany's intentions in their regard[109] and, thus advised, he drew up a rule and constitutions on 28 August 1821.[110] The title page of this work which was printed in 1826 credited Dr Delany with the authorship and Dr Doyle with the revision, approval and augmentation of the rule and constitutions. This was an act of generosity on Doyle's part to the memory of his episcopal predecessor, for in truth, Dr Delany had not drawn up a rule and constitutions. In his 1829 Relatio Status Doyle remarked only that he had 'reduced' the Patrician congregation 'to a more strict observance of their duties'.[111]

Generally there is no radical difference between the rule and the constitutions. The four great rules of the church were drawn up by Saints Augustine,

Basil, Benedict and Francis. Much of what constituted the Patrician rule and constitutions was similar to that of other male and female religious institutes. A comparison of the rules and constitutions of the Patrician congregation and the Presentation order reveal that the former was modelled on the latter. There are very great similarities and an identical text in many parts. The Presentation rule and constitutions (in turn based on the Ursuline rule) was approved by Pope Pius VII in 1805.[112] The parallels between the needs and observances of a lay female and a lay male institute coupled with the relative modernity and Irish origin of the Presentation order, probably made its rule an appropriate paradigm on which Bishop Doyle could base the Patrician rule.

The Patrician rule had a more detailed outline of the order of the day. Notable was the opening of their schools throughout the year at seven o'clock in the morning.[113] A distinctive feature was Doyle's emphasis on the importance of recreation (when permitted):

> Recreation should as often as possible be observed in common, and whilst it continues, it is not only lawful for the Brethren, but a duty incumbent on them, to indulge in a becoming freedom of proper exercise and unrestrained flow of cheerful, innocent conversation; in order to unbend at once the tension of their minds, from long close application, and promote their bodily health by necessary relaxation and exhilarating amusement.[114]

In 1819 representations were made to Bishop Doyle, probably by the secular clergy of his mensal parish of Tullow, that the Patricians wore white cravats and beaver hats and dressed like priests. In response Doyle commanded the brothers to wear black cravats and not to appear like clerics.[115] In 1823 the bishop considered it was time that the brothers, who until then had merely renewed their simple vows of poverty, chastity and obedience annually, underwent final profession. On behalf of his confrères, Brother Bernard Hayden plied Doyle with several anxieties about this step: would breaches of the rule be greater than before, after vows had been taken? If indefinite or general commands were imposed by the superior would each circumstance bind under pain of obedience? Doyle settled the brothers' doubts with a full answer. He drew up an act of profession for the Patricians and, on 31 January 1823, seven brothers were professed in the chapel of his residence at Old Derrig.[116]

Although the Patrician monastery at Tullow was begun in 1819, in 1823 it still remained unfinished, to the annoyance of the bishop. This delay was probably the result of bad management. Doyle forbade all further building until the finances were sufficient to allow it to be completed. To this end he entrusted to Brother Serenus Kelly a circular addressed to the people of England. Kelly began his quest in Dublin but, as the Pro-Cathedral was then being constructed, he had little or no success. He travelled to England where he remained for two years and collected about £2,000.[117] Kelly found on his return in 1825 that the monastery and schools were built. The brothers had assisted the tradesmen employed in the work. 'St Patrick's Monastic Seminary' was formally opened under the auspices of Bishop Doyle in 1825.[118] The brothers maintained both a pay school and a free school. Those brothers not engaged in teaching worked at trades. In 1826 Doyle gave Kelly a circular to enable him to make a quest in France to secure funds to add a wing to the monastery.[119]

In 1819 the Patricians were offered a site for a school in Clarenbridge, Co. Galway (diocese of Kilmacduagh) by Christopher and Joanna Redington of Kilcornan House.[120] In a strain of panegyric Doyle wrote to the bishop of this poor diocese, Dr Nicholas Archdeacon, underlining the moral improvement of the lower orders which the Patricians had accomplished in his own diocese.[121] The Clarenbridge filiation was established in 1823 after Brother Joseph Hickey had spent three years building it.[122] In 1827, the warden of Galway, Dr Edmund Ffrench (whom Doyle held in high regard), invited the Patricians to establish a filiation in his city. Brother Paul O'Connor and two others were sent to Galway in that year.[123] The Galway foundation proved to be a very successful one. A filiation in Castlecomer, diocese of Ossory, c.1827–9, appears to have been very short-lived.[124]

In summary we may agree with what Comerford has written of Doyle's influence on the Patricians: it was he 'who shaped their destiny'.[125] Under Doyle the Patricians were given direction; a written rule and constitutions was drawn up and instituted; the brothers professed for the first time and given a distinctive dress; a monastery built and an elementary school and a secondary level boarding school opened; two filiations were founded. Doyle secured the establishment of the Patricians as a teaching order.

FEMALE RELIGIOUS

Catholic orders of women were almost wiped out by the Reformation in Ireland. Only a handful of orders – the Poor Clares and the Dominicans among them – survived.[126] In 1771 the Ursuline order was invited to Ireland by Honora (Nano) Nagle who herself was to found the Presentation order in 1775.[127] The foundation of native female orders in Ireland was evidence of the relaxation of restrictions on Catholic education and further marked the slow re-emergence of the Catholic church from the penal era. The first post-Reformation nuns in the diocese of Kildare and Leighlin, were the Brigidine and Presentation orders, whose convents had been established during the administration of Bishop Delany.

The care with which Doyle scrutinised candidates for the priesthood was also applied with unrelaxed rigour to prospective entrants to the female orders: 'It is not in my power to admit any persons to a convent until I have examined personally into their dispositions'.[128] He required details of each candidate's age, bodily strength, habits of life, family and the exact amount of her fortune or dowry.[129] These details were then submitted to the convent which the applicant wished to enter; she was examined by the mother superior, assistant, and the mistress of novices, who decided on behalf of the convent whether they would receive her as a postulant.[130]

Convents supported themselves by virtue of the dowry system. In 1828 Doyle stated that 'no convent can receive a person not having such dowry for her future support and that would not be less than £600 for which sum an annuity is sometimes received – sometimes it may occur that a person with [a] smaller sum is received'.[131] Dowries were the financial mainstay of convents. The dowry or lack of it had ramifications of no small consequence for the status of the convent entrant throughout her life in religion. She who entered with the requisite dowry, which would support her for life in the convent, was received as a choir sister. As a result of the socio-economic standing of her family such a person would have received a private or a good convent education (almost invariably from the Ursulines) and would therefore be reasonably capable of teaching the 'dear little ones'[132] in the convent elementary school. Harriet Murdock, who entered the Brigidine convent in Tullow in 1829, began by teaching French and Music in their school.[133]

Inevitably when a dowry of approximately £600 was required, the choir sisters came from very prosperous and strong middle class backgrounds, sometimes indeed from what might be regarded as gentry families, including the occasional convert to Catholicism.[134] Sister Eliza Coslett, from Nutgrove, Co. Down, who entered Carlow Presentation convent in 1824 came of a judicial family. Sister Ellen Coughlin who entered the same convent the following year was the daughter of Owen Coughlin, Esq., of Rathoe, Carlow. Sister Anastasia Kinsella who entered in 1828, was the daughter of Gerard Kinsella of Nurney, Carlow, 'a respectable farmer who suffered persecutions at the time politics ran high in this county' (a very understated reference to the 1798 Rebellion). Alicia Nolan, daughter of John Nolan, Esq., of Killballyhue, Carlow, was received in 1830. Sister Teresa Taylor entered in 1832. Her father Joseph Taylor, Esq., of Nonsuch, County Westmeath, was described as a 'gentleman of great respectability'.[135] The profession of Sister M. de Chantal Wilmerding in Maryborough convent in 1825 by Doyle was attended by both Catholics and Protestants.

Suitably disposed and qualified candidates for the female religious life were highly valued. In 1826 Archbishop Curtis, in an angry letter, accused Doyle of, in effect, poaching a religious candidate from his diocese. He expressed 'deep disappointment' that Doyle had prevailed upon a Miss Harding not to join the Presentation convent in Drogheda

as she had resolved, wished and promised to do, and would have faithfully performed, had she only consulted her own feelings, and not been persuaded by Your Lordship that, merely taking the Habit in any Presentation convent, she might safely disappoint the just expectations she had caused in Drogheda.

Curtis requested Doyle – 'if my intercession be not rather a clog' – to persuade Miss Harding to enter in Drogheda. The archbishop received no satisfaction. The Maryborough Presentation convent register records that Alicia Harding (later Sister Peter) entered on 20 February 1826 and was professed by Bishop Doyle in the presence of a 'select congregation' on 8 September 1828. She was later joined by her sister in the same convent. The profession rite followed by some orders included a vow to remain in the convent where professed until death. In 1829, Doyle requested permission from Rome to remove any of the Presentation sisters from one convent to another in his diocese, when necessity required it, because their numbers were relatively small.[136]

The Presentation convent in Carlow made a ruling in chapter in 1833 that the property of each novice would have to be finally settled and secured to the convent, two to four months before the chapter to be held on her dispositions for admission to profession.[137] Even the small to middling farmer class who could just about afford to place a son in Carlow or Maynooth for five or more years of seminary training might find it exceptionally difficult, indeed virtually impossible, to place a daughter in religion for life as a choir sister. On the other hand, once ordained, the priest, by mass stipends, earned his own income. The conventual life of the choir or even the lay sister was probably beyond the potentiality of a female from a very poor background – it was perhaps rare for a religious disposition to blossom in a soul-destroying environment of grinding poverty. Illegitimacy was a canonical impediment to entry into the religious life. The Maryborough Presentation annals record that in 1826 'a candidate proposed to enter this convent highly qualified for the religious state by great piety – gifted with natural talents, assisted by an excellent education, with a fortune of £1,100, but was rejected from illegitimacy'.[138]

A female without the requisite dowry (and generally no more than an elementary education) could only be received into a convent 'in quality of a lay sister'. The lay sisters did not perform all the religious duties enjoined on the choir sisters, 'being destined for duties and services of another sort'.[139] They performed the menial tasks of the convent, worked in the kitchens and laundry, scrubbed and polished the floors, etc. Instead of Prime, Terce, Sext and None, lay sisters said the Pater Noster and the Ave Maria, and the Credo once; instead of Vespers and Compline, seven Paters and Aves; and in place of Matins and Lauds, ten. They were to assist 'as often as their duties will allow' at mass and other devotions.[140]

The lay sisters were set apart from the choir sisters by their practice of religion, apostolate and even dress. Their habits were neither as long nor as wide as those of the other sisters. They did not take their meals with the choir sisters. They had no say in the management of the convent 'having neither active nor passive voice';[141] they did not participate in the election of superiors as the vocals (choir sisters) did. In the convent chapel the lay sisters did not have a place in the choir, nor recite the office. Thus a form of religious apartheid distinguished the nuns in the house of God. One class was exalted, while the other was humbled to the level of servants of the former and had no status in the convent or the order.

In some ways, despite the almost caste like division of choir and lay sisters which must have thrown a shadow over true charity in convents, nuns are the silent heroines of the period we are examining. They devoted their lives to God, worked, prayed and did as they were told by their male superiors. The constitutions of the Presentation sisters, followed by the Brigidines, betray a male condescension to females that is typical of the era. Nuns were warned 'never to be found running giddily through the convent'.[142] The mistress of novices was admonished to eliminate from her charges 'those pettish and childish humours which, especially in the female sex, weaken the spirit, and render it vapid and languid'.[143]

The zeal and commitment to God, especially of those who willingly left comfortable, well-to-do families to lead the most detached, frugal, rigorous and austere lives, was remarkable. Both the Presentation and Brigidine constitutions demanded the complete renunciation of self. In both rules the following injunction was issued to the mistress of novices on the training of her charges:

> She shall study to make them truly sensible of the end they should have in view of quitting the world, and entering into the Religious state, which should be no other than to unite themselves more perfectly with God, by dying to themselves and to the world, mortifying their outward senses, and more particularly their interior passions, so as to apply all the powers and faculties of their soul and body to the service of their heavenly spouse, by a spirit of Evangelical poverty, divested of all earthly attachments; by the purest chastity, and by an unlimited obedience, grounded on self-denial, and a total abnegation of their own will. In short, that this congregation is, in a special manner, founded on Mount Calvary, there to serve a crucified Jesus, by whose example the Sisters ought to crucify their senses, imaginations, passions, inclinations, aversions, and caprices, for the sake and love of their Divine Master.[144]

These strictures were interpreted exactly and literally. Doyle warned his convents never to profess 'any one in whom the spirit of the world cannot be subdued'.[145] The sisters were to be like putty in the hands of God. Nuns sought to achieve a complete detachment from earthly ties. Dr Andrew Fitzgerald was taken aback when, speaking to a nun in Carlow convent, he alluded to her father and she calmly enquired: 'Is he alive?'[146] The austere conventual life 'certainly included amongst other penances the use of the Hair shirt and Discipline'.[147] In 1821 the Brigidine, Mother Mary Anne Lalor of Tullow convent, wrote to her spiritual director, Doyle:

> you gave me leave to try hair-cloth for a week. I did, and found it does me no harm. I wore it during Lent, leaving a day, sometimes two or three, between each week; and at the same time, I wore a chain of wire, two days out of three, I think it would be no prejudice to my health to go on that way at all times; I have two instruments of penance less severe: a hair girdle and a chain without points. I feel disposed to ask leave to wear one or other always.[148]

So great was the zeal manifested by many nuns that even Doyle found it necessary to restrain them, to urge them not to be too anxious for perfection; not to attempt what they could not achieve and to be content with their talents. Of one he jocosely remarked that she was attempting to reach heaven by forced marches. His stress on grace as far superior to free will was typically Augustinian: '... it is not he who runs that gains the prize but he whom God willeth'.[149]

The Presentation and Brigidine orders were neither fully contemplative like the Poor Clares nor did they work outside the convent enclosure like the Irish Sisters of Charity. Both attempted to marry a contemplative life of almost medieval asceticism to an educational apostolate within the confines of the convent enclosure. This juxtaposition posed tensions: 'the frequent conflict of active zeal with the opposing terrors of a breach of cloistral observance'.[150] Both Bishops Delany and Doyle restricted contact between their nuns and lay people. On a convent visitation in 1823 Doyle reflected:

> I could wish that the idea of asking people to sit, or talk, or eat or drink in a convent never entered the mind of any one – from these little trifles many evils take their rise, it is very difficult to preserve our heart and our mind in a community – but if the members of it can have recourse to friends or seculars – there is an end to all pure love of the religious state and to perfect union of heart.[151]

PRESENTATION SISTERS

At the suggestion of Dr Andrew Fitzgerald on the need for a school to educate the poor female children of Carlow town the first house of the Presentation order in the diocese was established on 29 January 1811 under the patronage of the parish priest, Dean Henry Staunton. Mother Francis de Sales Meighan, Sister Mary Anne Breen and Sister Mary Madden, religious from the Presentation convent in Kilkenny, formed the first community.[152] The Presentation order was specifically founded to teach the children of the poor and the nuns in Carlow opened a school immediately on their arrival. In 1819 a new school was founded and 130 children were admitted for tuition. In 1821 there were 300 children in the school and eight nuns in the convent.[153]

It seems not unlikely that Bishop Doyle's commitment to an unrelenting observance of the rule and constitutions conflicted with the modus vivendi of Carlow convent c.1819. 'I only sometimes fear that they are too comfortable,' he worried in 1820, 'as privations are the best property of a convent ...'.[154] In 1824 Mother Meighan and Sister Mary Madden returned to their convent in Kilkenny after thirteen years in Carlow: 'The ecclesiastical superiors deemed it prudent to counsel their return – the funds of the convent not being sufficient for their maintenance, as the annuity appropriated to them by Mr Meighan, brother of the foundress, had been withdrawn'. The extant annals record that the loss was a 'very severe one' and that both before and after the foundress's departure 'there were many trials to be endured'.[155] Unfortunately we cannot be more specific. The revised annals of the convent which date from c.1842 acknowledge the problem: 'On account of a large portion of the original annals having been suppressed by the foundress for reasons not transmitted to us many of the years will be found devoid of interesting material'.[156] The extant annals do not contain any references to Doyle's visitations of the convent so it may be inferred that such documentation was suppressed as well (possibly because the bishop excluded some nun(s) from the convent for failing to meet the conventual discipline he required).

Whatever the nature of the 'trials' which disturbed Carlow convent they did not prevent Doyle, in 1823, from deciding to establish another convent of the Presentation order – a filiation from Carlow – in Maryborough, the county town of Queen's County. This house was founded on 2 July 1824 by Mother M. Magdalen and two other sisters.[157] It was made possible through the cooperation of Doyle and the parish priest of Maryborough, Nicholas O'Connor. As has been noted[158] the bishop obtained a special Roman rescript allowing him (but not his successors) to utilise the dues of Ballyfin parish for the support of the convent. O'Connor had long sought the presence of the nuns in the town and he gave them his house for their convent.[159] In August 1824 a school was opened and 216 poor children – all that could be accommodated – were admitted.[160] In March 1825 teachers from Dublin were employed by the parish priest to instruct the children in 'the winding of silk' and the plaiting and knitting of 'Traunyne Grass' into an imitation of Leghorn for bonnets.[161] Most convents attempted to give their pupils some work experience which might be of use to them once their elementary education was finished and they were forced on to the labour market.

In 1833 there were nine professed nuns and four novices in Maryborough Presentation convent.[162]

The third Presentation convent in the diocese was established in the county town of Kildare. It owed its origins to a prosperous, levitical, Catholic middle class of Mahers, Cullens, Kennas and Lees[163] and specifically to the munificence of the brothers Patrick, Thomas and William Maher, 'three very pious men, and possessed of considerable wealth'.[164] Together with their Cullen and Verdon relatives they approached the parish priest of Kildare, Patrick Brennan, and helped him to purchase a site and buildings for the convent. The first nuns, Mother Mary Agnes Mooney, Sister M. Augustine Maher (sister of the above-mentioned Mahers and aunt of Dr Paul Cullen) and Sister M. Claire Dillon arrived in the town in Easter week on 15 April 1830; their school opened a week later. The Maher brothers made the nuns a gift of £450 on their arrival. It was little wonder that Doyle could write of the convent being 'comfortably established.'[165]

BRIGIDINES

If Bishop Delany's financial legacy to the Brigidine houses he founded at Tullow (1807) and Mountrath (1809) was very substantial, his pastoral legacy was very ill-defined indeed. His instructions for the regulation of these convents were far from approximating to a written rule and constitutions at the time of his demise. His intention that the Brigidines instruct the children of the poor and the middle classes alike had proved fraught with tensions in practice. In 1817 a considerable number of children was admitted into the Tullow school free of charge because their parents had kept them at home up to then as they could not afford the small fee required by the nuns for their education. However, 'the more respectable' people of Tullow 'objected to their children being mixed with the poor children'. In consequence the children were segregated into classes which reflected their socio-economic origins.[166]

On 29 November 1819, just two weeks after his consecration, Doyle made his first visitation of Tullow convent.[167] During his episcopacy Mother Mary Anne Lalor was repeatedly re-appointed superioress.[168] Doyle discerned the greatest need of education among the poor of Tullow. The middle class of the town possessed the means to look after themselves. He stipulated that the Brigidines concentrate on the poor. In 1820 the poor children whom the sisters catechised in their church Sunday school were invited into their lower school which soon became known as a free school.[169]

Where Dr Delany left clear instructions Doyle regarded them as binding on him. But it was precisely Delany's lack of precision which caused difficulty between Doyle and the Brigidines. At the beginning of his episcopacy Doyle was not well informed of Delany's conception of the Brigidine apostolate. This is hardly surprising given that Dr Delany himself appears to have had no clear idea of what he was trying to do. The result was that, in the early 1820s, possibly in 1820,[170] Doyle in effect attempted to turn the Brigidines into a branch or a replica of the Presentation order.[171] The Brigidine sisters, many of whom knew their founder personally, remained true to his intentions as they perceived them – chiefly to teach both rich and poor alike – and they 'respectfully objected'[172] to being subsumed into the Presentation order. The tenacity with which they held to their founder's wishes was understandable; by the very fact of not inviting the Presentation order into the diocese (until 1811) Delany had indicated that he sought something different in a female religious order from what they had to offer. A compromise between Doyle and the Brigidines appears to have been reached in 1828.[173] The exact framework of the Presentation order's rules and constitutions was retained by Doyle but modified to allow the Brigidines to retain their original name, to continue teaching the fee-paying middle classes and to instruct the children of the parish in church Sunday schools. On paper Doyle had grafted the Brigidines onto the Presentation order but in practice they maintained their distinctive identity.[174] None of Dr Delany's instructions however, in the form of letters of spiritual guidance to the original foundresses of Tullow and Mountrath,[175] were incorporated by Doyle into his Brigidine rule and constitution.[176] Doyle gave the Brigidines the black habit of the Presentation order.[177] On 9 March 1829 the sisters of the Mountrath convent received the habit in exchange for their previously worn black dresses with caps and bands.[178] Doyle's rule differed from that of the Presentation order in few respects other than those mentioned above. He allowed for dispensation from the rule at the discretion of the superioress; allowed nuns to go to an extraordinary confessor at any time, and did not delegate the government of the convent to a priest. The bishop would visit the convent every year – under the Presentation rule, the bishop made a visitation every third year 'if he deem it expedient'.[179]

Doyle held regular visitations, usually annually, of all his convents. His reform of the Brigidine convent of Mountrath involved the dismissal of nuns from the house. Two sisters, Brigid and Kate Delaney, and Sara Crosby (Sister M. Augustine) had been placed in the convent in 1811 by Bishop Delany. They 'did much to further the interests of the new foundation for many years, but were dismissed during the episcopacy of Doctor Doyle – Sister Augustine in 1821 and the Delaney sisters in 1823. The bishop considered their influence and example prejudicial to the good order and discipline of the community'.[180] In 1822 all the sisters in Mountrath made final profession having formerly only renewed their vows annually.[181]

On 21 April 1823, Tullow convent chapel, which took nine years to erect, was dedicated by the bishop.[182] On visitation in 1824 Doyle made a regulation that any sister who did not get up in the morning (at five o'clock) in accordance with the rule was not to go to communion on that day.[183] The rules of both the Presentation order and the Brigidine congregation stated that no nun was to receive communion on three successive days without the permission of the Mother Superior.[184] Doyle relaxed the restrictions on Brigidine diet – because of the labours of the classroom – allowing the nuns to take tea in the morning.[185]

In the early 1820s the Brigidine schoolrooms were too small to accommodate the number of children who flocked to them and 'for some years during the summer months, they were obliged to be taught in a field'.[186] In 1825 the nuns received Doyle's permission to build a new schoolhouse. The bishop prevailed on the Patrician brothers to give part of their adjoining garden for that purpose and in 1826 he blessed the newly erected school.[187] At this time the nuns received many orphan children, from Dublin orphan societies, who were boarded out in the town[188] as were many middle class children. This arrangement proved to be unsatisfactory. The nuns applied to Doyle for approbation to open a boarding school which they knew to be in accordance with Dr Delany's intentions. The bishop wrote to Mother Mary Anne Lalor assuring her that he approved of the plan and fully consented to it on condition that she likewise obtain the consent of Miss Judith Wogan-Browne. Apparently her consent, as a trustee of Dr Delany's will, was necessary before any building could be undertaken with the funds of his bequest. But she feared to take part in the responsibility and objected to boarders being accepted during her lifetime.[189]

In 1823 a Brigidine foundation was made in Roscrea from Mountrath. It was in the jurisdiction of the bishop of Killaloe and was independent of the Brigidine houses in Kildare and Leighlin. The entire community transferred to the Sacred Heart congregation in 1842. The Brigidines also had a short-lived foundation in Castlecomer, *c.*1829. The nuns there proved to be unsuited to the management of a school and there were 'divisions in the house'. A Castlecomer priest suggested to Doyle that the introduction of three or four Presentation nuns represented the only chance of preserving the convent.[190] It would seem that the Castlecomer filiation was abandoned in 1829. In 1830 two pious women formed a school in Paulstown with the sanction of the bishop and the cooperation of the local parish priest, James Maher. These lay devouts lived a religious life without taking formal vows and were joined by other women. In 1858 the Goresbridge Brigidine convent was opened and the two original founders of the Paulstown school became professed Brigidines.[191]

DISCALCED CARMELITES

Throughout the period 1823–1834, Doyle engaged in an extensive correspondence with the Discalced Carmelite convent of St Joseph in Ranelagh. Ninety-eight of his letters have survived. The level of Doyle's involvement with this convent was such that it is hardly an exaggeration to say that he directed Ranelagh from Carlow. The letters were advisory in both a temporal and spiritual sense. They make hardly any reference to public and political life, perhaps such matters were deemed inappropriate for discussion with an enclosed contemplative community. The letters guided the administration of the convent. They were edifying and amusing, warm and friendly though occasionally stern, and they manifest a very great attachment to the convent. Doyle actively sought the prayers of the convent both for himself – 'the prayers of my friends have often preserved me from evil' – and, from 1828, for the building of Carlow Cathedral.[192] The community at Ranelagh prayed for Doyle, its 'venerable friend and protector', on an on-going basis and there were many anxious expressions of concern about his poor health. Indeed under Ranelagh's influence the community of Discalced Carmelites at Lanherne in Cornwall also remembered Doyle in their prayers.

Doyle took care to instill confidence in the hesitant and to restrain the over-enthusiastic. The following is his advice to a potentially very zealous mistress of novices:

> Your novices when not tainted by bad example in the convent, are always too good, I mean they are too anxious to be so, and in their efforts to be perfect waste their minds and lose the liberty of the children of God. It is enough for you to keep them from evil, and to teach them fidelity in the observance of the rule and constitutions. The unction of the spirit will teach them interiorly, but by slow degrees, how to pray and suffer and love God. Don't occupy them much in the examination of their conscience or interior state, and still less indulge them in talking about what passes within their mind, nor are you to instruct them to pray by rule and compass as some do, but rather to let them follow the irregular motions of their own minds when these are not carried away entirely from God. Let them be always encouraged, and it is time enough to remind them of their faults the day after they occur, and then as mistakes to be avoided, not as faults to be punished. If this does not correct them send them out of the convent but let not reproof be almost ever found in your mouth.[193]

There was no shortage of vocations in Ranelagh. It was clear to Doyle that, in the past, persons had been admitted to the habit in Ranelagh who had no vocation to a religious state.[194] In advising on the case of a very difficult nun, the product of a mixed marriage, who was under strong Protestant and anti-Catholic influences, not least from her own sister, Doyle unburdened himself of some stringent comments on converts in religion: 'They are not called to religion who have not fully the spirit of Christ, above all his spirit of obedience, zeal and charity. Heretics after conversion and the children of heretics in nineteen cases out of twenty are proud and cannot deny themselves as obedience requires. They are scarcely ever fit for religious institutes. Heresy like original sin seems to be transmitted in its effects even after the guilt of it is taken away'.[195] Doyle disapproved for several reasons of the introduction of an English nun into an office at Ranelagh, among them: 'the natural hauteur of the English, even when virtue predominates in them – the total difference of their feelings and views from those inherent in the Irish character'.[196]

Doyle's correspondence with the Discalced Carmelites of Ranelagh began in December 1823 when the very young Mother Catherine Meade sought his advice on internal dissensions stemming from opposition by a considerably older generation to a reform movement within the convent. An earlier reform movement had resulted in the foundation of Warrenmount in 1813. Some nuns who were not supporters of the Ranelagh reform founded Clondalkin in 1824 and later in 1835 a number of nuns who were not disposed to the full observance of the primitive rule and constitutions moved to the Rehoboth convent in Dublin.

The Ranelagh convent had a serious dispute with the friars at Clarendon Street, Dublin, which dated from the actions of Rev Francis L'Estrange as Visitator in 1823.[197] Doyle professed his own unworthiness for having to deal with such problems: 'an affection of humility or distrust in myself would hardly become me, but I can tell you with great truth that my judgement is often weak and erroneous ...'. Nonetheless Doyle was prepared to hear from the convent on any subject and to give an opinion as often as the nuns required it. He advised that, in the first instance, the archbishop of Dublin, Dr Murray, 'the most holy and prudent man I know', should be consulted.[198] Murray was reluctant to interfere with the jurisdiction of the male provincial at Clarendon Street, over the convent in Ranelagh, even though he was well aware of Doyle's views on the case. Doyle's correspondence over several years indicates that he felt Murray's disposition was too mild. Doyle described Murray's approach in the following terms: 'his Grace's timidity', 'pacific dispositions', 'too indulgent', 'too tolerant'.[199] Writing of his own decision-making policy Doyle stated: 'I never desist from doing what is just and necessary thro' fear of consequences, I commit those to a just and good God, and it is to this uncompromising spirit that I am indebted under God to the good order which distinguishes this diocese even above many others'.[200] He later wrote: 'It is the business of nuns to pray, as it is ours to fight, you are to do the work of Joshua whilst we go down to the struggle'.[201]

Mother Meade was unhappy that the rule of St Teresa was not being followed rigorously enough; she gained no satisfaction from the male provincial who had allowed deviations from the rule of the order. Doyle asked Mother Meade not to resign as she was planning: 'The God of peace, as Saint Francis de Sales observed, is also the God of battles and when he calls us to combat we cannot desert our station without offending him'.[202] Doyle drafted the memorial to Rome of the reform oriented sisters of Ranelagh which was designed to effect the changes they wanted to bring about. The principal change which Doyle wished to see take place was to have the jurisdiction of Ranelagh taken from Clarendon Street and placed under the archbishop of Dublin.[203] The matter was referred to Murray who was not at first supportive. Rome also sought the opinion of a bishop outside Dublin, apparently Marum of Ossory, who reported as Doyle wished.[204]

Doyle wrote to the cardinal prefect of the Propaganda Fide congregation, urging him to procure a decision from the Holy Father on the memorial.[205] Ultimately Doyle received a long unfavourable letter from Cardinal Somaglia.[206] Doyle informed the Reverend Mother in Ranelagh: 'It is unfavourable and for the present at least, puts an end to all those hopes you entertained and in which I indeed participated'. The cardinal's letter, Doyle reported, communicated the sentiments which the pope, after the most mature deliberation, commanded him to write. These were:

> that his Holiness appreciates highly and commends greatly the zeal for religious discipline which animates you and your sisters, he prays you to continue to cherish it but to let it be confined within due bounds. He praises your zeal for the instruction of the poor, but whomsoever you may instruct his Holiness wishes you to feel that the instruction will be excellent and useful in proportion as you are all of one mind and heart. He concludes that the causes assigned for placing you under the jurisdiction of the Archbishop of Dublin however weighty are not so weighty as to warrant his Holiness in granting the prayer of your petition. This is the substance of the Cardinal's letter, it is, my dear sister, the decision of our Redeemer's Vicar on earth, and as such we are to presume it is conformable to the Will of God, and who are we to contravene his will.[207]

Events took a new turn when Rev. James Colgan, parish priest of Edenderry, informed Doyle that he was ready to establish a house of nuns in his parish. He sought Doyle's advice. Doyle immediately thought of the Ranelagh sisters and decided to establish them in his diocese. He wrote to Ranelagh informing them that one of his parish priests was prepared to make a spacious and good house and garden available, rent free, to a community of religious who would take charge of the education of the poor female children of his town.[208] As their regular superiors rejected the offer, Doyle sought the permission of the pope through the cardinal prefect for the transfer of six Discalced Carmelite nuns from Ranelagh to Edenderry. Such a move would allow the nuns to practise a more strict observance of the rule and devote a part of their time to the education of poor female children.[209] Propaganda informed Doyle that it had written to Archbishop Murray leaving the decision to him.[210] This time Dr Murray was favourably disposed.[211] But Doyle was not hopeful of success since he was now seeking a decision the reverse of the one recently given.[212]

By 21 January 1826, Doyle still had not heard from Rome: 'All that could possibly be done here, by the Prelate who was consulted from Rome as well as myself, has been done, so we must only suppose that our labours did not deserve the divine blessing or that the malice of the enemy prevailed against us or that Providence otherwise ordained'.[213] In fact the plan was not discussed by Propaganda until its meeting on 31 January 1826.[214] It was successfully opposed by the General of the Discalced Carmelites in Rome.[215] In March 1826 Doyle finally received the Roman reply from Cardinal Somaglia, 'which puts an end to all your hopes and mine relative to the sisters of your convent being enabled to change either their present discipline or found a new convent with better prospects'. He suspected that the Irish superiors of the order had engaged the friars in Rome to labour against them.[216]

The nuns had completely lost confidence in the Clarendon Street friars.[217] Doyle aided the Ranelagh nuns in their attempt to secure a papal inquiry into the manner in which they were treated by their male Carmelite superiors in Dublin.[218] Doyle once again intervened with Dr Murray for the sisters.[219] As he wrote to Mother Dolan in late 1826: 'St Francis de Sales seemed to think that Friars are not the best superiors of nuns and I have always been of that opinion ...'.[220] The nuns certainly did not see eye to eye with the Carmelite provincial, Rev. James Oates, and his successor in that office, Rev. Francis L'Estrange.[221]

Finally a successful outcome was attained when a papal bull of Pope Leo XII dated 11 January 1828 transferred the nuns from the jurisdiction of the friars to the archbishop. Doyle and Murray celebrated the occasion together in the convent on 7 February 1828. From then onwards, as is clear from the Doyle correspondence, life in the convent assumed a less strained dimension. The nuns accepted the spiritual direction of the Jesuits. Their spiritual director was Charles Aylmer who had been on the terna for Kildare and Leighlin in 1819. He persuaded the nuns between late 1828 and early 1829 to give up their boarding school as it was a distraction from the strict observance of the rule.[222]

A memorandum book maintained by Mother Dolan noted that Doyle, who was 'in a wretched state of health', preached a 'splendid sermon' on the occasion of the profession of three novices in the convent by Archbishop Murray on 9 February 1830.[223] Further worries by the convent about interference from the friars proved groundless.[224]

THE LAITY: FAITH AND MORALS

CONFRATERNITIES AND SUNDAY SCHOOL CATECHESIS

Bishop Doyle was cognisant that religious reform of the laity must begin with the instruction of the young and his pastoral achievement is perhaps nowhere more strikingly evidenced than in his transformation of catechetical teaching within his diocese. Trent required that prelates ensure that 'at least on the Lord's day and other festivals, the children in every parish be carefully taught the rudiments of the faith'.[1] Doyle's Diocesan Book for 1819–20 records the teaching of catechism in thirty-two parishes of the diocese for which information is given. There was apparently no parish in which the catechism was not taught. Doyle placed considerable emphasis on Sunday school teaching and on confraternities as a means of catechising the young. The Sunday school was a wholly catechetical occasion when Catholic children were instructed in the faith by pious young men and women of the Christian Doctrine and the Blessed Sacrament of the Eucharist confraternities. In 1825 Doyle remarked that 'The confraternities in my diocese are universally those conducting the Sunday schools'.[2]

Confraternities were voluntary associations of the Catholic laity, both men and women, normally segregated in practice, for religious purposes. This segregation was followed through in the Sunday schools where the sexes were separated. Canonically erected confraternities were regulated by ecclesiastical law and subject to religious superiors; their members often wore a distinctive dress and recited the office in common. Indulgences were communicated to the confraternities either directly by the pope or through the bishops. Confraternities had greatly multiplied in Counter-Reformation Europe.[3] However, on account of the penal laws, they developed slowly in Ireland. In the mid–eighteenth century the confraternity of the Holy Name, introduced in a number of dioceses to discourage profanity,[4] was one of the few then in existence in Ireland. The confraternity of the Blessed Sacrament of the Eucharist was founded in the mid-seventeenth century but only introduced to Ireland by Archbishop James Butler II in the 1780s.[5] Shortly afterwards it was erected in 'several' parishes of Kildare and Leighlin by Dr Daniel Delany who had a very strong devotion to the Blessed Sacrament.[6]

The confraternity promoted frequent communion. The principal duty of its members was to receive the eucharist once a month. In 1821 Bishop Doyle decreed that persons who wished to become enrolled as members of the confraternity of the Blessed Sacrament must be of good repute and have lived piously for a considerable time previous to entry. They had to make a general confession, and receive communion at least once a month for an entire year prior to their admission. They were received into the confraternity by Doyle on visitation. Confraternity members were required to assist the parish clergy at all times in their chapels, but particularly on Sunday mornings and before vespers, in 'instructing the ignorant', teaching the catechism, and reading books of piety aloud. They were also expected to prepare children for their first communion, and to assist sick persons, especially members of the confraternity, to die in the Lord. They were obliged to avoid all places of public gatherings, such as wakes, dances, alehouses, and idle company; to refrain from all conversation which might endanger their virtue or scandalize the weak, 'abstaining not only from evil, but from every appearance of evil'. Any member found acting contrary to the rules was to be expelled forthwith. Fitzpatrick commented melodramatically that shortly after Doyle's elevation 'dance houses, wakes and other midnight orgies, almost entirely ceased to scandalise'.[7] Confraternity presidents were to be elected annually – one from the members of each sex, in consultation with the priests, to watch over the duties thus prescribed, correct the faults of members, and if necessary report them to their priests.

Doyle ruled that confraternity members were not to wear any distinctive dress 'unless in such places as the custom of doing so is already clearly established, nor should we regret that even there it would go into disuse'. Members confessed their sins and received communion on the third Sunday of each month, or alternatively, on any other Sunday or holy day within the month. They were expected to observe 'great purity of life' and to promote, as much as possible, piety and devotion to the Blessed Sacrament. They recited a special short prayer at least once daily.[8] The only pre-condition necessary for gaining the indulgences granted to the confraternity was proper reception into it. Plenary indulgences, which could be applied by way of suffrage to the souls in purgatory were gained: on the day of joining the confraternity; at the time of death by invoking the name of Jesus with true contrition; on one day each year chosen for spending an hour in adoration of the Blessed Sacrament; once a month by spending an hour in the same manner; on the feast of the Epiphany; on the first Sunday of Lent; on Holy Thursday and on the Sunday within the octave; on the first Sunday in May; on Ascension Thursday; on the first Sunday of October; on the Sunday within the octave of all Saints; and on the first Sunday in Advent.

Partial indulgences could be gained by reciting the Lord's Prayer and Hail Mary five times each week in honour of the Holy Sacrament; an indulgence of seven years on the feast of Corpus Christi; of two hundred days by fasting the day before the feast; of one hundred days by saying a Pater Noster and Ave Maria for the sick and deceased members of the confraternity; of one hundred days by practising any of the spiritual and corporal works of mercy. Every member receiving communion who wished to gain a plenary indulgence offered up the Lord's Prayer and Hail Mary, each seven times, 'according to the intention of the Church', or recited the prayers usually set down in the prayer books for such occasions.[9]

Doyle drew attention to the fact that indulgences were not a remission of sin but of the temporal punishment which it might incur. Indulgences which were first granted by St Paul to the incestuous Corinthians and then by St Cyprian and other bishops in times of persecution, had always, in various forms, been granted by the church in favour of those penitents and 'such only' as laboured by their contrition and works of piety to atone, as far as they were able, for their sins. 'Indulgences are not granted to favour the indolent, but to support the weak, not to relax piety nor insure forgiveness, but to aid our exertions and strengthen our hope.'[10] The whole concept of works of supererogation must have made confraternity membership powerfully attractive to pious Catholics who were inspired by a lively fear of the devil and the eternal flames of hell.

The confraternity of the Christian Doctrine was closely related to that of the Blessed Sacrament of the Eucharist. Christian Doctrine schools were founded by Castellino da Castello in Milan in 1536 for the purpose of giving religious instruction. The confraternity was advocated by Cardinal Bellarmine, St Francis de Sales, and St Charles Borromeo, who drew up a code of rules and established it in every parish of his diocese.[11] Pope Pius V in his brief *Ex debito pastoralis officii* (6 October 1571) exhorted bishops to erect the confraternity in every parish of their dioceses. In 1607, Pope Paul V in his brief *Ex credito nobis* erected it into an arch-confraternity, with St Peter's in Rome as its head. From Rome it spread rapidly through Italy into Germany and France. In 1610 the Sacred Congregation of Indulgences ruled that the confraternity be established in every parish. Pope Innocent X in a 1686 encyclical recommended the confraternity to bishops. The afore-mentioned popes granted extensive indulgences which were further augmented by Pope Clement XII.[12] Despite this catalogue of Roman approval for the confraternity of the Christian Doctrine as an agency of the Counter-Reformation, it was, like its sister confraternity of the Blessed Sacrament, not established in Ireland until the 1780s. Archbishop Butler and Bishop Delany are credited with its introduction. In 1789 the bishops of the Cashel province recommended its establishment in every parish where such could be effected.[13]

Under Doyle, membership of the Christian Doctrine confraternity was less restrictive than that of the Blessed Sacrament: 'a greater number of persons and even those whose habits of piety are not of so long a continuance, or entirely so regular may be admitted into it'.[14] Entry was at the discretion of the clergy. Members were received into the confraternity simply by being enrolled by the parochial clergy. The obligation to teach catechism on Sundays and holy days and to give other religious instruction as requested by the clergy only applied to the better educated and most capable members. Doyle's regulations for the guidance of the confraternity were annexed, with only the slightest amendments, to the provincial statutes.[15] The 1831 statutes decreed expulsion for any member who frequented public houses or gave bad example in his parish.[16] There was no mention of restrictions on wakes or dances suggesting perhaps that these did not by then constitute a problem. A plenary indulgence was gained by those who, having confessed and received communion, were admitted into the confraternity. This indulgence was also granted on any day in each month on which a member confessed and received. An indulgence of seven years was gained each time a member taught catechism in public.[17]

In what condition were Sunday schools and confraternities in Kildare and Leighlin when Doyle became bishop? It appears that some efforts were made to re-organise the diocesan Sunday school network under Bishop Corcoran.[18] This suggests that the system had fallen into decay towards the end of Dr Delany's episcopacy or at least needed improvement. It is most unlikely that Sunday schools were widespread under Dr Delany. In his mensal parish of Tullow where the schools commenced in 1777,[19] Doyle found in 1820 that the catechism was taught in 'only one place' – presumably Tullow chapel. In 1823 there was catechetical instruction in both Tullow and Ardattin chapels.[20] Mere catechetical instruction was not enough for Doyle. On his first visitation of Arles parish he observed that the catechism was taught but 'little more' – apparently a reference to the need for pious readings in chapel. Although Sunday school was well attended in Leighlinbridge he noted 'catechism and nothing more in the chapels'.[21] Unfortunately in his Diocesan Book for 1819–20, Doyle gave no information on confraternities in sixteen out of the thirty-three parishes detailed. Doyle named eight parishes where confraternities were established. The confraternity of the Blessed Eucharist was mentioned for six of these parishes. In references to the parishes of Borris, Carbury and Clonmore, this confraternity was clearly linked by Doyle with the reception of monthly communion. In only three parishes was the confraternity of the Christian Doctrine found: Philipstown (which also had a Blessed Sacrament confraternity and a scapular society), Clonegal and Monasterevin. Doyle desired that the pious in Monasterevin be admitted into the Blessed Sacrament confraternity. Kildare had a scapular society but no other. Doyle named nine parishes where there were no confraternities: Arles, Balyna, Caragh, Clonbullogue, Edenderry, Kilcock, Killeigh, Maryborough and Tullow. Doyle's determination to improve this situation was rewarded with immediate results. In his 1820 Relatio Status Doyle referred to the confraternities of the Christian Doctrine and Blessed Sacrament which had been established in many parishes.[22] Doyle later explained why and how he had initiated confraternities at the outset of his episcopacy:

> When I came into that diocese, I found a few such societies existing in it, but from the advantages that I perceived to result from them, I myself recommended at the several visitations I held in the chapels, in the strongest

and most earnest manner, that such confraternities should be formed; and
I do not know that there is at present [1825] any one chapel in the diocese,
to which there is not a confraternity of the Christian Doctrine, as we call
it, attached.[23]

In his Lenten pastoral instructions in 1821, Doyle wrote:

It is to the members of those confraternities, when properly organised,
that we look with confidence, for the increase of holiness and good works
amongst all classes .... The formation of these societies, their increase and
good demeanour, will be to us ... a criterion of the piety of the faithful, in
the several parishes of these dioceses, and of the zeal of their respective
pastors and curates.[24]

The extant parochial visitation returns for twenty-nine parishes indicate the
extent to which Doyle's criterion was fulfilled. The Christian Doctrine
confraternity was established in virtually every parish in accordance with Doyle's
wishes. The Blessed Sacrament confraternity was also very prevalent. Some other
confraternities are also mentioned. The confraternity of the Blessed Virgin Mary
was established in the parishes of Ballinakill, Clonegal, Doonane, Newbridge
and Philipstown. Third orders were established in Doonane (St Francis and St
Dominic), Philipstown (St Dominic), Graiguenamanagh and Myshall (Carmel).
There were two unnamed orders of scapularians in Allen and Baltinglass. The
members of the Christian Doctrine confraternity in Baltinglass were also members of a purgatorian society.

Figures available for the diocese in 1829 reveal some remarkable data. Full
information on numbers in confraternities (and unfortunately no distinction is
made between the Blessed Sacrament of the Eucharist and the Christian Doctrine confraternities) is available for thirty-seven parishes.[25] Of the remaining ten
parishes, two, Tullow and Paulstown, are returned as containing 'a good number'
and one, Carbury, 'few' confraternity members. Data for seven parishes: Balyna,
Caragh, Carlow, Clane, Kilcock, Maryborough and Monasterevan – are not extant. In Naas in 1829 there was no confraternity because Gerald Doyle, P.P., had
no place to accommodate it. He reported to his bishop that 'the confraternity of
the Christian Doctrine went down at the time of the throwing down of the new
chapel and did not as yet revive'.[26] This state of affairs was probably only temporary but the parish is included as one of the thirty-seven for which we have information. These thirty-seven parishes had a total of 7,795 confraternity members,
an average of 210 per parish.

Statistics for the number of teachers in the Sunday schools of Kildare and
Leighlin are incomplete but it would seem probable that there were more than
twenty teachers, of both sexes, in most parishes. In Carlow parish in 1824 there

were no less than 129 Christian Doctrine teachers, seventy men and fifty-nine women.[27] The average number of teachers in six parishes (excluding Carlow) for which data are available – Bagenalstown (90); Ballon (63); Clonegal (41); Hacketstown (45); Portarlington (47); Rathvilly (25) – is fifty-one.[28] For the diocese as a whole it is probably safe to speak of an average of forty-five catechists in each parish. This cadre of catechists was certainly needed to cope with the numbers who attended Sunday schools. Figures available for summer 1824 which are based on twenty-one parishes indicate that 17,966 children were attending Sunday school instruction: an average of 855 children in each parish.[29] If we extrapolate from these average figures for the forty-seven parishes of the diocese, the scale of Doyle's pastoral achievement becomes clear. There were approximately 10,111 confraternity members (or no less than four per cent of the entire Catholic population) from whom were selected 2,115 catechists to teach 40,185 children. The teacher-pupil ratio was approximately 1:19. Thus Doyle was undoubtedly justified when he claimed in 1825: 'I am sure there is no part of Ireland in which Sunday schools are more diligently attended to than in my diocese'.[30] The magnitude of the numbers in the confraternities seems to suggest something broader than what Corish has called 'a more conscious commitment to religion on the part of the more economically secure',[31] and that is a desire for moral and doctrinal instruction which transcended class divisions. Religious belief rather than socio-economic status to a large extent determined participation in Kildare and Leighlin. In 1821 Doyle recommended to his pastors that 'the more virtuous of those who have lately been confirmed should be encouraged to enter in the confraternities'.[32] This statement helps to some extent to account for the large numbers in the confraternities.

The number of catechists in each parish was fairly evenly divided between the sexes. The parish clergy invariably testified to their high moral qualities: 'young, of good character',[33] 'excellent moral characters',[34] etc. These catechists were almost always members of the Christian Doctrine and the Blessed Sacrament confraternities, and rigidly adhered to their rules.[35] Teachers were drawn from 'the better instructed of our flock'.[36] They emerged from the ranks of the Sunday school pupils to become catechists themselves.

In Tuam diocese, Archbishop Kelly had no shortage of catechists in the towns but only two or three, in some instances, in country parishes. In these areas he relied heavily on schoolteachers.[37] But apart from one parish, no such problem existed in Kildare and Leighlin under Doyle. Carbury seems to have been the only significant parochial exception to the widespread pro-confraternity trend in the diocese. On visitation in 1823, Doyle recorded 'here great ignorance'; the catechism was taught by only a few in the parish and there was no confraternity.[38] Doyle's solution was to make use of the schoolteachers in the parish and the following year they attended Sunday schools in Carbury.[39] In Clane parish the catechists were 'schoolmasters and other individuals'.[40] In Monasterevan parish

the principal teachers of the Sunday schools in Monasterevan, Kildangan and
Nurney chapels were John Costigan, Martin Dowling and Martin Moore – respectively the masters of schools in Monasterevan, Derryaghta and Nurney.[41]
This connexion between the Catholic teachers of the day schools and the Sunday
schools was an important one. Children were instructed on Sundays by their
week-day teachers, or by catechists from their own part of the parish. It is more
than likely that there was a roll-call to check attendance.[42] The discipline of the
weekday class-room was maintained in the catechetical school. Indeed in many
places Sunday schools took place in the schoolhouses which were also the
dwellinghouses of the teachers.[43]

Sunday schools were held in all the chapels of the diocese and in schoolhouses and private houses which belonged to confraternity members in those
parts of parishes which were distant from the chapels. In Abbeyleix in 1824, less
than half the children of the parish were instructed in the chapels. Abbeyleix
chapel had 571 pupils, Ballyroan chapel an attendance of 580 but no less than
1,300 children were catechised elsewhere in Sunday evening schools.[44] In
Edenderry parish which had three chapels, the teaching of the catechism 'in
separate houses by pious persons' was still necessary in some remote parts of the
parish.[45] In the parish of Clane, where Doyle discovered the catechism taught in
only one chapel in 1823,[46] the distribution of 707 children in Sunday schools the
following year was:[47]

In Clane chapel,	240
In Rathcoffey chapel,	110
In Staplestown chapel,	150
At Mrs Dease's,	25
At Millicent,	10
At Hodgestown,	20
In Timahoe schoolhouse,	40
In Blackwood,	24
In Blackwood,	40
In Cooleragh,	24
In Timahoe,	24

In Clonegal parish in 1824 there were forty-one Sunday schools: two in the chapels
and thirty-nine in private houses.[48] In Suncroft parish in 1827 there was a Sunday school in the chapel and in every townland.[49]

In summer these Sunday schools held sessions lasting from two to four hours;
on average, perhaps, three to three-and-a-half hours.[50] The time of instruction
was usually divided between forenoon and afternoon with a preference for a longer
period of instruction in the morning in the chapels and probably in the afternoon
exclusively in other locations. In winter the instruction period was definitely

shorter, probably by as much as half, and in some places abandoned (as were the day schools) for the duration of the season. This fact caused Doyle some anxiety in December 1826 when the proselytising threat loomed large, leading him to introduce weekday catechetical classes outside normal school hours. Through his rural deans he advised his clergy:

> During the winter, be mindful to have the children of the several villages assembled at night to learn the catechism under the superintendence of some grave person, and to have them united on Sunday at the chapel, even for a short time before or after mass, to account to the members of the Christian Doctrine Society for what they have learned at their respective houses. I mention this, because in some places the custom of assembling the children at catechism on Sundays is interrupted during the winter months.[51]

What percentage of the young Catholic population attended Sunday school? The average attendance figure of 855 per parish would tend to suggest that probably only a small percentage, perhaps much less than ten per cent, were absentees. Poverty as a factor inhibiting attendance must always be taken into account. The brutal reality was that there were children who did not have the wherewithal to appear decently dressed. Seven hundred children attended Sunday school in the parish of Edenderry but the P.P. estimated that the figure would have been 1,000 but for impoverishment.[52] And this was in summer; in winter the problem became much more acute throughout the diocese. Want of suitable clothing was responsible for a diminution of up to half in attendance figures in day and Sunday schools.[53] Doyle calculated that the number of children attending day schools in the diocese in summer 1826 was between 36,000 and 37,000.[54] This writer has estimated the average annual number of children in Sunday schools at 40,185. The shortfall was made up of those children who were too poor to attend pay schools but who did attend Sunday schools which were free. It can hardly be over-emphasised that Sunday schools were non fee-paying. Their catchment area was thus wider than the fee-paying schools.

It has been stated that the rote method of learning failed to give pupils a deep understanding of their faith[55] – a criticism which could be applied to methods of teaching generally at this time and well into the next century. But as we shall see Sunday schools in Kildare and Leighlin strove to advance beyond mere rote learning. These catechetical schools had important literacy and educational functions and benefits for the Catholic population which have not been noted. Sunday schools provided the only schooling which many children received. They were attended by children whose parents were too poor to pay the modest stipend required to send them to pay schools or to purchase necessary school requisites. Being free, the Sunday school posed no such embarrassing difficulties but of course these children from very poor backgrounds were unable to read – a skill which normally took up to a year to acquire in the pay school.

In the Sunday schools of Abbeyleix parish seventy per cent of the children were unable to read in 1824;[56] in Carlow parish the figure was fifty-seven per cent,[57] but in Suncroft parish only twenty per cent were similarly unskilled.[58] Dr Michael Prendergast, V.G., observed that the desire to learn to read motivated Sunday school attendance among the very poor: 'many of the pupils cannot read, and not expecting to have at any time an opportunity of learning, they resort to the chapel for religious instructions'.[59] The implication, confirmed by other sources, was that Sunday school teachers instructed children to read as part of their provision of an adequate catechetical education. In Portarlington parish catechists utilised 'a set of spelling books and reading tablets, principally intended for the instruction of those persons who cannot attend on weekdays'.[60] Those unable to read were instructed separately from the readers.[61] Portarlington parish had 800 catechisms in stock; Paulstown, 500; and there is every indication from other parishes that they had ample catechisms to cater for all Sunday school pupils.[62] As we have seen, the number of readers varied from parish to parish but perhaps we can construe an average figure from the data for Hacketstown, Kildare and Portarlington parishes where fifty-per cent were able to read.[63] It seems probable that somewhat less than half the Catholics attending Sunday school in the diocese in 1824 were literate. But it is patent that the church was actively striving to promote full literacy in order to deepen the meaningfulness of catechetical instruction (which was largely from printed catechisms). Corish's remark that confraternity members were not of 'very poor' origin because 'their activities presuppose literacy'[64] may need to be qualified by this consideration. It was possible for an intelligent child from a very poor background to become a confraternity member and indeed a catechist in Kildare and Leighlin.

The most popular and extensively used catechetical text in the Sunday schools of the diocese was the *General Catechism*, closely followed by the *Abridgement of the Christian Doctrine* for advanced pupils.[65] The *General Catechism* was first produced by Archbishop Butler in 1775.[66] In fact, according to Doyle, the archbishop had merely translated a French catechism 'almost literally'.[67] Butler's catechism was later revised (1802) and approved for general use by the Irish archbishops. (Variously known as Butler's catechism, and the four archbishops' catechism, it is referred to here for convenience as the *General Catechism*.) There were several variant editions of the catechism, as originally approved by Dr Butler and the four archbishops, in circulation. The Irish Catholic church had no copyright on the text which was published, with no great fidelity to the approved text, by printers for profit in all the towns.[68] In 1820–21 Doyle issued a regulation declaring the use of the archbishops' version of the *General Cathecism* mandatory in the Sunday schools of the diocese.[69] In 1823 Doyle produced a 'revised, corrected and enlarged' edition of the *General Catechism* which was prescribed by him to be taught throughout Kildare and Leighlin. His revision made the catechism 'more plain and better fitted' for the instruction of 'the most precious portion' of his flock.[70] In his foreword he advised the Catholic children of his diocese:

> Be diligent in learning it; at home, in your schools, when resting from your employments, but especially on Sundays, under the eyes of your clergy, and with the assistance of those various masters and mistresses, who not only teach you by word, but also by example. We entreat you ... to read this catechism slowly, to think on the meaning of each word it contains, to answer your teachers in a slow, and clear manner ....[71]

Doyle required that certain prayers including the acts of contrition, faith, hope and charity, be said prior to the teaching of the catechism in the chapel Sunday schools[72] – a direction followed in the 1831 provincial statutes.[73] The forty-eight page *General Catechism* gave the Catholic child a thorough grounding in the essentials of the faith. In 1827 Doyle was obliged to publish a declaration stating that he had seen 'several spurious or inaccurate editions of the *General Catechism*' and especially one printed by J. Harvey, 26 Charles Street, Dublin, published 'as if approved and recommended by me'. He noted that Richard Coyne was the only authorised publisher of the catechism prescribed to be taught in Kildare and Leighlin.[74]

In December 1824, Archbishop Curtis of Armagh fully agreed with Doyle on the 'expediency, or necessity of rendering the style, if not the substance of the catechism somewhat more familiar and intelligible to the common people'. He hoped that this could be achieved by reducing the variety of existing catechisms in use: 'I know three of them which we have, all susceptible of improvement.' These three were the *General Catechism* (which Doyle, perhaps unknown to Curtis, had already revised); Bishop Plunkett's catechism in Meath diocese (which was only a variant of the *General Catechism*); and the diocesan catechism of Armagh and, Curtis believed, of all Ulster (which was the O'Reilly/Donlevy catechism[75]). There were, Curtis wrote, still further catechisms in the south and west with which he was not familiar but all of them constituted 'a great anomaly'. He ardently wished to see 'all Catholic Ireland making use of one and the same Catechism'. There was, he felt, contradicting himself, a need for two catechisms : one much more copious than the *General Cathecism* 'for those tolerably instructed and capable'; another much smaller one for children and beginners and 'those of very limited capacities', 'but both, so digested as to bear the most vigorous inspection and scrutiny'. The authorship of such catechisms, wrote the primate, would be an object worthy of Doyle's talents. Curtis assured Doyle that he and the rest of the episcopal bench would adopt Doyle's catechisms, adding significantly 'if properly applied to, and previously consulted'.[76] Whether Doyle had proposed to Curtis the adoption of one standard catechism is unclear but it seems unlikely that Doyle paid any heed to the primate's suggestions. He had already, as we have seen, revised the *General Catechism* which the archbishop's plan would have rendered redundant although that text had given general satisfaction for almost fifty years.

The second dominant text used in the Sunday schools of Kildare and Leighlin was the *Abridgement of the Christian Doctrine*. This work was composed by Henry Turberville of the English College at Douay in 1645 (and hence it was often known as the Douay Catechism). Like the *General Catechism* it was in question and answer format though much more elaborate. It was one of the most important of the early Catholic publications used in Dublin in the eighteenth century.[77] It was used 'generally' in the Sunday schools of Kildare and Leighlin and interestingly, 'in many instances', it had been introduced at the express desire of the confraternities themselves.[78] In 1827 Doyle prepared a new edition of Turberville's work. On 30 October 1827, in controversy with Dr Thomas Elrington, Anglican bishop of Leighlin and Ferns, Doyle informed him that 'some thousand copies have, since its revision by me, been distributed in these dioceses – a work which is now in the process of being stereotyped, and of which I earnestly wish there were a copy in the hands of every person in Ireland, who could read and understand it'.[79] Doyle's edition of the *Abridgement* was published especially for the catechetical use of the Christian Doctrine confraternities. He modernised its language and depolemicised its Counter-Reformation spirit of anti-Protestantism. Essentially he 'revised, corrected and occasionally altered or enlarged' the *Abridgement* making it 'more easy and simple, more plain and perspicuous as well as less harsh in its language and thereby more extensively useful'.[80] The *Abridgement* contained a detailed exposition of the faith at all times proven from scriptural sources. The Apostles' Creed, Our Father, Hail Mary, etc., were treated to a line by line textual analysis. The ten commandments, six precepts of the church, seven sacraments, etc., were explained and commented upon. The ordinary and canon of the mass, set out in parallel English and Latin columns, and the actions of the priest during its celebration, were expounded in a lucid fashion. Doyle's edition was a substantial 144-page tract.

One of the lesser known works attributed to Doyle is the corrected edition of Henry VIII's *Defence of the Seven Sacraments*, published *c*.1824.[81] King Henry, the editor asserted, was a 'pious and zealous Roman Catholic, until such times as he suffered himself to be borne away by an immoderate passion for women ...'. The editor praised the *Defence of the Seven Sacraments* as a 'work of considerable merit' for which Pope Leo X granted Henry the title 'Defender of the Faith' – a title 'still retained by his successors on the throne, though of a contrary religion'.[82] However, this work which was published in London does not appear to be from Doyle's hand; rather it cleverly makes use of his name on its title page as a selling device. The edition does not seem to have been much circulated in Ireland perhaps because it sold at half-a-crown. In 1830 Doyle's well-known Dublin publisher and printer, Coyne, was offering Doyle's edition of the *Abridgement* at six pence a copy; the bishop's edition of the *General Catechism* retailed at ten shillings per hundred copies which was little more than a penny per copy.[83]

Doyle also wrote introductions to two important religious texts, published by Coyne. On 1 July 1825 he wrote a preface for a new edition of the Augustinian William Gahan's two volume *Sermons and Moral Discourses,*[84] a popular work then out of print. Doyle praised the utilitarian value of Gahan's work at the expense of all other considerations:

> The great characteristic of Gahan's Sermons is not eloquence in the popular sense of the word; it is usefulness; we nowhere find in them the towering sublimity of a Bossuet, they do not have at all the captivating unction of a Massillon, they do not superabound in the learning and irresistible force of a Bourdaloue; but they instruct, they reprove, they persuade by the solidity of the thoughts, by the clearness and simplicity of the style, by the judicious introduction and application of the Sacred Scriptures, but above all, by the piety, sincerity and zeal of the writer, which they everywhere display.[85]

This edition of Gahan's work was extensively used throughout Kildare and Leighlin.[86]

In January 1833 Doyle wrote a preface[87] for a new edition of Alban Butler's *Lives of the Saints* which was designated by him as 'an historical supplement to the Old and New Testaments'. Hitherto, according to Doyle, the work was only available in twelve volumes. Coyne's edition, published with the approbation of the entire hierarchy (dated 29 January 1833) had the whole text in two extra large volumes for a 'low price'. Butler's great work was now placed, said Doyle, almost within the purchasing power of every Irish Catholic.[88]

Bishop Doyle required the confraternities of the Christian Doctrine to inquire regularly into the attendance of pupils at Sunday school. Furthermore they were to watch over their pupils' habits and morals on week-days as well: 'if you happen to see them in the commission of any fault correct them' but 'restrain them more by shame or favours than by fear'.[89] The provincial statutes recommended that the catechists should, as far as possible, be charged with the instruction of children in their own area and should 'at all times' watch over the conduct of their pupils.[90] In Carlow parish a large confraternity of the Blessed Sacrament of the Eucharist watched over public morals.[91]

Doyle recommended that children be arranged in class according to their proficiency in religious knowledge.[92] It was necessary in any case to separate the readers from the non-readers and to distinguish between pupils who were learning the *General Catechism* and those who had advanced to the *Abridgement of the*

Christian Doctrine. Sections of the catechism were marked out for readers to learn during the week to be examined the following Sunday. In Kildare and Leighlin there were four catechism classes and four catechisms or rather the *General Catechism* in three sizes and the *Abridgement of the Christian Doctrine*.[93] This arrangement of classes found favour in other dioceses as well.

We have useful information on this subject from the important Dublin city centre parish of SS Michael and John. There the Sunday school was divided into five classes. The first class was introduced to prayer and the next two studied gradated versions of the *General Catechism*; the fourth the *Historical Catechism* while the *Abridgement of the Christian Doctrine* described as 'the high-water mark of catechetical instruction'[94] was read by children of the fifth and final class.[95] A minute in the register of the Christian Doctrine confraternity dated 26 October 1828, recorded a resolution that 'the lads who receive catechetical instruction in this confraternity be not considered qualified to become teachers until they are fully instructed in the Large Abridgement and be otherwise particularly distinguished for their pious conduct'.[96]

Adult catechesis was also addressed by Doyle, particularly of those categorised as 'ignorant'[97] but it is difficult to find detailed hard information on this subject. In his 1820 pastoral, as has been mentioned, Doyle recommended the faithful during Lent to attend 'pious reading or instruction, in the evening at their respective chapels, or at their own houses'. Heads of families were exhorted at night-time to gather their children and domestics, who had not an opportunity of attending at chapel, for prayer and 'spiritual reading'.[98] An indulgence of one hundred days could be gained by parents who taught the catechism to their families in their own homes.[99] In Tullow, ten Brigidine nuns and forty female teachers instructed 256 female adults in the principles of Catholicism in 1824. Simultaneously in the same parish the Patrician brothers and a society of men teachers catechised 322 male adults in the duties of their religion for nearly four hours every Sunday.[100] In this respect Tullow was probably an exception. In general, adult catechesis may have been confined to an important instruction before mass on Sundays. Adults who could read did have access to the chapel libraries to which we now turn our attention.

CHAPEL LIBRARIES AND THE CATHOLIC BOOK SOCIETY

The chapel library, the object of which was the diffusion of religious knowledge, was an integral and highly successful aspect of Doyle's catechetical mission, particularly to adults. Steps were taken by him to initiate such libraries at the beginning of his episcopacy; in his 1821 pastoral he published typically all embracing and legalistic guidelines for the proper management of book societies in every parish. These societies were to be composed of those members of the Blessed

Sacrament of the Eucharist and Christian Doctrine confraternities who paid one shilling for that purpose. Every person of good character who regularly fulfilled his religious duties was eligible for admission to the society on payment of half-a-crown (so there was an obvious incentive to join a confraternity). Each society member was to pay two pence each month to promote the objects of the society; and, on omitting to do so for two successive months, ceased to be a member. The book society was governed by the parish priest or curate as 'perpetual president', and by a vice-president, secretary or librarian, and a treasurer 'who must be a layman'. The librarian kept the books under lock and key in the sacristy. The duties of the priest-president were to appoint, on a monthly basis, people to read in the chapel, and to superintend the children's classes and the teaching of the catechism. The society was free to make rules for the relief of any of its members who were in distress, and to have masses offered for their souls when deceased; it also granted premiums to children at their general examination in the catechism, and on the days of their first communion, and on other occasions of note. The bishop ordered that the rules of the book society be prominently displayed in the sacristy or chapel where parishioners and members could view them.[101] Doyle's rules were incorporated, with only the very slightest amendments, as an appendix to the provincial statutes.[102]

On his first visitation, Doyle outlined to the faithful 'at considerable length, in every chapel, the great advantages of a library of this kind, and how necessary it was to diffuse widely religious knowledge, and that the establishment of libraries was among the best means of doing so'. The Sunday following his visitation the clergy in their respective parishes made a collection from parishioners for the purchase of initial book stocks.[103] In theory the library was formed at the expense of the parish but in reality it seems that confraternity members were its overwhelming support, at least at the outset. In some parishes – Carlow, Clonegal, Hacketstown – it would appear that teachers or catechists alone had 'access' to the chapel libraries.[104] In Tullow both catechists and ordinary parishioners had access.[105] The catechists and confraternity members were undoubtedly among the best educated lay people and were those who made the greatest use of the libraries. The book society thus formed the inner circle of the chapel library but in time the rules became much more flexible and relaxed with regard to those non-confraternity members who could not afford the half-crown membership fee. In Clonbullogue parish in 1824 there were 106 volumes in the chapel library which were sometimes read in church on Sundays but more generally read by the parishioners in their homes.[106] In Portarlington in the same year there were thirty-seven volumes in the chapel library which had been purchased by the voluntary subscription of the parishioners who had the use of them at one penny a month for each book.[107]

The general practice of the diocese by 1825 was that those who could afford to pay did so – a penny per month – while the poor received books free. The

practice of lending books gratis was not contemplated in Doyle's original regulations but it was institutionalised in the provincial statutes;[108] it perhaps reflected
the success of the church in spreading literacy among the poor. The figures available
for 1820–23, which are admittedly incomplete, suggest that there were parochial
libraries in less than half the parishes of the diocese.[109] The deanery of Kilcock
was not a problem area. Vigorously denouncing the reading of Pastorini's *Prophecies* in his late 1822 pastoral directed against the Ribbonmen of that deanery,[110]
Doyle exhorted his flock to interest themselves in their parochial libraries, stating: 'all your chapels, dearest brethren, are provided with libraries; in which are
books containing tracts of piety, and explanations of the law; read and study them
and you will become wise unto salvation'.[111] A year later the organisation of chapel
libraries, while extensive, was not uniform. On 24 December 1823, Bishop Doyle
rejected an offer of Bibles from the (probably evangelically motivated) County
Kildare Ladies' Association, with the comment:

> Our poor people are tolerably well supplied with religious books from
> their parochial libraries which I have established in most of their chapels
> and am intent on increasing. So in that respect their wants are not great
> nor likely to be permanent.[112]

Specific instructions were issued by Doyle in his 1825 Lenten pastoral. These
were in part a response to the extraordinary number of tracts made available to
Catholics by the biblicals, which Doyle feared might lead to their seduction from
the faith. In consequence he made a major effort to ensure not alone that chapel
libraries were operative throughout the whole diocese but that religious books
were also available in family homes.

> In place ... of profane and irreligious books and pretended prophecies
> which distract your minds, corrupt your hearts and disturb your peace,
> we again, and most earnestly recommend to you the constant perusal of
> those books which compose your chapel-libraries; and we feel an earnest
> desire that not only libraries, but the houses of each of you be stored with
> books of piety and devotion ... an increased facility of doing so is now
> offered you in a great number of religious books of various sizes, and on
> every subject of faith and morals, which have lately been published by Mr
> Coyne of Capel Street, Dublin; and can be had of him, of Mr Nolan, or of
> Mr Price, in Carlow, for less than half of the prices at which they had
> hitherto been sold. We recommend therefore earnestly to you, dearest
> Brethren, that you procure those books, or at least a few of them for each
> family – and we exhort, nay we charge the Clergy, and the Religious
> Confraternities in each Chapel, not only to augment their own libraries,
> but to purchase the largest possible supply of these tracts and to distribute

a portion of them gratis to the poor, especially in the schools; and the better to promote this object, which is so near to our hearts, we desire as follows:– that a collection be made before or after Mass at each chapel in these Dioceses on the Second Sunday in Lent (notice having previously been given of it), and that an account of the amount of each collection – of the number of books purchased for it – and distributed as above, be rendered to us at our Annual Visitation of the Clergy in Easter Week.[113]

A month later on 18 March 1825 he claimed to have

established in every parish within the two dioceses of which I have care, parochial libraries which I have stocked with books of religious and moral instructions exclusively; these books are given out to heads of families, upon their paying a penny a week or a fortnight for the use of them; they are given to the poor gratis; when a man has read one of those books, he returns it to the librarian upon the Sunday; he then gets another, and thus every class of people in the diocese is instructed in their moral, social and religious duties.[114]

In 1822 Thomas Spring Rice, M.P., wished to promote similar lending libraries and sought Doyle's advice on the selection of books.[115] There were several hundred volumes in 'many' of his chapel libraries, the bishop replied, but he considered the following list of more than twenty works 'as valuable for instruction and moral improvement of the poor, that I have them placed in every parochial library and several copies of them in some':

Gobinet's Instructions for youth;
Commandments and sacraments explained by Dr Hornihold;
Bossuet's Exposition of the Christian Doctrine;
Butler's Lives of the Saints. His Feasts and Fasts and
posthumous works;
Gahan's Sermons;
Doctor Hays' Sincere and Pious Christian;
The Memorial of a Christian life by Lewis of Grenada;
Gother's works including his Exposition of the Gospels and Epistles;
Imitation of Christ by Thomas A Kempis;
Introduction to the Devout Life by St Francis de Sales;
Challoner's Meditation and Think Well On't;
Poor Man's Catechism;
Hornihold's Catechism of the Adult;
Sufferings of Christ;
Morality of St Augustine;

> Difference between temporal and eternal;
> Dorrell's Reflections;
> Elevation of the Soul;
> Manning's Moral Entertainments.[116]

Virtually all of these books are duplicated in an incomplete list of books which belonged to Suncroft chapel library.[117] Books on religious controversy were not allowed; neither did Doyle admit works on politics, history or science 'unmixed with religion'.[118] It seems likely that his own political works were excluded. The selection of other books apart from the basic foundation list was left to the discretion of parish priests and the book societies.[119]

The number of chapel libraries and books in them increased dramatically in the mid-1820s. By 1829 the average number of books in thirty-three parishes of the diocese for which data are available, containing seventy-two chapels, was 100 in each chapel library.[120] These parochial libraries were of such importance in promoting adult catechesis that in 1830 Doyle claimed: 'I do not know of any institution which has produced so such moral good in the country'.[121] Chapel libraries encouraged adult literacy and self-improvement. They simultaneously catered for a growing demand for religious knowledge while stimulating a more informed understanding of the faith. Doyle never ceased to extol the merits of these libraries. In his last pastoral letter (1834) he once again urged his flock to make more extensive use of them:

> Exchange ... those profane books, those idle and exciting publications, which disturb your peace, and too often embitter your minds, for the Gospel of God, the lives of the Saints, and those expositions of the Christian law which form your parish libraries, and are thus happily placed within your reach.[122]

The Catholic Book Society was a direct response by the Irish hierarchy to the perceived evangelical threat known as the New Reformation in 1827.[123] Occasional attempts by individuals to print and publish inexpensive Catholic literature for the widest possible readership generally proved, for whatever reason, unprofitable and unsuccessful. In Dublin in the mid-1820s a number of laymen and clerics were interested in establishing an organisation on a solid footing which would disseminate low-priced Catholic books and manuals throughout Ireland.[124] The most prominent advocates of such a departure were William Joseph Battersby, first biographer of Doyle, who is an important figure in the history of the Catholic press in Ireland,[125] and Rev. Dr William Yore. Battersby, an active catechist and Catholic social worker, who became a writer, printer and publisher, wrote several letters on the necessity of forming a Catholic book or tract society. In mid-summer 1824, Yore invited Doyle to join with him in promoting a book

society. Doyle responded enthusiastically with an entire programme and constitution for an 'Irish Catholic Society for the Diffusion of Religious Knowledge'.
It should, he suggested, be governed by a president, four vice-presidents, a treasurer, secretary and a committee of twenty-one members – none of whom was to
reside more than three miles from Dublin city. The committee should initiate a
correspondence with the Irish episcopacy and submit to the prelates a plan for
the formation of co-operative Catholic societies in the cities and towns of their
dioceses, and for the establishment or enlargement of useful circulating libraries.
Books 'calculated to excite dissensions amongst Irishmen [were to be] carefully
excluded' from the society's catalogue. Doyle advised Dr Yore to consult with
Daniel O'Connell and the Dublin cleric, Dean Lube O'Connor, on his recom-
mendations.[126] At a meeting in Dublin in November 1824 attended by Battersby
and several other Catholic laymen along with the Dublin clerics – Yore, Dowling,
Spratt, Deane, Canavan and White – rules and regulations, no doubt Doyle's,
were adopted.[127] Archbishop Murray, in whose diocese the project had been initiated, gave active encouragement. Battersby wrote of Doyle as the 'first prelate
out of Dublin' to support the enterprise warmly.

However, according to Battersby, 'circumstances delayed the complete adoption of the plan until February 1827'[128] when at Doyle's 'instigation'[129] the Catholic hierarchy agreed to sponsor the foundation of a 'Catholic Book Society for the
diffusion of useful knowledge throughout Ireland'. The objects of the Society
were, firstly, to furnish the Irish people, in the cheapest and most convenient
manner with 'useful information on the truths and duties of the Christian religion'; secondly (and indicating uneasiness over the New Reformation crusade)
'to supply all classes of persons with satisfactory refutations of the prevailing
errors of the present age'; thirdly, to supply 'the most approved books of elementary instruction' to schools throughout Ireland. The society began as a completely
clerical institution without lay assistance but during the course of its first year
W.J. Battersby was appointed registrar and general salesman, and his house, 33
Winetavern Street, became the Society's store and also the location for a weekly
committee meeting.[130] Doyle's influence can easily be discerned in the rules and
regulations of the Society which were ratified on 9 March 1827. The Society was
modelled on the guidelines he had drawn up in 1824. The primate, Dr Curtis,
was elected president; Doyle, the other archbishops, the president of Maynooth
College and the vicar-general of the Dublin diocese were named vice-presidents;
the remaining bishops were named guardians, and twenty one clergymen of the
Dublin diocese were appointed to the committee.[131] In Dublin, where inevitably
there was the greatest concentrated demand for its resources, the society was
supported by the 'special patronage'[132] of Archbishop Murray who was its treasurer.

The initiative to found the Catholic Book Society resulted more from the
renewed New Reformation campaign (itself partly inspired by near-famine con-

ditions when the greatest success in making converts was enjoyed) than from any other factor in 1827. Fear of the evangelicals is reflected in episcopal correspondence with Dr Murray. Bishop Kelly (Dromore) believed that the Society was 'of paramount importance at these perilous times'.[133] Bishop Egan (Kerry) agreed that more than usual exertions were called for to counteract 'unceasing enemies'.[134] Edmund Ffrench, warden of Galway, held that the Society was of the 'utmost importance at the present moment'.[135] O'Shaughnessy (Killaloe) stated simply that 'something is necessary'.[136] Bishop Keating (Ferns) was the only dissenting voice: 'when famine seems to approach us, and when the bulk of the people stands in much greater need of bread than of work', it was his decided opinion that there would be no success unless books were distributed free.[137] On the other hand Bishop Coen (coadjutor of Clonfert) felt that books would guard the flock 'against [the] inclinations of their enemies'.[138]

In April 1827 the Society's secretary, Rev. Matthew Flanagan, informed Doyle that 'a hundred thousand religious books will be circulated before the expiration of the next three months, which with the same liberal aid will be continued each succeeding quarter till every poor Roman Catholic family in Ireland will be furnished with a select library of religious and other useful books'.[139] But Flanagan was hopelessly over-optimistic and indeed in the first months of its existence the Society struggled to survive because of the failure of the committee to publicise its objectives properly. In theory every rural dean in each Irish diocese was to be an agent for the distribution of books and tracts but in practice only a few dioceses were properly organised, notably Dublin, Kildare and Leighlin, Limerick, Derry, Ardagh, Cloyne and Ross, and Meath.[140]

In June 1827, at the request of the Society, Doyle wrote an address on the function and objectives of the new organisation.[141] Doyle stressed the nationwide character and task of the Society. 'The guardians of the Society', the bishop wrote, 'are pledged to promote the circulation of religious books to the most remote parishes ... and to the most obscure cabin in Ireland'. Heretofore those anxious to promote a Catholic book society had been at a loss to institute an effective mode of proceeding. Now that had been overcome, a start had been made, and all that was required was Catholic co-operation which was neither 'laborious nor expensive'. The Society was established, Doyle contended, 'rather to gratify the desires than to excite the zeal of every good Catholic'. However he did emphasise as a 'principal object' its role in countering the proselytising threat of the New Reformation then at its zenith. The most important benefit, he commented, conferred on Catholics by the new Society, was the facility to purchase books at unusually low prices. In some instances the public could expect reductions of thirty-five per cent, in others of not less than fifty per cent.[142]

In September 1827 the secretary of the Catholic Book Society reported to Bishop Marum that in less than two months we shall have a tolerable supply of books having ordered for printing Manning's Short Way, Gulitzer's Defences, Gahan's History of the Old and New Testaments. Books published: Grounds of Christian Doctrine, Butler 1, 2, 3, sizes, O'Reilly's Catechism, 1st size ... 2nd size.[143]

Of necessity, the production of literature at a low, near cost price demanded tight financial management and subsidisation. Payments were made quarterly by recipients of the Society's stock. Doyle suggested, in his June 1827 address, that subscriptions or collections be taken in every parish and that every bishop, priest and confraternity member 'should consider themselves charged with the interests of the Society'.[144] Donations and subscriptions reached £882.7s.6d. in the first year of the Society's existence, but then sharply declined to only £242.2s.11d. in 1829.[145] The hierarchy agreed at its meeting in February 1829 that to assist the Society each of the prelates would accept £35 worth of books and requisites, not including catechisms. At this meeting Doyle moved a resolution urging the Catholic Association, prior to its expected voluntary dissolution, 'to vote from their funds such sum as would assist the committee to free the establishment confided to them from its present embarrassment'.[146] The Catholic Association which had already grant-aided the Society to the amount of £600 responded with a further £600.[147] At the hierarchy's annual meeting in 1830 Doyle again sponsored a resolution that the Catholic Book Society be given full support by every member of the episcopacy.[148] The great need of the Catholic Book Society in its first precarious years was for a capital injection which would have enabled it to enlarge its operations to meet the potential demand for its services.

In its first year to 31 January 1828, the Society circulated 29,704 catechisms, 10,200 *Grounds of Catholic Doctrine*, 2,300 of Gulitzer's *Defences of Catholic Principles* and 1,340 of Grou's *Exposition*. Receipts indicate that the diocese of Kildare and Leighlin purchased more books and requisites than any other diocese. The diocese bought the highest number (800 copies) of the *Grounds of Catholic Doctrine* and the smallest number (100 copies) of catechisms of all the Irish dioceses.[149] In its first three years, 1827–9, the Society printed 921,554 'books and school requisites' and circulated 680,297. The Society claimed that the higher figure almost equalled the number of books circulated by the government-aided Kildare Place Society in its seventeen years' existence. The Society asserted that it had reached only one-tenth of the number of books it could circulate if it had adequate capital.[150] In its first decade, despite this capital deficiency, the Society claimed to have printed five million books.[151] This was a considerable achievement to which Doyle significantly contributed. Nonetheless had the initiative been systematically organised in each diocese on a rural deanery basis it could have achieved far more.

PENANCE AND THE STATIONS

The main body of Doyle's pastoral instructions for Lent 1821 was taken up with an extended treatment of the sacrament of penance.[152] The bishop's purpose was to impress upon the faithful that confession was more than a mere cataloguing of sins and formed one part of the solemn and meaningful sacrament of penance. Leaning heavily on St Augustine as his authority[153] he outlined the nature of the sacrament warning against abuses such as the free commission of sin in the vain expectation of receiving ready forgiveness,[154] abstention from affected reverence, and private penance outside the confessional.[155] He progressed from a general introduction to the sacrament to a discussion of its three component parts: contrition, confession and satisfaction.

Contrition was sincere sorrow[156] and detestation of sin committed, joined with a firm purpose of amendment which required the penitent to repair, as far as possible, any injury done by him to the property or character of his neighbour. Doyle asserted that no practice was better calculated to produce a change of life in the sinner than confession. The embarrassment of having to confess sin acted as a powerful restraint on those who were thus deterred from acting criminally. For proper preparation for confession he advised the reading of the 'Table of Sins'. Those who were illiterate were recommended to compare their own lives with the commandments and the 'seven deadly sins'. A simple and brief confession was all that was required. It should not be couched in doubtful language calculated to deceive or conceal or preserve the good opinion of the confessor.[157]

The optimum age for first confession was between seven and ten years; frequent confession and communion were urged on all. This did not necessarily mean the weekly reception of communion. Doyle observed that the pious went to confession once a week or once a month and 'as opportunities may present themselves'.[158] He advised a nun that once a fortnight was sufficent so it seems unlikely that he expected any more frequent reception of the sacrament of penance from ordinary lay Catholics.[159]

Satisfaction, the third element of penance, was dealt with rather briefly by Doyle. His main emphasis was that sin may be forgiven yet the sinner may be chastised with temporal afflictions, which it is the purpose of satisfaction to arrest. Biblical references from Genesis, c. 3, v. 17; Numbers, c. 14, v. 20, 22; 2 Kings, c. 13 and 14; and Exodus, c. 32, 39, were adduced to support this statement.[160]

In 1825 Doyle gave important evidence on the frequency of reparation and restitution before the house of commons' committee on the state of Ireland.

> Have the instances of reparation and restitution, which have taken place within your knowledge, been numerous? – Numerous beyond the power of counting – and they are occurring almost daily. Every gentleman resi-

dent in Ireland, must well know what a common practice prevails there, of a priest coming and giving money to individuals, and telling them 'This is money which is restored for an injury that has been done to you': he cannot however tell the name of the person by whom the injury has been done, or any thing more about it. We clergymen frequently do this ourselves, but the reparation is much more frequently made in private, by the person who did the injury; we only become the channel through which it is made, where we find that the party concerned, cannot make it without exposing himself to be known, to which we do not oblige him.[161]

In a public letter to the parish priest of Abbeyleix in 1828, John Dunne, Esq., of Ballinakill, stated that he had received thirty pounds from the clergyman in question, Michael Keogh, 'the amount of principal with interest of property taken from me'. Moreover he noted 'the numerous instances that have come to my knowledge of restitution made through your instrumentality, and for sums of very considerable amounts – in one instance of seven hundred guineas ... You have worked a sincere reformation'.[162]

The confessional was absolutely secret and indeed would not have been frequented had it been otherwise.[163] Priests could not reveal information received in the confessional to anyone; but where a penitent went to confession it usually followed that he was prepared to make a clean breast of his sins and to make reparation for them. Where a penitent revealed an intention by himself or in the company of others to do injury to property or persons, the priest invariably endeavoured to dissuade him from such action and required him to dissuade his colleagues likewise or, failing that, to inform the endangered party or a magistrate. Absolution was refused unless the penitent undertook to follow the priest's instructions. Doyle acknowledged that he himself had often forestalled the commission of crime in this manner.[164]

On more than one occasion Doyle was obliged to warn female religious against scruples[165] and to admonish ordinary pious women against giving a history of their lives[166] every time they went to confession. In 1814, as has been mentioned, he warned of the dangers of allowing nuns to manifest their consciences on a monthly basis to their female superior. This was a practice, a form of sham confession, which could not, he felt, be observed without abuse.[167]

Parishioners were required to attend confession and communion in their own parishes under pain of mortal sin.[168] In 1823 Gerald Doyle, P.P., Naas, sought permission from the bishop to absolve parishioners who, in order to avoid complying with the discipline of the diocese, had gone into the adjacent diocese of Dublin to complete their Easter duty. Dr Doyle detected a certain indifference to religion in this behaviour and he refused the request: 'Better they should receive no sacraments than receive them unworthily'.[169]

In general, absence from the confessional was not a pastoral problem. If anything the contrary was the case. The *General Cathecism* posed the question: 'What must we do if we be so unhappy as to fall into mortal sin?' The answer: 'We must repent sincerely and go to confession as soon as possible'. 'Why should we go to confession if we fall into mortal sin?' 'That we may recover God's friendship, and be always prepared to die.'[170] The souls of Catholics who died in a state of mortal sin went to hell while those who died in venial sin went to purgatory. The injunction to attend confession as soon as mortal sin was committed was taken almost literally. But, more importantly, Catholics felt compelled not to go to communion without having been to confession. This created much work for the clergy. When a penitent was found not guilty of any mortal sin from the time of his last visit, absolution was not necessary and therefore was not given; instead the penitent received 'special leave' from his confessor to approach the altar.[171] Frequent communion was urged on all those who fell into mortal sin and indeed on all 'who desire to advance in piety'[172] but reception more than once a fortnight was probably very rare. In a circular letter to his clergy in 1821 Doyle requested 'that all Saturdays and vigils be set aside for hearing the confessions of pious persons only, and this in each chapel in rotation'. The pious penitents (presumably confraternity members) were to be admonished that 'as they occupy so such of the time and attention of the clergy' they should contribute liberally in offerings for their support 'on certain days'.[173] In 1796 the bishop of Ferns, Dr Caulfield, remarked that because he had only eighty priests, they were frequently compelled to sit in the confessional for eight, ten and even twelve hours a day, for almost the whole day, except during mass, meals and divine office.[174] In Dublin the zealous Rev. Henry Young 'often spent a whole night in the confessional'.[175] In Carlow (1814–19) Doyle laboured unremittingly in the confessional on Saturdays.[176] The parish priest of Carlow, William Fitzgerald, usually entered the confessional at four o'clock in the morning.[177] In 1821 Benjamin Joseph Broughall, P.P., Graiguenamanagh, complained that he often sat seven or eight hours in the confessional without interruption.[178] Illegal associations warned their members to keep their activities secret from the priest in the confessional. Such was the respect for the confessional that rather than adopt the sacrilegious expedient of making an untruthful confession, members of secret societies preferred not to attend.[179] So much so that one of the earliest signs of the activity of illegal associations in a parish was always the uniform absence from the sacrament of penance of those involved,[180] an indicator that confession was both understood and frequented. In times of distress, such as the cholera epidemic of 1832, the confessionals were crowded.[181]

The most striking evidence of all on pre-famine confessional practice in the diocese of Kildare and Leighlin was thrown up by Doyle's afore-mentioned dispute with the Jesuits.[182] It sheds new light on the extent of confessional practice and on church attempts to ensure that all Catholics fulfilled their Paschal duty. Whether the lenient reputation of the Jesuits as confessors was responsible for the crowds who thronged their confessionals at Clongowes is not known,[183] but the fact was that, late at night, penitents queued who were

> the poorest of the poor, who could not spare to receive the consolation of religion at other times: the same scene was regularly re-enacted in the morning with the dawn of day. Numbers from remote distances set out from their cabins in the dark to unburden their consciences at our confessionals at 3 or 4 o'clock in the morning and hasten back to their daily labour.[184]

Apart from its theological implications of hostility to the Society, Doyle's withdrawal of faculties from the Jesuits had two purposes: to uphold the due subordination of the flock to the pastor and to enable the P.P. to deduce that all parishioners had completed their Paschal duty. Parishioners were warned by their clergy that they did not comply with their Paschal duty if they went to confession at Clongowes or outside their parish.[185]

Dr Esmonde, S.J., wondered whether Doyle appreciated the circumstances which might occur to keep people from confessing 'in confidence and satisfaction' to their parish priest with whom they were perhaps very familiar; or the 'rational difficulty' that might be felt in confessing to a curate, especially if he were a young curate. Interestingly Esmonde reiterated this point: 'Just reasons might hinder the penitent from having full confidence in the curate'. Esmonde observed that when Catholics in Clane and Kill parishes had difficulty about confessing to their parochial clergy they went to Newbridge, Clongowes or Dublin.[186]

In allowing the Jesuits to exercise faculties once more in the diocese Doyle simultaneously introduced a restrictive confessional ticket system. The parishioner who wished to confess to a priest other than his parish priest or curate was required to have a ticket from his parochial clergy allowing him to do so; it was signed by the confessor as proof that the penitent had been to confession. This practice was well known in Italy. It had apparently been first used in country parishes in the diocese of Milan under Charles Borromeo. Esmonde contended that Doyle's ticket system gave a facility for fraud and hypocrisy because the penitent who had received a ticket was presumed to have gone to confession. Doyle ruled that, if the ticket were refused without just cause, application to the Ordinary or his vicars-general would bring speedy relief. But, as Esmonde maintained, it was scarcely realistic to expect the poor penitent to travel to Carlow to prove he had been unjustly denied a ticket – in the process incurring perhaps the displeasure of his parish priest.[187]

In response to Esmonde's complaints, Doyle made a new ruling that the ticket was never to be refused. Even so Esmonde claimed that there were some parishes in which tickets were refused 'wholesale' on the avowed principle that the church required all parishioners to confess at Easter to the parish priest or his curate. In answer to further tiresome complaints of this nature from Esmonde, Doyle allowed the Jesuits a discretionary power - apparently leave to hear confessions whether the penitents possessed tickets or not, to be exercised as they saw fit. Thus the ticket system of confessional practice may have been short-lived. It is unclear whether it applied to the whole diocese or just to the northern parishes of Kildare. It seems to have been a novel departure in the Irish context and it demonstrates the lengths to which Doyle was prepared to go in order to oversee the performance by the faithful of their religious duties.

The stations of confession (usually abbreviated to 'the stations') took place twice yearly in preparation for the most important holy days in the church calendar, namely Easter and Christmas. The stations were held in designated private houses by the parochial clergy and comprised the hearing of confessions and the celebration of mass. Failure to receive the sacraments of penance and the eucharist at least once annually at Easter (the minimum requirement which was known as the Paschal duty) resulted in ipso facto excommunication, exclusion from the sacrament of matrimony without leave of the bishop, and from a Christian burial even though such a person might have been attended by a clergyman prior to his or her death.[188]

In his Diocesan Book for 1819–20, Doyle noted with reference to several parishes that the stations were regularly observed by the clergy who left at the prescribed hour, six o'clock. The Christmas stations in Kildare and Leighlin under Doyle commenced immediately after 29 September and continued until the octave of the Epiphany, inclusive.[189] The Easter stations commenced on the first Monday in Lent and continued, where necessary, until Ascension. Stations were not to be held after Ascension, Doyle ruled, any custom to the contrary notwithstanding.[190] Because of difficulties facing the church in Ireland, Pope Paul V in his rescript, *Exponi nobis*, of 28 March 1607 extended the normal period from Palm Sunday to the Sunday after Easter, in which the faithful were required to fulfill the Paschal precept, to the period between Ash Wednesday and the feast of the Ascension.[191]

The 1821 diocesan statutes decreed that persons who omitted their Easter duty through wilful neglect could not be admitted to any sacrament until they applied to their bishop or their vicar forane to receive a penance proportionate to the grievousness of their sin. If they were absolved they were not, unless in cases of necessity, to be admitted to communion for six months from the time of their first application to confess.[192]

The presumed penal origin of the stations is somewhat obscure, although it is not difficult to imagine how such a practice might have developed in a society where attendance at the mass-house might have been hazardous. Corish has pointed out that the practice was well-established in Munster by the 1780s and universal thereafter.[193] Bishop Delany writing in 1800 stated that the stations were held in the houses of the upper sort of inhabitants ... for the purpose of accommodating the people in the vicinity with more convenient opportunity of performing certain religious duties ... The parish priest and his curate, unless otherwise engaged, uniformly breakfast and dine at those places on such occasions. The stations, in large populous parishes, generally exceed, sometimes considerably, one hundred in the year, from which of course, results a very capital saving in the article of house-keeping .... [194]

The stations in Tullow parish which never numbered more than fourteen or fifteen were 'wholly abolished' during Delany's episcopacy.[195] Keenan has claimed that Doyle wished to see the stations eradicated.[196] Conflicting statements by Fitzpatrick, who at one point stated that Doyle wanted the stations 'utterly abolished', are the source of this error.[197] In fact the exact opposite was the case. In 1819, Cardinal Fontana, prefect of Propaganda Fide, wrote to the Irish hierarchy urging the abolition of the stations and the administration of the sacrament of penance in church.[198] Doyle's diocesan statutes of 1820 refer to this matter:

De stationibus quas hic notavimus, rescripta Roma nuper venerunt, quibus hujus Regni Praesules monebantur, ut praedictas stationes ob abusus in illis occurrentes, omnino abolerent, atque ut sacramenta in Eclesiis tantum administrari sinerent; Nos vero (ex consilio Illus mi. ac Rev. mi. Metropolitani nostri ac Rev. rum Coepiscoporum hujus provinciae) duximus, Summae sedi morem quidem gerendum, simul vero et Utilitati Sacerdotum, et populi nobis commissi consulendum: Hinc omnes, quibus spectat, in Domino hortamur, ut primo mane ad Stationem se conferrant, et auditis confessionibus, sumptoque jentaculo, domum redeant; quod si praeter spem nostram, ac desiderium, etiam pro prandio detinentur, precipimus, ne post horam sextam vespertinam, ullo modo, moram ibidem trahant.[199]

Thus Doyle sought to reform and not to abolish the stations. At the prompting of one of his priests another reform of the stations – the abolition of the station dinner custom – took place in 1822.[200]

The station was always preceded, for the participants, by a period of fasting from midnight; the breakfast or dinner took place immediately after the station. In March 1822 the bishop received a convincing letter condemning this practice from 'Clericus Leighlinensis', who was probably Francis Haly, then administrator of Mountrath, subsequently bishop of Kildare and Leighlin, 1838–55. He stated that the tradition of station dinners developed during the penal period when priests were of necessity forced to accept the hospitality of their flocks. But the parochial revenues were now such as to allow clergymen to dine in dignity at home, without having recourse to the station dinner, which in worse times, they were compelled to accept 'by the great law of necessity'; 'But the cause in which the necessity originated having long since ceased to exist, the practice which it introduced should disappear with it'. 'Clericus Leighlinensis' argued that station dinners were hurtful to the Catholic community from both a spiritual and temporal point of view. The station day ought to be a time of recollection and of pious and devotional exercises but, where dinner was being prepared, it was impossible amid the hustle and bustle for the family of the house to give any attention to prayer. Their only concern was to provide a satisfactory meal and thus the main object of the station was lost to sight.

The habit of dining at station dinners, he contended, took away from the respectability of the priest. The station generally ended at 3 p.m. One hour later dinner was served. The priest took the head of the table, carved the meat, told jokes, and when he retired at six o'clock he had neither the time nor inclination for study. In its temporal aspect the station dinner put unnecessary expense on hard-pressed farmers. 'Clericus Leighlinensis' had often witnessed the young children of such farmers bereft of shoes or articles of clothing which the expense of the dinner would easily purchase. He estimated the average annual number of stations in each parish at eighty (forty in each cycle) and the cost of the dinner at two pounds, running up a total expense on each parish (or more accurately on forty to eighty parishioners, the great majority, farmers) of £160 sterling per annum: 'a very severe tax, no doubt at any time, but particularly during these times of unprecedented distress and why should the Catholic pastor conspire with the middlemen, the tithe proctor and the tax gatherer to draw the last shilling out of his impoverished and heart-broken parishioners?'[201] It will be recalled that Doyle had deliberately limited the number of clergy on the mission because he was aware that an impoverished flock could not support more. That his clergy should in any way contribute to the oppression of their parishioners was repugnant to him.

In response to 'Clericus Leighlinensis' Doyle abolished the station dinner custom as far as priests were concerned. He also sought the concurrence of Archbishop Troy and Bishop Marum for a similar measure in their dioceses. Dr Troy[202] readily agreed as did Dr Marum who pointed out that his own recommendation to end station dinners was of some years standing and had been adhered to 'by some of my priests'.[203] There is only one recorded instance of dissent from the new rule in Kildare and Leighlin. Michael Brennan, C.C., Bagenalstown, earned a rebuke from Doyle for violating the rule. He admitted that he had broken the rule but alleged that he had not infringed its spirit 'unless the object of the rule is to debar the priest from every social intercourse with the people, to make them strangers to each other'.[204]

Neither the Dublin provincial statutes nor the synod of Thurles made the removal of the stations from parishioners' homes to parochial chapels obligatory though it was strongly recommended.[205] The stations of confession are perhaps the classic example of how the non-institutional church under the penal code resolved its pastoral problems, not through dependence on Tridentine structures, but through centering the experience of religion on the home where a living-faith tradition was handed down in a distinctly Irish fashion.

The most notable source for mass attendance data in pre-famine Ireland is the first report of the commissioners of Public Instruction.[206] Corish has quite rightly warned that the 1834 statistics must be approached with 'great circumspection',[207] and indeed, while the report can be surveyed for obvious generalisations about national trends, its merit for detailed research purposes is suspect. The evidence presented contains too many imponderables to be more than casually useful. However, as it is the only statistical evidence available to us an effort must be made to assess it. The reliance to be placed on the finding of the report with regard to mass attendance depends to a great degree on the objectives of the commissioners and the methods by which their data were ascertained. The commissioners' primary function was to estimate the number in communion with the United Church of England and Ireland. They were prepared to stand over the accuracy of that part of their report above any of its other aspects.[208]

The commissioners submitted lists of queries to ministers of all persuasions in all the Protestant parishes of Ireland. One major problem was that the Established church parish which was the basic geographical unit of the census was not generally identical with the civil parish and the Catholic parish was not identical with either. From the clergymen of the Established church the commissioners received the greatest co-operation; they received replies relating to 1,390 parishes; from Catholic clergy relating to 868 parishes; and from Presbyterian ministers with reference to 210 parishes.[209] Where clerics failed to respond the queries were forwarded to 1,308 enumerators for answer 'in that branch of our enquiry which related to the census'.[210] The commissioners do not state with any degree of minuteness the particular mode of investigation adopted by them for obtaining mass attendance data. It seems likely that Protestant clergymen and enumerators were inclined in some cases to underestimate the size of the Catholic mass-going population. Given the denominational tensions of the time there probably was some difficulty, where Catholic clerical participation had not been secured in accurately computing Catholic mass attendance. Moreover, Catholics were always wary of government surveys and perhaps inclined to play down their numbers; it would also have been in Protestant interests to do the same. For Caragh parish the return stated: 'The chapel is crowded but no estimate could be obtained of attendance'. In Monasterevan the size of the Catholic congregation 'could not be ascertained': similarly, for individual chapels in Clonegal and

Bagenalstown.[211] It seems clear that all aspects of the work of the commission were not approached with the same degree of interest and scrutiny of the returns and that the enumeration of congregation size at Catholic places of worship was one of the least of the commissioners' priorities.

In 1975 Miller published the first paper to make extensive use of the evidence presented by the commissioners of Public Instruction.[212] Dealing with English speaking rural areas in dioceses bordering on Kildare and Leighlin he recorded a mass attendance figure of 53–60 per cent for the rural parishes between Kilkenny city and Callan in Ossory and a rate of 72 per cent in some rural parishes in Ferns; the latter he denominated 'unusually high' even for English speaking areas.[213] Miller presented much lower figures for the backward and denominationally heterogeneous counties of the north and west such as Cavan, Down and Donegal and this led him to the conclusion that nationally, attendance in English speaking rural areas, ranged between 30 and 60 per cent.[214] In the towns he estimated that attendance ranged between 80 and 100 per cent.[215]

Both Miller and Corish agree that the figures available are in many cases open to more than one interpretation and do not represent a modern socio-religious study.[216] Corish has asserted that: 'It may be that the figure given sometimes represents the attendance at one mass only, but if so, there is no way of establishing how many may have attended other masses – if there were other masses.'[217] Where statistical information given is capable of more than one interpretation Miller choses the lower figure. As Catholic attendance at chapel was rising in the vast majority of cases this was certainly unwise. The most serious criticism made by Corish of Miller's analysis is that he failed to allow for children under seven, nursing mothers, the aged, sick and otherwise impeded who were not required to attend mass. Indeed Corish has stated that 'it is a conservative estimate that one-fifth of the total population did not come to mass because the precept of attending did not bind them.' Corish corrects Miller's figures by this factor and arrives at a figure of between 37.5 and 75 per cent for attendance in English-speaking rural areas and effectively 100 per cent in the towns. Even so, in relation to the lower figures, he admonishes: 'These figures must be regarded as minimum figures rather than as firm figures, because of possible uncertainties in the data'.[218]

Murphy, in his study of the diocese of Killaloe, asserts that Corish significantly underestimated the number of Catholics who were not obliged to attend mass on Sundays. According to Murphy, Corish's figure of 20 per cent is 'far too low'. Murphy lays particular emphasis on problems arising from lack of respectable clothing, the condition of the roads and distance from chapels which involved hardship in bad weather as inhibitors of mass attendance in the west of Ireland where the lowest figures were returned by the commissioners. As Macaulay points out out theologians like St Alphonsus Liguori made allowances for these problems as justifiable reasons for non-mass attendance. Thus the seasonality and poverty factors which affected Sunday school catechesis also affected mass attendances.

Furthermore Murphy questions the statistics for mass attendance produced by the commissioners of Public Instruction in 1834, and the theories of Larkin and Miller which were largely based on these figures. He states that 'the figures for Killaloe diocese vary from accurate to wildly inaccurate and in most cases it is impossible to decide on the accuracy or otherwise of the data for a particular parish'. Among his remarks on specific data from the commissioners' report one notices the following: 'extremely slipshod', 'extraordinary anomalies', 'serious doubts', 'particularly puzzling'.[219] This confirms the view that detailed research is proving that the 1834 statistics must be treated with the greatest caution.

The data in the commissioners' report for Kildare and Leighlin have all the lack of clarity and peculiarities above-mentioned. Thus only the most tentative assessment can be attempted on figures available for forty-two of the forty-seven parishes.[220] In nearly three-quarters of the Catholic places of worship the average mass congregation was returned as 'increasing' in size. This increase can be attributed to an upsurge in Catholic religious practice and in part to the pre-famine increase in population. In a quarter of the chapels of the diocese the attendance was termed 'stationary' and in only one was it 'diminishing'.[221] In villages and towns attendance was very high; over 80 per cent in Carlow, and over 90 per cent in Ballinakill, Bagenalstown, Edenderry, Kildare, Philipstown and Tullow.[222] For the diocese as a whole (following Corish's conservative method of estimation) an average attendance of 61 per cent is suggested though it could conceivably have been as high as 74 per cent. To use Murphy's method of estimation would produce a still higher figure.

It is worth drawing attention to the fact that in thirteen parishes – more than a quarter of the parishes of the diocese – mass was available 'occasionally on weekdays'. In Carlow there was mass in the cathedral twice daily. An exceptional service was provided in Goresbridge parish: mass was available daily in Wells; three times a week from October to May and daily from June to September in Grange Sylvia; and in Shankill three times a week during about four months of the year with 'about 200' persons usually attending. In Bagenalstown parish, mass was celebrated daily during four months in the summer; and in Killeigh parish on Thursdays in summer and 'confession days'; in Edenderry parish on the 'second Saturday in every month'.[223]

Historians of Irish Catholicism have paid little attention to vespers (i.e. service of psalms, hymns and antiphons concluding with the 'Magnificat' traditionally sung in church on Sunday evenings and holy days). This is not surprising because information on the celebration of vespers in pre-famine Ireland is scarce. There is no mention of the devotion in the report of the commissioners of Public Instruction as it relates to Kildare and Leighlin. In a brief notice Corish has associated the service of vespers with urban areas in eighteenth century Ireland.

According to him there were sung vespers in Wexford town about 1750 and it was a regular service in the towns of Cloyne diocese in 1775.[224] It is impossible to determine what the practice was in Kildare and Leighlin under Doyle's predecessors. However, when Doyle became bishop it is clear that vespers was a well-established church service in most parts of the diocese. Details of vespers were entered by Doyle for twenty-six parishes in his Diocesan Book for 1819–20. Doyle found the service available in twenty parishes; no service was held in six parishes. No information was recorded for a further seven parishes. For Kildare parish Doyle noted 'no vespers but a rosary', and instructed that 'there will be vespers'. Where the service of vespers was available it was often offered in only one chapel in the parish. Doyle required vespers to be offered in all chapels. In this, as in other church matters, he anxiously sought to impose a uniformity of practice and observance.

As usual the statistics are not comprehensive but from data available for twenty-six parishes in 1820–23 it can be stated that the service was available in all the chapels of twenty-three parishes.[225] In Killeigh parish vespers were celebrated in two out of three chapels, but in four parishes: Borris, Clane, Edenderry and Graiguenamanagh, Doyle noted that the service was offered in one church only. There may perhaps have been a practice among parochial clergymen to say the office of vespers together. In Balyna parish Doyle recorded an entry of 'none' for vespers, neither were they said in Doonane or Leighlinbridge parishes. Nonetheless these three were the only negligent parishes out of the twenty-six for which information is extant. In only one instance – that of Glynn church in St Mullin's parish – did Doyle observe that vespers were actually 'sung'[226] implying perhaps that the service was recited elsewhere throughout the diocese. The significance of the service of vespers was that it brought an indeterminate number of Catholics to the church a second time on Sundays and holy days and was thus an important devotional practice. The service of vespers usually took place at four, five or six o' clock in summer and at two or three o' clock or immediately after last mass in winter. Vespers almost invariably followed catechetical instruction so the children of the parish were already present. The parochial visitation returns make it very evident that this was a standard procedure throughout the diocese. Thus the younger generation were in chapel on Sundays for mass, catechism and vespers.

Non-fulfillment of the Paschal precept was a problem dealt with by Bishop Gallagher in his diocesan statutes of 1748:

> Whereas, a great many are so careless of their salvation as not only to neglect approaching the Holy Sacraments of Confession and Communion often in the year, but, contrary to the express command of the general council of Lateran, even omit that duty at Easter, nay what is more deplorable, they pass several years without cleansing their consciences in the

laver of penance or feeding their souls with the flesh of the Immaculate Lamb. To remedy therefore so great an evil, we do hereby constitute and decree that as many as will not from the beginning of Lent to Trinity Sunday confess and receive from the hands of their respective parish priest or some other of their Ordinary's appointment, shall not be absolved by any but the said Ordinary or such as he deputes for that purpose, they shall all be excluded from the sacrifice of the Mass, and if they chance to die in that state, we declare them deprived of the prayers of the faithful and of Christian burial.[227]

These were indeed the traditional punishments for non-fulfillment of the Easter duty but Bishop Gallagher's language suggests that neglect of this fundamental requirement presented a pastoral problem.

The visitation returns for the Easter duty or Paschal requirement record invaluable details of the extent of Catholic practice and conformity in the diocese of Kildare and Leighlin. The figures available for thirty-three of the forty-two parishes in 1820 reveal that the clergy of the diocese had a very detailed knowledge of their parishioners. The twice annual stations in the Easter and Christmas cycles were the means by which this pastoral achievement was effected. (References to half-yearly communicants are to the Easter and Christmas reception of the sacraments.) It is clear that reception of penance and communion at Easter and Christmas were norms expected of Irish Catholics. Taken as a whole the visitation returns indicate that the number of absentees was very low.

Doyle's Diocesan Book, 1819–20, lists details of visitation returns made for thirty-three parishes. For four of these parishes – Allen, Arles, Caragh and Maryborough – no comments are made on the reception of the sacraments at Easter. Figures are extant for the remaining twenty-nine parishes. Figures are also available for twenty-four of the twenty-nine parishes for which the original visitation returns compiled on large single sheets survive. No data are given for the parishes of Allen, Bagenalstown, Clonbullogue, Leighlinbridge and Stradbally. Although they are usually undated these returns are for visitations made after 1820. For several of the twenty-four parishes there are two visitation returns and, for some, three returns. Comparison between these later returns and the 1820 returns evidences the improvements in rates of Catholic practice and also the rapid pace of population increase.[228]

In 1820 Doyle noted the remarkable fact that there were no absentees in Edenderry or Suncroft, 'few or none' in the parishes of Ballon, Carbury, and Philipstown. He stated that absentees were 'very few' in the parishes of Bagenalstown, Balyna, Clonmore and Killeigh. In Kildare and Rosenallis parishes there were 'only a few' absentees. Denis Lawlor, P.P. of Hacketstown, in his visitation return to Doyle of 11 August 1830, stated that in his parish there were 3,800 half-yearly communicants : 'I know of no one but Daniel Kirwan who obstinately

refuses to comply with the precept of the church as to confession and communion but I would humbly suggest that lenient measures might succeed with him'.
A visitation return for Arles parish stated that there were 'only seven who do not
go to their duty at Easter. We call them all in'. A second visitation report for Arles
stated that of the parishioners numbering 4,200 'all appeared at their respective
stations but four'. These four individuals: William Nolan, Balili-han; Tom Henry,
Strance; Pat Douge, Strance and William Moran, Ballickmoyler, were named for
the bishop's attention. In Doonane parish, Thomas Tyrrell, parish priest until
1823, stated that 2,500 adults made their Easter duty: 'the number of persons
absent from Easter duty this year is very small, not amounting to more than three
or four housekeepers. There may be some strollers who escape my knowledge,
but the number must be very small'. Tyrrell's successor but one in Doonane
parish, Eugene Kelly from 1826, recorded fifteen persons absent from their Easter
duty.[229]

In his Diocesan Book for 1819–20, Doyle stated that nearly one-third of the
parish of Kill were absentees. This may reflect the situation before Thomas Nolan
replaced his brother Daniel there as parish priest in 1823. Thomas Nolan was
able to report 1,234 half-yearly communicants in the parish. He stated in his
return 'there are 8 or 9 who did not comply with their Easter duty'. In Abbeyleix
where 2,500 approached the sacraments half-yearly the visitation report stated
'we have not more than about ten who don't present themselves for confession
every half-year and those few go occasionally'.[230]

Matthew O'Reilly, P.P., in a return for Philipstown, stated that 'reckoning
from about the age of eleven upwards there are about 3,450 in the parish very few
of whom do not present themselves at Easter and at Christmas especially at the
former time – not above 15 or 20'. James Maher, P.P. of Paulstown noted twenty
absentees in 1830. In 1820 there were 'several hundreds' absent in Clane, but
Malachy McMahon as parish priest made a later return which enumerated 3,000
annual communicants and a total of twenty absentees: ten in Staplestown, four in
Rathcoffey and six in Clane. Similarly in Killeshin a first visitation return noted
three hundred absentees but a second return gave only twenty. A change of parochial personnel may well have been responsible for this improvement. The number
of half-yearly communicants in Ballyadams was 4,347; 'the number who do not
approach the sacraments at Easter as nearly as can be ascertained – 21'.[231]

The visitation return for Rathvilly stated that 'not more than 30 neglect to
approach the Blessed Sacrament at Easter'. A second return gave the same figure. The 1820 figure for Newbridge noted about forty absentees. Thomas Nowlan,
P.P., Newbridge, commented that there were 1,800 adults as accurately as he
could ascertain and of those between thirty or forty neglected their Easter duty.[232]

Rev. Matthew Fanning in a visitation report of *c*.1830 stated that there were
2,920 half-yearly communicants in Raheen. There were about seventy absentees
'some of whom have since presented themselves'. In a second visitation return

dated 9 July 1832 Fanning numbered his half-yearly communicants at about 3,000. Absentees from the Paschal requirement were forty to fifty. He added incongruously that about 300 of the 3,000 had not approached communion that Easter – '200 of these have been Whitefeet'.

In Ballinakill parish in 1820 Doyle noted 400 absentees of whom forty were obstinate. Rev. Roger Molony, parish priest, in a later visitation return reported that 4,500 had received Easter confession: 'I calculate between 70 and 100 absent'. Stradbally parish in 1820 had eighty absentees. The first visitation return for Baltinglass enumerated 3,862 adults making their Easter duty: 'those who did not approach the sacraments last Easter, 80, obstinate sinners, 36'. A second return put the number of half-yearly communicants at 4,200 and stated that there were at least 100 absentees. A third return, dated 25 September 1832, listed 80 absentees. In Clonmore parish 4,152 adults made their Easter duty. John Kelly, parish priest, commented that 'of those who did not approach the sacraments or offered themselves before the time expired that had been allotted them, nearly 100'. This was an absentee rate of two-and-a-half per cent. A second return for Clonmore made during the administration of Philip Healy, P.P., from 1829 stated 'the absentees will be in the chapels' for the episcopal visit, undoubtedly to be publicly chastised by Doyle.[233]

In Borris parish in 1820 Doyle had noted 300 or 400 absentees. In 1832 when nearly 5,000 received at Easter there were 'obstinate nearly 200' or less than four per cent. In St Mullin's in 1820 Doyle listed 2,237 annual communicants and 100 absentees. In a later return for that parish, Thomas Moore, P.P., had 2,500 adults of whom about 150 did not approach the sacraments at Easter. He listed 26 names – for example: 'Larry Tobin, Ballyknockcrumpin, several years; Paddy Murphy, Drummond for years' – no doubt these received special attention from Doyle.

In 1820, 200 absentees were listed for Myshall, 'of these 6 or 8 are abominable'. This comment by Doyle would seem to imply that the vast majority of absentees could be made conform but some few could not be made amenable to Catholic norms. Laurence Cummins, P.P., Myshall, in a later visitation return stated that he had 2,300 half-yearly communicants and 'very few [were] totally absent from [the] Easter duty, several present themselves, and do not afterwards for a long time seek confession'.[234]

Maurice Kearney, administrator of Graiguenamanagh parish, stated that 4,500 persons frequented Easter and Christmas confessions, 'the greatest number absent are the inhabitants of Graigue, particularly boatmen'. A second visitation return gave the number of half-yearly communicants at 5,125 and recorded the number absent at Easter as 'at least 200'. Part of the explanation for this figure may perhaps be found in the major row between priest and people in Graiguenamanagh which has already been examined.

Bishop Doyle stated that Naas parish in 1820 had 'not many absentees, not more than 100'. This seems to be a benchmark figure for Doyle. Anything less

than 100 absentees in a parish seems to have been regarded as a reasonably satisfactory rating. A later return for Naas, signed by Gerald Doyle, P.P., and dated 21
October 1822, noted that the number of absentees was 'about 300'. The town
parishes of Tullow and Portarlington had 300 and 400 absentees respectively in
1820. This suggests that there may have been better fulfillment of the Paschal
requirement in rural areas than in town parishes. Rev. M.P. Malone in his visitation return for Tinryland parish, dated 16 June 1832, stated that he had 3,000
adults in Tinryland and Bennekerry and of that number nearly 300 had not received at Easter: 'those for the most part in the vicinity of Carlow'. Clonegal in
1820 had 500 absentees but 'few obstinate'. A later return by Martin Doyle, P.P.,
reported that the number of adults who approached the sacraments was 4,000 of
whom about forty did not approach. The numerically largest number of absentees in any parish was recorded for Mountrath, population 10,000, where the
visitation return stated that there were 'about one thousand who don't approach
the sacraments'. There may be an anomaly here as the population seems too high
and Doyle's 1820 return records only forty absentees.[235]

Overall the visitation returns for the Easter duty manifest firm evidence of
the very satisfactory levels of Catholic practice in the diocese of Kildare and
Leighlin in the 1820s and early 1830s. The rates of practice were clearly increasing during this period. Where there were parochial problems which related to
poor pastoral performance by particular priests, Doyle, by switching personnel,
invariably achieved improved rates of practice. The number of absentees *vis-à-
vis* the total Catholic population expected to be present is invariably very low in
percentage terms. The figures bespeak an impressive achievement by Doyle and
his parochial clergy.

In his 1820 and 1821 pastorals, Doyle admonished his flock to receive the
eucharist regularly. In the latter pastoral he stated that 'those Christians who do
not participate of the Blessed Eucharist are deprived of almost every source of
grace – like withered branches they are cut off from the tree of life, and are fit
only to become fuel for eternal fire'. Nor would affected reverence for the sacrament excuse the faithful 'from the disobedience you are guilty of by abstaining
from it'. In this pastoral the bishop encouraged the clergy and the faithful to
promote and augment the confraternity of the Blessed Sacrament in each parish.
No means were more efficacious for those 'anxious to become perfect in Christian virtue' than frequent participation in the eucharist.[236] The sacrament of communion was to be approached in a very reverent fashion and the manner of its
reception was very strictly delineated. Communicants were expected to be decently and modestly dressed and it was very disrespectful to approach the altar
unshaved, with unwashed face, hands or in dirty apparel, unless in cases of necessity.[237] The question of a clean set of clothes did pose problems for many. To
receive communion one was obliged to fast from midnight.

For many practising Catholics twice annual communion – one at Easter and the other at Christmas – was probably the norm. The average number of monthly communicants in thirty-three parishes of the diocese in 1820–23 was 272.[238] In a circular letter to his clergy in 1821 Doyle drew their attention to the fact that 'in some parishes'[239] (probably three: Ballyadams (600); Clonmore (450); Mountrath (500)), where there were only two officiating clergymen the number of monthly communicants exceeded 400. This was obviously a figure to be aimed for. There is as yet a dearth of information on Irish Catholic pre-famine communion practice. Hoppen and Corish have focussed on Waterford Cathedral where in 1840 the communicants averaged 350 each Sunday with over 600 on the first Sunday of the month.[240] Many parishes of Kildare and Leighlin compare favourably with this later Waterford datum. In 1820–23 the figure of 600 monthly communicants was returned for the parishes of Ballyadams and Tullow and in 1829 for Hacketstown and Rathvilly.[241]

For only four out of forty-one parishes for which we have data can we state with some certainty that the number of monthly communicants fell below 100 in 1820–23 and remained below that figure in 1829. In Carbury fifty to sixty 'devout persons' received monthly in 1820–23; we have no data for the parish in 1829 but Doyle returned an entry of 'few' for the number in the confraternities. Balyna parish had eighty parishioners who received monthly in 1820–23; we have no information for the parish in 1829. The backward parish of Rosenallis, for which we have no information in 1820–23 had only eighty monthly communicants in 1829. Clonaslee parish (erected out of Rosenallis in 1828) had eighty-seven monthly communicants and a similar number of confraternity members. The poor parish of Doonane (no data for 1820–23) had eighty monthly communicants in 1829.[242] No less than ten parishes in 1829 returned the same number of monthly communicants as confraternity members.[243] However in twenty-three parishes (for which we have information) the number of monthly communicants exceeded the number of confraternity members and there was little correlation between the figures.

MARRIAGE, CLANDESTINITY AND TAMETSI

Doyle and his clergy used every means in their power to prevent early and improvident marriages[244] but any diocesan clergyman who refused to marry a couple who were lawfully entitled to be married incurred suspension.[245] Among the poor and ignorant, those 'almost incapable of estimating the consequences of their own acts',[246] the highest incidence of marriage was recorded even though young couples in these circumstances had little means of subsistence for the inevitable multiple offspring of their unions.

The documentation on sexual behaviour generally is sparse. Public sinners were denounced by Doyle on visitation. Detail is extant in only a few cases. The parish priest was required to deliver in writing the names of public sinners with some account of their sins. A visitation return for Clonmore parish drew attention to 'John Tallon of Knockadumcoil [who] has lived for years in a state of concubinage'; 'Pat. Tallon of [the] same place has attempted a marriage with a female by whom he has a large family – he has done so knowing that his real wife is still living'; 'Denis Duigan ... is living in bad habits with a female'. An undated visitation return for Baltinglass parish stated: 'The poor, in general, in this town who have houses, receive as lodgers persons of the worst description of character. Idle and immoral young women find with them a home and live with them for months'. A pencilled note in Doyle's hand on the back of a Kill parish visitation return states: 'Pat. Murphy lives in the house with a woman with whom he had a child at Castlewarden – profligate female Margt. Keerane'. In 1830 Doyle detected a certain looseness in sexual morals among the poor, who 'are thrown together in the same huts, form intimacies that are often very criminal, and then seek escape from that state of criminality by entering into marriage'.[247] This was the only method of legitimising and making respectable a liaison which had perhaps resulted in pregnancy. Other solutions for an unwanted pregnancy – abortion, infanticide and desertion – were far from unknown but their frequency is virtually impossible to quantify. This is a little researched subject but attention has been correctly drawn to the fairly frequent occurrence of infanticide in pre-famine Tipperary.[248] In 1816 Bishop Corcoran gave Doyle power to absolve a penitent guilty of the crime of procuring abortion.[249] Before the parliamentary inquiry on the state of the Irish poor, Doyle acknowledged that he was aware of a 'good many' cases of infanticide but he was not prepared to elaborate: 'I know more than an ordinary person upon that subject, but my ministry is such that I think it would be prejudicial to its interest if I were to give the evidence sought for ..'. He had an extreme abhorrence of infanticide and felt that his opinions on the subject would not be objective.[250] He also attested to a 'good many' cases of child desertion.[251] Illegitimacy figures were above the national average in Carlow and Queen's County because the fathers of such children frequently refused to marry the mothers.[252] In at least one instance illegitimate children were excluded from daily attendance at a Catholic school in the diocese. In January 1831 the bishop wrote to the superioress of the Mountrath Brigidine convent stating:

> I do not wish you should admit to your school any illegitimate children, or the child of any person of bad repute; and though I feel the severity of visiting on the child the iniquity of the father, yet it is necessary in the present instance, in order to preserve the character of your school, and may operate to the correction of the parents.[253]

Doyle suggested that a place and time be set aside, once or oftener each week, to give religious instruction to those who were thus deprived of regular schooling

through no fault of their own.[254] The episcopal committee on church discipline
in 1829 recommended that none but married women be purified after childbirth.[255] Cohabitation outside the married state placed couples outside the pale
of Catholic society. It was claimed that the only convert made by the Protestant
crusade, in Carlow town in a two-year period, was an adulterous woman. Rev.
James Maher made the details of her case public:

> This unhappy woman ... had some years before been convicted of adul-
> tery before the bishop. Her husband, a poor labouring man, had accepted
> of £20 damages, paid to him by the author of his shame, through the hands
> of the Rt Rev. Dr Doyle and was again reconciled to his unfaithful wife –
> she returned to her 'accomplice' and has, until lately, lived with him in
> habits of gross and public delinquency. I myself have remonstrated with
> her, and to arrest the scandal arising from her conduct, have caused her to
> be excluded from the lodging houses of R.C.s. Still persevering in her evil
> ways she and her guilty paramour have been denounced in our chapels as
> public and scandalous sinners, driven as it were from C. Society, she pro-
> fessed herself a Protestant nearly two years past, and since that period has
> placed herself beyond the reach of our censure .... [256]

In conformity with the Council of Trent, Doyle's diocesan statutes of 1821
decreed that no marriage was to be solemnised, without sufficient cause, until
three days after the parties had prepared themselves by confession and communion. This was a regulation stressed by the episcopal conference in 1829.[257] Persons who eloped (as a means of forcing parental consent to their union) were not
to be married until the female had been 'removed from the power or influence of
the man'.[258] They were obliged to pay double the ordinary marriage fee but if any
impediment of which they were aware existed between them 'they need not entertain any hope of obtaining a dispensation'.[259] Doyle had a marked reluctance to
grant dispensations, the issuing of which he looked upon as tending to relax the
salutary discipline of the church.[260]

When Elizabeth Dowling and Maurice Prendergast of Monasterevan parish,
who were related in the second and third degrees, petitioned Doyle for a dispensation he refused on the grounds that their own parish priest did not recommend
it, because of parental objection. The couple eloped, probably hoping thereby to
obtain a dispensation more readily, but they were to be disappointed:

> Dr Doyle ... stated that from the conduct of the parties, he would never
> grant leave in their case, to their union – and when applied to a second
> time, he repeated his former decision, and added – the parties might ap-
> ply to the Holy See for relief.[261]

Archbishop Troy requested his suffragan to allow the couple's parish priest to write to Rome on their behalf.[262] Another case dating from 1832 clearly reveals Doyle's unwillingness to grant dispensations and the difficulties he faced in implementing church law on marriage. The bishop of New York, Dr Paul Dubois, wrote to the archbishop of Dublin, pleading for a dispensation permitting a 'modest and religious' couple, who had eloped to America, to reside in their native diocese of Kildare and Leighlin. Compliance with this request, replied Doyle, would only give rise to very great evils. The couple in question, he wrote, were

> as licentious, as wicked and as obstinate as any other pair who ever sought refuge in America. In their family incest, elopement with their usual consequences were household vices, and the strongest and unrelaxed efforts of the bishop and clergy of the district in which they lived were necessary to reform the habits of the people on the subject of marriage.[263]

This couple having first attempted to deceive their own bishop had now misrepresented themselves to the bishop of New York. Of the male party, Doyle commented:

> For the means to which he resolved to extort from me a dispensation were of the most malignant and abominable kind. He endeavoured also by bribes and terror to induce Mr Delany [P.P., Ballinakill] to second his views, but that clergyman acted as became him and exposed himself to the hatred of a wicked and numerous faction in his parish and the adjoining country rather than compromise his sense of duty. We have chiefly by our conduct in this case, succeeded in arresting a torrent of licentiousness in that part of the diocese where the ties of nature, the sanctity of marriage, parental authority and filial children were almost generally disregarded.[264]

Doyle asked his metropolitan to convey to the bishop of New York 'his inability to sanction in any way the cohabitation within my diocese of the persons mentioned'.[265]

Marriage within the forbidden degrees of consanguinity (which extended to the fourth degree or third cousin) required a dispensation from the Ordinary who in turn had to have permission from Rome. Doyle took care to fulfill the canonical requirement exactly.[266] In 1824 the archbishop of Armagh complained to his own vicar-general that his marriage dispensations had been limited by Rome – 'ever cautious in its proceedings' – to forty in six years although four hundred cases would occur in that time, so numerous were applications in his diocese.[267] Pre-famine Ireland was a very populous but intensely localised society where the kin group of medieval origin was still to be found in the more backward regions, as was probably the case in Ballinakill. Inevitably requests for relief from the impediment of consanguinity were frequent, but the number of dispensations allowed to each bishop was limited; the demand which exceeded the supply was satisfied by the irregular clergyman or couple-beggar who officiated at clandestine marriages. Catholic couples who married in the Protestant church obtained the sanction of civil law for their unions and were subsequently confirmed in their married state by the Catholic authorities. Although such a step avoided the complications of recourse to a couple-beggar it was not often resorted to, such was the extent of hostility among Catholics to the idea of marriage in a Protestant church. There is virtually no evidence of cohabitation as a stratagem to force a priest to rectify the scandal by the marriage ceremony: elopement, with its own particular and accepted rituals was the customary strategy employed.

The Council of Trent introduced the decree *Tametsi* to outlaw clandestine marriages which until then, though strictly forbidden, were not void. *Tametsi* stated :

> The Holy synod renders utterly incapable of conducting marriage, all those, who will attempt to contract it, otherwise than in the presence of the Parish Priest, or, another Priest, by leave of the parish priest, or Ordinary, and two or more witnesses; and she decrees, that all such contracts are null and void, as by the present decree she actually does invalidate them.[268]

Marriages otherwise contracted were clandestine and this included the widespread medieval practice where couples simply pledged themselves to one another without entering into a church ceremony.[269] *Tametsi* rendered all mixed marriages (between Catholics and Protestants) null and void unless entered into before a Catholic clergyman. This regulation conflicted directly with the civil law in Ireland. The penal statute, 19 Geo. 11, c. 13 (1746) laid down that a marriage contracted before a Catholic priest where one or both of the partners were Protestant, was void in law, and the officiating priest guilty of a felony.[270] A suspended priest was executed for officiating at a mixed marriage in 1726.[271] The penalty incurred by priests was not abolished until 1833 (3 & 4 Will. IV, c. 102)[272] although it was commuted to a fine in 1793 and more usually a sentence of imprisonment[273] (though mixed marriages so contracted remained void in law until 1870).[274]

Nevertheless *Tametsi* was published originally for most of the province of Armagh in 1587; much more definitely so for the province, with the exception of Meath, in 1678; it was promulgated in some dioceses of Tuam province in 1658 and over the whole province by 1745; in Cashel province the legislation was not introduced until 1775.[275] But most anomalous of all for the uniformity of Irish Catholic discipline was the fact that *Tametsi* had still not been published in the entire province of Dublin, the diocese of Meath and the wardenship of Galway in the first quarter of the nineteenth century. In these dioceses clandestine marriages, though forbidden, were valid whereas in the rest of the country they were null and void. The question of why this lack of uniformity prevailed for so long admits of no simple answer. One might expect that the province of Dublin, relatively the most organised and advanced in the Irish Catholic church, would have been to the forefront in the implementation of Tridentine legislation. However it also followed that in the Dublin province the Established church and indeed the administration of common law were well organised. Contiguity to the old Pale area and the dominance of Dublin diocese within the province, were factors inhibiting the publication of *Tametsi*. Corish has stated that the church authorities

> were reluctant to introduce the Tridentine *Tametsi* legislation, feeling it was better to live with the couple-beggar than face the possibility of civil legislation, which if it followed the lines of the 'Hardwicke Act' in England, would have obliged Catholics to marry in the Protestant parish church.[276]

The civil law had not interfered with Catholic marriage in Ireland and the bishops in the dioceses where *Tametsi* had not been promulgated did not wish to give the authorities any justification for so doing.

Where *Tametsi* was not in force, mixed marriages could take place before Protestant ministers without offending against Catholic canon law. Doyle acknowledged the reticence of the Irish Catholic church to punish couples who were married in this way, even where a couple were civilly married within the forbidden degrees of consanguinity; the 'uniform practice'[277] was to dispense with the existing impediments (unless they were such as were never dispensed with) so that couples could cohabit in a lawful religious union according to the Catholic church. As we have already stated it is perhaps surprising that this tactic was not resorted to with greater frequency by couples with consanguinity problems but the prevailing hostility to Protestantism prevented such a development. In England, Irish immigrants frequently refused to be married in the Protestant church as required by law from 1753.[278]

In Holland and Belgium, where *Tametsi* was published, serious difficulties resulted from Protestant hostility. In consequence Pope Benedict XIV issued a declaration of 4 November 1741 in which he pronounced mixed marriages valid provided they were in accordance with the civil laws, even if *Tametsi* was not observed.[279] The question of the validity of mixed marriages performed by a Protestant minister exercised and divided the Irish church in the decade from 1775 – the year in which the Munster bishops introduced *Tametsi* in their province in the belief that the 'Benedictine legislation' for the Dutch situation constituted a precedent.[280] Dr Troy (and later Dr Murray) did not approve of mixed marriages and in the case of the former supported the civil legislation against such marriages being performed by Catholic priests precisely because it hindered them.[281] Troy determined not to publish *Tametsi* unless Rome ruled that it did not apply to mixed marriages in Ireland.[282] In 1785 in consequence of a case stated to Rome, Propaganda, in a decree of 19 March, ruled that all marriages between Catholics and Protestants were valid in Ireland whether the Council of Trent's decree on matrimony were published or not.[283] Nevertheless Troy felt the times were not propitious for the publication of *Tametsi*. He probably influenced his successor Dr Murray on this question. The 1831 provincial statutes decreed that mixed marriages were surrounded by such difficulties and dangers that they could not be celebrated by the parish clergy without a licence from the Ordinary or vicar-general.[284]

If the Tridentine legislation on marriage was not published in the province of Dublin, the diocese of Meath and the wardenship of Galway, this did not imply that the existing penalties against clandestine marriage were less than ardently upheld. Bishop James Gallagher paid such attention to the problem in his 1748 statutes as to suggest that clandestine marriages presented the foremost pastoral problem in the diocese of Kildare and Leighlin at that time.[285] Clergymen guilty of this breach of church law were undoubtedly treated more severely than couples seeking to be thus married. Dr Gallagher drew up a list of graded punishments which indicated that clandestine marriages were commonplace in the diocese. Under Gallagher's legislation a parish priest was suspended for six months and from half the dues of his benefice for a first offence (that is marrying a couple who were not of his parish without permission). For a second offence he was suspended for six months and deprived of all emoluments of his parish. It was even necessary for the bishop to allow for a third offence for which the erring clergyman incurred ipso facto excommunication and deposition from his parish. A curate who committed the offence of sanctioning a clandestine marriage was suspended and lost any rights to a benefice in the diocese for seven years. For a third such offence he lost all rights to serve in the diocese. The penalty for those clerics who were, one supposes, the greatest offenders had no gradations and was much more severe: 'If any friar, of what order soever, or any other extern priest, marry clandestinely any couple in this diocese, we do hereby declare him excommunicated and to be denounced as such over the diocese'.[286]

Clandestinely married couples were excluded, by Bishop Gallagher's statutes, from mass and the sacraments until they proved their marital status by proper witnesses and by giving the name of the clergyman who married them, any oath or promise to the contrary (probably a frequent occurrence to protect the identity of the couple-beggar) notwithstanding; and until they had made public satisfaction for the scandal they had given.[287] Similar regulations were enforced in Ossory. In Cashel province (1777), Clogher (1789), and Dublin (1789), excommunication was extended not only to the celebrant and the contracting couple but also to witnesses and any persons who co-operated in the marriage arrangements.[288] It seems most probable that legislation similar to these regulations was also enacted for the diocese of Kildare and Leighlin.

Whether *Tametsi* was received or not (and allowing for the 1785 rescript) Doyle and his brothers on the episcopal bench did not consider clandestine, marriages which were solemnised by Catholic or Protestant clergymen regularly entitled to officiate even if the couples they married came from outside their parishes. Rather, the term 'clandestine' in the Irish context referred specifically to marriages performed by discredited clergymen of either Catholic or Protestant denomination, who were known as couple-beggars or 'Father Tackems'.[289] By the 1820s it was very unlikely that a Catholic priest of good standing would perform such a ceremony, but the couple-beggars had been excluded by the church from its jurisdiction and so they could do as they pleased. The state too was more concerned to penalise couple-beggars, of either church, than to punish priests regularly on the mission who celebrated mixed marriages. Between 1820 and 1832 six irregular Catholic priests were convicted for celebrating marriages where both parties were Protestant. They were each fined £500 and committed to jail for non-payment, but had their sentences remitted on application to the lord lieutenant.[290] At the Maryborough Spring assizes in 1831, Richard Sandys, a degraded Protestant clergyman, was sentenced to death for feloniously celebrating a marriage between two Protestants, and another between a Protestant and a Catholic at Mountrath. He was reprieved but received a similar sentence in 1835, and again in 1841.[291] Doyle's legislation on clandestine marriage was very definitely in the tradition of his predecessor Dr Gallagher. His 1821 diocesan synod decreed that:

> those married clandestinely and those who assist at such marriages being excommunicated are to be excluded from hearing mass or entering in to our place of worship, unless for the purpose of hearing sermons or spiritual instruction and from all the sacraments (except in articulo mortis) for six months after which they are henceforth *to be referred to us only or our vicar-general* to be further dealt with as their crime deserves. Note, the six months' exclusion from assisting at mass are to be spent in works of penance which on Sundays shall be public, such as kneeling outside the chapel door to beg the prayers of the faithful, whilst they enter, and should any of those concerned refuse to perform such penance they need not expect during their obstinacy to be loosed from their censure.[292]

Late in 1823 Doyle wrote to Propaganda indicating that he desired the Tridentine discipline on marriage to be established throughout Ireland. Clandestine marriages were valid in some dioceses, invalid in others, and this state of affairs was frankly unsatisfactory. He feared resistance from 'turbulent' priests but suggested that Propaganda should write to his metropolitan about the implementation of *Tametsi*.[293] Cardinal Consalvi wrote to Dr Murray stating that he had been informed that in certain dioceses *Tametsi* had not been promulgated and that 'gravia scandala' often arose in consequence. In dioceses where the decree had been published without much difficulty its implementation did not always follow. Propaganda greatly regretted this situation and asked that it be resolved. Consalvi asked Murray to inform him in confidence what exactly was the explanation for this situation. Could *Tametsi* be now published throughout all Ireland without causing disturbance?[294]

Archbishop Murray consulted the bishops concerned. Dr James Keating of Ferns was very definitely against the implementation of *Tametsi*; he feared 'unpleasant sensations in a certain quarter' if the decree were published – this may be an oblique reference to evangelical hostility. He believed that *Tametsi* would occasionally bring priests into conflict with the civil and ecclesiastical laws.[295] Dr Keating did not elucidate, but annulled clandestine marriages could give rise to disputes over property inheritance. The party to such a marriage who married again could be exposed to a charge of bigamy in civil law and the priest could be an accessory to the fact.[296] Bishop Keating maintained that his parochial clergy 'in many instances would feel great reluctance' in publishing *Tametsi*. Its introduction 'would increase our difficulties which are numerous enough'.[297] The bishop of Ossory, Dr Marum, favoured publication but even he warned that 'there may be local circumstances which would justify the non-observance of a law of this nature'.[298] The outlook of Dr Ffrench, Catholic warden of Galway, is not recorded. The only other prelate directly concerned was the aged Dr Plunkett of Meath. His opinion, as expressed in 1821, was that it was in the general interest of a uniform discipline that *Tametsi* be introduced.[299] There was however enough in this exchange of views on *Tametsi* unfavourable to its introduction to incline Archbishop Murray to his natural cautious approach.[300] He was not prepared to rush a decision. In his reply to Propaganda he requested more time to think the question over before giving his answer.[301]

The details of Doyle's efforts to effect the promulgation of *Tametsi* over the next three years are not extant but there were 'many delays and disappointments' for him before a consensus in favour of publication was established in 1827. In that year a joint requisition of the bishops concerned, in favour of *Tametsi*, was concurred in by the rest of the hierarchical bench and its implementation sanctioned by the Holy See for the whole of Ireland.[302] *Tametsi* was published in the parishes of Kildare and Leighlin on the first Sunday of Advent (2 December) 1827.[303] The decree required that the banns of marriage (the intention of the parties to marry) be published (announced from the altar) on three successive Sundays before the wedding was to take place. Publication of the banns served to bring the forthcoming marriage to public attention for the purpose of discovering any canonical impediments to its sanction. It frequently happened that the parents of one or other of the parties to be married, generally the parents of the man, refused to give their consent. This did not usually happen among the improvident but among those from the small farmer class and upwards[304] where the made match, the dowry system, and the economic and social consequences of marriage were more fully appreciated. Before the implementation of *Tametsi* the banns of marriage were not generally published in Kildare and Leighlin.[305]

Dr Marum expressed concern in 1824 that the 'enunciation of the banns' would be 'impracticable' in Ireland.[306] The banns were always, according to the bishop of Ossory, dispensed with, where the decree was published. In fact, as historians have noted, to fail to pay for a dispensation from the banns was universally regarded as a sign of great poverty; even the poorest deemed it imperative to obtain the exemption.[307] *Tametsi* allowed gratis for a dispensation from two publications of the banns. Only the vicar-general of the diocese or the rural dean of the district where the marriage was to take place could dispense from the third and final publication of the banns on receipt of one pound sterling to be charitably employed by the bishop.[308] A pound was the most appropriate sum for the dispensation, Dr Murray advised, for 'were any smaller sum sufficient the publication of the banns would go wholly into disuse as it has elsewhere'.[309] There may have been some discord among the bishops, even at the last, over the banns. Murray indicated to Doyle that he 'had not the temerity to send a copy of ... the Manifesto [the printed text of *Tametsi*] to the other prelates concerned in the affairs of the decree, I did mention to each of them the substance of what the rule would be in this diocese respecting the banns'. The archbishop feared that the warden of Galway was likely to experience some opposition to the decree.[310] In 1829 the hierarchical committee on church discipline complained that the banns were 'rarely published'.[311]

Once *Tametsi* was published in his diocese Doyle did not tolerate any deviations from its requirements however harsh the consequences. We may instance the following account dating from 1828 from his instructions to the parish priest of Graiguenamanagh in a case of clandestine marriage. Connolly,[312] misled by Fitzpatrick's poor editing,[313] mistakenly interprets this case as one of common adultery.

> tell the congregation that he and the woman living with him neither are or [*sic*] can be married; that you would marry either of them to any other person; that they and all who were present with them when they attempted to get married in Dublin are excommunicated ....
>
> Enquire if they be in the chapel, and if so, have them removed; and mention that mass cannot be celebrated there or in any place where they are known to be present. Inform the priests of the neighbourhood to whose chapels they might resort of the censure incurred by them; and request they may not permit them to assist at their mass or chapels. Should they present themselves for repentance, require the total separation of them; and the fortune, if paid, to be refunded, and some security that they will

not be found together; and should all this be done, impose some igno-
minious or painful humiliation, to continue till the Visitation. Should they
not repent, you will have less trouble, taking care from time to time to
warn the neighbours when you are down among them to hold no unnecessary communion with them.[314]

The publication of *Tametsi* for the whole of Ireland in 1827 was a reform
which Doyle took great satisfaction in having achieved. To his brother Peter he
commented: 'I have at length accomplished the publication of the Council of
Trent on which as you know I have been intent for some years'.[315] In his Diocesan
Book he recorded: 'It has long been much desired by me and my exertions to
obtain the enforcement of this salutary discipline were ... finally successful'.[316] It
has been claimed that the incidence of clandestine marriage (before 1827) clearly
indicates that the influence which the Catholic clergy 'could hope to exercise
over the marriages of their congregations was at best a limited one'.[317] This argument stretches a point. It must be asserted that couples who resorted to couple-
beggars were simply using a loophole in Irish church discipline to enter into a
valid marriage. Inevitably, while the loophole existed it was exploited. Clandestine marriages did not continue on any significant scale after the publication of
Tametsi in 1827.[318]

PATTERNS AND WAKES

Patterns and wakes were historically religious occasions which had overtones of
collective celebration for the Irish Catholic community. The word pattern is now
a standard corruption of the Irish *pátrún* meaning patron, and itself redolent of
time-worn tradition. In early nineteenth century Ireland the pattern centred on
a penitential parochial pilgrimage to the holy well of a particular saint on the
saint's feast day. Holy wells were (and are) almost invariably connected with ancient church sites, sometimes boasting the remnants of a round tower, though
more often stone crosses of early and medieval origin. The origins of holy wells
need not concern us here. The persistence into the nineteenth century and beyond of pilgrimages to these holy wells lays before us the striking tenacity and
resilience of the Irish Catholic experience over much more than a millennium.

In 1348 Friar Clyn recorded that pilgrims to St Mullin's waded through water, a detail of the pilgrimage made in the parish of that name, which could still
be witnessed in the late nineteenth century.[319] In the medieval period the religious element was the main component of the pattern day and even into the
modern period it was hardly ever lost sight of. The bloodied knees of pilgrims
making their penitential rounds or 'stations' were a familiar sight to many observers. The wells were believed to be sites of especial holiness, where through

the intercession of the patron saint, relief from illness might be granted. The curative powers of the water of the holy well were widely credited with the cure for numerous ailments and the myriad *ex voto* rags and sticks which usually decorated overhanging bushes or trees bore ample testimony to the strength of popular belief.

The church under the penal code adapted itself to the popular domesticity of the pattern day occasion. In Clane parish the pattern was accompanied by the stations of confession[320] and this arrangement seems to have been widespread. In Kiltennel, in Borris parish, which took its name from St Sennil, the pattern was held on 15 June annually, and many priests attended.[321] It is not difficult to imagine the potent superiority of religious custom and oral belief passed on through centuries relating to parochial saints and their ancient churches and holy wells over devotions in the post-medieval parish church, heretofore an impermanent thatched mass-house, if even that, and unlikely to have any such profound historical associations. The pattern day had, of course, more than just its religious aspect; it developed into an all-embracing communal celebration of the sacred and the profane which mirrored the temperament of early modern Ireland. Patterns such as those in Tullow and Myshall and at Glyn in Balyna parish had accompanying fairs on the same day.[322] Patterns became occasions that were not merely penitential but festive, accompanied by scenes of boisterous conviviality and often excessive drinking.

To present an accurate account of the precise numbers of holy wells and patterns extant in Kildare and Leighlin during Doyle's episcopacy is virtually impossible though the ordnance survey name and letter books (with the authority of O'Donovan and O'Curry) and the works of Comerford, O'Toole and Jackson make a detailed survey possible. A total of seventy recorded holy wells and fifty-three pattern day celebrations have been traced, in thirty-five parishes of the diocese.[323] No evidence has been discovered for this custom in twelve parishes or twenty-six per cent of the diocese. Allowance however should be made for two of these parishes – Arles and Ballyfin – both of which were originally part of larger ancient abbacies which had patron saints. Ballinakill, Ballyadams, Carbury, Clonbullogue, Kilcock, Stradbally and Suncroft apparently had no holy wells. Neither had Carlow nor the post-medieval new town parishes of Mountmellick and Portarlington. Although there was a holy well – St Brigid's – in the village of Rosenallis,[324] it was somewhat less usual to find holy wells in urban areas, but especially when they were modern towns.

Killeigh parish had at least seven holy wells; Balyna, six; Bagenalstown, five; Hacketstown and Monasterevan, four; six parishes: Ballon, Borris, Edenderry, Graiguenamanagh, Rathvilly, and Tullow, each had three wells reputed holy. The greatest number of holy wells was associated with St Brigid. Her dulia was carried on at nine holy wells. Brigid was the principal patron saint of the united diocese and the secondary patron of all Ireland. Surprisingly one finds no devotion to Conleth, first bishop of Kildare, another diocesan saint. Eight holy wells were associated with devotion on the universal church feast of the Assumption of the Virgin Mary on 15 August, a noted pattern and fair day throughout Ireland.

There were six patterns celebrating the feast of St John the Baptist on 24 June (two each in Hacketstown and Killeigh; one each in Monasterevan and Kildare) and probably several more. For instance St Lonn's day in Doonane parish was celebrated on 24 June. Connolly has associated evidence for a strong devotion to St John the Baptist with midsummer – an important time of celebration and feasting in the rhythmical annual work cycle which perhaps predated Christianity.[325] French authorities, however, insist that the festival of St John the Baptist had an integrity of its own; moreover that the idea that a number of pre-christian feasts were given respectability by the church is 'seductive but facile'. The leading folklorist, Van Gennep, has stated that

> you cannot read a book or an article on the feast of St John without finding the cliché: 'this is a remnant of sun worship from pre-christian times' with the rider: 'Sun worship existed in all peoples from the very remotest times'... the feast of St John cannot be either solar in general or solstitical in particular by its essence and origin because it does not coincide with the longest day of the year which all people could have determined.[326]

In the late eighteenth and early nineteenth centuries the popular festivities which took place on the eve and feast-day of 24 June were a source of dismay to many bishops particularly in the dioceses of Meath and Dublin.[327] St John the Baptist's day was a church holy day and this seems to have provided a convenient excuse for a pattern on this day to wells where the founding saint's dulia had fallen into desuetude. We shall later examine how Doyle went to the heart of this matter by seeking from Rome the abolition of Irish church holy days which had become notorious for public festivities.[328]

The national saint, Patrick, had four pattern days in his honour. The patron saint of Leighlin, Laserian, had two pattern days – at Bagenalstown and Old Leighlin respectively on 18 April; St Fintan of Clonenagh also had two patterns on 17 February in Mountrath and Raheen (which were divisions of the ancient abbacy of Clonenagh). St Fortchern's dulia took place in Bagenalstown and Tullow on 11 October; St Fionnan was commemorated in Killeigh and Rosenallis. Single holy wells were identified with twenty-one other saints of the early Irish church.[329]

Pattern day pilgrimages in early nineteenth century Kildare and Leighlin were impressive in number but weak in reality. In this respect the diocese is no different to the national trend; from the mid to the late eighteenth century, at least until the famine, the pattern day ritual went through a swift transition from strength to decay and disappearance. In this context it proved impossible to asso-

ciate twenty-three holy wells with their particular patrons. Their names had passed
out of the folk memory and the wells were given their nomenclature from their
immediate topography or less usually from association with a priest. The Catholic church was one agent in this process of change but not the only one. Everywhere, it seemed to knowledgeable observers such as John O'Donovan and Eugene
O'Curry, that the old customs and traditions of an archaic society were in rapid
retreat before the advance of modernising social and cultural influences. In
Clonaslee parish a pattern day had been celebrated at St Manmon's well but
O'Donovan in 1838 'met no one able to tell me the day or month in which this
pattern was held'.[330] In Doonane parish where the 'very famous' St Abban had
resided, he found that 'This Saint Abban is no longer venerated at Kilabban as
the patron or first founder of the church there'.[331] In Hacketstown parish,
O'Donovan significantly remarked that it was the 'old-fashioned' people who
were accustomed to perform the penitential stations until they were discontinued in 1833.[332] Of Killeigh parish he stated that the holy wells were resorted to
for various cures 'but the natives are now getting too sensible'.[333] In Edenderry
parish the people were 'all anglicised'.[334] Interestingly in this context it is probable that Bishop Doyle spoke Irish.[335] In the course of his lifetime the language
was lost to a large part of the country. Yet in his writings there is hardly a reference to the language or its decline.[336] That decline was surprisingly fast in the
pre-famine decades. A member of the ordnance survey reported from Aghaboe in
Queen's County that 'a few years will see the Irish language completely extinct
in this part of the country. Even at present we cannot expect to find a person in
every parish who can speak the language'.[337] Writing from Mountrath on 28 November 1838 O'Donovan was even less sanguine: 'the natives of this county ...
have lost their old language'.[338] Arriving in Castlecomer from Tullow, Eugene
O'Curry, made a curious but telling remark which captured the social and cultural transition he noticed between counties Carlow and Kilkenny:

> I am now on Irish ground, not so when at the east side of the Barrow
> where they have nothing but bad English, white frieze, good potatoes, and
> the girls all wearing shoes, stockings and bonnets but here, glory to them,
> they all speak fine Irish, and English, wear blue frieze, drink whiskey,
> dance and fight, the girls all going barefooted and bareheaded, in short
> here is every good manner and custom that ought to distinguish a decent
> country town in Ireland.[339]

Obviously Castlecomer presented a rich body of oral source material to the great
Irish scholar but there was much in O'Curry's romantic encomium for Old Ireland – poverty, lack of temperance and indiscipline – whose passing Doyle, for
one, did not regret.

There is no evidence, however, that Doyle sought to eradicate pattern days.

Although his ministry was marked by the imposition of Tridentine standards and procedures it was not Tridentine in the fashion in which Paul Cullen's was subsequently ultramontane, as for instance in the question of the stations of confession. Rather Doyle sought to contain what was too exuberant in the Irish religious tradition but to retain what had stood the test of time. What was best in the domestic religious tradition was blended into the Tridentine model. Restraint rather than condemnation or elimination marked his general approach to patterns. Speaking of patterns in 1825 he observed 'we endeavour to restrain that custom as much as we can'. Referring to the Lough Derg pilgrimage, allegedly the source of some notable abuses and a focus for fierce evangelical criticism, Doyle would only allow that 'It is hard ... to root out prejudices'.[340]

The suppression of five patterns which can be attributed to Doyle was relatively small *vis-à-vis* the total number of pattern days celebrated in the diocese during his episcopacy. In 1812 William Cullen, P.P., Leighlinbridge, suppressed the riotous pattern of St Laserian when a man was killed.[341] Doyle was undoubtedly the author of the suppression of the Doonane pattern to St Lonn's well on 24 June. Elderly natives recounted memories to Comerford of people flocking to the pattern where 'fields of tents [were] set up for their accommodation'. In the 1880s when patterns were again encouraged by the official church, the well was visited by pilgrims, especially on the festivals of the Blessed Virgin.[342] In the second half of the nineteenth century devotion to Mary was particularly encouraged by the Catholic church. The pattern of St Columcille at Sandyford in Hacketstown parish was discontinued 'in consequence of some abuses'.[343] It seems probable that the two other Hacketstown holy wells at which patterns were held on 24 June were also suppressed. 'In consequence of the bad effects of whiskey' a 'numerous pattern' in Killeigh parish on St John's day and SS Peter and Paul's day was abolished by the clergy.[344] The pattern of St Patrick in Rathvilly 'had to be discontinued on account of abuses'.[345] The Goresbridge pattern to Lady's Well on 15 August was prohibited by the parochial clergy, possibly by James Maher, P.P., 1830–33.[346] The parish of Tullow had three pattern days: St Torannan on 12 June; St Fortchern, who had a special local significance, on 11 October (there is no evidence of wells in either case); and the feast of the Assumption of Our Lady on 15 August. The pattern at Lady's Well was discontinued and a fair, held on 8 September, substituted and known as the pattern fair.[347] The suppression of most of these patterns was at the discretion, it would appear, of the parochial clergy rather than the bishop himself. This writer is inclined to the view, albeit from the negative evidence that Doyle makes no mention of patterns in his annual pastorals, that the abuse of such occasions did not constitute a major problem in his diocese.

It is perhaps surprising that the 'festive wake' was not a problem but such seems to be the case. This was probably due in part to Doyle's predecessor Bishop James Gallagher who in 1748 anathemised the festive wake in a series of famous strictures.[348] He inveighed against crowds who flocked to wakes 'to abandon themselves to unchristian diversions of lewd songs, of brutal tricks called fronsy fronsy' and decreed that the numbers admitted to the wake house should be strictly curtailed, a rule which must have been almost unenforceable in practice. More useful was his decree that no clergyman was to say mass where 'immodest songs, profane tricks or immoderate crowds are permitted'. Gallagher also forbade the 'heathenish customs of loud cries and howlings' which constituted keening and which the Catholic church had been opposing for centuries but which still lingered on. The diocesan clergy were commanded to banish the keen by imposing arbitrary punishment of prayer, fasting and alms on the keeners. Professional keeners who persisted in their occupation were to be excommunicated and denounced.[349]

Fitzpatrick refers to Doyle's annoyance at the mock levity of a wake he attended in County Wexford in 1810.[350] He also states that 'funeral entertainments' were among the first abuses tackled by Doyle.[351] As we have already noted, Doyle, in his 1821 pastoral, forbade confraternity members from attending wakes. The diocesan statutes stated:

> Night wakes, at which a large and indiscriminate concourse of persons attend, are prohibited; and the clergy are charged to encourage the recital of prayers and the reading of pious books at the obsequies of the dead; to dissuade the use of tobacco, and of whatever may be attended with expense, or become an incentive to sin; and to require that the corpse be interred at an early hour.

In the extant parochial visitation returns, wakes are only mentioned in two instances as public abuses worthy of the bishop's attention. The Baltinglass return of 25 September 1832 stated that plays at wakes were 'at least very prevalent' and 'rather more prevalent than in other parishes'. The St Mullin's return stated 'we understand that night wakes ... are getting some encouragement in some parts of the parish'.

No doubt Doyle tackled the abuse of wakes wherever such was found; yet the festive wake was evidently not one of his major pastoral concerns. The 1831 provincial statutes recommended that the funeral mass be celebrated in the church and not the home. Disorderly wakes were forbidden and were to be eliminated. Young persons and single people were prohibited from attending night wakes.[352] Nonetheless one does not get the impression that these were pressing problems in the Dublin province in 1831. The strictures were considerably milder than Bishop Gallagher's impressive fulminations of 1748.

DRINK AND TEMPERANCE

Drunkenness was the main abuse prevailing on festive occasions. Doyle's attitude to the problem can be examined under two headings: firstly his relations with the temperance movement which provide a general context for the subject; secondly his pastoral activity within the diocese.

In December 1829 Rev. George W. Carr,[353] a Protestant clergyman and secretary to the New Ross Temperance Society, one of the first such societies in Ireland, invited Doyle to found such a society in Carlow. The bishop professed a 'hatred and abhorrence quite peculiar'[354] of drunkenness. 'Every Christian,' he responded, 'must look upon drunkenness and excessive drinking as one of the most debasing and hateful vices which infest the humankind'. He did not lament the medical consequences of alcoholism, namely the death of the drunkard which was a blessing to the family he had scandalised or corrupted by his influence. But while he would have gladly co-operated with the Temperance Society, Doyle continued:

> I am not fitted in any one respect to undertake the formation of one; and, even if I were, I am not prepared to express to others a confidence which I do not feel, that such societies in this country, at this time, and with our present laws and social government, can be productive of any great, or extensive, or permanent good; but yet, as some good may be effected by them they certainly deserve support.[355]

These remarks from so influential a quarter, although indicative of goodwill, could only be construed as unhelpful if not damaging to the nascent temperance movement. Doyle had doubts about the social origins of the movement. The moral influence of the higher classes over the lower classes would be very small. Gentlemen temperance campaigners did not always practise what they preached. There would be difficulty embracing all ranks of society in temperance clubs. Somewhat resignedly Doyle posited another reason why the temperance movement would ultimately fail: in the towns 'where the vice of excessive drinking principally prevails', temperance lobbyists would have to face the diligent opposition of all the drunkards, publicans, brewers, distillers and grocers who retailed whiskey. But Doyle found the 'great and insurmountable obstacle' to the 'torrent of drunkenness' in the revenue laws. Temperance could be principally achieved if the chancellor of the exchequer deemed it more expedient 'to promote good morals than to secure a large revenue'. Doyle believed that the elimination of the drinking of spirits was impossible but that it would be perfectly practicable to reduce the use of spirits 'to one-fiftieth part of its present amount'. Acknowledging his own acquaintance with the making of malt and the brewing of beer, he had no hesitation in claiming that if malting and brewing were exempted from tax, the whiskey tax raised, the number of licenses reduced, then 'drunkenness in a little time would almost disappear from the country'.[356] In Doyle's view temperance was to be attained not primarily through societies with that aim but through an enlightened exchequer policy which would steer the country's drinking public away from highly priced spirits to the more attractively priced malt and beer. He advocated abstinence from spirits but at no point in this letter did he recommend teetotalism.

Doyle's letter on the drink problem, published in early January 1830, was naturally viewed by the temperance campaigners as prejudicial to their interests and as a check on their progress. James Henry, a Dublin temperance advocate, replied seriatim and cogently to Doyle. The bishop sought the unity of all ranks in temperance societies but, Henry replied, numerous societies from distinct classes had been successful. Doyle stated that the lack of upper class influence on the lower orders would hinder the inculcation of temperance but to date these societies had not been sponsored by the upper classes. In the United States where they had been joined by great numbers of the Presbyterian population, they were founded by ordinary clergymen. As to Doyle's reference to the opposition of the retailers of spirits, Henry countered succinctly : 'it is scarcely consistent to allege as an obstacle to their success, those very evils to remedy which they were instituted'.[357] On the revenue laws Doyle's correspondent took a fundamentalist stand. There would be no need to change the law if people simply stopped drinking. Temperance would hardly receive assistance from new laws; the reform must be spontaneous.[358] Unlike Doyle, Henry had no regard for the political dimension in curbing the excessive use of alcohol. Nevertheless Doyle was induced by such arguments to take a more favourable view of the temperance movement. His initial doubts about the movement as a new enthusiasm from the evangelicals (of whom G.W. Carr was one) disappeared as he foresaw the capacity of the movement to promote a moral reformation.

Two months later, in March 1830, Doyle corresponded with the Quaker, Dr Joshua Harvey, secretary of the Dublin Temperance Society, assuring him of his zealous co-operation. He confessed that the temperance societies' tracts had sharpened even his 'habitual horror'[359] of drunkenness which he now likened to a 'vice which enters like oil into the bones of a man, and is transmitted with his blood as an inheritance of woe to his children'. Teetotalism, which he compared to the example of individuals of heroic virtue, was something to be aimed for. Thus Dr Harvey's Temperance Society, Doyle maintained, had acted wisely in demanding the complete rejection of all alcohol in its rules, adding 'the imputed fault of their too great rigour or perfection is a mark of their wisdom and a presage of their future efficacy. What you want is publicity'.[360] This second letter on drunkenness was much more in accord with the temperance movement's ideas for the resolution of the problem than Doyle's first. It went even further than some temperance campaigners were prepared to go. A vote of thanks to Doyle was passed at the inaugural meeting of the Hibernian Temperance Society (formed from the Dublin Temperance Society) on 7 April 1830.[361] In 1832 Doyle was one of eighteen vice-presidents of this society.[362] A temperance society was founded in Carlow by Rev. James Maher in 1830.[363]

There were very many public houses in the diocese for licenses were cheap. In the barony of Maryborough East thirty-five licenses were held for the sale of spiritous liquors in 1830; fifty-two licenses were held in Maryborough West. In these two baronies between 1829 and 1831 there were only eight convictions for non-licensed public houses; virtually anyone who sought a license was given one, there were very few refusals.[364] It is difficult to assess to what extent unlicensed or shebeen houses proliferated throughout the diocese. Rev. Nicholas O'Connor stated: 'I never let one of them pass myself that I do not speak against in public', but he admitted 'when they escape my notice, as sometimes they do, it must be more difficult for the revenue officers to know them. I request to the people to give me information, but they are almost afraid to do it.' The shebeen owner was unlikely to be in good standing with the parochial clergy; his liquor often provided the inspiration for illegal activity. Rev. O'Connor maintained that the police did not interfere with unlicensed houses. He drew no distinction between licensed and unlicensed houses when it came to selling a 'bad spirit, half vitriol'.[365]

The subject of excessive drinking receives no more than passing mention in Doyle's pastoral letters with the exception of his final (1834) pastoral. Therein Doyle stigmatised the 'devouring flame',[366] of drunkenness with especial emphasis on spirit and whiskey drinking. In a powerfully expressive fashion he listed the evils of drunkenness. In his first letter on temperance and again in this pastoral, Doyle revealed en passant something of his protective yet dismissive attitude towards women (then so commonplace and not surprising given the status of women). He maintained that drunkenness had a worse effect on women than on men ('it stultifies and brutalises men – and as to women, it reduces their condition far below the condition of the brute').[367] Undoubtedly his main worry was that drunkenness weakened modesty and virtue and rendered the female 'more vile than the dung of the earth'.[368] In his urge to declaim against whiskey drinking Doyle painted a grim picture of the extent of the problem in his diocese:

> I could say with the Prophet, that 'my throat has become hoarse' crying out against that vice, and yet it prevails, nay it thrives and prospers in the midst of the nakedness, the starvation, the desolation which surround us. The cross-roads, the public ways, the streets of our towns and villages, are filled with ale-houses in which whiskey, mixed with a still more active poison, is preferred to the bye-stander at the lowest price; nay the very doors of our places of worship are beset by this iniquity .... [369]

Doyle in this pastoral repeated almost the very words of the 1831 provincial statutes which commanded the clergy to prohibit the sale of intoxicating liquor in the vicinity of churches by every means in their power. Priests were ordered to rebuke seriously and strenuously those who set up shop at almost the entrance to church and also those who frequented these houses 'even on the Sabbath day'.[370] In his invective against spirit drinking Doyle conjured up the fires of hell: 'The law of God condemns drunkenness as a crime which deserves hell ... hell is the proportion of the drunkard, the fire for him will never be extinguished, the worm that will gnaw him shall never die'.[371] Doyle was sorely tempted but ultimately not prepared to forbid diocesan Catholics from all recourse to whiskey drinking lest the injunction be disregarded. Instead he implored his people

> to desist altogether and entirely from the use of ardent spirits, unless after meals and mixed with water. If you use it then, and I wish you did not, let it be taken in small quantity, and not for gratification, but for your health's sake. The use of it for any other end is never free from sin.[372]

This last admonition certainly seems rigorist though perhaps a statement of fact in the context. Even if it were used for medicinal purposes he urged rejection of the idea that spirits were a necessary beverage. At fairs and markets and on journeys he recommended, not whiskey but wholesome food and 'good malt drink' for sustenance.[373]

THE HOLY DAYS' REFORM

Church holy days of obligation (namely days including Sunday on which the faithful were obliged to attend mass and abstain from servile labour) originated in the fourth century and developed in a sporadic and disorganised fashion until at least the mid-sixteenth century and often later.[374] Pre-Reformation England had forty or more holidays of precept (*festa chori et fori*)[375] which was the average number in western Christendom. The excessive number of these feast days was a source of annoyance to the civil rulers of post-Reformation Europe. The Council of Trent made some efforts to impose a uniform discipline. The Roman Breviary and Missal, published in accordance with Trent in 1568 and 1570 respectively, contained a church calendar which sought to regulate holy days throughout the Catholic world. Trent made this calendar obligatory on those who could not prove a prescriptive right of two hundred years in the enjoyment of their own distinctive feast-days.[376] The Tridentine regulation failed to achieve its purpose; it was not taken seriously. In practice there were marked national variations in the observance of holy days and new ones continued to be added to church calendars in several countries until Pope Urban VIII carried out a major reform. In *Universam per orbem*, 16 September 1642, he deprived bishops of the right to institute new ecclesiastical holy days without the permission of the Holy See and he limited the number of holy days to thirty-four.[377]

Pope Benedict XIII reduced the number of full holy days in Spain to only seventeen; there remained however many only partially abrogated holy days on which the hearing of mass was obligatory. Pope Clement XIV made concessions to the Empress Maria Theresa in 1772 but ordered the observance of sixteen full feast-days in Austria; a similar reduction was introduced in Bavaria in 1775.[378] In 1777 Pope Pius VI reduced the holy days of obligation to twelve in England. Work was permitted on two of these, Assumption and SS Peter and Paul, and it appears that only four – Ascension, Corpus Christi, Annunciation and All Saints – of the remaining ten were actually observed as holy days. In effect the Catholic calendar in England was almost equivalent to its Protestant counterpart.[379]

Throughout the eighteenth century, then, the number of holy days to be observed was reduced by Roman decree in several European countries. In the mid-eighteenth century there were thirty-four holy days in the Irish church calendar. In 1755 Pope Benedict XIV removed the obligation of abstaining from servile work on nineteen of these holy days but retained the obligation of attending mass.[380] This proved to be an unworkable compromise in practice because labouring Catholics found it impossible to attend mass and subsequently find employment on the same day. Popular observance of all holy days fell into disrepute through regular transgression. In 1778 at the urgent request of the Irish bishops the obligation to hear mass was removed on the holy days which had been partially abrogated.[381]

This reduction left fifteen full holy days in the Irish church year. Three or four of the moveable feasts sometimes fell on Sundays. In 1825 Bishop Doyle expressed concern that there were still too many Irish church holy days and informed the house of lords' committee on the state of Ireland that it was desirable that the number be further reduced.[382] Doyle's attitude was determined by a multiplicity of factors. The number of holy days applying in Ireland was, he believed, injurious to public industry, and especially to the Catholic labouring class. He estimated that this class numbered three million people and that it was losing two and a quarter million pounds sterling annually because of the prohibition on servile labour on holy days.[383] This temporal detriment was suffered by Catholic labourers to the advantage of their Protestant counterparts who could work on holy days; also benefitting were Catholics of such other groups as farmers, shopkeepers, traders and dealers of all kinds who were permitted by immemorial usage to hold fairs and markets on holy days.[384]

Doyle was also aware of several cases where the observance of holy days had become a source of interdenominational tension.[385] Protestant employers who were hostile to Catholicism occasionally used the powerful threat of redundancy to force Catholic labourers to work on holy days.[386] One Protestant employer, William Burton of Burton Hall, Carlow, complained to Doyle:

> I must have some value for money and think it better for the men to be at
> work than in a state of indolence on holy days, they will be better Catho-
> lics and better characters, half a day is all I claim from those who go to
> mass. But their having been at mass in the morning is to be the only ex-
> cuse for not working the whole day.[387]

Unlike Lord Cloncurry, Doyle did not think the abolition of holy days would
counter the problem of excessive drinking: 'for drunkards will drink at all times'.[388]
But he was cognisant of the scandal often arising from the manner in which the
labouring classes celebrated holy days:

> these idle persons of every age and sex, congregate in towns and villages
> on those days, where they resort in great numbers to taverns where they
> drink to excess, corrupt each others morals, learn to curse and blaspheme,
> enter into illegal combinations, or what is much more frequent quarrel
> and fight with each other, so that the holy day is generally not a day of
> holiness and prayer but a day of idleness, disputation, drunkenness and
> bloodshed, even so as to become an occasion of sin to many thousands and
> to bring reproaches innumerable upon our holy religion.[389]

On 21 August 1828, Doyle wrote to the prefect of Propaganda, Cardinal Capellari,
cogently outlining to him why the number of Irish church holy days should be
retrenched or relief given from the obligation of abstaining from servile work at
least in his own diocese.[390] The routine response of the cardinal prefect, later
Pope Gregory XVI, was to forward Doyle's letter to his metropolitan for an opinion on its contents.[391]

  This was a matter which concerned the entire Irish hierarchy. At the hierarchy's meeting, 5–12 February 1829, Doyle proposed that the pope be requested
to abolish the holy days on Easter Monday,[392] Whit Monday,[393] the festival of St
John the Baptist and the Annunciation. He was seconded by Bishop Kelly of
Waterford and Lismore. The proposal was carried but the motion on the Annunciation was passed by the narrowest of margins: ten votes for, nine against.[394]
Archbishop Murray wrote to Propaganda on behalf of the Irish bishops request-
ing the changes.[395] The Irish case for a reduction was enhanced by the fact that
the American episcopacy was also anxious to secure the same result.[396] The papal
decree, granted on 23 August 1829, abolished the Easter Monday and Whit Monday holy days; it was silent on the Annunciation and relieved the faithful of the
duty of abstaining from servile work on the feast of St John the Baptist but retained the requirement to attend mass, if the bishops unanimously approved of
the cessation.[397]

  Doyle asserted that the partial abrogation of the festival of St John the Baptist
would never have occurred if the pope's advisers had been familiar with condi-

tions prevailing in Ireland. He maintained that the rescript would bring the festival of St John into disrepute and that it was precisely to avert such transgressions that the Irish bishops petitioned Rome for the full abrogation of nineteen holy days in the late eighteenth century.[398] In January 1830 the hierarchy's annual meeting resolved that both the obligation to hear mass and to abstain from servile labour should continue together or cease together and the fast on the vigil of the feast should be abolished.[399] The bishops feared, like Doyle, that if the faithful were permitted to work on a day otherwise to be kept holy they would not fulfill the obligation to hear mass which 'from the fewness of our churches in country places, and the dispersed state of the population requires much time'.[400]

On 3 April 1830, Rev. Christopher Boylan, Roman agent of the Irish bishops and rector of the Irish College, informed Dr Curtis that the request to abolish the fast of the vigil of St John the Baptist's day had been granted but that the obligation to hear mass remained.[401] Curtis, Murray and Doyle were not prepared to accept this decision and were not prepared to implement it in their dioceses. Furthermore the Roman decree was not transmitted to the rest of the hierarchy because these bishops feared it would lead to a 'departure from that uniformity which we are desirous to establish'.[402] An episcopal meeting on 27 June 1831 again resolved, and this time probably with less division, to call for the full abrogation of St John the Baptist's day.[403] This time Rome granted the request.[404]

At he hierarchy's meeting in 1830 Doyle had also moved for an immediate application to the Holy See for a further reduction in the number of holy days – specifically proposing the abolition of Annunciation (25 March); Ascension (*c*.5 May); Circumcision (1 January); and the feast of SS Peter and Paul (29 June).[405] Twenty-two bishops were present at this meeting, of whom not more than eight were against the removal of any single holy day. Yet Doyle, as leader of the majority party of fourteen bishops, had to acknowledge that a 'considerable portion of their brethren, some from one cause and some from another, dissented from them'.[406] No doubt because they realised that division was fatal to their chances of success, the majority party postponed pursuing the matter at Rome. Later in 1830 Doyle drafted a lengthy letter to the pope on behalf of his metropolitan and suffragans, urging the cessation of holy days on the feasts above mentioned, for the province of Dublin alone.[407] The irony was that if this reduction had been granted it would have instituted a new anomaly in Irish church practice and a break from the uniformity which Doyle was so anxious to see established. It seems, however, that on reflection this letter was never sent to Rome. Reform could not be advanced at national level without a broad consensus among the hierarchy. Doyle thus failed to bring about the abolition of these four holy days. He had however achieved the removal for Ireland of the obligation to hear mass and abstain from servile labour on three days – Easter Monday, Whit Monday, and the feast of St John the Baptist. His main motivation in this matter was the transgression of church precept on holy days and the cost to the labouring poor of lost working days. As with the Tridentine legislation on marriage, Doyle, devoted much attention to the question of holy days, though without the same unqualified measure of success.

PUBLIC PEACE

Doyle had only just assumed the role of bishop when he first became aware of a potential pastoral problem with regard to secret societies. Reports reached him in January 1820 of combinations in 'remote' parts of his diocese, to which initially he did not give any credence as they did not emanate from his parochial clergy. However further reports represented King's County as more or less tainted by combinations. A magistrates' meeting at Parsonstown, chaired by Lord Rosse, held that much of the county had succumbed to the influence of agitators. On 19 January 1820, Doyle sought the observations of William Duanne, P.P., Mount-mellick, and rural dean of the reputedly disturbed area. Doyle was concerned that unless the 'infection' was checked by the intense winter cold it would commit some 'ravages amongst our poor people'. Doyle reflected that if the poverty of the peasantry were the cause of the disturbed state of the King's County a similar problem had not manifested itself in County Carlow where, 'so far from thinking of illegal associations, we are exerting ourselves daily to preserve the poor from perishing, for their distress is excessive'.[1] James Dowling, P.P., Killeigh, denounced the offenders as a 'parcel of beardless boys, without principal, property or religion'. He reported to Doyle that the Carders had lately ceased their activities when the leaders took advantage of a government pardon.[2] Doyle's 1820 Lenten pastoral mentions illegal associations only en passant.[3] But on his visitation round later that year he was obliged to preach against the agitators.[4] A difficult winter helped to aggravate the agitation.

By January 1821, 'a most critical situation' had arisen on the north-western borders of the diocese which were subject to the Peace Preservation Act. Three and a half parishes within Kildare and Leighlin were under the act's operation but, according to Doyle, only because of their proximity to the disturbed districts. This containment, the bishop explained, was

> owing to our exertion, and the confidence the government and magistracy have in us, but if we were to relax for a moment, all would be disorder. Hence I am obliged to be present everywhere, to stimulate the clergy, to encourage the virtuous portion of the people and terrify the wretched.[5]

Catholic clergymen had a number of stratagems at their disposal to quell agrarian unrest. Success or failure generally depended on their personal authority within their parishes. Priests regularly prevented serious incidents occurring in their parishes by the fact of their physical presence. James Delany, P.P., Ballinakill (whose administration did not always find favour with his turbulent parishioners), recounted an incident where a magistrate and a party of police having angered a Catholic crowd on its way to mass were obliged to retreat hastily to their barracks:

> I followed, and was literally obliged to throw myself between them and the exasperated multitude; and to remain at the barrack door for 15 minutes, biding the pelting that followed; if I had not been there the probability is that those police and the magistrate would have been immolated on the spot.

A more robust clerical approach was recounted by William St Leger Alcock, an officer in the 23rd regiment of the Royal Welsh Fusiliers. He described a stone throwing riot in Baltinglass on 9 February 1833 where he considered 'the police were too violent':

> For the few minutes that the volley of stones lasted they fell as thick as hail and then it was all over. The priest was on the spot immediately after the affray, and it was curious to see how he dispersed the mob. If any of them were at all refractory he instantly seized a stick and striking out right and left soon brought them to a sense of the situation.[6]

Interventions of this sort indicate that the priests were often more effective arbiters of the public peace than the police. Such interventions were commonplace in contemporary evidence and must be taken into account in any overall reckoning of clerical effectiveness in maintaining the public peace.

So many strangers had lately appeared in the county, a Carlow magistrate reported in January 1822, that 'in two cases the priests ... from their chapels exhorted their parishioners not to allow them to remain in their houses'.[7] The exclusion of known agitators or troublesome persons from attending Catholic places of worship was an important tactic in upholding the peace. Historically during the Whiteboy and Rightboy agitations, the mass-house as a meeting place had often been used by illegal combinations for swearing-in or recruiting purposes. Delany of Ballinakill was 'under the necessity of forbidding such characters to resort to [his] chapel' near Timahoe. Michael Keogh, P.P., Abbeyleix, feared that parishioners in one of his chapels would catch the spirit of combination from those evicted off the Cosby estate (in the late 1820s). He discovered that thirty-six parishioners 'of the lowest description' had been sworn-in but he 'succeeded after four or five Sundays in bringing them to Lord de Vesci, and prevailed upon them to make a solemn promise never again to be connected with illegal associations'.[8] In their Sunday sermons during periods of discontent priests generally appealed to farmers not to employ strangers on their lands.

Denunciation was probably the most powerful weapon available to priests against illegal societies. In 1822 Rev. Nicholas O'Connor, P.P., Maryborough, denounced two Tipperary Ribbonmen by name 'to intimidate others from coming to introduce any such system in the parish'.[9] In 1827 James Delany personally appealed to two journeymen masons to desist from swearing-in in his parish and when this had no effect he 'finally denounced the men by name and thus succeeded in removing them from the parish'.[10] In 1830–32 when members of the Whitefeet took up residence in Ballinakill and spread their agitation, Delany and his curate were forced 'in self-defence to expel them from the parish'. The conduct of the priests in this instance brought down on them the 'bitterest resentment' of the agitators.[11]

Parishioners were normally reluctant to give information against agitators to either the police or their priests. On 28 March 1832 Chief Constable Clancie of Stradbally reported to Dublin Castle that the police were 'so watched, and the fear and silence is so great, that it is by the merest chance alone we can do any good'.[12] There was however an equally great fear of informers which gave rise to an interesting form of peasant solidarity. Members of illegal societies normally travelled at least four or five miles to the scene of their crime so that they would not be known to the local inhabitants. 'It is a matter of notoriety', Rev. Delany observed, 'that the perpetrators of crime generally come from a distance'. But when an intended crime of this sort came to his notice, he added, 'I lose no time in writing to the parish priest in whose district the agents reside, and by our mutual co-operation and interference have in most cases frustrated their ambition'. He claimed more generally that his intervention as a cleric had prevented outrages in 'many, many instances'.[13] There is no reason to disbelieve him; but such intervention was not without its risks.

Combinations drew their support from the poorest and most destitute classes which were furthest from the ambit of clerical influence and for this reason priests faced very real difficulties in curbing their activities. In parliamentary evidence in February 1832 Doyle acknowledged that the 'general distress of the poor' was 'extremely great, and it is the chief cause of the existence of those combinations'.[14] However, some crime such as that of the Finnegan gang which was prominent in robberies in Carlow, particularly in early 1822, had no clearly discernible social, agrarian or political motive. Finnegan the elder held fifty acres of land and had thirty cows. Martin Doyle, P.P., of Clonegal advised one of the gang, Thomas Laughlin, who apparently had undergone a religious conversion, to give information to the magistrate Captain Pilsworth Whelan. At the trial, Chief Baron Smith in his charge to the jury, pronounced a lavish encomium on the conduct of Martin Doyle in helping, through his advice, to bring the Finnegans to justice. Michael and Hugh Finnegan, father and son, and William Nowlan were hanged in front of Carlow jail on 6 August 1822. They acknowledged the justice of their sentence. The parish priest of Carlow, Rev. William Fitzgerald, attended them on the platform. The hanging was witnessed by a crowd of both sexes estimated to be not less than 20,000.

Ribbonmen and Whitefeet were never pleased to see the efforts Catholic priests made to prevent their outrages or to see priests liaising with the law enforcement agencies. As a result priests often received notices advising them not to treat combinations harshly or had stones thrown at their persons. Rev. James Delany reported that 'the people complained of my conduct and said I overstepped my duty and was rather officious'.[15] In 1822 a Ribbonman threatened the life of the parish priest of Maryborough and he prudently 'kept out of the way for some time'.[16] In 1822 also, Doyle was obliged to remove a clergyman from the deanery of Kilcock 'through a strong apprehension which he entertained, and in which I also participated, that if he continued in the parish where he laboured to check this evil he might be assassinated'.[17] A decade later, there was 'an attempt to shoot Mr Maher', P.P., Paulstown, which undoubtedly related to efforts on his part to remove Whitefeet agitators from his parish.[18]

In his Lenten pastoral for 1821 Doyle instructed his flock against the illegal associations which were 'said to exist' on the confines of the diocese. Doyle stated that the threats of the illegal societies were determining the rents landlords could charge, the lands tenants could occupy, the labourers farmers could employ and the wages they could pay. Worse, combinations were enforcing their arbitrary measures by unjust and barbaric acts on the alleged offenders and even animals. Doyle denounced these combinations as opposed to the civil obedience which Catholicism commanded to the state and to Catholicism itself. The oath which initiates took, said Doyle, was 'in every sense unlawful'. His diocesan clergy, however, 'had not been without effect' in preventing their parishioners from joining combinations even though he characterised the offenders as bereft of land, character or religious beliefs 'which alone' would deter others from entering into combinations by taking unlawful and sacrilegious oaths.[19]

In his 1821 pastoral the bishop held the rights of property to be sacrosanct. The landlord might be oppressive 'but there is no authority, not even in the state, which can deprive him of his property, or compel him (unless for the public good) to dispose of it otherwise than according to his own will'.[20] He asserted with ill-considered biblical imagery that the poorest people of his diocese had not been goaded into illegal activities by distress:

> No: for where is the landlord amongst you, who is an oppressor? Where is the employer who is not humane? When have you been sick and they have not relieved you? When have you been naked and they have not covered you? When have you been hungry and they have not fed you? When have you been homeless and they have not sheltered you? And if you could point out exceptions are they not rare as the stars that fall from heaven?[21]

This paean to landlordism is remarkable for its lack of social realism. The relatively peaceful recent history of the diocese, Doyle's own social milieu and his years spent teaching in New Ross and Carlow may have sheltered and distanced him somewhat from the harsher realities of Irish life. Some years later he drew a line through his Sermon on the Mount analogy.[22] His 1821 pastoral adduced a biblical justification for loyalty to the state. Doyle pointed out that the Bible asserts that Catholics should be submissive, even to unjust rulers, because these had a divine right to rule. Jesus had said to Pontius Pilate who judged him unjustly: 'thou wouldst not have any power over me, if it had not been given to thee from above'.[23]

Doyle also rejected the idea of illegal associations from a purely pragmatic point of view. He maintained that the government was simply too powerful for them and they they would be crushed as the Whiteboys, Rightboys, Peep-o-days, Defenders, Hearts of Oak, United Irishmen and, incongruously, Orangemen, had been. The hangman's noose put an end to these conspiratorial organisations while on the other hand the advice of government was 'never productive of evil'. Members of illegal societies were admonished to abandon them and to repent of the sins they had committed mainly through ignorance. But, Doyle warned, if anyone persisted in defying the law of God and country by bringing terror and (as a result) taxation into a hitherto peaceful diocese, he would resort to the 'severest chastisement' vested in him.[24]

North Kildare was disturbed in late 1822. A meeting on 3 November of thirteen magistrates petitioned the lord lieutenant for the enforcement of the Peace Preservation Act in the parishes of the union of Kilmeague and Rathmore, Feighcullen, Thomastown, Pollardstown and Dunmurry, Cloncurry and Rathangan.[25] On 19 November 1822 Doyle directed a powerful pastoral letter against the activities of Ribbonmen in the deanery of Kilcock. He stressed, more than in any subsequent pastoral, the tenets of Catholicism in relation to civil allegiance, the justification for which was found in the Bible. His anxiety to demonstrate the doctrinal foundations for the allegiance of Catholics to the state was very evident. On earth Christ paid allegiance to the state and required the Apostle Peter to follow his example. Consequently when persecuted in one city Peter fled to another but he 'never spoke the language of resistance'. On the contrary Saint Peter said: 'be you subject to every human creature for God's sake, whether it be the king as excelling, or to the governors as sent by him for the punishment of evil doers, for so is the will of God'.[26] It was ironic that these were the very words later quoted (perhaps deliberately) against Doyle by the authors of the Maynooth Manifesto attacking the sentiments of his letter on the union of the churches.[27] Doyle also quoted in this pastoral from Paul's epistle to the Romans on the principles of Catholic obedience to the state:

> Let every soul be subject to the higher powers, for there is no power but
> from God, and those that are, are ordained of God; therefore, he that

resisteth the power, resisteth the ordinance of God, and they that resist, purchase to themselves damnation; for rulers are not a terror to the good work, but to the evil. Wilt thou then not be afraid of the power? Do that which is good, and thou shalt have praise from the same,. for he is the minister of God to thee for good; but if thou do that which is evil, fear; for he beareth not the sword in vain, for he is the minister of God, an avenger to execute wrath upon him that doeth evil: wherefore, be subject of necessity, not only for wrath, but also for conscience sake. Render therefore, to all men their dues, tribute to whom tribute is due, custom to whom custom, fear to whom fear, honor to whom honor ....

[Doyle concluded:] The design then into which, it appears, some of you have entered, of subverting the state, and overthrowing the government established in this country by divine permission, is opposed to the maxims and example of our divine redeemer; and of his apostles; and to the uniform doctrine of that church whose faith you profess.[28]

Political objections buttressed theological opposition to the Ribbonmen. Doyle deprecated the occasion of the outbreak when King George IV had just visited Ireland 'like a common father' dispensing among all classes the spirit of peace and goodwill.[29] (Privately Doyle had favoured an address to the king during his visit on the 'profound grief and intense pain' suffered by Catholics under the existing laws, but there had been objections to it.[30]) Doyle referred to the appointment of a new lord lieutenant (the Marquis Wellesley, who was not named) 'for the avowed purpose of dispensing the laws impartially'.[31] (In his *Letters on the State of Ireland*, Doyle argued that unjust laws could not be impartially administered.[32]) Doyle also indirectly alluded to the Irish attorney general, W.C. Plunket, 'the strenuous and powerful advocate of our rights as Catholics'.[33] To the paternalism of George IV, Doyle added the maternalism of England which had 'with the anxiety of a mother', supported a million starving Irish people in 1822 while she forgot crimes committed in southern Ireland which 'called to heaven for vengeance against us'.[34]

Analysing the *raison d'être* of the Ribbonmen, Doyle found that their most obvious motivation lay in sheer poverty which he allowed was 'general and great' but which 'in many instances cannot be remedied by human power' – a fatalistic outlook which was soon transformed into a relentless advocacy of an Irish poor law. Contradicting his own views then and later, in an unusually weak piece of special pleading, Doyle believed it remarkable that he never knew of anyone who was compelled by distress to enter into combinations; 'idle tradesmen, boatmen, servants without families, and young inexperienced youths of the labouring classes' comprised the membership of these societies, but none did so from poverty – 'of this you are all conscious'. In any case employment could hardly be secured by upsetting the social fabric of society.[35] Doyle also attributed Ribbon motivation to the obverse and reverse faces of religious identity – love of Catholicism and hatred of Orangeism. But he insisted the Orangemen were 'our brethren in Christ'; the great Christian precept was 'to love God above all things and your neighbour as yourself for the love of God' and this included all men, even those who differed from Catholics in religious belief.[36]

In this pastoral Doyle warned his flock against belief in prophecies which were in circulation, especially the work of Pastorini which was interpreted as portending the downfall of Protestantism in 1824 or 1825. Though chiliastic prophecies of the Pastorini variety were probably not much circulated in the diocese of Kildare and Leighlin because of the vigilance of Doyle and his clergy the Protestant population, in common with most of their co-religionists elsewhere, displayed considerable signs of alarm. In Carlow on Christmas Eve 1824 Protestants fortified their strongest houses and waited in expectation of a Catholic onslaught which never materialised.[37] Before the lords' committee on the state of Ireland in 1825 Doyle blamed *agents provocateurs* for circulating printed extracts from Pastorini among the peasantry, particularly in the south, 'to excite dissension ... and to produce appearances of disturbances'.[38] In his 1825 Lenten pastoral Doyle described Pastorini's *Prophecies* as 'the impious production of an overheated mind'[39] and he doubted, he informed the lords' committee, 'whether any noble lord could designate it more strongly'.[40] It was not politic to mention to the lords that in this same pastoral he had also classed the *Prophecies* with the 'ravings of itinerant Biblemen' and the ridiculous publications of (evangelical) tract societies.[41] Doyle's analogy captured the spirit of the times. In the early 1820s it is not insignificant that millenarian rumours suggesting the imminent overthrow of Protestantism were prevalent at a time when evangelicals were forecasting the imminent demise of Catholicism in Ireland. In general Pastorini was denounced by the Catholic hierarchy and clergy as a very mischievous work. Doyle was persuaded in 1825 that his efforts to check the influence of Pastorini had been successful: 'there is no one in my diocese who gives the least countenance to it'.[42]

Nationalism was undoubtedly the most interesting of the influences which Doyle associated with the rise of the Ribbon society in 1822 – 'your object is to make your country free and happy'. Significantly Doyle was not prepared to argue the merit of this objective, which 'even if it were laudable, could not justify the employment of unlawful means'.[43] But secret societies were composed of men without education, finance, weaponry, judgement or the leadership qualities necessary to oppose a regular army. Doyle unhistorically recalled that all denominations, Catholic, Protestant and Dissenter, had united without success in 1798 to overthrow the government. What chance then had the contemptible conspiracies of the secret societies? Doyle's purpose was polemical rather than informative and in consequence the more forceful the impression created by the pastoral the better. In this famous pastoral Doyle's portrayal of society and the interaction of the classes that composed it was essentially static and conservative. He compared the body of a nation to the human body:

> The different ranks and orders which compose it are ordained of God, that the whole may be preserved entire. If any of them should seek to usurp the place of the other discord would ensue. If your feet, seeing your hands are idle, would refuse to walk: if your hands would undertake to do the duties of the head, how monstrous and absurd would it not appear? So in the state, if those whom God has appointed to labour should abandon their station and seek to govern; if the ignorant would take the place of the wise; the soldier the place of the peasant; the tradesman that of the magistrate; the schoolmaster that of the bishop or judge, how could society exist?[44]

Doyle looked upon the ranks and orders of society 'as an ark projected by the finger of God, for the preservation of the species'.[45]

This pastoral against Ribbonism was one dimensional: an outright attack on a secret society which was seen to be acting without sense or reason. Nothing could mitigate such behaviour. By contrast with his approach in the 1821 pastoral Doyle did not wax lyrical about the benevolence of landlords who were not mentioned as a class. It is worth noting that, on balance, Doyle's pastoral deduced that the Ribbonmen acted more from political and religious than economic motives – although poverty was the primary cause of the outbreak. It was most unusual for a Catholic bishop to acknowledge that nationalism and sectarianism rather than purely local grievances influenced the activity of Irish secret societies. Generally the hierarchy preferred to play down or avoid any reference to political motives for rural disturbances.

This powerful pastoral against Ribbonism brought its author significant public attention as its national relevance was immediately recognised. Doyle himself was anxious to influence opinion where it counted. The attorney general, W.C. Plunket, (in response to a letter from Doyle enclosing a copy of the pastoral) found the tract valuable not only for the effect it would have on lawless associations but because it would familiarise the public with the 'liberal and enlightened' thought of a member of the Catholic hierarchy.[46] Archbishop Murray was naturally more forthcoming than Plunket; the pastoral had been a 'high treat' for him and he mistakenly hoped that it might weaken Protestant animosity towards Catholicism in Ireland.[47] Archbishop Curtis, who found the address 'excellent', complained that it had been derided by the irreconcilable enemies of conciliation 'as well as of True Religion' in Ireland.[48] The whig M.P., Thomas Spring Rice, was even more hyperbolical: the pastoral was, he said, 'one of the most useful documents which has ever appeared'.[49]

The pastoral enjoyed great popularity in the public press and was printed in many pamphlet editions (including one in Irish by Scurry in 1826). It was also commented upon favourably in the English press. Several hundred copies of a small edition were sold in Dublin on 25 November 1822, notwithstanding the fact that the pastoral appeared in two morning papers of the same day.[50] Dublin printers published several editions for their own profit.[51] The *Dublin Evening Post* advised the Irish government to circulate several thousand copies of the pastoral.[52] Sir John Lambert, commander of the army in the south of Ireland, published an edition in Cork. The public authorities of Galway city did likewise. The duke of Leinster ordered 400 copies.[53] O'Connell was later to claim that the pastoral did more to tranquillise the country than the Insurrection Act and that the government had printed 200,000 copies for distribution.[54] Fitzpatrick gave a figure of 300,000 copies printed by the government.[55] No government documentation has yet come to light which would verify whether either of these figures were at all plausible or wildly inaccurate, the latter being the more likely.

Doyle believed that his pastoral would fall on deaf ears unless it was sustained by his own exertions and those of his clergy. He spent several weeks visiting the parishes of the deanery of Kilcock, preaching in the chapels and even 'sometimes by the wayside'.[56] On 26 November 1822 Major James Tandy reported to the chief secretary, Henry Goulburn, that no outrage had been committed or attempted in the most disturbed part of County Kildare since the police were stationed there by Goulburn's orders.[57] Stands of arms were returned to their rightful owners in virtually all the disturbed parishes; in fact, according to Doyle, there was 'nothing more common'.[58] The Catholic clergy acted as a conduit for this process; it was much less common for stolen firearms to be returned directly to their owners or the law enforcement agencies. Doyle directed that if arms were being given by clergymen to magistrates it was to be done privately or at least without publicity in the press. He gave two reasons for this injunction to Francis Haly, P.P., Kilcock: first, 'let us do all the good we can for the love of God and our country but never seek the favourable consideration of those in power'; second, he deemed it prudent that parishioners should not know what became of arms given up to their priests.[59] This was useful advice for clergymen had to be careful to retain an independent middle ground.

Doyle's pastoral against Ribbonism of November 1822 was his last to advocate passive obedience. While it still upholds the law, there is a noticeable new departure in his June 1823 pastoral:

> you will ask me, are we then to suffer in silence and not vindicate our good name? Far from it Brethren – you should uphold, by every lawful means, your own character, and promote your own interests. These interests are the interests of truth and justice, and they must advance. The ways of their progress are obvious, and nothing can retard them but your own imprudence ....

You have increased in property, in numbers, and in strength; these give you a moral weight, which carries you forward with an accelerated motion. Education has arrived to a state of excellence amongst those of you who are blessed with the means of obtaining it, and is united with a pure and sound morality. These will illuminate, and enliven, and direct the movements of our body, that we may act in concert, dissipate prejudice, make our merits manifest, and attach to our cause the virtuous and the intelligent of every creed and class.[60]

From 1822 there was no pastoral from Doyle's pen for a further seven years on the subject of illegal societies. In 1825 it was unnecessary for him to do more than strongly recommend a continuation of the 'good order and peaceable demeanour' which pertained throughout the diocese. He had enough confidence in his flock to propose that persons organising oath-bound societies should be arrested and handed over to a magistrate or informed upon. He starkly accepted the likely consequences of such a course of action and stated that not even death should deter the law-abiding: 'you should not fear the assassin who would seduce you to your ruin', especially when the law would afford its protection. He acknowledged that, in Ireland, informers were doubly infamous on account of their historic associations with the penal laws but to inform against sanguine combinations was 'not infamous but truly honourable'.[61] Doyle's injunction was inculcated by his clergy even though the person who gave information or appeared for the state at an agrarian outrage trial could not safely return to his native abode and more usually had to be spirited out of the country.[62] Catholic clergymen themselves were extremely reluctant to give evidence or prosecute to trial their own parishioners.[63]

Sheer hunger arising from a reduction in labourers' wages and the eviction of tenants consequent upon falling prices were the only possible reasons Doyle could adduce for an outbreak of agrarian agitation in the deanery of Maryborough in 1829.[64] The bishop asserted that Catholics and Protestants were united together in the revolt though there seems to be very little evidence for this claim. The parish priests of Abbeyleix, Ballinakill and Maryborough alleged that evictions taking place from 1827 onwards, which gave rise to the agitation, were motivated at least in some cases by heightened evangelical prejudices, namely landlord anger at the refusal of Catholic parents to send their children to schools disapproved of by their clergy.[65]

The evicted endured considerable hardship as they were bereft of any means apart from their own labour of providing for themselves. During the summer of 1831 they were virtually naked and 'living upon ... the yellow weeds that grow in corn'.[66] Members of evicted families often became the leading and most violent agitators. Their fate turned them savage. As Rev. Nicholas O'Connor remarked: 'when men become reckless of character and principle by intolerable misery, they disregard every moral obligation'.[67] Most of those turned out in the parishes of Ballinakill and Maryborough took refuge on waste land in the colliery district of Abbeyleix adjoining the Castlecomer coalfields in the diocese of Ossory.[68] The agitators were motivated by pure revenge; they acted in groups without committee management or careful premeditation with the one exception that they rarely acted in their own immediate area. Their plans, such as they were, generally involved the seizure of firearms, and were often hatched in shebeen houses under the malignant influence of cheap whiskey.[69] Their principal object was to maintain labourers' wages at a level they could live on and to intimidate landowners from turning tenants off their lands.[70] They were joined by those who feared the same fate as themselves – eviction – and who hoped they might be able to prevent it. Intimidation was a powerful weapon in their hands, used both against landowners and to force others to join their ranks under pain of a beating or worse.[71] Occupants of slated houses were thought to be above intimidation. The Carlow newspaper commented that the Queen's County was in such a disturbed state that 'men have been compelled to abandon their work in the fields, by large bodies of those illegal associations, called White Boys'. At the Queen's County summer assizes on 31 July 1829, Lord Chief Justice Bushe stated that 'the utmost exertion was necessary to repress a system that would erect the dominion of the mob over that of the higher orders'.[72] The agitators of the 1829–32 period were not manifestly as politically aware as the Ribbonmen of the early 1820s though they did decry the uselessness to them of emancipation (which had been presented as a panacea for all Ireland's ills).[73] Attacks generally took place by night but in desperation and as they grew bolder, they attacked their victims in broad daylight.[74]

'No man does evil for evil's sake', wrote Doyle consolingly if somewhat optimistically when, in his (November 1829) pastoral, he pinpointed hunger and distress as the causes of the violence. But, he continued, these did not justify revolt in the year of emancipation. The penal code, 'the greatest cause of our national misfortunes has been removed'. The road to improvement in Ireland lay open and the work of improvement had already been commenced by government: 'In other times ... if I saw you in want, or driven to combine I [would – erased] might hesitate before I should take up the arms of the Gospel, lest I should seem to range myself on the side of guilt in power against guilt in distress'. But distress was no longer the precursor of despair. Distress was, he wrote, utilising a sharp but easily understood simile, like the agony of childbirth; if borne with patience it would lead to happiness - in this case the resurrection of Ireland. If provocation justified any transgression, no offence would be committed by the violation of any law. Therefore association or combination not authorised by the law was not justifiable. Doyle wrote, but suppressed, lines which justified the combinations he sought to condemn:

> Associations or combinations into which men enter urged thereto by want
> or oppression are not justifiable unless in those cases where the oppres-
> sion or want is insupportable or extreme, and that the laws or the govern-
> ment after having been respectfully applied to neglect or refuse to remove
> the oppression or supply the extreme want.[75]

Here, Doyle was giving meaning to his understanding of the constitution: the
contract between the government and the governed was being stretched to breaking point. The advanced social radicalism espoused here – ultimately to the effect that the poor were entitled to find some means of supporting themselves,
legal or otherwise, rather than starving to death – was channelled by Doyle into
his somewhat lonely crusade for an Irish poor law.

In 1829 Doyle's pastoral letter was read from every altar by the parochial
clergy in the deanery of Maryborough. Immediately after the publication Doyle
himself addressed various congregations in several parishes of the disturbed districts, as for instance in Luggacurren in Ballyadams. Several stands of arms were
handed up to Rev. Cummins, one of the Catholic curates in Ballyadams. He had
made repeated remonstrances to the malcontents among his flock. He delivered
up the arms to the magistracy. In an address from the altar to his parishioners,
the parish priest of Maryborough argued that the government seemed ready to
bring into practical effect the inestimable benefits of emancipation and thus he
'succeeded in obtaining from them all the firearms and weapons in the parish'.
The timely and judicious activities of Doyle and his clergy prompted an 'extensive return of arms'. This decisive action by Doyle and the strenuous and repeated exhortations of his clergy appear to have been critical in reducing the
number of disturbances in the deanery of Maryborough. In April 1830 Doyle
expressed himself 'satisfied that evil combinations which were greatly extended
in a part of the diocese of Leighlin have been lately and everywhere dissolved'.[76]

Glimpses of the iron fist behind the velvet glove can be seen in Doyle's private correspondence. In 1830 he supported the notable clerical agitator, James
Maher, P.P., Paulstown, in leading the opposition to threatened evictions which
were politically motivated on Viscount Beresford's estate at Ballinkillen in
Bagenalstown parish. According to Walter Blackney, J.P., the reason for the evictions was that Beresford 'will not now, or in time to come, let any of his estates, to
persons, who might by any possibility be under the influence of Popish Priests.
These men have had nothing to do in the events of the late election. But they are
Catholics ... and this is the fruit and substance of their crime'.[77] Bishop Doyle
drew up a list of resolutions opposing the evictions to be passed by James Maher
at a meeting to be held in Ballinkillen chapel. The resolutions included the stricture that 'whosoever by act or deed will aid or abet or concur in the principles' of
Beresford and his land-agent, Doyne, 'shall be deemed by us an enemy to the
public peace and an accomplice in deeds of injustice and tyranny and therefore

be excluded from all religious and civil intercourse with us or our families'. With indignation Doyle cast trenchant aspersions on both the perceived oppressor and the oppressed:

> This is a crisis for the Co. Carlow. They, are to be sure a pusillanimous race as Ireland could furnish, and especially there, but if they dare to free themselves the way is open. If not let them be slaves ....
>
> If the matter go forward we must be prepared to sustain it at all risks, and the people must adhere rigorously to the non-intercourse system ....
>
> If the men we have were to be depended on we would humble to the earth this *Bastard race of tyrants*.[78]

The incisiveness and forcefulness of commentary such as this gives us a real insight into what made Doyle such a formidable figure to both friends and enemies alike.

At the beginning of the 1830s, parallel with his efforts to curb agrarian agitation, Doyle was playing a leading role in the sanguine tithe war. We are not here concerned with the issue of tithe per se which is examined elsewhere.[79] Suffice it to state that from late 1830, tithe agitation raged with the support of the Catholic church. This issue divided magistrates from Catholic clergymen in their efforts to maintain the peace and resulted in a breakdown in communication between the two groups. The agrarian agitation of late 1829 in the deanery of Maryborough simmered during 1830 and erupted in 1831 to reach new heights of violence in spring 1832. Judge Baron Smith in his address to the Maryborough assizes of summer 1831 concentrated on attacking Catholic failure to uphold the law of tithe and on proving a nexus between agrarian outrage and the tithe agitation which was denied by all Catholics. Baron Smith did not mention Doyle by name but all his charges and addresses were designed to counter the bishop's anti-tithe arguments. Even as late as the spring assizes of 1832, Smith stated that 'between present outrage and late tithe resistance, there exists some unperceived derivative connection, some lurking and dark relation of cause and effect'. Doyle responded with the anonymous publication, *Church of Ireland, Tithes!!! A most important dialogue between a bishop and a judge*.[80]

On 10 June 1831 thirty-seven Queen's County magistrates decided to counter the agrarian agitators by forming a 'Volunteer Armed Association' to be composed of 'respectable and well-disposed' subjects 'of all denominations'. A public notice recommended that 'every individual who wishes to prove his loyalty to the king, his attachment to the laws, and his desire to co-operate with his respectable neighbours, should enrol his name and be admitted a member of the Association'.[81]

This project failed for related reasons which had much to do with divisive party passions in Ireland. With the tithe war raging and O'Connellite politicians denouncing the activities of local yeomanry corps, the government was almost as reluctant to arm Protestants further as the magistrates were reluctant to arm Catholics. The Catholics for their part were very cautious about being mobilised to enforce the collection of tithes.

Almost a year later, Chief Secretary Stanley pointed out in the house of commons that in the Queen's County no patrol had been formed and no application made to the government for arms. James Grattan, M.P., stated that he had spoken to his tenantry in favour of the 'Volunteer Armed Association' and forty of them had declared their willingness to bear arms for the preservation of the peace of the county. He communicated this information to the magistrates but had not heard a word since then. He lamented the 'supineness of the magistracy' and contended that if the original offer had been accepted the agrarian troublemakers would have been swiftly curtailed.

Sir Henry Parnell claimed that a supply of arms had been requested from the government but that it was refused 'on the ground that the parties to whom arms were intended to be supplied were exclusively Protestants'. Sir Charles Coote suggested that the armed association had failed because the system of intimidation in the Queen's County prevented the peasantry, who resided in thatched cabins, from participating through fear of personal violence. In the house of lords, the earl of Roden held that the initiative had failed because the Catholic clergy had set their faces against it. Stanley maintained that to place arms in the hands of any 'particular class' in the Queen's County would be 'exceedingly unwise and improper' and, far from preventing trouble, would 'tend in no small degree to augment the disturbances'.[82]

When the parish priest of Ballinakill returned several stands of arms to a magistrate, he was accosted by a parishioner with the rebuff: 'You are very anxious and zealous in your efforts to withdraw from the peasantry some few useless guns, while there is a yeomanry corps being formed in the next village, and about to be entrusted with arms'. Catholics had not joined or been invited to join the 'Volunteer Armed Association' and this fact was used as an argument for why arms should not be handed up to the priest.[83]

Doyle's late November 1831 pastoral referred to those combined under the 'unmeaning appellations' of Whitefeet and Blackfeet in the Queen's County portion of his diocese.[84] The distinction, if any, between the Whitefeet and the Blackfeet is unclear, though both were in the 1829 tradition of violent dissent. Various reasons have been suggested for the origin of their names: among them that the original leaders of the Whitefeet or Whitelegs wore white stockings and that the stocking colour became a party emblem;[85] another, that the Blackfeet wore shoes and the Whitefeet went barefoot.[86] There was nothing particularly original in their names. Irish agrarian societies had a long tradition of deriving their nomenclature from some article of apparel. The Leinster head of police, Colonel Sir John Harvey, posited that the two groups often met to fight which would suggest that there were issues of personal dispute rather like factionalism between them. He believed the Whitefeet were anti-clerical while their rivals, the Blackfeet, took more notice of their clergy.[87] Nicholas O'Connor, P.P., could not discern any difference between the groups though he gave evidence that the Blackfeet did not take an oath but instead made a vow on their knees.[88] The doctrine of oaths and the crime of perjury were treated with the utmost seriousness by Doyle who frequently preached on this theme during visitation. In May 1829, after the disqualification of the forty shilling freeholders, he addressed a pastoral solely on the requirements for the registration of freeholders for the ten pounds' franchise, which dealt at length with the dangers of perjury. This pastoral was re-published, with some new opening remarks, in early August 1830 and again in May 1831 (before the general election).[89]

Doyle's late 1831 pastoral was occasioned by an affray on the border of the diocese with Ossory three miles from Castlecomer on 25 November. Eight alleged Whitefeet were being taken by the police with a military escort under a Captain Mathews, from Newtown colliery to Castlecomer jail when they were attacked and pelted with stones by a would-be rescuing crowd at Cloneen turnpike gate. According to Captain Mathews, the police opened fire on their assailants without orders and five would-be rescuers were killed and several wounded. The following day Doyle went to that part of Abbeyleix parish which bordered on Castlecomer and denounced the Whitefeet before very large congregations in the chapels of the vicinity. He ordered that those wounded in the affray be denied the spiritual attendance of the priests and that those killed be denied Christian burials. So great was the effect of Doyle's preaching that the Leinster head of police was able to walk unaccompanied the next day through a subdued population which two days earlier had been in a state of insurrection. He witnessed the funeral procession of one of those killed taking place to unconsecrated ground without the attendance of a Catholic clergyman.[90] In Doyle's opinion an extreme pastoral problem called for an appropriately severe ecclesiastical remedy.

In his pastoral of late November 1831, Doyle once more acknowledged that hunger, the threat of starvation, and the desire for revenge were the causes of this particular outbreak of agrarian discontent. But he contended that the legislative and governmental systems responsible for the 'oppression of the poor' were 'now waxing old and going to decay'. The spirit of reform ran rather too optimistically through this pastoral. Illegal combinations, he advised, would only postpone this reform and heighten oppression. It is evident that Doyle had high hopes of change under the whigs, and that he believed with some justification (as for instance in the passing of Catholic emancipation and the 1832 Reform Act) that he lived in an era experiencing profound changes in its political system.

The pre- and post-emancipation periods in Ireland were likened by Doyle to the pre- and post-penal eras. A few people, and he classed himself among them, understood that Ireland could pass from the penal epoch, her 'state of bondage' to freedom, 'only through the narrow obedience to the law and the unqualified allegiance to the ruling power'. By this method emancipation had been achieved. Rural revolt, then as before, posed the greatest internal threat to legislative progress for Ireland:

> The poor, and the oppressed, and the ignorant people of Ireland, goaded by the old and inveterate enemies of all freedom and justice, could not comprehend that resistance to an all powerful oppression is as wicked as it is vain; wicked because it confirms the power of the oppressor; vain, because no effort by a disorganized rabble can ever be productive of success. Whilst we, therefore, the clergy, the gentry, the educated and the intelligent of the Irish people, by pleading and urging incessantly the justice of our cause, you who combined illegally against pastoral or general oppression, afforded to the common enemy a justification of those harsh laws by which ourselves and our country were kept enslaved.[91]

It was clear, the bishop maintained, that if emancipation could be achieved by constitutional means then other reforms could also be attained by the same process. The legislature could not be expected to remove all the ills of Ireland overnight. The government would have to be given time for this purpose but the prospect of reform was within view. Doyle looked upon the passage of emancipation as the harbinger of a new beginning in Anglo-Irish relations. He posited a legal provision for the poor as one partial remedy for the destitute unemployed. He urged petitions to parliament on the subject. The merit of a poor law, he stated, was 'a truth as certain as the rising of tomorrow's sun'.[92] The problem with Doyle's pastoral was that it was probably only fully understood by a reasonably educated audience. The political situation at national level meant little to the poorest of his flock. The parish priest of Maryborough acknowledged that 'all the enlightened part of the people' looked to a reformed parliament to do them justice 'but the very poor people do not look to government or the parliament at all, or any means, except what nature has given them, to prevent their being turned out, they abandon their clergy, and we can have no influence over them'.[93] In his parliamentary evidence in 1832, Doyle stated that: 'though I have conversed with a considerable number of the unfortunate people engaged in them [illegal associations], I find that they are of that class which have no education, suffering great privation, and who scarcely know the end or object of their combination'.[94]

Doyle's late November 1831 pastoral failed to suppress the activities of illegal agrarian associations in the Queen's County; even though the *Carlow Morning Post* printed several thousand copies of the pastoral in a cheap and convenient form for circulation in the disturbed area. Despite the very energetic efforts of the bishop and his diocesan clergy, the combinations continued to disturb the public peace. In Queen's County during April 1832 alone, there were thirty-one robberies, fifty-one serious assaults and 149 attacks on houses.[95] In that month, a Queen's County magistrate reported to his superiors that 'armed parties of men parade the district [of Stradbally] at noon-day without disguising their arms in the least; and as for outrages, they are innumerable, and the peaceful part of the community are in the utmost state of intimidation'. The strong farmer, Patrick Lalor of Tennakill, resented the private meetings of the magistrates which did not involve the middle classes in their proceedings. In a letter to the editor of the *Carlow Morning Post*, he complained that it was without precedent that 'no man's person or property is safe' and the county was as unsafe by day as it was by night.[96]

During April the bishop visited Maryborough to denounce the on-going agitation. From there Doyle addressed a correspondent stating that he was 'in the midst of an impious confederacy called Whitefeet, which has immersed itself in all kinds of iniquity, and has put all authority of God and man at defiance'. Rev. O'Connor remarked that Doyle's 'first address spread through the country with an electrical effect'. His preaching had a great impact on a 'considerable number of the deluded'. There were not twenty members of the Whitefeet who did not abandon their combination immediately after Doyle's exhortation though there were some few, as O'Connor admitted, 'almost beyond the hope of conversion', on whom no advice from the altar seemed to have any effect. A stipendiary magistrate, Captain Anderson, who heard Doyle preach advised O'Connor that the bishop's address should be printed and circulated.[97] This was the origin of Doyle's brief but very pointed pastoral of 5 May 1832.[98]

Doyle attributed the disorders of every sort effected by the Whitefeet to the influence of the devil yet he hesitated to excommunicate the combinators and thus 'give them over to Satan'. Instead he imposed very severe pre-conditions on the Whitefeet before they could return to the Catholic fold. Clergymen were forbidden from hearing the confessions of Whitefeet members unless such persons had publicly renounced their involvement in the presence of their former companions and until they had made reparation at the expense, if necessary, of all their possessions, and even at the risk of their own lives, for the damage they or their associates had caused. If these extremely strict requirements for confession were met, the erstwhile combinator was to perform as penance the stations of the cross for one year in chapel,[99] or to hear read on bended knees in church, the seven penitential psalms with the litanies and the prayers attached to them. If this penance was performed to the letter the penitent was to be admitted to confession at the end of the year. If extraordinary sorrow was manifested the period of one year might be shortened. Any person who had benefitted in any way from the activities of the Whitefeet or Blackfeet was not to be admitted to the sacrament of penance until he had returned what he had unlawfully gained.[100]

Before he issued this rigorist pastoral Doyle had taken counsel with his clergy at Mountmellick. The vicar-general, John Dunne, P.P., Portarlington, was not present at this meeting but he advised Doyle by letter against 'extremes'. He urged him to withhold his strictures at least for some time longer and noted that the confessionals were 'already more crowded' because of the cholera panic.[101] Dunne advised Doyle to give *pro tempore* faculties to every priest to absolve in all cases of reservation except those which called for reference to the Ordinary or vicar-general. If the agitation continued he expressed his willingness to contemplate the suppression of mass for some weeks in the disturbed parishes stopping short of formal excommunication.[102] However the vicar-general's letter arrived too late to influence Doyle's pastoral.

As an afterthought to this pastoral, Doyle added, in a foreword to his diocesan clergy, an injunction to encourage and assist 'by every means' the formation of self-defence associations among property owners and the well-disposed of all classes for the protection of their persons and property against the agrarian agitators. The self-defence associations should, he recommended, patrol the countryside day and night and dismiss the disaffected from their employment. This strategy he believed would defeat the combinations and restore order.[103] On 20 May 1832 Doyle informed a correspondent that the best means of proceeding was to swear in the peaceable as special constables. Persons thus sworn should however publicly refuse to be employed in the tithe gathering process or in the levying of church cess.[104] In the union of Grangeford in County Carlow the form of an oath to be taken by members of an association founded for the protection of life and property was submitted to the Catholic clergyman, Thomas Tyrrell, P.P., Tirryland. It was assented to by him on the promise of William Duckett, J.P., that 'no person swearing should be employed to recover tithes'.[105] The priests themselves did not propose to carry arms or (with the exception of James Maher) to take the field with these associations.[106] In fact Doyle disapproved of the use of firearms by the special constables. He was prepared to support only moderate measures to restore a semblance of order; with an uncharacteristic resignation born out of a sense of helplessness, he commented: 'if force and terror be resorted to, I shall stay silent to witness and deplore the result'.[107]

Doyle's pastoral inspired prosperous tenant-farmers to defend themselves against the Whitefeet confederacy. They were 'exceedingly anxious' for an association of the type proposed by Doyle because they felt themselves to be without protection. In this matter 'the priests were merely the organs of public sentiment'.[108] Of their own accord they were perhaps reluctant to go beyond advice and exhortation. In response to public demand a deputation of clerics from the deanery of Maryborough waited on the magistrate, Viscount de Vesci, the major landowner in Abbeyleix parish, to negotiate the 'formation of a protection society of all good men of every class and creed, without distinction'. Its modus operandi was to be in accord with Doyle's pastoral instructions: to traverse the countryside night and day and to co-operate with the constituted authorities. It was intended that the patrols should be accompanied by a small contingent from the ranks of the police or military. The protecting society's patrols were to call at the houses of suspected persons or check on their whereabouts and 'as they are generally servants or labourers, they could be dismissed with safety under the protection of such an association'. The priests' address to de Vesci claimed that 'even the towns are no longer secure, as they are at present invaded by the repeated visits of nightly marauders'.[109] However the protecting society proposal never became a reality in the Maryborough deanery. De Vesci, a good natured but apparently not very efficient peer, consulted the neighbouring magistrates and they decided that they would await the issue of the Special Commission (which opened in Maryborough on 23 May to try offenders who had been charged).[110] Relations between priests and magistrates in the deanery were not amiable. Fundamentally neither party wished to be forced into an accommodation by the Whitefeet outrages. The magistrates were jealous protectors of their authority and zealous upholders of the law when it suited them. Although they themselves had little time for tithe they were aware that if the proposed protecting society's members were sworn in as special constables they would not do duty in the collection of tithe or church cess. Some prejudiced magistrates murmured that the priests would arm the Whitefeet who towards the end of their agitation apparently did involve themselves in the anti-tithe campaign. The magistrates did not wish to countenance any apparent diminution of their authority or to aid an agency which did not give wholehearted support to the totality of the law.[111]

During the Whitefeet agitation the peasantry in Queen's County lost confidence in the magistracy.[112] Magistrates' courts were abandoned in favour of clerical jurisdiction. Priests were 'tormented' by parishioners visiting their homes seeking arbitration in disputes.[113] The Irish Catholic hierarchy in 1829 had warned against the development of clerical courts.[114] Frowned upon by the administration and by the church itself, clerical courts do not appear to have been more than isolated occurrences at periods of intense local agitation and crisis.

Doyle's pastoral of 5 May 1832 was issued at the very moment when the Whitefeet agitation came to a climax. The Queen's County crime statistics for May 1832 reveal a very definite decrease on the previous month's total: five robberies, twenty-three serious crimes and forty-three attacks on houses. By mid-July 1832 the worst was over and there had been a general surrender of arms in which the clergy were again prominent. The exertions of police and priests, the convictions at the Special Commission in Maryborough[115] and some improvement in social conditions all contributed to a major reduction though far from a complete cessation in the outrage reports.

Under the heading 'Whitefootism – delivery of arms – the Catholic clergy', the *Carlow Morning Post* of 28 June 1832 reported that a memorial had been forwarded to the government praying that an amnesty should be granted to all Whitefeet who would deliver up their arms and who had not been guilty of murder or robbery. The government did not actually consent to this arrangement, but tacitly approved of it, and in consequence Rev. Kelly of Clonbrock, Doonane parish, in Queen's County, had received from fifteen to twenty stand of arms, and means had been adopted for securing the delivery of more. A meeting held at Wolfhill in Ballyadams parish, had been addressed by Revs Kelly, Hickey, Doran, Hart, Cummins and Walsh who strenuously implored the Whitefeet to give up their arms.

It is clear that Doyle and his clergy played a sterling role in maintaining the public peace in the diocese of Kildare and Leighlin. While Doyle was always conscious of the national political situation, his pastoral letters on rural discontent were carefully considered. Doyle's pastoral letters were very different from his polemical political works; the purpose of the latter was to stimulate constitutional agitation, that of the former to quell violent agitation. In his pastoral letters Doyle counselled obedience and loyalty within the law to the constituted authorities to save his flock from the folly of certain defeat in agrarian or political rebellion. In 1825 Doyle informed the lords' committee on the state of Ireland that the position of the Irish Catholic clergy was 'one of extreme difficulty; one in which we are endeavouring to conciliate the upper orders, and to keep quiet the feelings of the lower orders'.[116]

CONCLUSION: THE TRIDENTINE EVOLUTION OF IRISH CATHOLICISM

Doyle's health, which had often been poor, deteriorated from 1832. He was suffering from consumption or tuberculosis. On 17 March 1833, Rome granted Doyle six months leave from his diocese – which was somewhat more time than he had sought – so that he might recuperate in a warmer climate. Paul Cullen hoped that Doyle might stay in Rome.[1] Doyle did not leave the diocese. He was quite prepared for death and did not see why it should be a source of concern to anyone. He was annoyed with friends who expressed great anxiety about his declining health:

> If I were not a Christian I should not set much value on my own life or that of any person, but being a believer and having access to God through Christ if I be not a prevaricator, and knowing that his Providence disposes even the smallest things it appears to me irreligious to be very solicitous about the life of anyone.[2]

There were occasional improvements but the overall pattern was downwards. In November 1833 Doyle was reported to be in a state of steady and progressive convalescence.[3] At the dedication of the new chapel of Kildare in December 1833, prayers were offered for Doyle's full and speedy recovery.[4] In a letter to Mother Dolan of the Discalced Carmelites of Ranelagh on 13 January 1834, Doyle offered this unusually revealing account of his health:

> I recovered partially during the latter end of Autumn but the Winter has thrown me back to my former position – renewing or aggravating all my old complaints. I sometimes on Sundays endeavoured to celebrate Mass in my little oratory but could not, latterly, attempt to do so. When I walk upstairs my breathing becomes difficult, I feel fatigue or exhaustion, and at no time am I able to continue walking, however slowly, for a quarter of an hour. My rest at night is often interrupted by a severe cough and headache. Withal, I am in appearance tolerably well, my spirits are never depressed, and though my patience is often on the point of failing it generally remains unbroken.[5]

Michael Slattery, Doyle's old colleague on the staff of Carlow College, who through

Doyle's influence had become president of Maynooth College in 1832 spent a week with Doyle at Braganza after Christmas 1833. Slattery was awaiting the arrival of the Bull from Rome confirming his appointment as archbishop of Cashel and Emly.[6] On the occasion of the consecration of Slattery as archbishop in late February 1834, the *Tipperary Free Press* commented that there was a general feeling of regret on account of the absence of Doyle who had intended to be the consecrating prelate, if his health had permitted.[7] The *Evening Freeman* reported in April on the severe and dangerous illness Doyle faced and how he was in 'almost a hopeless state'.[8]

Doyle hoped that by appointing a coadjutor he might be able for health purposes to take extended leave of the diocese in a more congenial climate. He addressed a circular letter to his parish priests dated 3 April 1834 inviting them to Carlow Cathedral on 21 April to vote for a coadjutor bishop with right of succession. Archbishop Murray and Bishop Kinsella presided in the absence of Doyle. The result of the ballotting was publicly declared. Edward Nolan, vice-president of Carlow College, with thirty-eight votes was declared dignissimus on the terna. Michael Flanagan, vicar-general and parish priest of Balyna, with thirty-one votes was named dignior and Denis Lawlor, parish priest of Hacketstown with twenty-six votes was declared dignus. Support for other candidates from both home and abroad ranged between one and twelve votes.[9] Doyle did not influence or interfere in any way with the choice of his parish priests. Privately he made reference to 'that boy in Rome', Paul Cullen, as a worthy successor, chiefly on the grounds that, as he had no pastoral experience in the diocese, he would not be compromised by anything he might have to deal with on the mission.[10]

Throughout May some of Doyle's clergy were in constant attendance at Braganza. Edward Nolan administered extreme unction to Doyle at the end of May.[11] The end finally came at nine o'clock on the morning of 15 June 1834. Doyle died on a narrow truckle bed with only a straw mattress beneath him, thus adding bodily penance to his emaciating illness. The remains were visited by the public at Braganza. The funeral hearse was drawn by six horses. But the people as a mark of respect insisted on drawing the hearse the entire way from Braganza through the main streets of the town to the Cathedral. The County Carlow M.P.s, Walter Blackney and Thomas Wallace were among the pall-bearers. The procession was led by nearly 1,000 school children of the convent, national and Catholic schools in Carlow. These were followed by the members of the charitable societies established in Carlow, and all were decorated with scarves and hatbands. To these succeeded the students of Carlow College and all the inhabitants of the town. On 19 June, Archbishop Murray presided at the obsequies assisted by Archbishop Slattery, Bishop Murphy of Cork, Bishop Kinsella of Ossory and Bishop Keating of Ferns. Dr Fitzgerald, president of Carlow College, wept so freely at the funeral 'as to attract and excite the sympathy and feelings of all present'. In its issue reporting Doyle's death and interment, the *Carlow Morning Post* appeared with black borders and black lines as if marking a royal death. Its obituary, written by a Carlow College professor, described Doyle as 'the most eminent of all ecclesiastics of his own, or any other creed in Great Britain and Ireland'.[12] This mirrored a comment in the *Morning Chronicle* in 1831 which asked 'who is there of the established clergy, either of England, Ireland or Scotland, for instance, to compare with Dr Doyle ?'[13]

Doyle had desired to be buried with his episcopal predecessor James Keefe in the 'Old Graves' beside the river Barrow but, almost inevitably, he was buried before the high altar of the Cathedral he had built and consecrated less than a year earlier. The inscription on his burial stone, which is in the form of a cross, reads :

> I.H.S. Underneath are deposited, in the hope of a glorious resurrection, the mortal remains of The Right Revd James Doyle, Bishop of Kildare and Leighlin. He was consecrated, on the 14th of Novr., 1819, and died on the 15th of June 1834, in the 48th year of his age. The powerful energies of his great mind were unremittingly exerted for the interests of religion and his country; but the special objects of his public labours and pastoral solicitude were the poor. And it was his dying wish that they should be reminded, by a simple inscription on his tomb, to pray for the repose of his soul. Eternal rest give to him, O Lord, and let perpetual light shine unto him.

The *Dublin Evening Post* and the *Carlow Morning Post* both poured scorn on the propagandistic and malicious reports carried in Protestant papers that Doyle had apostasised on his death-bed.[14] Bishop Kinsella delivered a panegyric at the month's mind mass in July.[15] Richard More O'Ferrall, M.P., acted as chairman, with Robert Cassidy as secretary, of a meeting held in Carlow College on 17 July to consider the erection of a fitting memorial to Doyle. The meeting appointed a managing committee of gentry and priests to gather subscriptions for the Doyle monument fund.[16] A full record of their endeavours is extant in the archives. John Hogan was commissioned to sculpt a statue of Doyle. Hogan's very highly regarded statue was unveiled in 1840 in Carlow Cathedral.[17]

The opening chapter of this work discussed Doyle's early life before he became bishop. The second chapter assessed the impact of Doyle's predecessors on the diocese he came to rule in 1819 and it examined important aspects of Doyle's own pastoral administration. It has been seen that Bishop Delany had difficulty managing his mensal parishes not to mention effectively governing a large diocese. His pastoral shortcomings led to the growth of many of the abuses which Doyle as bishop set out to eradicate. Doyle's reform activity was apparently concentrated more on his clergy than on the laity per se, though this may be because the surviving source material is mainly in the form of correspondence with his clergy, and apart from regular visitations, Doyle administered the diocese through his clergy.

Doyle re-instituted the diocesan deanery system which had been neglected by Delany and his incapacitated successor, Corcoran. Doyle chose not to restore the diocesan chapter which had lapsed, thus concentrating power in his own hands. Ecclesiastical power in the diocese was centralised in Carlow parish, in which were located Carlow College, a major Catholic lay college and seminary, and Braganza (from 1826) the first permanent residence or seat of the bishops of Kildare and Leighlin.

Doyle's concern for his flock was such that, though Carlow College provided him with an annual supply of new priests, he chose to maintain an under-staffed diocese rather than impose the burden of further clergy on the poor. (Similarly, after much heart-searching, Doyle was prepared, in years of great poverty, to relax the full rigour of Lenten observance to help relieve the poor.) An under-staffed diocese did not however mean pastoral neglect. Doyle's emphasis was placed on the quality of clerical pastoral performance rather than on the number of priests on the mission. It is also clear that the socio-economic profile of a parish dictated the type of priest appointed to minister in it.

The Council of Trent provided Doyle with a source-book of ecclesiastical government. Aspects of his episcopal management, such as the holding of annual diocesan synods, his scrupulously executed visitations and the excommunication of incorrigibles, were all in strict conformity with Trent.

An extraordinary surge of church-building permeated the diocese in Doyle's time providing the physical facilities to accommodate an increasing population. All classes, including the Protestant gentry, contributed to this vigorous expansionism, according to their means, either financially or in the supply of labour. It has proved difficult to quantify the input of the Catholic middle class in the erection of these churches partly because of the lack of documentation but as this class provided sons and daughters for the church, it may be assumed that it was prominently involved. The building of Carlow Cathedral in only five years was remarkably fast by Irish standards in the nineteenth century.

Chapter three analysed Doyle's influence on the education of his secular clergy and his role in the shaping and determining of their lifestyle and conduct. Doyle was the architect of reforms and improvements, not only in Carlow College but also in Maynooth College and in the Irish College, Paris. Candidates for the priesthood in Carlow were well-educated and thoroughly examined before they were allowed to proceed to ordination. During Doyle's episcopacy, the college had a justifiably high reputation. In an effort to attain even higher standards in 1824, Doyle invited a French order, the Paris-based Sulpicians, to take over the management of the college. Indeed many of Doyle's reforms bear a close resemblance to the renewal taking place in the French church at this time. In Carlow College, Doyle ran an examination-based post-graduate pastoral course in catechesis and preaching to prepare newly ordained priests for the needs of the mission. On the mission, priests preached and catechised every Sunday.

In Doyle's administration, theological conferences became an integral part of the ecclesiastical round for seculars and regulars in the diocese. The harshness of the penalties imposed for absence from conferences in Kildare and Leighlin was but one indication that these conferences were in no sense purely ritual exercises. They followed a very detailed programme of renewal and revision of ecclesiastical knowledge in the fields of moral and dogmatic theology, as laid down by Doyle, who usually attended in person. Apart from this on-going attention to ecclesiastical education, the theological conference also helped to promote uniformity of observance within the diocese and an esprit de corps among the clergy. Annual retreats also provided temporary breaks from the rigours of the mission and gave clergymen an opportunity to concentrate on their spirituality and to re-dedicate themselves to the things of the spirit. On such occasions, Doyle invariably preached on the duties of the priest. His leading national role as a preacher, as for instance, his sermon at the dedication of the pro-cathedral in Dublin, has been recognised en passant.

Under Doyle, the public image of the priest took on a uniform character. Priests were required to dress in black or blackish cloth; their attendance at public amusements and festivities was normally prohibited. A new sense of separateness was fostered by Doyle's neo-Tridentine emphasis on clerical appearance, dress and public decorum. There was perhaps a diminution of that ease and familiarity of social intercourse which were features of the priest-people relationship in the penal era. The priest now had increased status and a more professional dimension to him but this did not mean that he was any less concerned about his flock: it simply meant that he was more conscious of the role and dignity of the clerical state and that he performed his functions in a more accomplished manner. An exact attention to the rubric of the liturgy and to the cleanliness of all sacred vessels and vestments was strictly required. The phenomenon of farmer-priests provided another example of how Doyle distanced the priest from the lay-man. He curtailed the activities of farmer-priests whose farming backgrounds and in some cases contiguity to their native heaths were very strong incentives to participate in the agricultural economy. Such reform inevitably led to the professionalisation of priests as specialists in only one distinct and well-defined discipline and to the formation of a sort of clerical caste. Although Doyle was a rigorist, his methods of dealing with troublesome priests were characterised by a strict fairness; a forewarning of priests whose conduct was unacceptable; a disposition to take counsel from fellow bishops and a willingness, if necessary, in almost democratic fashion to hear the opinions of parishioners themselves, before disciplinary action was taken. After initially dealing with some clerics Doyle found few faults with the great majority of his priests apart perhaps from occasional inattention to the exact rubric of the liturgy.

In 1823 and again in 1831 Doyle praised the 'piety and zeal' of his missionary priests.[18] In the latter year, he noted their 'oft-proved disposition to second my efforts in all that regards the interests of religion'.[19] In his 1829 Relatio Status, Doyle could fairly state of his diocesan priests that 'their morals are with scarcely any exception good, and they are among the most learned and disciplined of the Irish clergy'.[20]

Doyle acted, at all times, to uphold the dignity of religion where he perceived it to be endangered and he was not prepared to tolerate recalcitrants. In accord with this perspective was the bishop's regulation of clerical incomes. He was concerned to spare the poor from avaricious clergymen. Parishioners were expected to contribute to the support of their clergy in accordance with their means: thus the majority of the poor, who had nothing, gave nothing. Doyle considerably improved the status of the hitherto lowly curate by regulating the manner in which he was supported by his parish priest. The parallels between Doyle's diocesan reforms and the provincial statutes of 1831 are many and striking.

In chapter four, Doyle's relations with the Augustinians elucidated three difficulties facing all the orders: namely the problem of unsuitable entrants to the religious life, of internal wrangling in monasteries, and of the hostility of some members of the episcopacy to the regulars. Doyle's own adminstration of his monastic and conventual religious was chiefly characterised by an unrelenting insistence on discipline and order. In his Relatio Status for 1829 Doyle informed Rome that the regulars 'tho' few in number ... have not been exempt from faults which I was obliged to meet with punishment'. Of the nuns, he reported that, though their enclosures were not complete 'no abuses have crept into their monasteries'.[21] Punished most severely were the strolling friars who were entirely banished from Kildare and Leighlin under Doyle. These wandering friars were a legacy of the penal era who, free of regular occupation and communal discipline, had degenerated into a lax and easy-going observance. The circumstances under which they had been tolerated no longer prevailed. They consequently lacked a *raison d'être* and Doyle was unprepared to accept their continued presence in his diocese as he pursued a policy of ecclesiastical *aggiornamento*. Their lifestyle was an affront to Doyle's conception of the religious life. Punished also were the Calced Carmelites whose Irish province was in disarray in the 1820s. As a result of their indiscipline the Carmelites lost their monastery in Leighlinbridge during Doyle's episcopacy. Doyle's bruising dispute with the Jesuits at Clongowes (even if faculties were restored) could hardly have failed to leave the Jesuits under any illusions about his views on the alleged 'lax' theology of the Society of Jesus.

The foundation of the Brigidines and the Patricians has been regarded as the high-point of Bishop Delany's pastoral achievement. However the formation of these congregations was peculiarly nebulous and they were given neither firm direction nor a distinctive character by him. That definition of direction and character was very largely Doyle's achievement though he preferred to highlight Delany's role. Even in his 1829 report to the pope, Doyle only allowed that he had 'reduced' the Brigidine 'rules to better order and given them a more religious appearance'.[22] In fact, however, Doyle had provided the Brigidines and Patricians with a rule and had established them on a solid and successful teaching basis.[23]

While it is necessary to emphasise the reforms of the orders carried out by Doyle (and the re-organization of Delany's congregations), sight must not be lost of the substantial progress made by religious themselves in Kildare and Leighlin, as the fabric of institutional Catholicism rose to prominence amid an expanding landscape of church building in the diocese. In particular the history of the Dominicans, Patricians, Brigidines and the Presentation order under Doyle is one of growth, expansion and the erection of new monasteries, churches and schools, the latter being consistent with the bishop's strong pastoral stress on the education of the poor.

Given that Doyle was an extremely vigilant pastor and a remarkably keen observer of the contemporary Irish scene, his evidence on the state of religious practice within Kildare and Leighlin and the changes taking place in religious behaviour generally is especially valuable. On the whole, Doyle was very satisfied with what he found. Indeed, in 1823, he could write that 'the progress of our religion ... is such as to excite even our own surprise'.[24] On his first pastoral visitation he witnessed 'many striking proofs' of the laity's 'unbounded zeal'; 'in many places, the piety manifested by you has filled our hearts with gratitude to Heaven'. He did complain that public scandals had occasionally come to his attention but this seemed very much an aside in the flow of praise.[25] His 1823 Lenten pastoral was more forthcoming and was outspoken against those among his flock who were drunkards, blasphemers, adulterers, fornicators, liars, usurers, oppressors of the poor, thieves and slanderers – 'these many of you were ... and these many of you still are; these things we often charged you with before God, and Jesus Christ to renounce, but you have not done so'.[26] But this was not a wholesale indictment of the flock as is clear from his June 1823 pastoral: 'we speak not to those few incorrigible sinners ... but ... to you ... who compose almost the entire population'.[27]

Doyle's main concern was to provide a church infrastructure to support the many who evidently displayed a disposition and anxiety to deepen their faith. In his 1821 Lenten pastoral, he remarked on 'the desire of religious instruction which pervades all classes' yet he lamented that even

> where the most zealous clergymen are constantly employed in attending to the instruction, and other spiritual wants of their numerous congregations, that yet great numbers remain ignorant of what it would be desirable they should know, and that only a few acquire that intimate knowledge of

our holy religion, and its sublime morality which is so necessary for arriving at the perfection of a Christian life.[28]

It was in this context, as was seen in chapter five, that Doyle encouraged and extended Sunday school catechesis, confraternities and chapel libraries throughout his diocese. In 1824 he was more sanguine than he had been three years earlier, commenting that 'amongst our people there may often be a want of religious instruction though much less than is supposed'.[29] He concentrated on a simple but effective organisation. There were two main catechisms in use in Doyle's Sunday schools, both of which were edited by him; as there were two main confraternities in his diocese, both of which were structured and regulated by him. Any more at that time would have diffused Catholic energies too much for his liking. The provincial statutes made the establishment of the confraternity of the Christian Doctrine mandatory in every parish (where it did not already exist) within a year; likewise every parish was to have its chapel libraries, and the confraternity of the Blessed Sacrament of the Eucharist was recommended.[30]

Doyle made catechetical instruction by the confraternities an important and integral part of the lives of young Catholics and extended Christian instruction to the adult population through before mass readings on Sundays and through the formation of chapel libraries. His instigation of the Catholic Book Society was an attempt to extend this policy thoughout the entire Irish church by providing cheap religious and devotional literature to a new generation of literate Catholics. The perceived threat from the New Reformation tract and bible distributing campaigners acted as a spur to this form of Catholic renewal.

Doyle endeavoured to form Catholics well instructed in the faith, namely young people who could read and bring an informed conscience to bear on their lives in accordance with Catholic teaching. The extraordinary data available for the numbers in the Sunday schools and the confraternities, the number of catechists and the quantity of books in the chapel libraries, attest to the success of Doyle's endeavour. Indeed it is hardly an exaggeration to claim that, through Sunday school catechesis, confraternities and chapel libraries, Doyle accomplished a catechetical revolution in Kildare and Leighlin. It is doubtful whether any other diocese could lay claim to a comparable achievement.

In the critically important matter of lay Catholic religious practice, a number of findings were suggested by the somewhat fragmentary evidence. Firstly, there is strong evidence that confessional visits were frequent. It would appear that Catholics were under the impression that they had to attend confession before each individual reception of communion whether they had committed mortal sin or not. The 'stations of confession' were retained and reformed (not abolished as some historians have suggested) by Doyle. This practice supposedly originated in the penal era and undoubtedly held, in early nineteenth century Ireland, an important place in the church year for ordinary Catholics. Doyle was among those bishops who resisted a Roman rescript to abolish the practice in private houses and to remove the hearing of confessions solely to the churches.

Mass attendance figures present particular difficulties as the evidence is very tentative but, based on on the report of the commissioners of Public Instruction (which has been challenged), a 61 per cent average for the diocese was suggested rising possibly as high as 74 per cent. However, this writer, in common with others such as Patrick J. Corish, Ignatius Murphy and Ambrose Macaulay, is inclined to the view that the statistics supplied in the report of the commissioners of Public Instruction are surrounded by so many imponderables as to be unreliable. They are too vague to be accepted as authoritative. Doyle, who is certainly a reliable witness, did not draw any attention to a pastoral concern over mass attendance. On the contrary, his pastoral of June 1823 lauded the 'multitudes' who attended mass, their 'pious demeanour' and 'strict integrity'.[31] Attendance at Easter duty was of even more fundamental importance and here the evidence was highly satisfactory from the church perspective. The visitation returns reveal an extremely detailed knowledge of the faithful by the parochial clergy. In some parishes there were no absentees recorded, in many parishes absenteeism was not more than two or three per cent and in only one parish in the entire diocese, were ten per cent of the total Catholic population deemed to be absent from their Easter duty. Little attention has been focussed up to now by historians on the incidence of week-day masses which in Kildare and Leighlin were celebrated in over a quarter of the parishes of the diocese in 1834; also neglected has been the service of vespers which was an important devotion throughout the diocese, bringing parishioners to the parochial chapels a second time on Sundays.

It seems probable that the difficulty of receiving communion with regularity during the penal era created a climate in which infrequent reception of communion was the norm. Doyle expressed dissatisfaction with the figures for annual communicants in a number of parishes in 1820–23 but it is noticeable how these figures were revised upwards in his 1829 survey of the diocese. Monthly reception of communion was the ideal inculcated by the clergy and it is probable that only the religious themselves received more often on a regular basis. Doyle urged the laity to receive the sacrament frequently and noted an affected reverence as an inhibiting factor.

Doyle was responsible for three significant ecclesiastical initiatives at hierarchical level which influenced the Irish church nationally. He was the architect and motivating force behind the successful Catholic Book Society which could have achieved more had it been supported generally by the Irish church. The implementation throughout Ireland of *Tametsi*, the Tridentine decree on marriage, took place largely at Doyle's insistence. It put an end to the singularly anomalous position where clandestine marriages, though strictly prohibited, were valid in some dioceses though null and void in most others. The removal of three of the most abused holy days from the Irish church calendar was primarily Doyle's achievement. He was also the most influential Irish Catholic churchman to support the temperance movement before Fr Mathew's crusade.

Patterns were popular religious practices in Kildare and Leighlin. As with the stations of confession – another instance of inherited popular religious practice – Doyle did not abolish patterns, but rather endeavoured to restrain the tradition where boisterous conviviality threatened or overwhelmed the religious content of the occasion. Perhaps surprisingly, no evidence has been found of wake abuses presenting a significant pastoral problem.

In his 1829 Relatio Status, Doyle confirmed his overall satisfaction with the practice of religion among the laity of Kildare and Leighlin, informing Rome that 'the morals of the people are excellent and are each year more and more exemplary. There is no abuse prevailing which the ordinary authority cannot correct'.[32] This comment represented a very definite seal of approval from a severe and non-compromising exponent of the need for the uniform application of neo-Tridentine standards.

Chapter six examined Doyle's efforts to contain and eliminate the activities of illegal agrarian and political secret societies in his diocese. In his first pastoral letters Doyle advocated an *ancien régime* style conformity to the crown. This approach reached its zenith in his November 1822 pastoral against Ribbonism in the deanery of Kilcock. The submissiveness which Doyle advocated rested on theological grounds: the duty of Catholics to give their allegiance to the duly constituted temporal power. This pastoral was also notable for Doyle's direct recognition of political disaffection stemming from nationalism, the evidence for which members of the hierarchical bench normally sought to minimise. Doyle's June 1823 pastoral revealed a decidedly new approach: passive obedience was cast aside; the biblical justificiations for Catholic allegiance to the temporal power omitted. In their stead, Doyle emphasised the legal and constitutional right of the subject to agitate for redress of grievance.

In other writings, the right to rebel was acknowledged by Doyle but, as the failure of rebellion would only compound the difficulties of the Irish Catholics and as failure was the most likely outcome of such an undertaking, he privately dismissed it as impractical and publicly preached the necessity for undivided allegiance to the throne.

Doyle's efforts to maintain the public peace were neither a complete success nor a complete failure (though by his own standards he probably considered his endeavour a failure in the final two years of his life). Agrarian disturbance had its origin in social, economic and political factors which lay outside clerical control. Where the wealth of society was so unevenly distributed, with consequent social injustice, it was perhaps inevitable that the marginalised and the recalcitrant would take the law into their own hands. Thus, despite unwearying exertions and occasional personal risk (though it was rare enough for threats to be carried out in the

1820s and for clergymen to be in danger of their lives), the church was ultimately unable to quell agrarian outrage completely. Nonetheless it is arguable that the Catholic church was the most powerful force for peace and good order in the country. The church did much to maintain the law and, even if in the last analysis it was often unable to preserve the public peace, it prevented a bad situation from becoming much worse. Throughout the pre-famine decades the voice of the church defused the potentially explosive forces within peasant society.

To what extent was clerical control over the poor weakened by the church's opposition to Ribbonism? The evidence of the Queen's County parish priests – O'Connor, Delany and Keogh – suggests that they were able to influence those on the margins of secret societies but held no sway with the committed and the completely disaffected who were generally those at the bottom of the social ladder. Yet this disaffected group left no permanent record of anticlericalism. As has been pointed out, 'the level of anticlerical violence is insignificant when set beside the full extent of clerical involvement in the maintenance of law and order'.[33]

Where national political issues influenced local agitation (as in 1822, according to Doyle) the Irish terrorist was always able to make a distinction, which rationalised if it did not explain, the dichotomy between his Catholic code of religious beliefs, and the non-Christian reality of his violent politics. It would seem that a hereditary belief in the fundamental justice of the 'cause' took precedence over orthodox religious considerations. The politics of revenge superseded religion, and instinct had ascendency over religious formation. Viewed objectively, this co-existence is a considerable paradox but one which the Irish mind lived with, not uncomfortably, and without long-term detriment to religious observance or the status of the church, for most of the nineteenth century.

This book has stressed the evolutionary development of Irish Catholicism within a fully Tridentine and neo-Tridentine framework once the penal laws had been removed from the statute book. The 1820s however do appear to have been a critical decade in the development of the Irish church in the nineteenth century. It was a decade which witnessed a renaissance of Catholic politics in a self-confidently aggressive form; which saw the further identification and cementing of denominational beliefs and political attitudes in Irish life. An assessment of the extent to which these trends in political life and religious controversy acted as a catalyst and an accelerator of religious devotion in Ireland has lain outside the scope of this work. The political, interdenominational and education questions of this period form the subject of the author's other book on Doyle.[34]

The implications of this present work for the Larkin thesis are obvious. The Larkin thesis of a 'Devotional Revolution in Ireland, 1850–1875' was predicated on an unawareness of the nature of pre-famine Catholicism. For instance, Larkin contended that 'Most of the two million Irish who emigrated between 1847 and 1860 were part of the pre-famine generation of non-practising Catholics, if indeed they were Catholics at all'.[35] In work published in 1991, the present writer offered a refutation of the Larkin thesis by stressing the 'Tridentine evolution' of modern Irish Catholicism over a much longer time period.[36]

Doyle's pastoral administration within Kildare and Leighlin was exceptionally impressive. His rigorist 'hands-on' approach touched every branch of diocesan administration. There was no aspect of Catholic practice within the diocese which did not receive his attention. By the time of his death, Doyle certainly had the best organised diocese in the country. Rarely had an Irish bishop made the provisions of the Council of Trent on the role of the active, resident bishop, so completely his own. However, as has been seen, his achievement transcended his own diocese. He was a national figure and very much the dominant force within the hierarchy. The energy and commitment Doyle brought to his ministry made him the leading church reformer in Ireland. The hierarchical bench relied on Doyle to draft national pastoral letters for them. No major question was contemplated without Doyle's opinion first being sought. Prelates such as Murray of Dublin and Curtis of Armagh, depended on Doyle for advice and guidance and acknowledged the value of his ideas to them. By those standards – the standards of his own diocesan administration and of his national contemporary influence – Bishop Doyle's pastoral achievement was an extraordinary one.

APPENDICES

Parish	Baptisms	Marriages
Abbeyleix	6 June 1824 – 23 Aug. 1830	2 July 1824 – 28 July 1830
Allen	15 Oct. 1820 – 31 Oct. 1852	17 Oct. 1820 – 26 Oct. 1876
Arles	20 Mar. 1831 – 22 Jan. 1843	28 Sept. 1831 – 27 Feb. 1843
Bagenalstown	1 Jan. 1820 – 27 June 1841	8 Jan. 1820 – 26 June 1841
Ballinakill	14 Oct. 1794 – 19 Mar. 1815	27 Oct. 1794 – 7 Feb. 1815
	16 Jan. 1820 – 26 May 1820	15 Jan. 1820 – 7 July 1820
	4 Nov. 1820 – 29 Sept. 1872	3 Nov. 1820 – 25 Nov. 1875
Ballon	2 Jan. 1785 – 10 Sept. 1795	10 Aug. 1782 – 10 Dec. 1795
	2 July 1816 – 26 Dec. 1830	8 Jan. 1820 – 14 Feb. 1825
	9 Jan. 1820 – 14 Feb. 1825	10 Aug. 1816 – 26 Nov. 1868
	6 Jan. 1831 – 27 Dec. 1868	
Ballyadams	3 Jan. 1820 – 28 Feb. 1847	12 Jan. 1820 – 24 Nov. 1853
Ballyfin	10 Oct. 1824 – 3 Aug. 1862	1 Aug. 1819 – 27 Aug. 1862
Baltinglass	31 May 1807 – 18 Feb. 1810	2 Feb. 1810 – 16 Apr. 1811
	8 July 1810 – 4 Apr. 1811	20 Nov. 1813 – 12 Sept. 1815
	4 Oct. 1813 – 19 Jan. 1830	25(?) Apr. 1816– 25 Apr. 1831
	7 Mar. 1830 – 12 July 1857	28 Jan. 1830 – 19 May 1857
Balyna	17 Oct. 1785 – 27 Oct. 1801	5 Nov. 1797 – 23 May 1799
	6 Nov. 1801 – 17 July 1803	13 Nov. 1801 – 31 Jan. 1802
	24 Aug. 1807 – 21 Oct. 1811	1 Oct. 1807 – 26 Oct. 1811
	15 Jan. 1815 – 22 Feb. 1815	22 Jan. 1815 – 7 Feb. 1815
	1 Feb. 1818 – 12 Apr. 1829	7 Apr. 1817 – 21 Aug. 1830
	1 Feb. 1818 – 21 Dec. 1865	23 Mar. 1818 – 15 Nov. 1880
Borris	2 May 1782 – 23 Dec. 1813	26 Jan. 1782 – 4 Dec. 1813
	2 Feb. 1825 – 15 Mar. 1840	8 Feb. 1825 – 3 Mar. 1840
Caragh	Registers date from 1849	
Carbury	1 Oct. 1821 – 22 May 1850	2 Nov. 1821 – 27 Oct. 1850
Carlow	15 Nov. 1787 – 14 Jan. 1789	1 Jan. 1820 – 17 June 1845
	7 Dec. 1793 – 17 Dec. 1793	
	19 Jan. 1794 – 17 Dec. 1795	
	1 Jan. 1799 – 9 May 1804	
	10 Jan. 1806 – 15 Apr. 1806	
	2 Jan. 1807 – 5 Feb. 1807	
	1 Jan. 1809 – 9 May 1809	
	5 Jan. 1811 – 13 Jan. 1811	
	1 Jan. 1820 – 19 Aug. 1834	
Clane	17 Mar. 1785 – 4 Sept. 1785	10 Apr. 1825 – 2 June 1828
	1 Feb. 1786 – 3 July 1786	15 Nov. 1829 – 5 June 1840
	8 Dec. 1788 – 8 Apr. 1789	
	28 Feb. 1825 – 28 Feb. 1827	
	6 Sept. 1829 – 31 May 1840	

Parish	Baptisms	Marriages
Clonaslee	Registers date from 1849	
Clonbullogue	7 Nov. 1819 – 14 June 1869	2 Jan. 1808 – 14 June 1869
Clonegal	7 Jan. 1833 – 27 Nov. 1842	14 Feb. 1833 – 20 May 1871
Clonmore	23 Nov. 1819 – 26 Feb. 1860	14 Feb. 1813 – 19 Feb. 1860
Doonane	c.1821–1856	c.1821–1856
Edenderry	2 Jan. 1820 – 29 Dec. 1838	9 Jan. 1820 – 20 Nov. 1837
Graiguenamanagh	from 1838	6 July 1818 – 26 Nov. 1868
Hacketstown	29 Aug. 1820 – 20 Apr. 1823	31 Aug. 1820 – 1 Dec. 1827
	10 July 1826 – 7 Sept. 1826	3 Mar. 1829 – 28 Nov. 1863
	a few entries for 1815–20	
	in this volume	
	14 Oct. 1827 – 27 Mar. 1877	
Kilcock	6 July 1771 – 4 Dec. 1786	28 Jan. 1770 – 28 May 1787
	14 Aug. 1816 – 23 Dec. 1826	27 Feb. 1791 – 1 May 1791
	9 Oct. 1831 – 28 June 1834	7 Aug. 1816 – 29 Sept. 1822
Kildare	1 Nov. 1815 – 31 Dec. 1837	1 Nov. 1815 – 30 Nov. 1837
Kill	Registers date from 1840 and 1843 respectively	
Killeigh	Registers date from 1843 and 1844 respectively	
Killeshin	23 Nov. 1819 – 16 Oct. 1845	20 Jan. 1822 – 24 Nov. 1846
Leighlinbridge	1 Jan. 1783 – 22 Oct. 1786	9 Feb. 1783 – 14 Jan. 1788
	1 Dec. 1819 – 26 June 1827	13 Jan. 1820 –27 Feb. 1827
	6 July 1827 – 16 Nov. 1844	12 July 1827 – 22 Nov. 1880
Maryborough	14 May 1826 – 4 Feb. 1838	27 Apr. 1826 – 30 Jan. 1838
Monasterevan	1 Jan. 1819 – 22 Feb. 1835	11 Sept. 1819 – 26 Feb. 1835
	28 Mar. 1829 – 15 Aug. 1833	
Mountmellick	1 Jan. 1814 – 23 Dec. 1837	2 Feb. 1814 – 27 Apr. 1843
Mountrath	12 Oct. 1823 – 21 Apr. 1867	13 June 1827 – 28 July 1869
Myshall	11 Feb. 1822 – 3 May 1846	17 Sept. 1822 – 30 Jan. 1845
Naas	1 Mar. 1813 – 24 Jan. 1865	28 Feb. 1813 – 15 Aug. 1877
Newbridge	2 Aug. 1786 – 18 Jan. 1795	6 Aug. 1786 – 20 Jan. 1795
	14 Jan. 1820 – 18 Aug. 1832	17 Aug. 1820 – 15 Aug. 1846
	1 Jan. 1834 – 1 Oct. 1846	
Paulstown	9 July 1824 – 19 Apr. 1846	21 Jan. 1824 – 28 Nov. 1840
Philipstown	12 Aug. 1795 – 23 Sept. 1798	7 Jan. 1820 – 3 May 1855
	6 Jan. 1820 – 18 Feb. 1855	
Portarlington	1 Jan. 1820 – 22 Nov. 1846	24 Nov. 1822 – 16 July 1845
Raheen	5 Apr. 1819 – 19 Dec. 1880	20 Jan. 1820 – 30 Sept. 1880
Rathvilly	19 Oct. 1797 – 15 Jan. 1813	5 Oct. 1800 – 13 Feb. 1812
	29 June 1813 – 25 Apr. 1842	29 June 1813 – 27 Nov. 1880
Rosenallis	21 Oct. 1765 – 19 Jan. 1777	12 Oct. 1765 – 10 June 1777
	1 Feb. 1782 – 13 Aug. 1782	7 Feb. 1782 – 10 June 1782
	3 Aug. 1823 – 27 Dec. 1879	? July 1823 – 24 July 1859
St Mullin's	4 Sept. 1807 – 3 Mar. 1810	25 Oct. 1807 – 8 Mar.(?) 1813
	19 Jan. 1812 – 16 Apr. 1814	10 Aug. 1832 – 30 Nov. 1871
	8 Feb. 1816 – 25 Mar.(?)1816	
	6 Jan. 1820 – 30 July 1832	
	10 Aug. 1832 – 31 Dec. 1871	
Stradbally	2 Jan. 1820 – 18 May 1855	20 Jan. 1820 – 24 June 1849
Suncroft	29 Mar. 1805 – 26 Dec. 1880	15 Mar. 1805 – 29 July 1880

Parish	Baptisms	Marriages
Tinryland	28 Mar. 1813 – 24 May 1833	20 June 1813 – 24 Feb. 1843
	2 June 1833 – 20 Dec. 1857	
Tullow	13 Aug. 1763 – 10 Jan. 1781	7 May 1775 – 20 Feb. 1776
	19 Jan. 1798 – 1 Jan. 1802	18 Jan. 1799 – 27 Feb. 1800
	5 June 1807 – 4 July 1831	19 June 1807 – 20 May 1830
	23 Aug. 1830 – 18 Apr. 1858	20(?) Nov. 1830 – 20 Feb. 1860

Parish	Deaths
Ballinakill	30 Oct. 1794 – 25 Feb. 1815
Ballon	9 Aug. 1825 – 6 Dec. 1834
Baltinglass	12 Aug. 1824 – 11 Sept. 1830
Doonane	c. 1821–1856
Rosenallis	14 Oct. 1824 – 21 Sept. 1827

APPENDIX 2: PAROCHIAL CHURCH BUILDING, 1819–29[1]

Parish	Churches	*1819–1829*
Abbeyleix	Abbeyleix	Built
	Ballyroan	Improved
Allen	Allen/Kilmeague	Enlarged
	Milltown	Improved
Arles	Arles	Enlarged
	Ballylinan	Enlarged
	Killeen	Planned
Bagenalstown	Bagenalstown	Enlarged
	Newtown	Improved
	Ballinkillen	Improved
Ballinakill	Ballinakill	Improved
	Knockardagun/Mountain	Enlarged
Ballon	Ballon	Improved
	Rathoe	Improved
Ballyadams	Ballyadams	Enlarged
	Luggacurrin	Enlarged
	Wolfhill	Improved
Ballyfin	Ballyfin	Built
Baltinglass	Baltinglass	Built
	Bumba Hall/Grange Con	Improved
	Stratford	Enlarged & Improved

Parish	Churches	1819–1829
Balyna	Johnstown	Built
	Nurney/Garrisher/Clogherinkoe	Enlarged
	Broadford/Kilreny	Improved
Borris	Ballymurphy	Improved
	Rathana	not mentioned
	Borris	Built
Caragh	Prosperous	Improved
	Caragh	Improved
Carbury	Carbury/Derrinturn	Improved
	Dunfort/Kilshinroe	Enlarged
Carlow	Cathedral	Building begun, 1828
Clane	Clane	Improved
	Rathcoffey	Enlarged
	Staplestown	Enlarged
Clonaslee	Clonaslee	Built
Clonbullogue	Clonbullogue	Enlarged
	Brackna	Enlarged
	Walsh Island	Built
Clonegal	Clonegal	Built
	Kildavin/Barragh	Improved
Clonmore	Clonmore	Improved
	Kilquiggan	Improved & Enlarged
	Knockballestein/Ballyconnell	Not mentioned
Doonane	Doonane	Improved
	Mayo	Built
Edenderry	Edenderry	Improved
	Croghan	Built
	Rhode	Not mentioned
Graiguenamanagh	Graiguenamanagh	Improved
	Scaughvasteen	Built
Hacketstown	Hacketstown	Built
	Kilanmote	Enlarged
	Knockanana	Enlarged
	Mountain/Askanagap	Built
Kilcock	Kilcock	Improved
	Newtown	Improved

Parish	Churches	*1819–1829*
Kildare	Kildare	Improved
	Rathangan	Built
Kill	Kill	Built
	Lyons	Not mentioned
Killeigh	Killeigh	Improved
	Ballinagar	Enlarged
	Raheen	Enlarged
Killeshin	Killeshin	Improved
	Graigue	Enlarged
Leighlin	Leighlinbridge	Improved
	Ballinabranna/Millford	Built
Maryborough	Maryborough	Built
	Heath	Improved
Monasterevan	Monasterevan/Passlands	Improved
	Kildangan	Not mentioned
	Nurney	Built
Mountmellick	Mountmellick	Improved
	Clonoughadoo	Built
Mountrath	Mountrath	Improved
	Clonard	Improved
Myshall	Myshall	Improved
	Drumfea	Improved
Naas	Naas	Built
Newbridge	Newbridge	Enlarged
	Two-mile-house	Built
Paulstown	Paulstown	Improved
	Goresbridge	Built
Philipstown	Philipstown	Greatly Enlarged
	Kilclonfert	Improved
	Ballycommon	Planned
Portarlington	Portarlington	Not mentioned
	Emo	Improved
	Killenard	Built
Raheen	Raheen	Not mentioned
	Shanahoe	Improved

Parish	Churches	1819–1829
Rathvilly	Rathvilly	Improved
	Kiltegan	Built
	Englishtown	Improved
Rosenallis	Rosenallis	Improved
St Mullin's	Glynn	Built
	Drummond	Improved
Stradbally	Stradbally	Not mentioned
	Esker	Not mentioned
	Timahoe (replacing Esker)	Erected 1832
	Vicarstown	Erected 1836
Suncroft	Suncroft	Not mentioned
Tinryland	Tinryland	Not mentioned
	Urglin/Bennekerry	Not mentioned
Tullow	Tullow	Improved
	Ardattin	Improved
	Grange	Built

APPENDIX 3: PAROCHIAL SUNDAY SCHOOLS AND CONFRATERNITIES IN 1829[1]

Parish	Sunday Schools	Nos.	Confraternities
Abbeyleix	Abbeyleix ch.	571	
	Ballyroan ch.	580	
	Other schools	1300	
			310
Allen			100
Arles	Arles ch.		200
	Ballylinan ch.		150
	Killeen ch.		80
Bagenalstown	Bagenalstown ch.	461	76
	Newtown ch.	493	90
	Ballinkillen ch.	432	95
Ballinakill	Ballinakill	7/800	435
Ballon	Ballon ch.	188	52
	Rathoe ch. & school	138	36

Parish	Sunday Schools	Nos.	Confraternities
Ballyadams	Ballyadams ch.	290	
	Wolfhill ch.	300	
Ballyfin	Included with Mountrath		30
Baltinglass	Baltinglass ch.		
	Bumba Hall ch.		
	Stratford ch.		454
Balyna	–	–	–
Borris	Borris ch.		
	Ballymurphy ch.		
	Rathana ch.	–	313
Caragh	Caragh ch.	170	
	Prosperous ch.	360	
Carbury	Carbury &		'Few'
	Dunfort chs.	420	
	Other schools	180	
Carlow	Carlow ch.	1118	–
Clane	Clane ch.	240	
	Rathcoffey ch.	110	
	Staplestown ch.	150	
	Other schools	207	
Clonaslee(1828)	See Rosenallis parish		87
Clonbullogue	Clonbullogue ch.		45
	Brackna ch.		52
	Walsh Island		10
Clonegal	Clonegal ch.		
	Barragh ch.		
	39 Other schools	873	48
Clonmore	Clonmore ch.		
	Kilquiggan ch.		
	Knockballestein ch.	225	–
Doonane	Doonane ch.		
	Mayo ch.	–	67
Edenderry	Edenderry ch.		
	Rhode ch.		
	Croghan ch.		
	Other schools	700	250

Parish	Sunday Schools	Nos.	Confraternities
Graiguenamanagh		-	450
Hacketstown	Hacketstown ch.		
	Kilanmote ch.		
	Knockanana ch.		
	Mountain ch.	700	17
Kilcock	Kilcock ch.	105	
	Newtown ch.	130	
	Tiermoghan	70	
Kildare	Kildare ch.	544	
	Rathangan ch.	324	
Kill	Kill ch.		78
	Lyons/Ardclough ch.	225	70
Killeigh	Killeigh ch.		
	Ballinagar ch.		
	Raheen ch.	-	195
Killeshin	Killeshin		84
	Graigue		97
Leighlin	Leighlinbridge		
	Ballinabranna/Millford	-	109
Maryborough		-	-
Monasterevan	Monasterevan ch.	500	
	Kildangan ch.	280	
	Nurney ch.	200	
Mountmellick	Mountmellick ch.	550	
	Clonoughadoo ch.	150	
Mountrath	Mountrath ch.		
& Ballyfin	Clonard ch.		200
	Ballyfin ch.	1800	-
Myshall	Myshall		
	Drumphea	-	305
Naas	Naas ch.	-	-
Newbridge	Newbridge ch.		
	Two-mile-house	average 1000	-
Paulstown	Paulstown ch.	500	
	Goresbridge ch.	300	'Many'

Parish	Sunday Schools	Nos.	Confraternities
Philipstown	Philipstown ch.		
	Kilclonfert ch.		
	Ballycommon ch.	–	170
Portarlington	Portarlington ch.		302
	Killinard	627	285
	Emo		258
Raheen	Raheen ch.		100
	Shanahoe ch.		100
Rathvilly	Rathvilly ch.		
	Kiltegan ch.		
	Englishtown ch.	275	196
Rosenallis	Rosenallis ch.	400	55
& Clonaslee	Clonaslee ch.	440	
St Mullin's	Glynn ch.		
	Drummond ch.	–	130
Stradbally	Stradbally ch.		
	Esker ch.	–	'Perhaps 300'
Suncroft	Suncroft ch.	360	10
Tinryland	Tinryland ch.		
	Bennekerry ch.	–	200
Tullow	Tullow ch.	1022	
	Ardattin ch.		
	Grange ch.	–	'Many'

APPENDIX 4: PAROCHIAL CHAPEL LIBRARIES IN 1829[1]

Parish	Churches	Library vols.
Abbeyleix	Abbeyleix	80
	Ballyroan	80
Allen	Allen	66
	Milltown	–
Arles	Arles	110
	Ballylinan	104
	Killeen	80

Parish	Churches	Library vols.
Bagenalstown	Bagenalstown	120
	Newtown	150
	Ballinkillen	120
Ballinakill	Ballinakill	118
	Knockdargun/Mountain	103
Ballon	Ballon	95
	Rathoe	134
Ballyadams	Ballyadams	113
	Luggacurrin	96
	Wolfhill	94
Ballyfin	Ballyfin	25
Baltinglass	Baltinglass	110
	Bumba Hall	56
	Stratford	80
Balyna	Johnstown	'small no.'
	Nurney/Garrisher	40
	Broadford/Kilreny	43
Borris	Borris	309
	Ballymurphy	157
	Rathana	200
Caragh	Prosperous	–
	Caragh	–
Carbury	Carbury	7
	Dunfort	–
Carlow	Carlow	360
Clane	Clane	–
	Rathcoffey	–
	Staplestown	–
Clonaslee	Clonaslee	28
Clonbullogue	Clonbullogue	100
	Brackna	171
	Walsh Island	–
Clonegal	Clonegal	36
	Barragh	62
Clonmore	Clonmore	70

Parish	Churches	Library vols.
	Kilquiggan	75
	Knockballestein	58
Doonane	Doonane	–
	Mayo	–
Edenderry	Edenderry	140
	Rhode	–
	Croghan	–
Graiguenamanagh	Graiguenamanagh	77
	Scaughvasteen	60
Hacketstown	Hacketstown	10
	Kilanmote	74
	Knockanana	14
	Mountain	–
Kilcock	Kilcock	–
	Newtown	–
Kildare	Kildare	231
	Rathangan	336
Kill	Kill	22
	Lyons	40
Killeigh	Killeigh	90
	Ballinagar	90
	Raheen	95
Killeshin	Killeshin	107
	Graigue	73
Leighlin	Leighlinbridge	72
	Ballinabranna	6
Maryborough	Maryborough	–
	Heath	–
Monasterevan	Monasterevan	298
	Kildangan	186
	Nurney	182
Mountmellick	Mountmellick	200
	Clonoughado	80
Mountrath	Mountrath	200
	Clonard	–

Parish	Churches	Library vols.
Myshall	Myshall	68
	Drumfea	40
Naas	Naas	350
Newbridge	Newbridge	–
	Two-mile-house	–
Paulstown	Paulstown	113
	Goresbridge	–
Philipstown	Philipstown	150
	Kilclonfert	50
	Ballycommon	30
Portarlington	Portarlington	121
	Emo	84
	Killinard	76
Raheen	Raheen	39
	Shanahoe	36
Rathvilly	Rathvilly	200
	Kiltegan	150
	Englishtown	130
Rosenallis	Rosenallis	90
St Mullin's	Glynn	60
	Drummond	–
Stradbally	Stradbally	42
	Esker	8
Suncroft	Suncroft	100
Tinryland	Tinryland	30
	Bennekerry	30
Tullow	Tullow	200
	Ardattin	–
	Grange	–

APPENDIX 5: ANNUAL AND MONTHLY COMMUNICANTS, 1820/23, 1829

Parish	1820/23		1829	
	Annual	*Monthly*	*Annual*	*Monthly*
Abbeyleix(1824)			2500	310
Allen	–	300	–	200
Arles	4000	200	3000	–
Bagenalstown	–	–	5000	400
Ballinakill	5000	500	4000	435
Ballon	1200	200	–	222
Ballyadams	3500	600	4200	400
Ballyfin	1600	300	2000	300
Baltinglass	3284	300	4064	454
Balyna	2400	80	–	–
Borris	3000	130	5400	313
Caragh	–	–	–	–
Carbury	1300	55	2000	–
Carlow	2000	450	2600	500
Clane	3000	250	–	–
Clonaslee (1828)			2368	87
Clonbullogue	–	–	2500	130
Clonegal	–	–	3994	374
Clonmore	–	–	4800	600
Doonane	–	–	2623	80
Edenderry	3000	300	3000	500
Graiguenamanagh	5000	500	4400	450
(divided, 1823)				
Hacketstown	3855	200	3260	600
Kilcock	1527	115	–	–
Kildare	–	–	3600	400
Kill	900	60	1000	220
Killeigh	3460	205	4000	300
Killeshin	–	–	3200	350
Leighlinbridge	4000	100	3398	109
(divided, 1823)				
Maryborough	–	300	–	–
Monasterevan	–	–	3200	270
Mountmellick	–	–	3500	300
Mountrath	(?)4000	500	2500	400
Myshall	2200	260	2639	350
Naas	1300	120	1756	50
Newbridge	(?)2000	120	–	250
Paulstown	–	–	3000	500
Philipstown	3450	300	3200	270
Portarlington	–	–	1416	250
Raheen	2590	350	2500	200
Rathvilly	1900	340	4100	600
Rosenallis	–	–	1800	80
St Mullin's	2367	200	3050	130
Stradbally	2300	150	3000	200
Suncroft	–	–	1300	100
Tinryland	–	300	1900	400
Tullow	3274	600	4000	(?)450

APPENDIX 6: HOLY WELLS AND PATTERNS

Parish	Holy Wells and Patterns	Details
Abbeyleix	Lady's Well dedicated to the Blessed Virgin pattern day, 15 August	Sited in the direction of Rosconnel just outside Ballinakill parish bounds.[1]
Allen	St Brigid's Well, esteemed holy	In 1880s 'generally known as Fr Moore's Well' after C.C. who died in 1826. May once have been known as the Black Well. Located at Rathbride: stone crucifix three feet high beside well; four wooden crosses stand at some distance from each other around the well – and a number of ex voto crutches were to be seen there in the 1880s. 'This place is still much resorted to.'[2]
	St Peter's day	Formerly a pattern day.[3]
Arles	St Guaire's Well	Saint still remembered in the 1830s.[4]
Bagenalstown	St Laserian's Well pattern was held on 18 April	In Lorum: round tower once stood here.[5]
	St Lappan's Well called Tobar-Molapog feast day, 3 November	At Dunore, a church site.[6]
	St Fortchern's Well, festival was kept in Idrone barony on 11 October	In Killoughternane: 'the existence of which had been well nigh forgotten. It is resorted to by numerous pilgrims at the present time [1880s] and many cures are said to have been effected, in evidence of which numerous ex voto crutches, etc., have been deposited in the ruins of the church'.[7]
	St Brigid's Well[8]	
	St Andrew's Well, pattern day 30 November[9]	
Ballinakill	–	
Ballon	Blessed Well named Tobar-croagh	Ballon Hill: said to have gone dry in consequence of an act of desecration.[10]
	St Patrick's Well	Kellistown.[11]
	Holy Well beside Protestant church	Ahade.[12]
	St Catherine's Well	In Castlemore within Eustace's demesne 'much frequented by pilgrims up to recent times'.[13]
Ballyadams	–	
Ballyfin	–	

Parish	Holy Wells and Patterns	Details
Baltinglass	St Patrick's Well, pilgrimage and stations made on his festival, 17 March	At Knockpatrick: O'Toole states that it was abolished when a man was killed at a faction fight there.[14] Comerford has a folklore account that it was filled in *c.*1780 by a Protestant farmer with grave consequences to himself.[15]
	St Bernard's Well, 20 august	Pattern discontinued *c.*1780.[16]
	Several other wells in this parish[17]	
Balyna	Holy Well of Tober-crogh neeve, 'The well of the Holy Cross'	In Carrick: 'now totally neglected and its site scarcely known, it was once highly venerated and its healing powers greatly esteemed ...'.[18]
	St Colman's Well	Visited on St Peter's day.[19]
	Lady's Well	At Glynn: 'A fair and patron are held here in August'.[20]
	Tobernakill[21]	
	Trinity Well[22]	
	Toberaulin[23]	
Borris	Lady's Well, pattern on last Sunday in June	In Clonagoose.[24]
	Sunday pattern, 15 up to 24 June, feast of Bishop Sennil	In Kiltennil.[25]
	Tober-Modalamhan (St Magdalen's Well)	In Kiltennil.[26]
	Kilcullen Well	In Ballynagraine: 'was, within the memory of people still living, resorted [to] by pilgrims'.[27]
Caragh	St Farannan's Well 12 June or July	In the civil parish of Downings to the west of the church where stations were formerly performed. Farannan considered the patron saint.[28]
Carbury	–	
Carlow	–	
Clane	Sunday Well	On west side of the river Liffey: 'A Patron and Stations used to be held at it within the memory of some still living'.[29]
	St Peter's day, pattern, 29 June	In Donadea parish: pattern had died out by 1830s.[30]

Parish	Holy Wells and Patterns	Details
Clonaslee	St Manmon's Well	Pattern formerly celebrated near it. John O'Donovan 'met no one able to tell me the day or month on or in which his pattern was held' in 1838.[31]
Clonbullogue	–	
Clonegal	St Brigid's Well, pattern on her festival, 1 February	In Moyacomb: pattern held up to close of eighteenth century probably discontinued in 1798.[32]
	Sunday's Well or Tober-Ri an Domhnaigh	In Curra townland in Moyacomb.[33]
	Cronavana Well, pattern day, 3 May[34]	In Barragh: discontinued 1798.[35]
Clonmore	St Martin's Well	Croneleigh: dedicated to St Martin of Tours or possibly St Martin the elder, a missionary companion of St Patrick.[36]
	St Mogue's Well, pattern, 1 February	Discontinued c.1800.[37]
	Chapel Well	In Domnach-Fiacc associated with St Fiacc.[38]
	Tobar-Nahan	Pattern held until c.1780–90.[39]
Doonane	St Lonn's Well, pattern, 24 June	In Killgorey (St Guaire – patron of Sruille): withered trunk of an ancient tree decorated with ex voto rags was to be seen there in the 1880s. Old natives told of people flocking to the pattern and of 'fields of tents set up for their accommodation. As has so frequently been the case, abuses resulting from these assemblages, caused the Patron to be discontinued; but even still, the well is resorted to by pilgrims, especially on the festivals of the Blessed Virgin'.[40]
Edenderry	St Patrick's Well	Hill of Croghan: 'resorted for cures even still'.[41]
	Two other sacred wells	Associations forgotten.[42]
Graigue-namanagh	Ancient Well	In Auchailtean: associated with St Bairfion whose feast day is given as 8 November in the Martyrology of Donegal.[43]
	St Fiachra's Well, pattern day, 8 February	'on which day many old people still attend to make their penitential rounds, and perform their devotions' – 'no one from the district would think of emigrating without providing himself with a bottle of the water, as a preservative against shipwreck.'[44]

Parish	Holy Wells and Patterns	Details
	St Michael's Well, pattern, 29 September	In Tinnehinch: well known fair on Michaelmas day – 'festival even still a special day in the neighbourhood; a curious custom is kept up here of eating mutton pasties on that day' – also the custom of the Michaelmas sheep and "Michael's portion".'[45]
Hacketstown	Blessed Well, pattern, 24 June	Near Protestant church: in 1880s pattern still within the memory of old inhabitants.[46]
	St John's Well – Tobar Eoin pattern, 24 June	In Rathdangan.[47]
	St Columbkill's Well, pattern, 9 June	In Sandyford: 'in consequence of some abuses, this celebration was discontinued about 60 years ago [1820s]'.[48] O'Donovan stated that 'old-fashioned people were accustomed to perform stations until the year 1833'.[49]
Kilcock	-	
Kildare	St Brigid's Well	
	St John's Well	both wells in East Tully.[50]
	Sunday Well	In Ballycook.
Kill	Tobar Brighde	In Hartwell townland.[51]
	Lady/Sunday Well	In Whitechurch parish near old church – not frequented in 1830s.[52]
	Well	Near ruin called 'the castle', name forgotten.[53]
Killeigh	Three wells sacred to St Fionnan	In Ballykean civil parish near old church 'at which crowds of pilgrims were accustomed to perform stations about three generations back but now [1830s] entirely neglected'.[54]
	Tobar-Brachain, St Brachan (or Berachan's) Well, pattern, 3 December	In Clonsast civil parish near old church. Patron 'vividly remembered' in the 1830s to be St Brachan 'whose memory was annually celebrated with great devotion'.[55]
	St Brachan's Well	In Clonshannon townland, Clonsast. In the 1830s still visited by a 'few pilgrims'. 'Until a very late period, a numerous pattern was held on the field adjoining this well, and the church on St John's day, and on St Peter and St Paul's, but in consequence of the bad effects of whiskey, the clergy have thought proper to abolish it.'
	Killeigh Holy Wells	Nine holy wells near the village of Killeigh

Parish	Holy Wells and Patterns	Details
		in Geashill civil parish. O'Donovan was of opinion that they should probably be called 'St Sincheall's wells'.[56]
Killeshin	St Diarmuid's Well[57]	
	St Fiacc's Well	O'Donovan in 1838 stated that this well was 'now stopped up'.[58]
Leighlin	St Laserian's Well commonly known as St Molashog's Well, pattern, 18 April	Near St Laserian's Cathedral in Old Leighlin. Pattern suppressed by P.P. in 1812 after a man had been killed in a fight.[59]
Maryborough	Holy Well	At Rathleague in Straboe civil parish. Greatly frequented by pilgrims until the early nineteenth century when it became known as 'Tobar a ghadaigh' because the Tipperary highwayman, Jeremiah Grant, resorted there. He was hanged in Maryborough, 1813.[60]
Monasterevan	Tubbercorcar (St Corcar, 8 March)	In Laccagh: 'was formerly much frequented for the cure of mental maladies'.[61]
	Fuaran Well, pattern, 29 June & 15 August	Mylerstown in Harristown civil parish (Nurney).[62]
	Tobar Righ an Domhnaigh (Sunday's Well)	Ricardstown, Nurney.[63]
	St Brigid's Well	Near Riverstown demesne, Kildangan.[64]
		No holy well near the site of the monastery or its vicinity. The well near the site of the monastery which probably bore the name of St Evin was called Lord Henry Moore's Well in the 1830s because it was enclosed by him.[65]
Mountmellick	Cavagh's Well	Near old burying place in Killeen townland. In 1830s inhabitants knew little about well.[66]
Mountrath	St Fintan's Well, pattern, 17 February	Site of St Fintan's monastery.[67]
Myshall	Holy Well, pattern, 14 September. The feast of the exaltation of the Holy Cross	Adjacent to church ruins. Pattern fair of Myshall a 'great sheep fair'.[68]
Naas	Sunday's Well	In Naas east, pattern held at certain periods. St David venerated in parish on 1 March. 'Green leeks' worn on the occasion.[69]
Newbridge	St Augustine's Well	Site of Augustinian priory of Great Connell founded 1202.[70]

Parish	Holy Wells and Patterns	Details
Paulstown	Lady's Well, pattern, 15 August	In Low Grange: 'much frequented ... up to a period within the recollection of the old inhabitants. In consequence of abuses the clergy thought it well to put a stop to the Patron'.[71]
Philipstown	Lady's Well(?), pattern, 15 August	In Kilclonfert: pattern still held in the 1880s – 'A family named Mangan who regard themselves as the hereditary guardians of the well, attend punctually on the Eve of the Assumption to ... put the place n order for the next day's celebrations'.[72]
Portarlington	-	
Raheen	St Fintan's Well, pattern, 17 February	In Cremogue (Raheen was part of the ancient abbacy of St Fintan). In the 1880s Comerford stated: 'The penitential rounds used to be performed here on the festival of the Saint, and at the present time, pebbles taken from the bottom of this well are eagerly sought for and treasured up, as preservatives against shipwreck or accidental death'.[73]
Rathvilly	St Patrick's Well, pattern, 17 March	In Highfield – Pattern 'had to be discontinued on account of abuses. It is still occasionally visited by pilgrims'.[74]
	St Brigid's Well	In Kilranelagh.[75]
	Well believed holy	In Straboe.[76]
	St Columbcille's well, pattern, 9 June	In Rathdonnil townland at Drumquin.[77]
Rosenallis	St Brigid's Well	In village: parish dedicated to St Brigid.[78]
	St Fionan's Well	In Rearymore – near ruins of old church of Reary.[79]
St Mullin's	St Moling's Well, patterns: 17 June, 25 July (St James's day)	Site of St Moling's church which gives its name to the parish and of a very famous pattern.[80]
Stradbally	-	
Suncroft	-	
Tinryland	St Brigid's Well	In Graig-na-Spiddogue, Tullowmagrinagh.[81]
Tullow	Feast of St Fortchern celebrated on 11 October	Fortchern was one of Patrick's disciples.[82]
	Feast day of St Torannan celebrated on 12 June[83]	

Parish	*Holy Wells and Patterns*	*Details*
	Lady's Well 'formerly the patron well of Tullow'	Water reputed to have been efficacious for the cure of all diseases. 'The Patron has been discontinued, and a fair, held on 8 September, substituted in its place, called the Patron Fair'.[84]

NOTES

ABBREVIATIONS

Acta	Acta Congregationum, Archives of the Congregation of Propaganda Fide, Rome.
Battersby, *Life of Doyle*	[W.J. Battersby], *The life of the Rt Rev Dr Doyle, compiled from authentic documents by the author of the 'Priesthood Vindicated'* (3rd ed., improved and enlarged, Dublin, 1860).
——, *Hist. of the Augustinians in Ire.*	W.J. Battersby, *A history of the abbeys, convents, etc. of the order of St Augustine in Ireland* (Dublin, 1856).
Birch, *St Kieran's*	Peter Birch, *Saint Kieran's College, Kilkenny* (Dublin, 1951).
Bossy, *Eng. Cath. Comm.*	John Bossy, *The English Catholic community 1570–1850* (pbk ed. London, 1977).
Brenan, *Schools*	Martin Brenan, *Schools of Kildare and Leighlin A.D. 1775–1835* (Dublin, 1935).
Brigidine Rule	*Rules and Constitutions of the religious congregation of the Sisters of St Brigid ... established in the town of Tullow for the instruction of female children; conformably to the rules and constitutions prescribed by the founder ... Dr Delany, Bishop of Kildare and Leighlin, and by his Lordship's successor in the above Sees. – James Doyle, D.D.* (Dublin, 1850).
Butler, *Near Restful Waters*	Thomas C. Butler, *Near Restful Waters – The Augustinians in County Wexford* (Ballyboden, 1975).
Council of Trent	*Canons and decrees of the sacred and oecumenical Council of Trent celebrated under the sovereign pontiffs, Paul III, Julius III and Paul IV* (London, [1848?]), translated by Rev. J. Waterworth.
C.C.A.	Carlow College Archives.
Castlereagh (ed.), *Memoirs and Correspondence*	Viscount Castlereagh (ed.), *Memoirs and Correspondence of Viscount Castlereagh*, 4 vols (London, 1848–9).
Cath. Ency.	*Catholic Encyclopaedia*, 16 vols (1st ed., New York, 1907–1914).
Cloncurry, *Personal Recollections*	Lord Cloncurry, *Personal Recollections of the life and times with extracts from the correspondence of Valentine Lord Cloncurry* (Dublin, 1849).
C.S.J.A.	Clongowes Wood, Society of Jesus Archives.
Comerford, *Collections*	Michael Comerford, *Collections relating to the dioceses of Kildare and Leighlin*, 3 vols (Dublin, 1883–6).
Connolly, *Priests and people*	S.J. Connolly, *Priests and people in pre-famine Ireland 1780–1845* (Dublin, 1982).
Corish, *Cath. Comm.*	Patrick J. Corish, *The Catholic Community in the seventeenth and eighteenth centuries* (Dublin, 1981).
——, *Ir. Cath. Experience*	——, *The Irish Catholic Experience – A historical survey* (Dublin, 1985.)
Decreta Synodi ... Thurles	*Decreta Synodi Plenariae Episcoporum Hiberniae apud Thurles habitae anno MDCCCL* (Dubin, 1851).

Delumeau, *Catholicism between Luther and Voltaire* — Jean Delumeau, *Catholicism between Luther and Voltaire: a new view of the Counter-Reformation* (Eng. ed., London, 1977).

Disturbed Counties' evidence — *Minutes of evidence taken before the Lords Select Committee appointed to inquire into the state of the disturbed counties in Ireland, with the immediate causes which have produced the same, and with the efficiency of the laws for the suppression of outrages against the public peace*, H.L. 1831–32 (677), xvi, 1.

Doyle/J.K.L.,

——, *Diocesan Book* — Bishop Doyle's 'Diocesan Book' (MS in Kildare and Leighlin Diocesan Archives).

——, *Pastoral, Lent 1820* — ——, 'Pastoral letter on the Lent of 1820' (printed copy in Kildare and Leighlin Diocesan Archives).

——, *Pastoral, Lent 1821* — ——, *Pastoral instructions for the Lent of 1821 ...* (Carlow, [1821]).

——, *Pastoral, Nov. 1822* — ——, *Pastoral letter addressed to the Roman Catholic clergy ...* (corrected ed., Dublin, 1823).

——, *Pastoral, Lent 1823* — *A second excellent pastoral letter from the Rt Rev Dr Doyle, Catholic Bishop of Kildare and Leighlin* (Dublin, 1823).

——, *Pastoral, June 1823* — *Miracle wrought by Prince Hohenlohe in the person of Miss Maria Lalor ...* (Dublin, [1823]).

——, *Vindication* — *A vindication of the religious and civil principles of the Irish Catholics ...* (Dublin, 1823).

——, *Defence of Vindication* — *A defence by J.K.L. of his vindication of the religious and civil principles of the Irish Catholics* (Dublin, 1824).

——, *Letters on a re-union of the churches* — *Letters on a re-union of the churches of England and Rome, from an to the Rt Revd Dr Doyle, R.C. Bp of Kildare, John O'Driscoll, Alexander Knox and Thomas Newenham* (Gloucester, [1824]).

——, *Pastoral, Lent 1825* — ——, *Pastoral instructions for the Lent of 1825* (Carlow, 1825).

——, *Letters on the state of Ire.* — *Letters on the state of Ireland addressed by J.K.L. to a friend in England* (Dublin, 1825).

——, *Essay on the Cath. Claims* — *An essay on the Catholic claims addressed to the Right Honourable the Earl of Liverpool K.G. etc, etc, etc by the Right James Doyle* (Dublin, London, 1826).

——, *(ed.), Abridgement of the Christian Doctrine* — *An abridgement of the Christian Doctrine with proofs of scripture on points controverted by way of question and answer composed in 1649, by H.T. of the English College at Douay, now revised by the Right Rev. James Doyle, D.D. and prescribed by him to be used in the United Dioceses of Kildare and Leighlin* (Dublin, 1828).

——, *Formation of nat. lit. inst.* — ——, *Letter to Daniel O'Connell, Esq., on the formation of a national literary institute for the extension of science to all classes by Irish youth* (Dublin, 1829).

——, *Pastoral, Nov. 1829* — ——, 'Pastoral letter addressed to the faithful of the Deanery of Maryboro' (MS in Kildare and Leighlin Diocesan Archives).

——, *Pastoral, Jan. 1831* — 'Pastoral letter on the building of Carlow Cathedral' (printed copy in Dublin Diocesan Archives).

——, *Pastoral, Dec. 1831* — ——, 'Pastoral letter to the deluded persons combined under the unmeaning appellation of "Blackfeet" and "Whitefeet" in that part of the Queen's County which lies within the diocese of Leighlin' (printed copy in Kildare and Leighlin Diocesan Archives).

———, *Letter to Spring Rice*
———, *Letter to Thomas Spring Rice, Esq., M.P. etc, etc on the establishment of a legal provision for the Irish poor and on the nature and destination of church property* (Dublin, London, 1831).

———, *Pastoral, May 1832*
'Pastoral letter against illegal combinations 5 May 1832' (MS in Kildare and Leighlin Diocesan Archives).

———, *Pastoral, 1833*
'Pastoral letter on Jubilee' (printed copy in C.S.J.A.).

———, *Pastoral, Lent 1834*
'Pastoral letter for the Lent of 1834' (printed copy in Central Catholic Library, Dublin).

D.D.A.
Dublin Diocesan Archives.

D.E.P.
Dublin Evening Post.

Education Inquiry
First report of the commissioners of Irish education inquiry, H.C. 1825 (400), xii.

Fitzpatrick, *Doyle*
W.J. Fitzpatrick, *The life, times and correspondence of the Rt Rev Dr Doyle, Bishop of Kildare and Leighlin*, 2 vols (Dublin, 1890).

Gibbons, *Glimpses*
Margaret Gibbons, *Glimpses of Catholic Ireland in the eighteenth century: Restoration of the daughters of St Brigid by Most Rev Dr Delany* (Dublin, 1932).

I.A.P.A.
Irish Augustinian Provincial Archives, Ballyboden, County Dublin.

K.L.D.A.
Kildare and Leighlin Diocesan Archives, Bishop's House, Carlow.

MacSuibhne (ed.), *Knockbeg*
Peadar MacSuibhne (ed.), *Knockbeg Centenary Book* (Carlow, [1948]).

———, *Cullen and his contemporaries*
Paul Cullen and his contemporaries 5 vols (Naas, 1961–1977).

Meagher, *Murray*
William Meagher, *Notices of the life and character of his Grace Most Rev Daniel Murray, late Archbishop of Dublin ...* (Dublin, 1853).

O'Connell Corr.
M.R. O'Connell (ed.), *The correspondence of Daniel O'Connell*, 8 vols (Dublin, 1973–81).

O'Hanlon and O'Leary, *Queen's Co.*
John O'Hanlon and Edward O'Leary, *History of the Queen's County* (Kilkenny, 1981 reprint).

O'Riordan, *Delany*
Mary O'Riordan, 'Life of Dr Delany: Bishop of Kildare and Leighlin' (typescript in Brigidine Convent, Paulstown, Co. Kilkenny).

Patrician Rule
The Rules and Constitutions of the Congregation of St Patrick, written by the Rt Rev Dr Delany, Bishop of Kildare and Leighlin, who founded this Congregation at Tullow, February 2, AD 1807 [recte 1808]. *Revised, approved and augmented by his successor, the Rt Rev Dr Doyle* (Manchester, 1826).

Presentation Rule
Rules and Constitutions of the Institute of the Religious Sisterhood of the Presentation of the ever blessed Virgin Mary established in the city of Cork, for the charitable instruction of poor girls, conformably to the rules of the late Pope Pius VI ... (Dublin, 1809).

Scritture (Irlanda)
Scritture riferite nei congressi, Irlanda, Archives of the Congregation of Propaganda Fide, Rome.

S.O.I. evidence
(for *state of Ireland evidence*) *Second report from the select committee appointed to inquire into the state of Ireland, ...* H.C. 1825 (129), viii, 173.

———,
Third report from the select committee appointed to inquire into the state of Ireland, ... H.C. 1825 (129), viii, 193.

———,
Minutes of evidence taken before the Lords' select committee appointed to inquire into the state of Ireland, ... H.L. 1825 (181), ix, 1.

S.P.I. evidence
(for *state of the poor in Ireland evidence*) *Minutes of evidence taken before*

the select committee on the state of the poor in Ireland, H.C. 1830 (654),
vii, 1.

Stat. dioec. prov.   Statuta Dioecesana, per provinciam Dubliniensem observanda, et a RR
    Dublin, 1831   mis DD. Daniele Murray, Archiepiscopo Dubliniensi; Jacobo Keating,
                      Episcopo Fernensi; Jacobo Doyle, Episcopo Kildarensi et Leighlinensi; et
                      Guilielmo Kinsella, Episcopo Ossoriensi, in suis respective Synodis Dioec-
                      esanis edita et promulgata, Hebdomada quarta mensis Julii, A.D. 1831
                      (Dublin, 1831).

Tithe evidence   Second report from the select committee appointed to inquire into the
                      collection and payment of Tithes in Ireland ... H.C. 1831–32 (508), xxi,
                      245.

——,   Second report from the select committee of the house of lords appointed to
                      inquire into the collection and payment of Tithes in Ireland ... H.L. 1831–
                      32 (663), xxii, 181.

T.3.A.   Tullow Brigidine Archives.
T.?.A.   Tullow Patrician Archives.

CHAPTER 1

1 Cf. 'Notes on the Ryan family', p. 8, typescript written by Rev. Nicholas Ryan, O.M.I., in
   1937, now in the possession of the Ryan family, Mullinderry. The Ryan family have lived
   in Mullinderry since 1785. Their house is on the site of the original castle. Rev. Nicholas
   Ryan was born in this house in the mid-nineteenth century. The present owner farms 120
   acres there. See also 'some historical notices' on 'Tintern and its locality' by 'Antiquarian'
   in the Wexford paper, The People, 3 May 1913. Fitzpatrick, Doyle, passim, has no mention
   of Mullinderry though the opening pages of his first chapter are devoted to proving the
   venerability of the Doyle family, e.g. 'The branch of the family from which Bishop Doyle
   descends has been for centuries resident in the county Wexford' (ibid., i, 2). Though this
   statement is probably correct Fitzpatrick was unable to provide genealogical information
   which would confirm it.
2 Information from his gravestone in St Mary's churchyard, New Ross. He died on 5 October 1818, aged sixty-three.
3 From a pencilled note on the inside cover of vol. 1 of Fleury's Histoire Ecclésiastiqué
   (Bruxelles, 1716), bearing the J.K.L. monogram, in the bishop's library, Bishop's House,
   Carlow.
4 See Doyle, Letters on the state of Ire., p. 175: 'Individuals of my own family have spent
   some years in the Company's service'.
5 Fitzpatrick, Doyle, i, 5–6; The People, 3 May 1913.
6 Fitzpatrick, Doyle, i. 6; Doyle, Vindication, p. 49, acknowledged Protestant 'blood' relations.
7 Fitzpatrick, op. cit., i. 6.
8 G.D. Burtchaell and T.U. Sadleir (ed.), Alumni Dublinenses (Dublin, 1935 ed.), p. 243.
   Patrick Doyle is stated to be the fifth son of James Doyle. Sizars were allowed free education in consideration of performing certain, at one time menial, duties (ibid., p. viii); see
   also Edward Keane, P.B. Phair and T.U. Sadleir (ed.). King's Inns Admission Papers 1607–
   1867 (Dublin, 1982). p. 142.
9 Doyle to Mary Coney, 17 Feb. 1814 cited in Fitzpatrick, op. cit., i, 58.
10 Baptismal registers are not extant for 1786 in either New Ross or Cushinstown parishes. It
   is an interesting curiosity that the child was delivered by his half-brother, James Doyle,
   who had a successful medical practice in New Ross.

11 Fitzpatrick, op. cit., i. 5. It seems plausible that the mother's maiden name would have been used to differentiate between the two James's.

12 Fitzpatrick, *Doyle* (1862), i, 23.

13 MS massbook 'Missale no. 3' in O.S.A. priory, New Ross; Thomas Pakenham, *The year of liberty* (London, 1972 pbk. ed.), p. 228 quotes James Alexander, who stated that 2,600 died. Most of the dead rebels wore scapulars.

14 Fitzpatrick, *Doyle*, i, 9.

15 Ibid.

16 W.G. Carroll, *A memoir of the Right Rev. James Thomas O'Brien, DD* (Dublin, 1875), p. 48.

17 Fitzpatrick, *Doyle*, ii, 433 fn.

18 Doyle, *Letters on the state of Ire.*, p. 149.

19 Fitzpatrick, op. cit., i. 11.

20 Butler, *Near Restful Waters*, pp 80, 97, 148. For the Anglo-Norman Rossiters see F.X. Martin, 'The Rossiters of Rathmacknee Castle I, 1169–1627' in *The Past* no. 5 (1949), pp 103–16; 'The Rossiters of Rathmacknee Castle II' in *The Past* no. 6 (1950), pp 13–25; 'II John Baptist Rossiter, O.SA.' in ibid., pp 26–44.

21 Housebook '1798–1830', entry, for 22 Aug. 1800 (MS in O.S.A. priory, New Ross).

22 O.S.A. housebooks, passim, New Ross.

23 Butler, *Near Restful Waters*, p. 98.

24 Housebook '1798–1830' (MS in O.S.A. priory, New Ross).

25 Butler, op. cit., pp 102–3.

26 Ibid., p. 103.

27 Fitzpatrick, *Doyle*, i, 11, 19.

28 Doyle to John Gibbons, O.S.A., Provincial, 17 Oct. 1823 (I.A.P.A.); for Dr John A. Furlong see Butler, op. cit., p. 55.

29 William Carleton points out in his largely autobiographical short story 'The Lough Derg Pilgrim' that on the strength of his prospective candidacy for the priesthood, he became godfather before he was nineteen years old, to many godchildren. In Cushinstown parish register, the name of James Doyle is given as sponsor on 5 May 1801, 20 Feb. 1804, 7 Dec. 1804 and 18 Dec. 1805. See N.L.I. microfilm p. 4259.

30 Fitzpatrick, *Doyle*, i, 13.

31 Butler, op. cit., p. 32.

32 W.H. Grattan-Flood, *History of the diocese of Ferns* (Waterford, 1916), pp 207–8.

33 Ibid., p. 118.

34 Martin Doyle (1781–1861) was born in Ballinvegga near Ballygalvert. For the cousin reference see Doyle to Martin Doyle, 4 Feb. 1817 (K.L.DA.). See also MacSuibhne (ed.), *Knockbeg*, pp 89–92.

35 On this point see: Doyle to Miss Devereux, ? Feb. 1814, cited in Fitzpatrick, *Doyle*, i, 60; Doyle to Nicholas Clayton, O.S.A., 14 Dec. 1814 cited in ibid., i, 68; and also Doyle to Austin McDermott, O.S.A., undated, cited in ibid., i, 198.

36 *Essay on the Catholic claims* (Dublin, London, 1826), pp 233–4.

37 Doyle to Daniel O'Connor, O.S.A., Provincial, 25 Jan. 1828 (I.A.P.A.). See also Doyle to Nicholas Clayton, O.S.A., 14 Dec. 1814, cited in Fitzpatrick, op. cit., i, 68.

38 'Grantstown A/C Book 1804–42' (MS in I.A.P.A.); Butler errs on the date in *Near Restful Waters*, p. 31.

39 Clayton became a very distinguished Augustinian but died young (Fitzpatrick, *Doyle*, i, 68). Hanlon was from south Wexford and a fellow novice with Doyle in Grantstown. He died in Limerick in 1818 aged thirty-one. McDermott served for most of his life in the Galway house of the Augustinians. Rector-provincial, 1827 (Battersby, *Hist. of the Augustinians in Ire.*, p. 65).

40 In a letter written in 1822 Doyle contended that 'to suppress or secularise most of the convents of men in Portugal would be a good work' (quoted in Fitzpatrick, *Doyle*, i, 36).

41 According to Doyle there were 2,200 students in the university and 'more than twenty

particular colleges', Doyle to Mrs Crosbie, 2 July 1806, from Coimbra, cited in Fitzpatrick, op. cit., i, 18. Not all the students in Doyle's college attended the university (*S.O.I. evidence*, p. 243, H.L. 1825 (181), ix, 1). Unfortunately the records of the Augustinian province in Portugal were deliberately burned in 1836 (information communicated to the writer by Rev. Carlos Alonso, O.S.A., Estudio Augustiniano, Valladolid, 26 April 1986); for Doyle's registration see 'Relaçao dos Estudantes Matriculados na Universidade de Coimbra no anno lectivo de 1807 para 1808', p. 43, Archives of the University of Coimbra, Portugal.

42 Doyle, *Letters on the state of Ire.*, pp 55–7. Fitzpatrick, a fervent Catholic, earnestly but melodramatically wrote of the young ecclesiastic that he 'breathed contagion and was smitten'. Furthermore 'whether Doyle was right or wrong in thus imperilling his faith, we shall not now discuss ... it cannot be denied that he was for a time completely staggered by the well-put points of infidel minds' (Fitzpatrick, *Doyle*, i, 23). It is interesting to note that Doyle's much older half-brother James became a free-thinker while studying in Enlightenment France (ibid., i, 90).

43 Doyle, untitled and unpaginated MS journal in K.L.D.A., hereafter referred to as Doyle, 'Journal, 1811–12'.

44 Ibid., F.L. Ford, *Europe 1780–1830* (London, 1970), p. 209.

45 Doyle, 'Journal, 1811–12' (MS, K.L.D.A.).

46 Fitzpatrick, *Doyle*, i, 27, 29.

47 Ibid., i. 28.

48 Ford, op. cit., p. 209.

49 *Lord Liverpool* (London, 1984), p. 72.

50 Fitzpatrick, *Doyle*, i, 31.

51 Doyle, 'Journal 1811–12' (MS, K.L.D.A.).

52 Ibid. For de Lemos see Damiao Peres's edition of Fortunato de Almeida's *Historia da Igreja de Portugal* 4 vols (Barcelos and Porto, 1967–1971), iii, 515–18; also Samuel J. Miller, *Portugal and Rome c.1748. An aspect of the Catholic Enlightenment* (Rome, 1978), passim. De Lemos had strong links with the Portuguese Royal court and was suspected of 'Jansenism'.

53 Doyle, *Pastoral, June 1823*, p. 8.

54 Fitzpatrick, *Doyle*, i, 32; 'Dr Doyle informed the Rev. W. Yore in 1821 that he had been engaged on the diplomatic service in Portugal' (ibid., i, 30).

55 Ibid., i, 37.

56 Book 37, p. 84 of the Registers of the University of Coimbra in the Archives of the University of Coimbra, Portugal; Doyle, *Pastoral, June 1823*, p. 9.

57 *An account of Ireland, statistical and political* 2 vols (London, 1812), ii, 628.

58 Fitzpatrick, *Doyle*, i, 38, 40, 43.

59 Crane was provincial from 1807 to 1811 and again from 1819 to 1823. He was rector of New Ross from 1811 to 1815 (Battersby, *Hist. of the Augustinians in Ire.*, pp 64–5, 213–14). See also F.X. Martin, 'The Irish Augustinians in Rome, 1656–1956' in J.F. Madden (ed.), *The Irish Augustinians in Rome* (Rome, 1956), pp 16–74 at p. 38.

60 Housebook, '1809–1879', entry in Doyle's hand (MS, O.SA. priory, New Ross).

61 Butler, *Near Restful Waters*, p. 123.

62 Battersby, *Hist. of the Augustinians in Ire.*, pp 64–5.

63 Doyle, 'Journal, 1811–12', entry for 12 Mar. 1812 (MS, K.L.D.A.).

64 *General Rules for the governing of New Ross Houghton fever hospital and dispensary* (Waterford, 1829), passim; Doyle, *S.P.I. evidence*, p. 409, H.C. 1830 (654), vii, 1. Neither the parish priest nor rector of New Ross at the time of writing (joint chairman on a monthly rotating basis of the new Houghton hospital) was able to shed any light on the existence of the minutes of the old hospital.

65 *Ir. Cath. Experience*, p. 149; there was no interdenominational tension in the south Wexford baronies of Forth and Bargy even in the 1840s (ibid.).

66 *The emergence of modern Ireland 1600–1900* (Dublin, 1983), p. 216.
67 Doyle, 'Journal, 1811–12', entry for 14 Dec. 1812 (MS, K.L.D.A.).
68 Ibid.
69 In a letter to Daniel O'Connor, O.SA., Provincial, 3 Dec. 1829 ('MS Book no. 70' I.A.P.A.), Doyle, after giving a description of his recent illness, wrote: 'I am now T.G. weakly but well and will I suppose improve still more. The world is much in error about my labours – the truth is I seldom labour, and am never so well as when obliged to use much exertion. It is inactivity-indolence and a consequent neglect to take exercise which are the cause of my occasional illness. When called upon I work very hard and if I worked always I would be always well, but a perverse nature fastens me to an old chair or sofa and some old book'.
70 Doyle, 'Journal, 1811–12', entry for 12 Apr. 1812 (MS. K.L.D.A.).
71 See Doyle, *Formation of nat. lit. inst.*, preface. unpaginated; also Fitzpatrick, *Doyle*, i, 184.
72 Doyle. 'Journal, 1811–12', passim.
73 Doyle, 'Journal, 1811–12', entry for 3 May 1812 (MS, K.L.D.A.).
74 Ibid.
75 Doyle, 'Journal, 1811–12', entry for 28 Nov. 1811 (MS, K.L.D.A.).
76 Ibid., entry for 25 Dec. 1811.
77 Ibid.
78 Doyle, 'Journal, 1811–12', entries for 19 May, 8 Oct. 1812 (MS, K.L.D.A.).
79 Ibid., undated entry. A half page of Doyle's foolscap journal has been excised below this quotation.
80 *S.O.I. evidence*, p. 180, H.C. 1825 (129), viii, 173. If a veto were granted Doyle made it clear that he would resign – no less than three times (ibid., pp 210, 221).
81 *S.O.I. evidence*, p. 227, H.C. 1825 (181), ix, 1.
82 A license to open a Catholic school had to be procured from the Church of Ireland bishop under Gardiner's Act of 1782 but this requirement was abolished in 1792 (MacSuibhne (ed), *Knockbeg*, p. 11).
83 *Freeman's Journal*, 22 Sept. 1785; Peadar MacSuibhne, 'The early history of Carlow College' in *I.E.R.*, fifth series, lxii (July–Dec. 1943), pp 230–48. A very good case can be made for the 1782 date. In 1800 Bishop Delany wrote of the origins of Carlow College : 'No sooner had the repeal of the Penal Statutes taken place [27 July 1782], that before opposed an insuperable bar to the erection of Popish schools in this kingdom, than Dr Keefe, late Roman Catholic Bishop of Kildare and Leighlin, in conjunction with the actual incumbent, instantaneously availed themselves of the auspicious moment, and, with eager zeal, vigorously set about at once commencing this foundation ...'. See Castlereagh (ed.), *Memoirs and Correspondence*, iv, 143.
84 MacSuibhne, loc. cit.; Charles Topham Bowden, *A tour through Ireland* (Dublin, 1791), pp 95–100. The origin and foundation of the college is further discussed in the present writer's 'Bishops of Kildare and Leighlin, 1752–1819' – a paper read to the second annual history seminar in Carlow College on 25 April 1986.
85 Castlereagh (ed.), *Memoirs and Correspondence*, iv, 144–7.
86 Comerford, *Collections*, i, 167–9, iii, 100, 402; MacSuibhne (ed.), *Knockbeg*, pp 9–15. For a glowing account of Staunton's reforms as parish priest of Carlow see Roger McHugh (ed.), *Carlow in '98. The autobiography of William Farrell of Carlow* (Dublin, 1949), pp 39–40.
87 Comerford, *Collections*, i, 169, iii, 169 fn. Four of the eight were parish priests under Doyle: Thady Duane, Rosenallis, 1802–28; Daniel Nolan, Kill, 1804–23, Paulstown, 1823–9; Matthew Reilly. Philipstown, 1805–25; and John Walsh, Borris, 1805–36. Nolan caused Doyle some problems dealt with below.
88 See Birch, *St Kieran's* (Dublin, 1951), pp 1–61; Comerford, *Collections*, iii, 169 fn.
89 Comerford, *Collections*, i, 169–70.
90 He was offered the position of sub-prefect of the lay seminary in Maynooth in 1801 and

the chair of sacred scripture in 1814 both of which he declined. See Archbishop Troy to Fitzgerald, 13 Nov., 12, 15 Dec. 1801 in MS 1562, N.L.I. and the *Irish Catholic Magazine* vol. 1 (Sept., 1829), p. 288 for a list of persons appointed to positions in Maynooth College who declined them.

91　Comerford, op. cit., i. 170–1; Birch, *St Kieran's* (Dublin, 1951), pp 60–1. P.J. Brophy, 'A pioneer Irish educationist' in *Carlovian* (1949), pp 19–30.

92　Comerford, op. cit., i. 171–2; Birch, *St Kieran's*, pp 79, 84, 98–9.

93　MacSuibhne, *Cullen and his contemporaries*, i, 7.

94　MacSuibhne, *'98 in Carlow* (Carlow, 1974), p. 110.

95　John Healy, *Maynooth College: its centenary history, 1795–1895* (Dublin, 1895), pp 631, 735.

96　Comerford, *Collections*, i, 172–6. The *Carlow Morning Post* reported on 13 Sept. 1832 that Bishop England was on a visit to the College. He received and replied to an address from the students. The newspaper credited England as a student with giving public instruction in the parish chapel and establishing the Magdalen Asylum and the Catholic free schools of Carlow town.

97　Ibid.

98　Fitzpatrick, *Doyle*, i, 49–53.

99　P.J. Brophy, 'A pioneer Irish educationist' in *Carlovian* (1949), p. 24.

100　A detached note in Doyle's hand in a New Ross housebook indicates that he was still in the priory on 13 October 1813 (Housebook '1788 (1795)', MS, O.S.A. priory, New Ross).

101　*D.E.P.*, 30 Nov. 1813 cited in P.J. Brophy, 'A pioneer Irish educationist' in *Carlovian* (1949), pp 24–5.

102　Fitzpatrick, *Doyle*, i, 56.

103　Ibid., i, 53–4.

104　Fitzpatrick, *Doyle*, i, 55.

105　*Irish Catholic Magazine*, vol. i (Sept., 1829), p. 293.

106　Fitzpatrick, op. cit., i, 56.

107　Therry was one of the founders of the Catholic church in Australia (Comerford, *Collections* i, 179–84). Kinsella (1797–1845) was on the staff of Carlow College from 1818 occupying key chairs including theology until his appointment as bishop of Ossory in 1829 when still only thirty-two years of age. Kinsella was the author of *Controversial letters in reply to Rev. Mr Pope, Rev. Mr Daly, Rev. Dr Singer and others. Also remarks on the canons of the scriptures* (Dublin, 1826), (Comerford, op. cit., i, 191–2). Maher (1793–1874) was uncle of Paul Cullen and a significant and contentious figure in nineteenth century church history in his own right (ibid., i, 177–8). Clowry, the least well known but not the least distinguished of these students took a prominent part in the famous controversial discussion at Carlow on 18, 19 November 1824. In 1827 he published *Controversial letters in reply to Rev. Mr Daly, Rev. Dr Singer, etc., etc.; to which are added the letters signed B.E.* [Doyle] (Dublin, London, 1827). Clowry also published a two volume translation of Bossuet's, *History of the variations of the Protestant churches*. (See Richard Coyne's advertisement in *D.E.P.*, 30 Nov. 1830). As administrator of Tullow mensal parish in 1829 he died aged thirty-five. A memorial erected by Dr Doyle bore the inscription 'His zeal, his eloquence, and polemic writings placed his name, when he had only arrived at manhood, among the most distinguished in the church of Ireland' (Comerford, op. cit., i, 192).

108　For example: James Delany, P.P. Ballinakill, 1824–74; William Kinsella, P.P. Ballon, 1825–72; Daniel Lalor, P.P. Baltinglass, 1831–71; Terence O'Connell, P.P. Portarlington and Emo, 1832–75; James Maher, P.P. Leighlin, 1827, died P.P. Killeshin (Carlow-Graigue) 1874; Thomas Nolan, Adm., Tullow, 1829, P.P. Abbeyleix, 1838–86 (Comerford, op. cit., iii, 109; 122–3; 161; ii, 319; i, 177–8; and MacSuibhne (ed.), *Knockbeg*, pp 44–5.

109　Doyle letter, 25 May 1816, cited in Fitzpatrick, *Doyle*, i, 76.

110　'Two unpublished MSS of J.K.L.' in *Carlovian* (1914), pp 116–21 at pp 119–20.

111 Ibid., p. 118.
112 'Two unpublished MSS of J.K.L.' in *Carlovian* (1914), pp 117–18.
113 Ibid., p. 118.
114 Joseph de Ghellinck, 'Denis Petau (Dionysius Petavius)' in *Cath. Ency.*, xi, 743–4.
115 Antoine Degert. 'Honoré Tournely' in ibid., xiv. 800.
116 Louis N. Delamarre, 'Jacques-Bénigne Bossuet' in *Cath. Ency.*, ii, 698–702; J. Derek Holmes and Bernard Bickers, *A short history of the Catholic church* (London, 1983), p. 175.
117 Delahogue was certainly studied in Carlow in 1824, see Carlow parish report on education, 1824 (MS in K.L.D.A.).
118 In bishop's library, Bishop's House, Carlow.
119 Fitzpatrick, *Doyle*, i, 136–8. In 1824 Delahogue and Anglade were the leading authors of the 'Maynooth Manifesto' (*D.E.P.*, 5 June 1824).
120 Acta, vol. 184, p. 113; Scritture (Irlanda), vol. 23, p. 414.
121 Doyle's statement in 1825 that '... we are not concerned about it ...' was quite accurate. See *S.O.I. evidence*, p. 314, H.L. 1825 (181), ix, 1.
122 The four articles are outlined in Patrick J. Corish. 'Gallicanism at Maynooth: Archbishop Cullen and the Royal Visitation of 1853', in Art Cosgrove and Donal McCartney (ed.), *Studies in Irish history presented to R. Dudley Edwards* (Dublin, 1979), p. 176. For a politically Gallican and pragmatically minimalist position adopted in the course of the struggle for Catholic emancipation at a crucial stage see Doyle's parliamentary evidence on the state of Ireland in 1825: *S.O.I. evidence*, pp 223–48, 308–17, H.L. 1825 (181), ix, 1; ibid., pp 173–222, H.C. 1825 (129), viii, 173, passim. See also his *Essay on the Cath. Claims*, addressed to the prime minister, Lord Liverpool, in 1826, passim.
123 For a defence of the primacy of Rome and theological ultramontanism espoused against Protestant controversialists see Doyle's *Defence of Vindication* pp 84–6; Doyle to Thomas Newenham, 29 June 1824 in *Letters on a re-union of the churches*, p. 25; and especially *A reply by J.K.L. to the late charge of the Most Rev. Doctor Magee protestant archbishop of Dublin* ... (Dublin, 1827), pp 32–54.
124 See Maureen Wall, 'Catholic loyalty to king and pope in eighteenth century Ireland' in *Ir. Cath. Hist. Comm. Proc.*, (1960), pp 17–24.
125 'Two unpublished MSS of J.K.L.' in *Carlovian* (1914), p. 119.
126 'Two unpublished MSS of J.K.L.' in *Carlovian* (1914), p. 119; for Locke's emphasis on the rationality of belief, see Gerald R. Cragg, *The church and the age of reason, 1648–1789* (London, 1983 pbk. ed.), pp 75–7.
127 Doyle to relative, 27 Jan. 1814, cited in Fitzpatrick, *Doyle*, i, 57; Doyle to Dr Martin Howlett, 9 Apr. 1815, cited in ibid., i, 72; Doyle to Martin Doyle, C.C. Clonegal, 30 Jan. 1818 (K.L.D.A.).
128 Fitzpatrick, op. cit., i, 81–4. In 1817 the evangelical Robert J. McGhee applied to Maynooth and Carlow colleges for a statement of the Catholic doctrine on the reading of scripture. Doyle's reply of 31 October 1817 was mentioned by McGhee in his book, *The bible, the rights of conscience and the Established Church vindicated* (Dublin, 1818). For Doyle's letter see Fitzpatrick, op. cit., ii, 512–15.
129 Doyle to Mary Howlett, 17 Feb. 1814, cited in Fitzpatrick, op. cit., i. 59.
130 Doyle to Miss Devereux, 12 Feb. 1814, cited in Fitzpatrick, *Doyle*, i, 59.
131 P.J. Brophy, 'A pioneer Irish educationist' in *Carlovian* (1949), p. 26 states that Fitzgerald continued to teach scripture after being appointed president and this was probably the case for at least one year. The terna result, 1819, refers to Doyle as professor of theology and sacred scripture (MS, K.L.D.A.). For Doyle's influence on Slattery's subsequent career, see the present writer's 'Archbishop Slattery and the episcopal controversy on Irish national education, 1838–1841' in *Arch. Hib.*, xxxix (1984), pp 13–31 passim.
132 Doyle to Dr Bartholomew Crotty, president, Maynooth College, draft, undated [mid-1817], (K.L.D.A.).

133 Doyle to Rev. Martin Doyle, undated (K.L.D.A.).
134 Fitzpatrick, op. cit., i, 78. The journalist and old Carlow College boy Maurice Lenihan redressing the balance in the *Limerick Reporter and Tipperary Vindicator*, 16 Nov. 1866, remembered Fitzgerald affectionately as a very punctual priest. The late Monsignor P.J. Brophy who wrote on Fitzgerald suggested orally to the present writer that Fitzgerald may have been 'lazy'.
135 Fitzpatrick, *Doyle*, i, 72, has the reference but does not mention Fitzgerald by name although the clue 'Dr F ———— d' could hardly be mistaken.
136 Doyle to Rev. Martin Doyle, 3 June 1817 (K.L.D.A.).
137 Doyle to Nicholas Clayton, O.S.A., 14 Dec. 1814, cited in Fitzpatrick, op. cit., i, 68–9. This is Fitzpatrick's only reference to Doyle's attempts to move to Maynooth College.
138 Doyle to Bishop Marum, copy, undated [early June 1816], (K.L.DA.).
139 Bishop Marum to Doyle, from Kilkenny, 14 June 1816 (K.L.D.A.).
140 Doyle to Archbishop Troy, undated copy [25 June 1816], (K.L.D.A.).
141 Doyle to Dr Bartholomew Crotty, undated [mid to late June 1816], (K.L.DA.).
142 Troy to Doyle, 29 June 1816 (K.L.D.A.).
143 Doyle to James Bolger of Ballinabarney, undated copy [June 1816], (K.L.D.A.); for a brief notice of the Bolger family see E.W. Hughes, 'On penal day sites in the Barrow Valley' in *Old Kilkenny Review*, vol. 2, no. 2 (1980), pp 46–7.
144 Bolger to Doyle, 23 June 1816 (K.L.D.A.).
145 Sir Edward Bellew to Bolger, 5 July 1816 (K.L.DA.).
146 Doyle to Bolger, 26 July 1816, copy (K.L.D.A.). Doyle was absent from Carlow in mid-July.
147 Doyle to Sir Edward Bellew, undated copy [early August 1816], (K.L.D.A.).
148 Ibid.
149 Doyle to Rev. Martin Doyle, 16 Nov. 1816 (K.L.D.A.).
150 Doyle to Bishop Corcoran, undated [Nov. 1816], (K.L.DA.).
151 Doyle to Dr Bartholomew Crotty, undated [mid-1817], (K.L.D.A.).
152 Doyle to Bishop Corcoran, undated [Nov. 1816], (K.L.D.A.).
153 Doyle to Rev. Martin Doyle, 14 Nov. 1816 (K.L.D.A.).
154 Ibid.
155 Letter in K.L.D.A.
156 Doyle to Dr Bartholomew Crotty, undated [mid-1817], (K.L.D.A.); see also Doyle to Sir Edward Bellew, undated [mid-1817], (K.L.D.A.).
157 Fitzpatrick, *Doyle*, i, 85; also Doyle to Mary Coney, 25 Dec. 1818: 'People may treat about me and dispose of me, but they shall not do it unknown to myself; and perhaps their views and mine differ very widely' (ibid., i, 88).
158 Letter of 14 Dec. 1816 (K.L.D.A.).
159 Doyle to Martin Howlett, 1 Oct. 1814, cited in Fitzpatrick, op. cit., i. 61.
160 Doyle to Nicholas Clayton, O.S.A., 14 Dec. 1814, cited in ibid., i. 86.
161 Bishop Corcoran to Doyle, 28 Feb. 1816 (K.L.D.A.).
162 Bishop Corcoran to Doyle, 20 Nov. 1818 (K.L.D.A.).
163 Fitzpatrick, *Doyle*, i, 79; Doyle to Mary Coney, 19 Oct. 1817, has the following: 'I believe there is no one of the many candidates spoken of more indifferent about the result than myself (cited in ibid., i, 80).
164 Doyle to Rev. Martin Doyle, 30 Jan. 1818 (K.L.D.A.); Doyle to niece, 19 Mar. 1818, cited in Fitzpatrick, op. cit., i. 89.
165 Doyle to Mary Coney, 25 Dec. 1818, cited in Fitzpatrick, op. cit., i, 88.
166 Fitzpatrick, *Doyle*, i, 88.
167 In 1810 he denounced the reading of lost-and-found notices at mass (ibid., i, 40).
168 Ibid., i, 42. Doyle to Rev. Martin Doyle, 14 Dec. 1816 (K.L.D.A.).
169 Doyle to Dr Martin Howlett, 1 Oct 1814, quoted in Fitzpatrick, op. cit., i, 61.

170 Ibid., i, 43, 74, 80.
171 MS in Doyle's hand in K.L.D.A. Bodily mortification, a not uncommon practice at this time, was indicative of the interior, spiritual life of resurgent Catholicism.
172 Doyle admitted as such in *S.O.I. evidence*, p. 187, H.C. 1825 (129), viii, 173.
173 'Account Book, no. 4' [1812–1818], (MS, C.C.A.).
174 Fitzpatrick, *Doyle*, i. 76.
175 Doyle to Rev. Martin Doyle, 17 Oct 1816 (K.L.D.A.); Doyle's letter of May 1817 cited in Fitzpatrick, op. cit., i. 83.
176 Doyle to Mary Coney, 23 Oct. 1820 cited in Fitzpatrick, op. cit., i. 135; ibid., i, 296–7 reveals that, as bishop, Doyle was negligent of claiming dues and that his bursar had to keep a tight rein on his finances.
177 Financial MSS, passim (K.L.D.A.).
178 Terna result, unsigned and undated (MS, K.L.D.A.); *D.E.P.*, 25 Mar. 1819. For the care Doyle took not to compromise himself in the election see Doyle to James Conran, vicar capitular, 7 Mar. 1819, quoted in Fitzpatrick, *Doyle*, ii, 521. Doyle was apparently the only priest in the diocese with a knowledge of the correct procedure to be followed by the vicar capitular.
179 Fitzpatrick, op. cit., i, 90.
180 Terna result, unsigned and undated (MS, K.L.D.A.).
181 Doyle, *S.O.I. evidence*, p. 188, H.C. 1825 (129), vii, 173.
182 Acta, vol. 182, pp 167–8.
183 Doyle, Diocesan Book.
184 Doyle to Mary Coney, 24 Mar. 1819, quoted in Fitzpatrick, *Doyle*, i, 89.
185 Doyle, Diocesan Book. A rambling and opinionated letter from Edward Hay to Doyle, 25 June 1824 (K.L.D.A.), noticed that a recent publication asserted Dr Doyle 'was the government nominee to the See he fills'. On this letter an indignant Doyle wrote: 'I have written to Mr Hay in the most express terms ... such statement in all its parts is untrue, totally untrue'; see also Doyle to Edward Hay, 27 Jan. 1825 (copy in 'Letters of J.K.L. and Hay, 1825', Section 60/2, file xvi, Proceedings of the Catholic Association, D.D.A.). See *Carlow Morning Post*, 23 June 1819 for the farewell address of the students of theology of Carlow College to Doyle and his reply dated 20 June 1819. The consecrating bishops were Drs Troy, Murray, Marum, Keating and Everard of Cashel and Emly. See Comerford, *Collections*, i, 94.

CHAPTER 2

1 These topics are treated thematically, as they relate to Doyle's pastorate, in chapter 5; for a short note on Gallagher's pastorate see Doyle's Diocesan Book – one of the very few sources of information on this prelate. His sermons 'comprise the most popular work, with a single exception, ever printed in Irish'. Cf. Aodh de Blacam, *Gaelic literature surveyed* (Dublin, 1973 ed.), p. 304. The most popular printed work in Irish was Teig Gaelach O'Sullivan's 'Pious Miscellany' – a collection of devout poetry. O'Sullivan who died in 1800 was a close friend of Edmund Rice, founder of the Irish Christian Brothers (ibid., pp 331–2).
2 Doyle to Mrs Gurley, 6 May 1823, quoted in Fitzpatrick, *Doyle*, i, 239.
3 There is a good description of these penal mass stations and priest hunters in O'Hanlon and O'Leary, *Queen's Co.*, ii, 571–93. See also E.W. Hughes, 'On penal day sites in the Barrow Valley' in *Old Kilkenny Review*, vol. 2, no. 2 (1980), pp 44–48.
4 Doyle, Diocesan Book; also Martin Brenan, 'Bishop Keefe of Kildare and Leighlin, A.D. 1702–1787' in *I.E.R.*, fifth series, L (July to Dec. 1937), pp 113–26.

5 Corish, *Ir. Cath. Comm.*, p. 75.
6 Comerford, *Collections*, iii, 398.
7 E.A. D'Alton, 'Penal laws in Ireland' in *Cath. Ency.*, xi, 616.
8 For the harassment, imprisonment and transportation of John Taaf, parish priest of Carlow, *c.*1743–51 see Comerford, *Collections*, iii, 53; Brenan, loc. cit., pp 116–17 and John Brady, *Catholics and Catholicism in the eighteenth century press* (Maynooth, 1965), pp 79–80. Taaf was an unregistered priest.
9 Doyle, Diocesan Book.
10 He succeeded to the primacy in 1787 and ministered until his death in 1818. He was a member of the wealthy O'Reilly family of Kildangan Castle, Monasterevan. He had a private income and hence became the first post-Reformation Catholic archbishop of Armagh to live in the manner expected of a primate (Comerford, *Collections*, i, 87; Ambrose Coleman, 'Armagh' in *Cath. Ency.*, i, 732).
11 Castlereagh (ed.), *Memoirs and Correspondence*, iv, 141.
12 Ibid., iv, 152.
13 Ibid., iv, 141–2.
14 Annals, p. 3 (MS, Mountrath Brigidine convent).
15 Ibid.
16 Castlereagh (ed.), *Memoirs and Correspondence*, iv, 153.
17 Comerford, *Collections*, iii, 300–301; Linus H. Walker, *The purpose of his will* (Galway, 1981), p. 20.
18 See reports on education from the parishes of Carlow, Paulstown (then in Leighlinbridge parish), Mountmellick, Rathvilly, Rosenallis, 1824 (MSS in K.L.D.A.).
19 O'Riordan, *Delany*, p. 36.
20 Annals, four-page insert unpaginated between pp 42–3; no specific date given (MS, T.B.A.).
21 Dr O'Riordan has stated that the sisters were withdrawn in consequence of an attack by a party of 'Orangemen' on a clerical conference meeting in their schoolhouse (*Delany*, p. 39) Fitzpatrick, *Doyle*, i, 107, stated that this attack took place in 1798. Comerford, *Collections*, iii, 310, gave the date as 1793.
22 There is a 'shroud of vagueness around these "Brigidines" at Clonegal' (O'Riordan, *Delany*, p. 39).
23 Purcell's 'manners and disposition brought Goldsmith's village parson very forcibly to my mind' stated Charles Topham Bowden, *A tour through Ireland* (Dublin, 1791), p. 108.
24 Doyle to Martin Doyle, 14 Nov. 1814 (K.L.D.A.).
25 O'Riordan, *Delany*, p. 40.
26 Clonegal parish report on education, 1824 (MS in K.L.D.A.).
27 O'Riordan, *Delany*, p. 40.
28 Ibid., p. 160.
29 Ibid., p. 246.
30 Linus H. Walker, *To build and to plant* (Carlow, n.d.), pp 7–9.
31 Annals, pp 25, 35 (MS, T.B.A.).
32 O'Riordan, *Delany*, p. 179.
33 Fitzpatrick, *Doyle*, i, 132.
34 Ibid., i, 107.
35 Castlereagh (ed.), *Memoirs and Correspondence*, iv, 139.
36 O'Riordan, op. cit., p. 73.
37 Doyle, *Letters on the state of Ire.*, pp 100–1; 'Kildare and Leighlin diocesan statutes, 1820', printed p. 1 (K.L.D.A.). For dates of origin of extant parochial registers in the diocese see Appendix 1.
38 Fitzpatrick, *Doyle*, ii, 519 and O'Riordan, *Delany*, p. 84 incorrectly state that this friar was not under Delany's jurisdiction.
39 O'Riordan, op. cit., p. 180; Comerford, *Collections*, iii, 392–3.

40 Castlereagh (ed.), *Memoirs and Correspondence*, iv, 148.
41 Delany to Bishop Moylan, 30 Dec. 1808, in Evelyn Bolster, 'The Moylan correspondence in Bishop's House, Killarney: Part 1', *Collect. Hib.*, no. 14 (1971), p. 137.
42 Fitzpatrick, *Doyle*, i, 132.
43 Delany to Troy, 14 Nov. 1788, cited in Comerford, *Collections*, iii, 157–60 at p. 157.
44 Annals, p. 38 (MS, Mountrath Brigidine convent).
45 Fitzpatrick, op. cit., i, 129 fn.
46 Myles V. Ronan, *An apostle of Catholic Dublin – Father Henry Young* (Dublin, 1944), p. 235.
47 E.J. Cullen, *The origin and development of the Irish Vincentian foundations 1833–1933* (Dublin, [1933]), pp 51, 57–63.
48 Delany to Troy, 14 Nov. 1788, cited in Comerford, *Collections*, iii, 157.
49 MacSuibhne (ed.), *Knockbeg*, p. 83.
50 '... I found you suspended for life under the Bull of Gregory XV "Universi dominici gregis".' See Doyle to O'Neill, draft, undated [Mar. 1820] in response to O'Neill to Doyle, 4 Mar. 1820 (K.L.D.A.).
51 Doyle to O'Neill, undated [Mar. 1820], (K.L.D.A.).
52 Cited in Gibbons, *Glimpses*, pp 321–2.
53 James Delany to Fitzpatrick, 10 June 1861, cited in Fitzpatrick, *Doyle*, i, 128–9 fn.
54 These calculations are based on figures given in Castlereagh (ed.), *Memoirs and Correspondence*, iv, 149–51.
55 Doyle, Diocesan Book.
56 Out of thirty three votes cast in the diocesan election Murphy received twenty-three; Michael Corcoran, eight; and Michael Prendergast, P.P. Bagenalstown, three votes. In a letter to Archbishop Troy of 24 Nov. 1814, Murphy renounced the bishopric pleading motives of conscience. Corcoran was particularly recommended by the bishop of Ferns. See Acta, vol. 178, pp 55–6, 74; Doyle, Diocesan Book.
57 Doyle, Diocesan Book.
58 Fitzpatrick, *Doyle*, i, 86.
59 Ibid., i, 127.
60 Doyle, Diocesan Book. For an interesting expression of Bishop Corcoran's liberal political principles on the separation of church and state and opposition to the veto, see Corcoran to Sir Henry Parnell, M.P., 17 Dec. 1816 (Congleton MSS, Ebbesbourne Wake, Salisbury, Wiltshire, in the possession of Lord Congleton).
61 See terna result, 1819 (MS in K.L.D.A.); *D.E.P.*, 25 Mar. 1819.
62 Doyle to Peter Doyle, P.P., Tintern, 4 Aug. 1822 (K.L.D.A.).
63 Doyle, *S.O.I. evidence*, p. 185, H.C. 1825 (129), viii, 173; ibid., p. 231, H.L. 1825 (181), ix, 1.
64 Doyle, Diocesan Book. On 20 Oct. 1823 the administrator of Graiguenamanagh parish complained to Bishop Doyle that if he was to cope with the Goresbridge portion of his parish (Upper and Lower Grange and Barrowmount) he would require the townland of Duninga 'which the overzeal of the late Dean Cullen of Leighlin wrested from the parish of Graig in Doctor Delany's time' (Maurice Kearney to Doyle, K.L.D.A.). A month later all the townlands mentioned were annexed to the new parish of Paulstown (Goresbridge). Both Leighlinbridge and Graiguenamanagh were in the pastoral care of administrators in 1823 and this gave Doyle the opportunity to create the new parishes from them.
65 Doyle to Francis Haly, P.P., Kilcock, 18 Feb. 1824 (K.L.D.A.). Doyle stated that he was under 'the disagreeable necessity of seeking to provide two pastors for Ballinakill henceforth to be divided into two parishes'. The death of the parish priest of Ballinakill, Roger Molony, provided Doyle with the opportunity for the division. For a notice of Molony see Comerford, *Collections*, iii, 65.
66 Clonaslee parish was created on the death of Thady Duane, P.P., Rosenallis, 6 Apr. 1828. Cf. Comerford, op. cit., ii, 329.

67 See Doyle, Diocesan Book. Comerford, op. cit., ii, 266.
68 For a reference to the 'conference of Ballyroan' meeting c. 1815 see James O'Neill to Doyle, 4 Mar. 1820 (K.L.D.A.).
69 Doyle, Diocesan Book.
70 Doyle to James Conran, rural dean, 10 Dec. 1819, in Latin (K.L.D.A.); also the article by David Dunford entitled 'Dean' in *Cath. Ency.*, iv, 659–60, especially section on rural deans.
71 For theological conferences see chapter 3.
72 Doyle to James Conran, rural dean, 10 Dec. 1819, in Latin (K.L.D.A.).
73 Doyle to Dr Michael Prendergast, rural dean, 12 Dec. 1819, quoted in Fitzpatrick, *Doyle*, i, 113–14.
74 See Doyle, Diocesan Book. Battersby, *Life of Doyle*, pp 26–7 for details of Kildare and Leighlin deaneries as of 4 May 1827; also cited in Comerford, *Collections*, i, 317–18.
75 Cf. W.H.W. Fanning's article 'Chapter' in *Cath. Ency.*, iii, 582–4.
76 Comerford, op. cit., ii, 343–4, iii, 402.
77 Doyle, Diocesan Book.
78 Doyle to Rev. Martin Doyle, undated [1816 or 1817], (K.L.D.A.). Cullen died in 1823. Comerford, op. cit., ii, 343, states that John Dunne who died in 1832 was dean of Kildare for sixteen years.
79 Doyle to Rev. Martin Doyle, undated [1816 or 1817], (K.L.D.A.).
80 *D.E.P.*, 21 Mar. 1821; see also ibid., 16 Feb. 1821. The first and second letters of J.K.L. to Edward Hay and Laicus [Thomas Finn] are on the merits of domestic nomination in the general context of the veto question.
81 W.H.W. Fanning, 'Vicar General' in *Cath. Ency.*, xv, 402–3.
82 The appointment of the forty-year-old James Maher as vicar-general was controversial within the diocese (Fitzpatrick, *Doyle*, ii, 498). As Maher was appointed professor of theology and sacred scripture in Carlow College in 1837 (Comerford, *Collections*, i, 178) it cannot have been on the grounds of his lack of theological acumen.
83 Italian translation of Doyle's letter to John Rice, O.S.A., Rome, [?] Nov. 1819 in Scritture (Irlanda), vol. 22, pp 316–17. Until his transfer to the priory at Callan, County Kilkenny in 1825, John Rice acted as Bishop Doyle's agent in Rome. For Doyle's erection of Raheen parish, see Comerford, *Collections*, iii, 337.
84 Doyle to John Rice, O.S.A., in Italian, [?] Nov. 1819 (Scritture (Irlanda), vol. 22, pp 316–17).
85 Prendergast to Doyle, 25 Feb. 1820 (K.L.D.A.).
86 Propaganda to Troy, 24 April 1820 (Scritture (Irlanda), vol. 23, p. 184), and Troy to Propaganda, undated (Acta, vol. 184, pp 108, 113).
87 Doyle, Diocesan Book.
88 Doyle to Propaganda, 8 Oct. 1823 (Latin copy in K.L.D.A.).
89 Propaganda to Murray, 6 Dec. 1823 (File 30/7 (1823), no. 60, D.D.A.).
90 Propaganda to Doyle, 21 Feb. 1824 (K.L.D.A.). This letter is acknowledged in Doyle to Propaganda, 12 May 1824 (Scritture (Irlanda), vol. 24, p. 164).
91 Ibid. See also Comerford, *Collections*, iii, 135.
92 Doyle, Diocesan Book.
93 Doyle, Relatio Status, 13 May 1829 (Scritture (Irlanda), vol. 25, pp 160–1).
94 Doyle, *S.O.I. evidence*, p. 230, H.L. 1825 (181), ix, 1; Relatio Status, 1829.
95 Doyle, Diocesan Book.
96 Doyle, *Tithe evidence*, p. 97, H.L. 1831–32 (663), xxii, 181.
97 Connolly, *Priests and people*, p. 36.
98 Doyle, *Pastoral, Lent 1821*, p. 4.
99 Doyle, *S.O.I. evidence*, p. 199, H.C. 1825 (129), vii, 173.
100 *D.E.P.*, 16 Jan. 1827; at the same time Doyle had several unemployed curates. Appointing, James Hayden, C.C., to St Mullin's, Doyle remarked to the P.P.: 'nor wd I employ Hayden

but that he is a pauper and his living here [in Carlow] is not creditable to the ministry'. Cf. Doyle to Thomas Dowling, 19 July 1826 (K.L.D.A.).

101 Doyle, Diocesan Book.
102 Connolly, *Priests and people*, p. 36.
103 Corish, *Ir. Cath. Experience*, p. 159.
104 Doyle to Martin Doyle, 16 June 1816 (K.L.D.A.).
105 See chapter 3.
106 Doyle, *S.O.I. evidence*, p. 186, H.C. 1825 (129), viii, 173. The mountainous Hacketstown parish seems to have been regarded as an undesirable posting ('You will be sorry to leave even Hacketstown ...', Rev. P. Healy to Rev. Christopher Doyle, C.C., Hacketstown, 26 Sept. [1818], K.L.D.A.).
107 *Council of Trent*, Sess. XIV, Decree on Reformation, c. 12; for how a right to patronage was to be proved see ibid., Sess. XXV, Decree on Reformation, c. 9. For patronage in some Irish dioceses see Desmond J. Keenan, *The Catholic church in nineteenth-century Ireland* (Dublin, 1983), p. 56.
108 One of these cases, that of Rev. Anthony Goss, is dealt with in chapter 3.
109 Kavanagh to Doyle, 22 Jan. 1821 (K.L.D.A.); for Lalor see Comerford, *Collections*, iii, 78.
110 For Hickey see Comerford, ibid.
111 Ibid., ii, 123.
112 Dominick O'Reilly to Doyle, 9 Nov. 1822 (K.L.D.A.). O'Reilly was a relation of Richard O'Reilly, archbishop of Armagh, 1787–1818. The family had financed the erection of Kildangan chapel in 1792 (Comerford, *Collections*, ii, 243). The fact that in his letter O'Reilly stressed the wishes of the parishioners would seem to indicate that his was not a claim of patronage.
113 Comerford, *Collections*, ii, 245.
114 See Doyle's letter to him of 22 Mar. 1830 quoted in chapter 3.
115 William Scully to Doyle, 27 June 1825 (K.L.D.A.); for Matthew O'Reilly see Comerford, op. cit., ii, 306.
116 Doyle to William Scully, 1 July 1825 (K.L.D.A.).
117 Dowling to Doyle, 25 Jan. 1820 (K.L.D.A.). Dowling also made a severe complaint against his second curate, Cornelius Dowling, who, he said, had been removed by the vicar capitular, James Conran, in 1819, for giving scandal in the parish. This did not prevent Cornelius Dowling however from becoming parish priest of Doonane in 1823.
118 *D.E.P.*, 5 July 1825.
119 Ibid., 9 July 1825.
120 He ministered in the parish from 1825 to 1850, see Comerford, *Collections*, ii, 306.
121 Doyle to Gerald Doyle, P.P., 12 Feb. 1830 (K.L.D.A.); Doyle to Philip Healy, C.C., Ballinakill, 9 Oct. 1825 (K.L.D.A.). For the appointment of curates by parish priests see Corish, *Ir. Cath. Experience*, p. 201.
122 See chapter 3.
123 Fitzpatrick, *Doyle*, i, 126.
124 Doyle to William Tierney, C.C., Clonegal, 10 Sept. 1831 (K.L.D.A.). Tierney was appointed P.P. of Caragh and Downings.
125 Fitzpatrick, *Doyle*, i, 126.
126 Ibid., i, 138.
127 *Stat. dioec. prov. Dublin., 1831*, p. 14.
128 Ibid., p. 36.
129 Doyle, *S.O.I. evidence*, p. 246, H.L. 1825 (181), ix, 1.
130 Fitzpatrick, *Doyle*, i, 289, has the details but not the P.P.'s name. He was probably John Kelly, P.P., Clonmore (1813–28 Sept. 1828). A successor was not appointed to the parish until 1 Feb. 1829 by which time the house had apparently been recovered. See Doyle to Philip Healy, C.C., Philipstown, 1 Feb. 1829 (K.L.D.A.).

131 Doyle, *Tithe evidence*, p. 339, H.C. 1831–32 (508), xxi, 245. For Doyle's own will see Fitzpatrick, op. cit., ii, 503.

132 Doyle to Dr Jeremiah Donovan, 8 Mar. 1823, letter quoted in Fitzpatrick, *Doyle*, ii, 67. Donovan published the first English translation of the *Catechism* in 1829.

133 Corish, *Ir. Cath. Experience*, pp 222, 254–5.

134 L.M. Cullen, *The emergence of modern Ireland 1600–1900* (Dublin, 1983), pp 132–4.

135 John Bossy, 'The Counter-Reformation and the people of Catholic Ireland, 1596–1641' in T. Desmond Williams (ed.), *Historical Studies*, viii (Dublin, 1971), pp 155–69 at p. 169.

136 Archbishop Curtis of Armagh, (born *c.*1745) was an *ancien régime* style courtier of doubtful political judgement. He spent most of his life in the Irish College, Salamanca, where Archbishop Murray (born 1768), was one of his pupils. Murray's first fourteen years as bishop, were spent as coadjutor to the able Archbishop Troy who transmitted much of his penal era caution to his successor. Murray ruled Dublin in his own right for almost thirty years, 1823–52.

137 See Doyle's circular letter to his clergy, undated [1821], (printed copy in K.L.D.A.); Report of sub-committee of the hierarchy on Irish church discipline, 1829 ('Bishops' Minute Book, 1829–49', MS, D.D.A.).

138 *Council of Trent*, Sess. XXIV. On reformation, c. 2.

139 Doyle, Relatio Status, 13 May 1829 (Scritture (Irlanda), vol. 25, pp 160–1). The subject matter of Doyle's diocesan statutes is discussed thematically throughout this work rather than chronologically here.

140 See Doyle, 'Kildare and Leighlin dioceses statutes, 1820' (printed copy in K.L.D.A.); there is a reference to the synod in Doyle, *Pastoral, Lent 1821*, p. 33; see also Fitzpatrick, Doyle, i, 121.

141 Doyle, 'Kildare and Leighlin diocesan statutes, 1821' (MS, K.L.D.A.). 'Excerpta ex Statutis, synodalibus dioceseon unitarum Kild. et Leighlin. A.D. 1824' (printed copy, pp 11, in K.L.D.A.).

142 *Council of Trent*, Sess. XXIV, Decree on reformation, c. 2.

143 Meagher, *Murray*, p. 111; the seventeenth century statutes were published in *Constitutiones Provinciales et Synodales Ecclesiae Metropolitanae et Primitalis, Dublinensis* (n.p., 1770); a summary is given in Comerford, *Collections*, i, 245–57.

144 Meagher, op. cit., p. 112.

145 Ibid. Comerford, op. cit., i, 254; *Council of Trent*, Sess. XXIV, Decree on the reformation of marriage, c. 1.

146 *Council of Trent*, Sess. XXIV, On reformation, c. 18.

147 Comerford, *Collections*, i, 246, 249.

148 *Council of Trent*, Sess. XXII, Decree concerning the mass, c. 9.

149 Ibid., Sess. XXV, Decree on reformation, c. 12.

150 Comerford, *Collections*, i, 254.

151 Ibid., i, 257.

152 Corish, *Ir. Cath. Experience*, p. 197; see ibid., p. 201 where the author writes 'It is hard to find anything in Thurles that had not been laid down at Trent'. Cf. Corish's 'The Catholic community in the nineteenth century' in *Arch. Hib.*, xxxviii (1983), pp 26–33 at p. 31; Connolly, *Priests and people*, p. 71; Meagher, *Murray*, p. 130.

153 Doyle, *Tithe evidence*, p. 98, H.L. 1831–32 (663), xxii, 181.

154 Doyle, *Tithe evidence*, p. 312, H.C. 1831–32 (508), xxi, 245.

155 Murray to Doyle, 26 July 1831 (K.L.D.A.). Murray was however quite within his rights. Cf. Owen Chadwick, *The Popes and European Revolution* (Oxford, 1981), p. 202.

156 Murray to Doyle, 30 July 1831 (K.L.D.A.).

157 Comerford, *Collections*, i, 108; Bishop Kinsella's chapter, one of a total of twenty-seven, was on the duties of the vicar-general and vicar forane. See *Stat. dioec. prov. Dublin, 1831*, pp 25–6.

158 *Council of Trent*, Sess. XXIV, Decree on Reformation, c. 3.
159 Doyle, *Tithe evidence*, p. 98, H.L. 1831–32 (663), xxii, 181.
160 See for example Doyle to Catherine Finn, 29 Aug. 1824, quoted in Fitzpatrick, *Doyle*, i, 357: 'I had been drudging in the country, all day, as I have been incessantly for the last month ...'.
161 See letter from 'B.E.' [Doyle] in *D.E.P.*, 14 Sept. 1824; MS copy of this letter is in Doyle's hand in K.L.D.A.
162 Doyle, *Pastoral, Lent 1820*, p. 3.
163 Fitzpatrick, *Doyle*, i, 463. These returns survive for Kildare and Leighlin. Doyle's Diocesan Books contain much information clearly derived from them.
164 Doyle, circular letter to his clergy, undated [1821], (printed copy in K.L.D.A.).
165 Letter of 'B.E.' [Doyle], in *D.E.P.*, 14 Sept. 1824.
166 Doyle, *Pastoral, Lent 1820*, p. 3.
167 Doyle's Relatio Status, 6 Nov. 1820 (Scritture (Irlanda), vol. 23, pp 300–1 at p. 301).
168 Ibid. Fontana to Doyle, 24 Feb. 1821 (K.L.D.A.); Doyle, Diocesan Book.
169 Council *of Trent*, Sess. XXV, Decree on Reformation, c. 3.
170 Doyle, *S.O.I. evidence*, p. 312, H.L. 1825 (181), ix, 1.
171 Fitzpatrick, *Doyle*, i, 379–80.
172 Ibid., i, 512–13.
173 Ibid., i, 397.
174 Doyle, *S.O.I. evidence*, p. 312, H.L. 1825 (181), ix, 1. In its temporal effects, Doyle claimed, excommunication generally amounted to a nullity as its religious effects were considered sufficient deprivation of the recalcitrant. This was perhaps to play down the effect of Catholic solidarity on the offender.
175 See statement of Rev. Nicholas O'Connor. P.P., Maryborough, in *Disturbed Counties' evidence*, p. 196, 1831–32 (677), xvi, 1.
176 All fourteen pastorals are listed in the bibliography and twelve have been listed in the abbreviations. Those not listed there are Doyle's *Pastoral address on the education of the Catholic poor* (2nd ed., Dublin, 1827). This pastoral received its first newspaper publication in *D.E.P.*, 26, 29 Aug. 1826; and also Doyle's 'Pastoral letter on the Freeholders' Qualification Oath' which was published in *D.E.P.*, 28 May 1829; MS of original is in K.L.D.A. This latter pastoral was re-published with some new opening remarks in early Aug. 1830 and again in May 1831. See *Carlow Morning Post*, 9 Aug. 1830 and 2 May 1831.
177 These were: (1) 'Pastoral charge of the archbishops and bishops of Ireland on Bible societies' (*D.E.P.*, 6 Jan. 1825); (2) *Pastoral instructions of the archbishops and bishops of the R.C. church in Ireland on the subject of the General Jubilee* (Dublin, 1826); (3) 'Pastoral address on education' dated 25 Jan. 1826; and (4) 'Address of the Roman Catholic Prelates in the year 1830' dated 9 Feb. 1830.
178 See chapter three of Thomas McGrath, *Politics, Interdenominational Relations and Education in the Public Ministry of Bishop James Doyle of Kildare and Leighlin, 1786–1834* (Dublin, 1998).
179 Young has not yet received the attention he deserves but for a useful account see Myles V. Ronan, *An Apostle of Catholic Dublin – Father Henry Young* (Dublin, 1944), passim.
180 For Doyle's reference to 'my friend, the Rev. H. Young, of Harold's Cross', see his *Defence of Vindication*, p. 20. For Doyle's reference to Rev. Henry Young as 'one of those few whom the light of God always directs' see Doyle to Mother Dolan, 15 Nov. 1832 (archives of the Discalced Carmelite convent, Malahide, Co. Dublin).
181 Comerford, *Collections*, iii, 149–51. On p. 149 the author writes: 'After the lapse of nearly 60 years, the apostolic labours of this saintly priest are still distinctly remembered in the parish'.
182 Myles V. Ronan, op. cit., p. 215. See also Lady Georgiana Fullerton, *A sketch of the life of the late Father Henry Young of Dublin* (London, 1874), pp 100–2, 104.
183 Henry Young to Doyle, 7 Apr. 1828 (K.L.D.A.).

184 Comerford, *Collections*, iii, 149. Lady Georgiana Fullerton states that Young gave a mission of four months' duration at Stratford-on-Slaney in Baltinglass parish. See Fullerton op. cit., p. 98.

185 A jubilee is a period of remission from the penal consequences of sin granted under certain conditions (usually confession, communion and frequentation of churches) which must be fulfilled within a specific time.

186 Meagher, *Murray*, p. 102.

187 The text of this encyclical is given in Claudia Carlen, *The Papal Encyclicals* (1740–1981), 5 vols (n.p. [McGrath Publishing Co., U.S.], 1981), i, 205–8. The encyclical ended with the admonition 'It is in no manner permitted to anyone to infringe upon this page of our indiction, promulgation, concession, exhortation, rogation, and desire or to go rashly against it. If any one may have presumed to do so, let him know that he will incur the indignation of the omnipotent God and the blessed Apostles Peter and Paul'.

188 See Curtis to Doyle, 30 Sept. 1824 (K.L.D.A.).

189 Curtis to Murray, undated [late Sept./early Oct. 1824], (File 214/1, D.D.A.).

190 Doyle, *S.O.I. evidence*, p. 315, H.L. 1825 (181), ix, 1.

191 The prophecies of 'Pastorini', the cause of this scare are examined in chapter 6.

192 Carlen, *The Papal Encyclicals*, i, 209–15.

193 The *Bull of His Holiness, Leo XII, extending the Universal Jubilee to the whole Catholic world* (Dublin, 1826), pp 1–18, to which is annexed with consecutive pagination the *Pastoral instructions of the archbishops and bishops of the R.C. church in Ireland on the subject of the General Jubilee* (Dublin, 1826), pp 21–36.

194 *Pastoral instructions of the archbishops and bishops of the R.C. church in Ireland on the subject of the General Jubilee* (Dublin, 1826), pp 31–2.

195 Doyle to Somaglia, 19 Mar. 1826 (Scritture (Irlanda), vol. 24, p. 571).

196 The *Bull of His Holiness, Leo XII, extending the Universal Jubilee to the whole Catholic world* (Dublin, 1826), p. 17 allowed for such an extension to a maximum of two years.

197 Meagher, *Murray*, p. 107.

198 Ibid., pp 106–7.

199 See Doyle, *Pastoral, 1833*, 3 pp. The usual ample faculties with respect to censures and reserved cases were granted to approved confessors 'so that when once the penitent is truly converted, he may select, among all the confessors approved by the Ordinary, the individual of his preference, and unbosom to him his spiritual miseries, how grievous soever they may be, without incurring the risk of being referred by him to any higher authority'. Persons excommunicated, suspended, or interdicted by name, were excepted from the benefits of the Jubilee unless they made reparation during it.

200 These rules are outlined in detail in Doyle's published pastoral letters for 1820 and 1823 and also in his 'Lenten regulations, 1829' (MS, K.L.D.A.).

201 Doyle, *Pastoral, Lent 1825*, p. 10. Children were not mentioned in earlier pastorals. In response to a statement from the authorities of Clongowes College that the establishment would suffer if flesh meat were not given to the children during Lent, Doyle gave permission for the use of meat on Sundays, Tuesdays and Thursdays until Palm Sunday inclusive. See Doyle to Bartholomew Esmonde, 14 Mar. 1824 (C.S.J.A.)

202 Doyle, *Pastoral, Lent 1823*, p. 12.

203 Fitzpatrick, *Doyle*, i, 236.

204 Bishop Marum to Doyle, 29 Jan. 1827 (K.L.D.A.); see also Archbishop Murray's Lenten pastoral dated 24 Feb. 1827 (File 30/10 (1827), no. 1, D.D.A.).

205 Doyle to Murray, 6 Jan. 1832 (File 31/3 (1831-32), no. 129, D.D.A.). In this letter Doyle stated that he and Bishops Kinsella and Keating were willing to follow Dr Murray's fast and abstinence regulations for 1832. The threatened outbreak of cholera led Doyle to comment that 'if that scourge arrived we should seek to appease heaven by humiliation and prayer, and oppose the visitation not by fasting but by cheer'.

206 Doyle, *Pastoral, Lent 1834*, passim.
207 Ibid., p. 6.
208 Doyle, *Pastoral, Lent 1834*, p. 6. Fitzpatrick, *Doyle*, i, 237.
209 Fitzpatrick, op. cit., i, 238.
210 Archbishop Troy's Lenten pastoral for 1823 (printed copy in File 30/6 (1822–23), no. 13, D.D.A.).
211 Archbishop Troy's Lenten pastoral for 1823 (printed copy in File 30/6 (1822–23), no. 13, D.D.A.).
212 Archbishop Murray's Lenten pastoral dated 24 Feb. 1824 (File 30/8 (1824), no. 1, D.D.A.).
213 Archbishop Murray's Lenten pastoral dated 24 Feb. 1827 (printed copy in File 30/10 [1827], no. 1, D.D.A.). This pastoral is identical with Murray's 1824 pastoral.
214 Doyle to Murray, 6 Jan. 1832 (File 31/3 (1831–32), no. 129, D.D.A.).
215 Archbishop Troy's Lenten pastoral for 1823 (printed copy in File 30/6 (1822–23), no. 13, D.D.A.).
216 See notes 212 and 213.
217 Marum to Doyle, 29 Jan. 1827 (K.L.D.A.).
218 Doyle, *Pastoral, Lent 1823*, pp 4–5.
219 Archbishop Murray's Lenten pastoral dated 24 Feb. 1824 (File 30/8 (1824), no. 1, D.D.A.).
220 Doyle, *Pastoral, Lent 1834*, p. 6. On strict interpretation of fast and abstinence law during the penal period see Maureen Wall, *The Penal laws, 1691–1760* (Dundalk, 1976), p. 47; Comerford, *Collections*, i, 250–1; and especially Meagher, *Murray*, pp 112–13. The author writes that in the seventeenth century Irish Catholics devoted considerably more than half the days of the year to fast and abstinence.
221 Fitzpatrick, *Doyle*, i, 327; ii, 62.
222 Dr Jeremiah Donovan to Doyle, 26 Mar. 1823 (K.L.D.A.).
223 Doyle to Mrs Mary Coney, 26 Apr. 1823, quoted in Fitzpatrick, op. cit., i, 238.
224 See especially Doyle, *Pastoral, Lent 1834*, passim.
225 Doyle, *Pastoral, Lent 1834*, p. 15. Fitzpatrick, *Doyle*, i, 237–8.
226 Doyle, *Pastoral, Lent 1825*, pp 5–9.
227 Ibid., pp 15, 9.
228 *Pastoral, Lent 1823*, p. 12. For Carlow chapel, see Doyle to Mother Dolan, 6 Mar. 1828 (archives of the Discalced Carmelite convent, Malahide, Co. Dublin).
229 *Pastoral, Lent 1820*, p. 3.
230 Doyle, *S.O.I. evidence*, p. 198, H.C. 1825 (129), viii, 173. See also Doyle, *Defence of Vindication*, p. 75.
231 Doyle, *S.O.I. evidence*, p. 198, H.C. 1825 (129), viii, 173. The roof of Abbeyleix parish church fell in twice, rather embarrassing the parish priest, Michael Keogh. See *Disturbed Counties' evidence*, p. 279, 1831–32 (677), xvi, 1.
232 See *Carlow Morning Post*, 6 May 1819, 2 May 1822, 28 April 1828, 1 May 1828; Propaganda to Doyle, 3 June 1821 (K.L.D.A.); Comerford, *Collections*, i, 316–317; Doyle, *S.O.I. evidence*, p. 198, H.C. 1825 (129), viii, 173; P.J. Brophy, 'The parish of Killeshin in the 19th century' in *Carloviana*, vol 1, no. 1 (Jan., 1947), pp 8–9. In July 1819 Doyle consecrated the new chapel at Tinryland at a solemn high mass. His sermon was very positive with regard to the state of Ireland ('No longer did we hear persecution preached .... The country was protected by laws, the priesthood respected by government, and revered by the people.'). Perhaps such words were intended for the ears of the Protestant gentry present who included Sir Thomas Butler, James Butler, Hugh Falkiner. Once more the band of the Carlow Militia staff was in attendance. See *Carlow Morning Post*, 15 July 1819.
233 Fitzpatrick, *Doyle*, i, 283–4.
234 For a list of these churches see Appendix 2.

235 For an interesting paper on this subject see Kevin Whelan, 'The Catholic parish, the Catholic chapel and village development in Ireland' in *Ir. Geography*, 16 (1983), pp 1–15.

236 Kevin Whelan, 'The Catholic Church in County Tipperary, 1700–1900' in William Nolan and Thomas McGrath (ed.), *Tipperary: History and Society* (Dublin, 1985), pp 215–55 at pp 231–2. But for a contrary opinion see Jarlath Glynn, 'The Catholic Church in Wexford town, 1800–1858' in *The Past*, no. 15 (1984), pp 5–53 at pp 32–3.

237 Much research remains to be done in this area but for the numerous levitical relations of the middle-class Cullens and Mahers see MacSuibhne, *Cullen and his contemporaries*.

238 Castlereagh (ed.), *Memoirs and Correspondence*, iv, 141, 152–3.

239 Doyle, *S.O.I. evidence*, p. 198, H.C. 1825 (129), viii, 173. Newspaper references to Protestant liberality towards Catholic church building enterprises are not unusual. For the very interesting resolution, dated 2 July 1821, of the Protestant parishioners of Clonegal to assist in the building of a new Catholic chapel in the parish, see Peadar MacSuibhne, *Conegal parish* (Ballon, 1975), pp 58–9. In 1828 a parish meeting of Tinryland Catholics acknowledged its gratitude to Field Marshal Beresford 'for his truly liberal grant of the ground for ever, rent free, for our Parochial House, Chapel and School Houses, which are thereon erected – it stands as a lessons to the less liberal Protestants of our county'. See *Carlow Morning Post*, 17 January 1828. In 1829, Patrick Brennan, P.P. of Kildare, received thirty pounds from Robert La Touche, Esq., M.P., towards the erection of a new Catholic chapel in Kildare. See *Carlow Morning Post*, 18 June 1829. In 1830, Peter Gale, Esq., a Protestant magistrate of the Queen's County, contributed handsomely towards the repair of Graigue chapel. He had previously given a considerable donation towards the erection of Doyle's Cathedral. See *Carlow Morning Post*, 10 June 1830. Doyle himself paid a very warm-hearted and generous tribute to the liberality of the landlord of Tullow, Robert Doyne, Esq., in a letter to the editor of the *Carlow Morning Post* written from Clongowes Wood College on 11 April 1832. Doyle acknowledged that Doyne, unsolicited, had promised fifty pounds to assist in building a belfry for Tullow Catholic chapel. Doyle commented: 'This gentleman bestowed to my predecessor the ground upon which the chapel and convent with all their appurtenances in Tullow, now stand; he assisted me to purchase a residence for the clergy in that town, and annexed to it, without any charges, a piece of land. He was amongst the earliest subscribers to the building of our Church in Carlow, and in that case, as in every other, wherein I received favours from him, the kind manner in which he bestowed his gifts, greatly enhances their value. The improvements undertaken and executed by Mr Doyne in Tullow, his paternal care of his tenantry, and the extensive and unceasing charities administered by himself and every member of his family, especially in seasons of distress, to all the poor of the neighbourhood, deserve for him the utmost esteem of the public, and that reward from above which is never withheld from men of goodwill upon earth. I feel a singular pleasure in thus noticing the steady and uniformly benevolent conduct of Mr Doyne, in a county which had often been distracted by party spirit, and which requires only the union of its inhabitants to be the happiest spot in Ireland.' See *Carlow Morning Post*, 16 April 1832. The context in which Doyle wrote this letter is unclear. The letter is unusual as the Doynes do not appear to have been regarded as a blessing in Tullow.

240 Browne of Browne's Hill to Doyle, 21 Dec. 1822 (K.L.D.A.); Doyle to John Dunne, P.P., Portarlington, 1 June 1829, re Lord Portarlington's 'extraordinary' munificence (K.L.D.A.); *D.E.P.*, 11 June 1829.

241 Doyle to William Wellesley Pole, [?] Apr. 1820; Wellesley Pole to Doyle, 7 Apr. 1820 (K.L.D.A.). For Doyle's good relations with Pole who in 1821 was created Baron Maryborough see *Defence of Vindication*, p. 62: 'my Lord Maryboro ... a Nobleman whom J.K.L. should not mention without acknowledging the obligations he owes to his Lordship ...'. Maryborough was a brother of the duke of Wellington and Marquis Wellesley.

242 James Grattan, M.P., to Doyle, 6 Aug. 1825 (K.L.D.A.).

243 Walter Berwick to Doyle, 24 Feb. 1825 (K.L.D.A.).
244 Comerford, *Collections*, iii, 372.
245 Doyle, Relatio Status, 13 May 1829 (Scritture (Irlanda), vol. 25, p. 161).
246 Cf. Connolly, *Priests and people*, pp 30–1.
247 For the Carlow public meeting of 10 Mar. 1822 see *Carlow Morning Post*, 14 Mar. 1822. Letter of 'Friend to true religion' in *D.E.P.*, 4 Apr. 1822.
248 Doyle to Martin Doyle, P.P., Graiguenamanagh, 18 Nov. 1829 (K.L.D.A.).
249 Ibid.
250 The only reference to this dispute is in Fitzpatrick, *Doyle*, ii, 456.
251 See the Maurice Kearney case in chapter 3.
252 Oral tradition in Clonegal and Graiguenamanagh regarded Martin Doyle as a man who exacted dues.
253 Under the stewardship of Rev. Louis Moore, P.P., 1805–1818, two galleries were erected by voluntary groups who were given occupational rights to them. The gallery in the north transept was at the disposal of the Trades Society ('Tradesmens' Gallery') while that of the south transept was reserved for the Barrow Anchor Society ('Boatmen's Gallery'). 'Each had its own rules and was rather strict – and they exercised their rights in the Abbey up to the commencement of the 1974/80 restoration [though in a less strict manner than originally exercised]. In fact only the pews at ground level in the Abbey could be occupied by the general public without any reservations'. Cf. Rev. Patrick Dunny and Michael O'Leary, *The village of the monks – Duiske Abbey, Graiguenamanagh* (Freshford, 1980), p. 18.
254 Martin Doyle to Doyle, 14 July 1829 (K.L.D.A.).
255 Thomas Cloney, 1774–1850, was imprisoned in Fort George in Scotland for four years for his part in the 1798 rebellion. He afterwards moved from his native Wexford to Graiguenamanagh (his uncle Laurence Cloney had been P.P., 1747–96) where he resided until his death. Cloney's narrative (1832) of the 1798 rebellion is well known. He became a local symbol of resurgent Ireland, visited at Graiguenamanagh by his friend Daniel O'Connell, Rev. Theobald Mathew, and even the Young Ireland leaders, William Smith O'Brien and John Blake Dillon, as they raised the standard of rebellion in July 1848. Cf. Comerford, *Collections*, iii, 220; Thomas Pakenham, *The year of liberty* (London, 1972, pbk. ed.), passim; Corish, *Cath. Comm.*, p. 99.
256 Doyle to Rev. Martin Doyle, 18 Nov. 1829 (K.L.D.A.).
257 Doyle to Rev. Peter Doyle, 15 July 1820 (K.L.D.A.).
258 Comerford, *Collections*, i, 329.
259 Doyle to Rev. Gerald Doyle, 7 Jan. 1828, cited in Fitzpatrick, *Doyle*, ii, 438.
260 Doyle, Diocesan Book. See also *Carlow Morning Post*, 10 Apr. 1828. Rev. D.W. Cahill of Carlow College preached on the occasion. In the evening Doyle presided at dinner in Coffey's Hotel for fifty gentlemen. For an interesting article on the building of the Cathedral see Thomas McDonnell, 'From a humble chapel to a fine Cathedral' in *Carlow People* (Supplement), 26 June 1997, pp 4–5.
261 Fitzpatrick, op. cit., ii, 65.
262 Doyle, Diocesan Book.
263 Ibid.
264 Doyle to Lord Cloncurry, 14 Oct. 1829, cited in Cloncurry, *Personal recollections*, p. 382.
265 Cobden was a Protestant and a member of the vestry of St Mary's church, Carlow. See T.P. Kennedy, 'Church building' in Corish, *Ir. Catholicism*, v, 3, 30; William Garner, *Carlow architectural heritage* (Dublin, 1980), passim.
266 Doyle, Diocesan Book.
267 Ibid., Doyle, as might be expected, attributed the main lay support of the cathedral to the Leighlin end of the diocese.
268 Shrewsbury to Doyle, 25 Apr. 1828 (K.L.D.A.); Leinster to Doyle, 25 Apr. 1828 (K.L.D.A.);

D.E.P., 6 May 1828 for contributions from Lord Clifden and Colonel Latouche; Doyle to Cloncurry, 14 Oct. 1829 cited in Cloncurry, *Personal recollections*, p. 382.

269 Doyle to relation, 6 Dec. 1828, cited in Fitzpatrick, *Doyle*, ii, 100.

270 Doyle to Lord Cloncurry, 14 Oct. 1829 cited in Cloncurry, op. cit., p. 382.

271 Doyle to Rev. Martin Doyle, 7 Jan. 1830 (K.L.D.A.).

272 See file on Carlow Cathedral (K.L.D.A.).

273 Doyle to Brother Serenus Kelly, 11 Sept. 1830, cited in Fitzpatrick, *Doyle*, ii, 216–17. For the text of Doyle's circular to the English public, see *The Catholic magazine and review*, vol. 1, no. 1 (Feb. 1831), p. 64.

274 Doyle to Brother Serenus Kelly, 9 Nov. 1830, cited in Fitzpatrick, *Doyle*, ii, 224.

275 Doyle to Brother Serenus Kelly, 11 Sept. 1830, cited in Fitzpatrick, *Doyle*, ii, 224.

276 Serenus Kelly's Journal cited in ibid., ii, 225. Doyle was the recipient of many naive letters from the baroness on the subject of the priest in politics, cf. K.L.D.A. passim.

277 Fitzpatrick, op. cit., ii, 217.

278 Ibid., ii, 227.

279 Ibid., ii, 224.

280 Doyle, Diocesan Book. The Maher brothers of Kilrush were the major benefactors responsible for the foundation of the Presentation convent in Kildare town in 1830. See chapter 4.

281 Doyle, *Pastoral, Jan. 1831*, published in the diocese on 23 Jan. 1831 (printed copy in File 31/2 (1829–30), no. 83, D.D.A.). Doyle to Mother Dolan, 24 Oct. 1830 (archive of the Discalced Carmelite convent, Malahide, Co. Dublin).

282 The point was stressed twice in the pastoral. The parishioners of Naas had just built a new church and Doyle informed the P.P.: 'were they to refuse all aid to the cathedral fund I would not resent their doing so, but feel gratified for any contribution, however small ...'. Doyle to Gerald Doyle, 11 Jan. 1831, quoted in Fitzpatrick, *Doyle*, ii, 439.

283 Doyle, *Pastoral, Jan. 1831* (File 31/2 (1829–30), no. 83, D.D.A.).

284 From a circular letter to the Catholic priests of the diocese printed with the pastoral.

285 See file on Carlow Cathedral in K.L.D.A.; this seems to have been a collection in the parishes of Leighlin.

286 Fitzpatrick, op. cit., ii, 342.

287 Doyle to Mother Dolan, 11 Apr. 1832 (archives of the Discalced Carmelite convent, Malahide, Co. Dublin); Fitzpatrick, op. cit., ii, 343.

288 Comerford, *Collections*, i, 105.

289 Doyle to unnamed nun, 10 Dec. 1833 cited in ibid. The final cost was £9,000 and not £30,000 as stated by Connolly, *Priests and people*, p. 94 and other writers.

CHAPTER 3

1 Corish. *Ir. Cath. Experience*, p. 185, states that Carlow College 'must have been poles apart' from other Irish seminaries.

2 F.J. Brophy, 'A pioneer Irish educationist' in *Carlovian* (1949), p. 30.

3 Quoted in Fitzpatrick, *Doyle*, ii, 478 fn., from 'Mem. of the late Rev. H. Rorke, S.J.,' no page given. I have been unable to trace this memoir in Jesuit libraries where it is unknown so it may have been only in manuscript form.

4 Doyle to Daniel O'Connor, O.S.A., 14 August 1824 (I.A.P.A.).

5 Doyle, *S.O.I. evidence*, p. 244, H.L. 1825 (181), ix, 1.

6 These peculiarities have been silently corrected where they do not interfere with the context throughout this work.

7 Doyle to Murray, 4 Jan. 1824, quoted in Fitzpatrick, *Doyle*, i, 369–70; Doyle to Murray, 24 Jan. 1824 (File 30/8 (1824), no. 8, D.D.A.), incorrectly dated 15 Jan. 1824 in *Arch. Hib.*,

xxxvi (1981), p. 61; Doyle to Murray, 15 Jan. 1824 (File 30/8 (1824), no. 9, D.D.A.). See also Doyle to 'Master Hartigan', 12 July 1830 (File 31/2 (1829–30), no. 81, D.D.A.).

8 Doyle, *S.O.I. evidence*, p. 244, H.L. 1825 (181), ix, 1. Doyle required that intending seminarians spend at least 'one year, or two' in Carlow lay college.

9 Fitzpatrick, *Doyle* (1862), i, 86; Doyle, *S.O.I. evidence*, p. 200, H.C. 1825 (129), viii, 173, implied that student numbers in 1825 were between forty and sixty.

10 Rev. John B. Taylor to Propaganda Fide, 19 Jan. 1823, quoted in MacSuibhne, *Cullen and his contemporaries*, i, 357. Taylor was a professor of classics in Carlow College.

11 Doyle, *S.O.I. evidence*, p. 200, H.C. 1825 (129), viii, 173.

12 Doyle, *S.O.I. evidence*, p. 244, H.L. 1825 (181), ix, 1; *D.E.P.*, 10 July 1824; ibid., 7 July 1825, noted that the pupils underwent a very strict examination from Dr Doyle in law. The syllabus studied in science and languages is outlined in the *Irish Catholic Magazine*, vol. 1 (Sept., 1829), pp 294–6. For reference to these annual literary exhibitions in the lay college see *Carlow Morning Post*, 3, 6 July 1828, 5 July 1830, 11 July 1831. For the awarding of prizes in the ecclesiastical department, see the *Carlow Morning Post*, 21 June 1830.

13 Fitzpatrick, *Doyle* (1862), i, 86. This comment is not to be found in the later edition.

14 Doyle, *S.O.I. evidence*, p. 199, H.C. 1825 (129), viii, 173; Maynooth College experienced financial difficulties until Peel increased its grant in 1845.

15 Doyle, *S.O.I. evidence*, p. 244, H.L. 1825 (181), ix, 1.

16 Doyle, *S.O.I. evidence*, p. 200, H.C. 1825 (129), viii, 173; for examples of priests with farming backgrounds who ministered in Co. Tipperary 1850-1891, see James O'Shea, *Priest, Politics, and Society in post-famine Ireland – A study of County Tipperary 1850–1891* (Dublin, 1983), pp 307-312.

17 Carlow parish report on education, 1824 (MS in K.L.D.A.).

18 Doyle, Relatio Status, 6 Nov. 1820 (Scritture (Irlanda), vol. 23, p. 301).

19 Doyle, *S.O.I. evidence*, p. 200, H.C. 1825 (129), viii, 173.

20 Doyle to Mrs Coney, 'Twelfth day' [6 Jan. 1830], quoted in Fitzpatrick, *Doyle*, ii, 181.

21 Doyle to relation, 20 Oct. 1814, quoted in Fitzpatrick, op. cit., i, 74.

22 Birch, *St Kieran's*, p. 106.

23 'Two unpublished MSS of J.K.L.' in *Carlovian* (1914), p. 120; from the death of Bishop Lanigan in February 1812 until the consecration of Bishop Marum in March 1815, Ossory was without a bishop and the affairs of St. Kieran's College appear to have been unsettled. See Birch, op, cit., p. 80 and passim. There were two students from Leighlin, Eugene Kelly and Edmund Murphy, in Birchfield in 1813–14 (Birch, ibid., pp 93–4).

24 Dr Bartholomew Crotty to Doyle, 24 Oct. 1819 (K.L.D.A.).

25 Dr Bartholomew Crotty to Doyle, 2 Dec. 1822 (K.L.D.A.).

26 Bishop James Keating to Doyle, 26 Oct. 1823 (K.L.D.A.).

27 *D.E.P.*, 29 July 1824.

28 Connolly, *Priests and people*, pp 117–18.

29 *D.E.P.*, 7 Aug. 1824; William Talbot to Doyle, 7 Aug. 1824 (K.L.D.A.); Bishop Sweetman of Ferns included a stricture against priests who 'act the fairy doctor' in his 1771 diocesan regulations. See Corish, *Ir. Cath. Experience*, p. 135. The boundary line between religion and superstition may have been unclear to some practising Catholics. Degraded or suspended priests who were dependant on their wits to make their living outside the official church took advantage of peasant credulity for their own gain. Interestingly such priests enjoyed reputations of great sanctity and supernatural power which were no doubt encouraged by themselves in order to make ends meet.

30 'Bishops' Minute Book, 1829–49' (MS, D.D.A.).

31 Doyle, *S.O.I. evidence*, p. 201, H.C. 1825 (129), viii, 173.

32 Ibid., p. 200.

33 Henry Young, *Catholic Directory* (Dublin, 1821), p. 42.

34 Doyle, *S.O.I. evidence*, p. 200, H.C. 1825 (129), viii, 173; in 1824 Dr. Andrew Fitzgerald

stated that the syllabus in the ecclesiastical college was 'Scripture, church history of Reeves, Delahogue's Theology, Denn's Theology, The Trinity College course of Natural Philosophy and Astronomy, Darre's Geometry, the Logic, Metaphysics and Ethics of Lyons, and Locke's Essay'. See Carlow parish report on education, 1824 (MS in K.L.D.A.).

35 Murray to Doyle, 4 July 1822 (K.L.D.A.).
36 Murray to Doyle, 30 Mar. 1823 (K.L.D.A.). Murray wanted Doyle present at the next board meeting for a discussion of the Dunboyne establishment.
37 Murray to Doyle, 26 May 1823 (K.L.D.A.).
38 'Minutes of the trustees of Maynooth', p. 99 (MS, President's Office, Maynooth College).
39 Doyle, *S.O.I. evidence*, p. 243, H.L. 1825 (181), ix, 1.
40 'Minutes of the trustees of Maynooth', p. 115 (MS, President's Office, Maynooth College); see also Curtis to Doyle, 28 Apr. 1828 on points of discipline for the Maynooth meeting (K.L.D.A.).
41 'Minutes of the trustees of Maynooth', p. 181 (MS, President's Office, Maynooth College).
42 Doyle, Diocesan Book.
43 Duclaux to Doyle, 28 Aug. 1824, cited in Comerford, *Collections*, ii, 353–4.
44 There are no letters from Doyle in the Sulpician archives in Paris though there is one from Dr Andrew Fitzgerald to Rev. Antoine Garnier, dated 22 May 1824, expressing a desire to send some students to Paris to be educated at St Sulpice. This letter is preserved in the Archives de St Sulpice, 6 rue du Regard, 75006 Paris.
45 Doyle, *S.O.I. evidence*, p. 201, H.C. 1825 (181), ix, 1.
46 Henry Young, *Catholic Directory* (Dublin, 1821), pp 41–2.
47 Walsh to Doyle, 6 Dec. 1825 (K.L.D.A.).
48 Bishop Peter Baines (on behalf of Collinridge) to Doyle, 25 Mar. 1826 (K.L.D.A.).
49 William Poynter to Doyle, 13 Oct. 1825, quoted in Comerford, *Collections*, i, 181.
50 Flaget to Doyle, 5 Mar. 1826 (K.L.D.A.).
51 Corish, *Ir. Cath. Experience*, p. 215 states that 100 were ordained annually by the end of the nineteenth century. This figure is far too high.
52 Doyle, *S.O.I. evidence*, p. 215, H.C. 1825 (129), viii, 173; ibid., p. 243, H.L. 1825 (181), ix, 1.
53 MacSuibhne, *Cullen and his contemporaries*, i, 7.
54 Paul Cullen to Rev. James Maher, 10 Oct. 1829, quoted in MacSuibhne, op. cit., pp 148–51.
55 Doyle, *S.O.I. evidence*, pp 202–3, H.C. 1825 (129), viii, 173.
56 Ibid., p. 202, H.C. 1825 (129), viii, 173.
57 Patrick Boyle, 'Irish colleges on the continent' in *Cath. Ency.*, viii, 162–3. Boyle's history, *The Irish College in Paris (1578–1905) with a brief sketch of the other Irish Colleges in France* (London and Dublin, 1905), is cursory.
58 Doyle, *S.O.I. evidence*, p. 201, H.C. 1825 (129) viii, 173.
59 Ibid., p. 202.
60 Doyle, Diocesan Book. Murray to Doyle, 23 Dec. 1819 (K.L.D.A.).
61 Doyle, Diocesan Book.
62 Birch, *St. Kieran's*, p. 323.
63 Patrick Magrath to Doyle, from Piltown, Co. Kilkenny, 31 Aug. 1827 (K.L.D.A.).
64 Dr Patrick McSweeney to Doyle, 25 May 1828, from Paris (K.L.D.A.).
65 Dr Patrick McSweeney to Doyle, 25 May 1828, from Paris (K.L.D.A.); Doyle, Diocesan Book.
66 Doyle, Diocesan Book.
67 See the report of Murray and Doyle to the meeting of the Irish hierarchy on 5 Feb. 1829 in 'Bishops' Minute Book, 1829–49' (MS, D.D.A.).
68 According to Fitzpatrick, *Doyle*, ii, 87, Doyle offered the rectorship to Patrick Brennan, P.P., Kildare and to James Maher, P.P., Leighlin, but they both declined it.

69 'Bishops' Minute Book, 1829–49', for 1829 (MS, D.D.A.).
70 Murray to Doyle, 19 Apr. 1824 (K.L.D.A.). This letter includes Blake's prospectus for the new college dated 1 Apr. 1824. He saw the college functioning to produce priests of superior character, both urbane and ultramontane. Irish students in Rome 'should acquire a general knowledge of books, libraries, and of the world, particularly of ecclesiastical and charitable institutions; they should learn the most correct notions of good taste for building and ornamenting churches, convents, etc; they should select the best pieces of church music; and, as far as their means would allow, might collect paintings, prints, medals, books, etc., on the cheapest terms; which, on their return to Ireland, would serve for improving our national taste, and edifying the piety of our people'.
71 Myles V. Ronan, *An apostle of Catholic Dublin – Father Henry Young* (Dublin, 1944), p. 131.
72 Michael O'Riordan, 'The Irish College in Rome' in *Cath. Ency.*, viii, 158.
73 Boylan to Murray, 14 Mar. 1828 (File 30/11 (1828), no. 19, D.D.A.).
74 Boylan to Doyle, 23 June 1829 (K.L.D.A.).
75 Propaganda Fide to Murray, 2 July 1831 (File 31/3 (1831), no. 70, D.D.A.).
76 Propaganda Fide to Murray, 7 Jan. 1832 (File 31/3 (1831), no. 147a, D.D.A.).
77 He was the best student in the Lisbon college according to Rev. Benjamin Joseph Broughall in 1827 (Broughall to Doyle, 11 Nov. 1827, from Lisbon, quoted in Comerford, *Collections*, i, 291–4 at p. 293).
78 Doyle, Diocesan Book.
79 W.H.W. Fanning, 'Ecclesiastical Conferences' in *Cath. Ency.*, iv, 213–14.
80 'Conferences', a four page MS, in Doyle's hand, undated [1819], (K.L.D.A.).
81 Fanning, loc. cit., p. 213.
82 Ibid.
83 Corish, *Cath. Comm.*, p. 29.
84 In Doyle's library there was a copy of *The ecclesiastical conferences, the synodal discourses and episcopal mandates of Massillon, bishop of Clermont on the principal duties of the clergy* (Dublin and London, 1825), 2 vols translated by Rev. Christopher H. Boylan of Maynooth College. On p. xxiii, a list of seventeen clerical subscribers, including Bishop Doyle, of the diocese of Kildare and Leighlin, is given. This book is now in the bishop's library, Bishop's House, Carlow.
85 Corish, *Cath. Comm.*, p. 101.
86 Discussed in chapter 2.
87 Ballon deanery seems to have been subsumed into the Carlow deanery for the purpose of theological conferences. It may have been that Bishop Doyle was unhappy with Conran's theological knowledge.
88 Doyle, Diocesan Book.
89 Cf. Fitzpatrick, *Doyle*, i, 131, 240, 365.
90 See Doyle to Dr Thomas Browne, 8 Feb. 1831 (K.L.D.A.). Doyle informed Browne, president of Downside Abbey, that 'the attention of the clergy at conferences is often turned to the mode of administering the sacrament of penance'.
91 Doyle's own copy is in the bishop's library, Bishop's House, Carlow.
92 This example and two more are given in Fitzpatrick, *Doyle*, ii, 201.
93 Doyle to Murray, post marked 27 Jan. 1824 (File 30/8 (1824), no. 108, D.D.A.).
94 Donal A. Kerr, *Peel, priests and politics* (Oxford, 1982), pp 232–3, 236–7.
95 Whether this was a specially printed treatise or a book extract is unclear. The modernity of Doyle's approach to communication was notable for its time. He generally printed pastorals and circular letters to his clergy.
96 'Conferences' (MS, K.L.D.A.).
97 Doyle to M. Coleman, convent, Leighlinbridge, 8 June 1820 (K.L.D.A.).
98 'Conferences' (MS, K.L.D.A.).

99 Doyle 'Commonplace book', 1820' (MS in K.L.D.A.); Fitzpatrick, *Doyle*, ii, 516.
100 Fitzpatrick, Doyle, ii, 516.
101 'Kildare and Leighlin diocesan statutes, 1821' (MS, K.L.D.A.); the general framework of the theological conferences as outlined by Doyle was followed in the provincial statutes. See *Stat. dioec. prov. Dublin., 1831*, p. 24.
102 Doyle, Relatio Status, 13 May 1829 (Scritture (Irlanda), vol. 25, p. 160).
103 Fitzpatrick, op. cit., ii, 200.
104 *Stat. dioec. prov. Dublin., 1831*, pp 23–4.
105 Fitzpatrick, op. cit., i, 101.
106 Doyle to Rev. Matthew Fanning, 1 May 1820 (K.L.D.A.).
107 Fitzpatrick, *Doyle*, i, 129.
108 Ibid.
109 Desmond J. Keenan, *The Catholic church in nineteenth-century Ireland* (Dublin, 1983), p. 221.
110 Doyle to Peter Doyle, 15 July 1820 (K.L.D.A.); Doyle, Relatio Status, 6 Nov. 1820 (Scritture (Irlanda), vol. 23, p. 300).
111 Doyle to Peter Doyle, 21 July 1821; see also same to same, 30 Jan. 1821 (both letters in K.L.D.A.).
112 Fitzpatrick, op. cit., i, 297.
113 Ambrose Macaulay, *Dr Russell of Maynooth* (London, 1983), p. 16.
114 *Council of Trent*, Sess. V, Decree on Reformation, c. 2; see also ibid., Sess. XXIII, Decree on Reformation, c. 1 and Sess. XXIV, On Reformation, c. 4.
115 Corish, *Ir. Cath. Experience*, p. 176.
116 Doyle to Dr Jeremiah Donovan, 13 Feb. 1820, cited in Fitzpatrick, *Doyle*, i, 121. In this letter Doyle congratulated Donovan (professor of classics in Carlow College, 1816–20) on his appointment to the chair of rhetoric in Maynooth College.
117 *Council of Trent*, Sess. V. c. 2.
118 Ibid., Sess. XXV, Decree concerning Purgatory.
119 Fitzpatrick, *Doyle*, i, 70.
120 *Stat. dioec. prov. Dublin., 1831*, pp 69–71 particularly at pp 70–1.
121 Charles William Russell described Doyle as 'the finest preacher he had ever heard'. Cf. Ambrose Macaulay, *Dr Russell of Maynooth* (London, 1983), p. 16.
122 Fitzpatrick, op. cit., ii, 495.
123 Doyle, *S.O.I. evidence*, p. 197, H.C. 1825 (129), viii, 173.
124 Murray to Doyle, 26 Mar. 1823 and same to same, 30 Mar. 1823 (both letters in K.L.D.A.). The latter letter noted that Doyle had declined to preach and stated that Murray intended to ask Peter Kenney, S.J., rector of Clongowes Wood College, instead. Kenney was an outstanding preacher. Kenney must also have declined Archbishop Murray's invitation as Keogh, another redoubtable pulpit orator, was asked to deliver the panegyric, but at the last moment he was unable to do so and Doyle stepped from the congregation to take his place (Fitzpatrick, *Doyle*, i, 258).
125 *D.E.P.*, 15 Nov. 1825; the sermon has been printed in Comerford, *Collections*, i, 308-16.
126 Fitzpatrick, *Doyle*, i, 257.
127 *D.E.P.*, 19 Aug. 1823.
128 Doyle to Daniel O'Connor, O.S.A., 2, 21 Oct. 1827 (I.A.P.A.); Fitzpatrick, op. cit., ii, 37. Cards of admission to Bishop Doyle's sermon were issued at ten shillings each. A copy of the printed invitation to this event is in the Cork Archives Institute, Day Collection, vol. 2, no. 23. See Hugh Fenning, 'Cork imprints of Catholic historical interest 1805–1830: a provisional check list (part 2)' in *Jnl. of the Cork historical and archaeological society*, vol. 101 (1996), pp 115–142 at p. 139.
129 *D.E.P.*, 28 Apr. 1829; Fitzpatrick, op. cit., ii, 135.
130 Myles V. Ronan, *An Apostle of the Catholic Dublin – Father Henry Young* (Dublin, 1941), p. 241.

131 M.C. Normoyle, *A tree is planted – the life and times of Edmund Rice* (2cd ed., private circulation, n.p., 1976), p. 102; J.D. Fitzpatrick, 'The beginning of the Christian Brothers – their relations with various ecclesiastical authorities' in *Proc. Ir. Cath. Hist. Comm.* (1961), pp 23–7 at p. 25.

132 William Young to Henry Young, 30 Mar. 1828, enclosed with Henry Young to Doyle, 7 Apr. 1828 (K.L.D.A.). Comerford, *Collections*, iii, 150–1, prints the letter but omits the words 'fix the tickets at almost any price'.

133 O'Connell to Doyle, 26 Jan. 1823 (K.L.D.A.).

134 For listings of all the charity sermons preached in Dublin see Henry Young, *Catholic Directory* (Dublin, 1821), pp. 38–9 and the *Irish Catholic Directory*, 1836, p. 51. There was scarcely a Sunday in the year on which there was not a charity sermon in Dublin in 1836. On many Sundays there were two sermons, sometimes three.

135 There was also among this class an appreciation of a good sermon almost as if it were an art form.

136 *Council of Trent*, Sess. XIV, Decree on Reformation, c. 6.

137 Fitzpatrick, *Doyle*, i, 106; see W.H. Grattan-Flood, *History of the diocese of Ferns* (Waterford, 1916), p. 219 for dress reforms introduced by Bishop Patrick Ryan.

138 Fitzpatrick, op. cit., i, 106.

139 F.X. Martin, 'The Rossiters of Rathmacknee Castle II' in *The Past*, no. 6 (1950), p. 33.

140 Fitzpatrick, op. cit., i, 119 fn.

141 'Kildare and Leighlin diocesan statutes, 1820', p. 2 (of three page printed copy in Latin, K.L.D.A.).

142 *Stat. dioec. prov. Dublin., 1831*, pp 16–17.

143 'Kildare and Leighlin diocesan statutes, 1820', p. 1 (K.L.D.A.).

144 *Council of Trent*, Sess. XIV, Decree on Reformation, c. 6.

145 Fitzpatrick, *Doyle*, i, 283.

146 Ibid., ii, 359.

147 Ibid., i, 286.

148 New chalices are found in parish churches from the early 1820s. A chalice in Stradbally parish church is inscribed: 'This chalice purchased by the parishioners for the use of the parish chapel. Very Rev James Doyle, Prelate. Rev Patrick Dowling, P.P., A.D. 1820'. Cf. Peadar MacSuibhne, *Carlovia* 3 (Carlow, 1977), p. 80.

149 Fitzpatrick, *Doyle*, i, 285. Doyle was appalled to find threadbare vestments in a turf basket. He tore them in two but the priest had them sewn together again. The bishop's practice subsequently was to burn such vestments in the sacristy fire. For the case of a priest who was in straitened circumstances and claimed that he could not afford to purchase respectable clothes see chapter 3.

150 Fitzpatrick, op. cit., i, 286, hinted at the name which MacSuibhne, *Carlovia 3* (Carlow, 1977), p. 36 has deduced. When dying Dowling did not appoint a priest of the diocese as his executor. Doyle nonetheless preached his panegyric. See also MacSuibhne (ed.), *Knockbeg*, pp 84–5.

151 'Bishops' Minute Book, 1829–49' for 1829 (MS, D.D.A.).

152 Letter of May/June 1824 cited in Fitzpatrick, *Doyle* (1862), i, 351.

153 Fitzpatrick, *Doyle* (1862), i, 111; Shortly after Fitzpatrick's biography was first published, Michael Coyle of Athy, wrote to the author, on 4 July 1861 stating 'I have met a priest of Kildare who was very bitter about the *Stations – the Priests' Farms and Tallyho*' (cf. Fitzpatrick MS 15495, N.L.I.).

154 See James Godkin, *The religious history of Ireland* (London, 1873), p. 222; E.R. Norman, *Church and society in England 1770-1970* (Oxford, 1976), pp 69–70; Connolly, *Priests and people*, p. 66 gives 'Pax Vobiscum' following the toned down version in the later edition of Fitzpatrick, *Doyle*, i, 104.

155 Doyle, *S.O.I. evidence*, p. 199, H.C. 1825 (129), viii, 173.

156 Doyle, *Pastoral, Lent 1825*, p. 8.
157 'Kildare and Leighlin diocesan statutes, 1820', p. 2 (K.L.D.A.).
158 Fitzpatrick, op. cit., i, 286.
159 Fitzpatrick, *Doyle*, i, 287.
160 Archbishop Murray carried leniency to such lengths 'as to excite not barely the surprise, but the open disapproval of wise and worthy observers'. Murray relied upon a maxim of St Francis de Sales that it was very hard to know the exact point where clemency should cease and severity begin. 'Even abuses he suffered to remain, when he saw reason to dread that their suppression would but eventuate in aggravated scandal, or in new evils as dangerous as those of which he had to complain.' Doyle used to designate Murray 'that angel of a man' but he felt 'provoked occasionally at what seemed to him excess of lenity' in Murray. Cf. Meagher, *Murray*, pp 23, 22, 65. It seems probable that Murray thought Doyle too severe.
161 Doyle, *Essay on the Cath. Claims*, p. 181.
162 Doyle to Gerald Doyle, P.P., Naas, 2 June 1825, quoted in Fitzpatrick, op. cit., ii, 437. 'I should be glad my judgement could be always as favourable to you as my feelings are partial' (ibid., ii, 435).
163 'Bishops' Minute Book, 1829–49', for 1829 (MS, D.D.A.).
164 *Stat. dioec. prov. Dublin., 1831*, pp 9–10.
165 *Decreta Synodi ... Thurles*, pp 30–1.
166 Edward MacLysaght, *Irish life in the seventeenth century* (Dublin, 1979 ed.), p. 298; see 'Notes' compiled by the mid-nineteenth century Cashel diocesan priest, Thomas O'Carroll (Cashel Diocesan Archives).
167 James O'Shea, *Priest, politics and society in post-famine Ireland – a study of County Tipperary, 1850–1891* (Dublin, 1983), pp 21, 317–18. Only two of these P.P.s held more than 100 acres (110 and 115 acres respectively).
168 Ibid., p. 22.
169 Fitzpatrick, *Doyle*, i, 104, 138.
170 James Dowling, P.P., to Doyle, 25 Jan. 1820 (K.L.D.A.).
171 Cited in James A. Reynolds, *The Catholic Emancipation crisis in Ireland, 1823–1829* (Westport, Connecticut, 1970 reprint), p. 53. The best known case of a pre-famine farmer priest is perhaps that of Dr James Murray, P.P. of Clonmellan, who twice headed the terna for the diocese of Meath. He was, Archbishop Curtis acknowledged, a 'learned, pious and exemplary clergyman' but he cultivated an 'extensive portion of lands'. In 1830 the bishops of the Armagh province felt they could not in conscience recommend Murray to Rome for the See. His votes in the terna, said Curtis, were 'supposed to have been given by the farming, jobbing and selling priests, so common over the diocese of Meath, whom Dr Murray if appointed would not be able or willing to put down, or reform, but would rather encourage by his own example' (Curtis to Christopher Boylan, 1 June 1830, in Scritture (Irlanda), vol. 25, pp 306–7.).
172 Fitzpatrick, *Doyle*, i, 139.
173 Ibid.
174 Fitzpatrick, *Doyle* (1862), i, 144. In the 1880 edition, vol. 1, p. 139, this remark has been toned down: 'He fed the lambs and sheep, though not always in a scriptural sense'. Nolan's name is not given in either edition.
175 Cloncurry to Doyle, 8 Feb. 1830 (K.L.D.A.); MacSuibhne (ed.), *Knockbeg*, pp. 25, 59. Nolan was one of the first priest-students in Carlow College and thus a very young parish priest. Cf. chapter 1, note 87.
176 Cloncurry to Doyle, 8 Feb. 1830 (K.L.D.A.).
177 Fitzpatrick, op. cit., i, 139.
178 Cloncurry to Doyle, 8 Feb. 1830 (K.L.D.A.).
179 Doyle to Robert Cassidy, 19 Feb. 1829, quoted in Cloncurry, *Personal recollections*, p. 381.

180 Fitzpatrick, op. cit., i, 119–20 fn.
181 Doyle to Robert Cassidy, 19 Feb. 1829, quoted in Cloncurry, *Personal recollections*, p. 381. For the dispute between Lord Cloncurry and the Nolan brother-priests see Cloncurry to Doyle, 26 Feb. 1824 (K.L.D.A.); Doyle to Cloncurry, 10 Mar. 1824 in Cloncurry, *Personal recollections*, p. 386; Doyle to Robert Cassidy, 20 Feb. 1829, in ibid., p. 381; Doyle to Cloncurry, 20 Feb. 1829, in ibid., pp. 381-2; Cloncurry to Doyle, 15 Feb. 1830 (K.L.D.A.); Doyle to Cloncurry, 16 Feb. 1830 (K.L.D.A.).
182 Dowling to Doyle, 25 Jan. 1820 (K.L.D.A.).
183 Doyle, *Tithe evidence*, p. 97, H.L. 1831–32 (663), xxii, 181.
184 Doyle to Rev. Philip Healy, 1 Feb. 1829 (K.L.D.A.).
185 Doyle, *S.O.I. evidence*, p. 235, H.L. 1825 (181), ix, 1.
186 Doyle, *S.O.I. evidence*, p. 235, H.L. 1825 (181), ix, 1.
187 *Decreta synodi ... Thurles*, p. 39.
188 *Stat. dioec. prov. Dublin.*, 1831, p. 9.
189 Doyle, *Tithe evidence*, p. 97, H.L. 1831–32 (663), xxii, 181.
190 Ibid., p. 98.
191 Doyle, *S.O.I. evidence*, p. 235, H.L. 1825 (181), ix, 1.
192 Doyle, *S.O.I. evidence*, p. 390, H.C. 1830 (654), vii, 1. James Conran, V.F., P.P. Ballon, disapproved of his farm labourers fasting during Lent (MacSuibhne (ed.), *Knockbeg*, p. 78).
193 Doyle, *Tithe evidence*, p. 98, H.L. 1831–32 (663), xxii, 181.
194 *Stat. dioec. prov. Dublin., 1831*, p. 9.
195 *Decreta synodi ... Thurles*, p. 40.
196 *Council of Trent*, Sess. XIV, Decree on Reformation, proem.
197 Doyle, *S.O.I. evidence*, p. 186, H.C. 1825 (129), viii, 173.
198 Doyle, *Pastoral, Lent 1821*, p. 3.
199 See Rev. P. Healy to Christopher Doyle, C.C. Hacketstown, 26 Sept. [1818], (K.L.D.A.). This is a jocose letter congratulating the latter on his transfer to Ballyfin parish ('it was a pity to have such a genius buried in the fogs of Hacketstown'). The letter also seems to hint at a somewhat relaxed easygoing clerical lifestyle: 'you must drop your debenture buying and live hospitably. I see a long train of pleasures before you. Here there are no back or belly aches nor sore throats – all is joy and comfort and care and happiness – good diet – good potteen and fine air'. Nonetheless, Doyle, in 1834, considered Healy had the qualities necessary for a bishop.
200 Not surprisingly the cases of these priests are generally absent from the historiographical literature of the diocese.
201 Doyle, *S.O.I. evidence*, pp 186–7, H.C. 1825 (129), viii, 173.
202 Doyle to John Dunne, V.F., P.P., Kilcock, 22 Mar. 1821 (K.L.D.A.) and same to same, 30 Mar. 1821, quoted in Fitzpatrick, *Doyle* (1862), i, 146, but without revealing the priest's name.
203 MacSuibhne (ed.), *Knockbeg*, pp 31, 89; Henry Young, *Catholic Directory* (Dublin, 1821), p. 43.
204 Doyle to John Dunne, V.F., P.P., 22 Mar. 1821 (K.L.D.A.).
205 Ibid.
206 Doyle to John Dunne, V.F., 30 Mar. 1821 quoted in Fitzpatrick, *Doyle* (1862), i, 146.
207 Doyle to John Dunne, V.F., 22 Mar. 1821 (K.L.D.A.).
208 Doyle, Diocesan Book.
209 Ibid., Doyle's entry on Hanrick has been heavily inked over; part of it is illegible.
210 Troy to Doyle, 23 Mar. 1820 (K.L.D.A.).
211 Plunkett to Doyle, 27 Mar. 1821 (K.L.D.A.). Doyle's letter to Plunkett was written at the request of one of his diocesan clerics who had a complaint against the Meath priest.
212 Doyle, Diocesan Book, 1819–20, and Doyle, Diocesan Book. Moore was replaced by Rev.

John Gahan as administrator. When Rev. Moore died in 1839 Gahan became parish priest. Cf. Comerford, *Collections*, i, 122; iii, 352; MacSuibhne (ed.), *Knockbeg*, pp 27, 79; ibid., Liam O Fearghail, 'Fr John Gahan, P.P., Rathvilly,', pp. 103–4, states that Rev. Moore was an invalid and nearly blind. Doyle makes no mention of this. Moore was still only seventy-three years of age when he died. For reports on Rathvilly parish in 1822, 1829 and 1830 see 'Rathvilly Baptismal Register, 29 June 1813 – 25 Apr. 1842' on microfilm, p. 4189, in N.L.I.

213 Doyle, Diocesan Book.
214 Chapter 1, note 162.
215 Comerford, op. cit., iii, 266.
216 Doyle to John Rice, O.S.A., [?] Nov. 1819 (in Italian in Scritture (Irlanda), vol. 22, p. 317). Michael McDonald, C.C. Killeshin from 1817 until his death in 1823 appears to have carried out most of the work of the parish, including the building of Killeshin church in which Doyle erected a tablet to his memory stating that he had 'improved by his labours and example the morals and piety of this parish'. Cf. Comerford, *Collections*, iii, 248.
217 Fitzpatrick, *Doyle* (1862), ii, 446. The last sentence of this quotation is omitted in ibid., (1890), ii, 500.
218 Doyle, Diocesan Book.
219 *D.E.P.*, 3 June 1823, 12 Apr. 1830.
220 Doyle, Diocesan Book.
221 *Tithe evidence*, p. 38, H.L. 1831–32 (271), xxii, 1; evidence of Rev Samuel Thomas Roberts, a Kilkenny magistrate and friend of Rev. Goss.
222 Fitzpatrick, *Doyle*, ii, 358–9, 450.
223 Doyle to Thomas Spring Rice, 29 Nov. 1832, cited in Fitzpatrick, *Doyle*, ii, 450.
224 Comerford, *Collections*, ii, 341.
225 Maurice Kearney to Doyle, 10 Jan. 1825 (K.L.D.A.).
226 Maurice Kearney to Doyle, from Suncroft, 27 Oct. 1821 (K.L.D.A.).
227 Benjamin Joseph Broughall to Doyle, 22 June 1821 (K.L.D.A.).
228 Broughall to Doyle, 30 Aug. 1822, from Paris (K.L.D.A.); and same to same, 26 Oct. 1822 (K.L.D.A.). For Broughall's recurring ill-health and colourful wanderings around the Mediterranean see his letters from Lisbon, Alexandria and Naples documented in Comerford, *Collections*, i, 287–303. He died with a reputation of great sanctity in the Benedictine monastery of Monte Cassino in 1850. On the question of lawful absence from a parish see *Council of Trent*, Sess. VI, Decree on Reformation, c. 2.
229 Kearney to Doyle, 30 Oct. 1823 (K.L.D.A.). This was the parish where the tithe war began seven years later.
230 Ibid.
231 Kearney to Doyle, 11 Sept. 1822 (K.L.D.A.).
232 Kearney to Doyle, 30 Oct. 1823 (K.L.D.A.).
233 Thomas Cloney to Doyle, 16 Aug. 1824 (K.L.D.A.).
234 Kearney to Doyle, 26 Aug. 1824 (K.L.D.A.).
235 Kearney to Doyle, 8 Sept. 1824 (K.L.D.A.).
236 Cloney to Doyle, 8 Sept. 1824 (K.L.D.A.).
237 Kearney to Doyle, 8 Sept. 1824 (K.L.D.A.).
238 [Cloney's] Memorial from Graiguenamanagh parishioners to Bishop Doyle, undated (MS, K.L.D.A.).
239 [Kearney's] Memorial from Graiguenamanagh parishioners to Bishop Doyle, undated (MS, K.L.D.A.).
240 Kearney to Doyle, 8 Sept. 1824 (K.L.D.A.). For an extended discussion of this conflict see the present writer's unpublished paper: 'Priests and people in Graiguenamanagh in the early nineteenth century'. A paper delivered as a public lecture in Graiguenamanagh on 10 November 1988.

241 Kearney to Doyle, 14 Sept. 1824 (K.L.D.A).
242 Kearney to Doyle, 10 Jan. 1825 (K.L.D.A.).
243 Doyle, Diocesan Book. The 1831 provincial statutes devoted much attention to a forceful
    denunciation of clerical avariciousness. Cf. *Stat. dioec. prov. Dublin., 1831*, p. 13.
244 Kearney to Doyle, 12 Feb. 1825 (K.L.D.A.). The last remark is perhaps a reference to
    Mark Kennedy, P.P., Clane, 1810–21.
245 Doyle to Thomas Spring Rice, 29 Nov. 1832, cited in Fitzpatrick, *Doyle*, ii, 450.
246 Comerford, *Collections*, ii, 114. In Clane, Rev. Kearney spent much of his time at Clongowes
    Wood College where the students joked that he came when he caught the smell of dinner
    cooking. See Arthur Griffith (ed.), *Meagher of the Sword* (Dublin, 1916), pp 273-9.
247 See Doyle to Fanning, 1 May 1820 (K.L.D.A.).
248 Archbishop Troy to Doyle, 23 Feb. 1820 (K.L.D.A.). Troy was paraphrasing Garry's at-
    torney who had personally approached him requesting his intervention to stop a legal
    action.
249 Ibid. Stephen Garry to Doyle, 27 Feb. 1820, from Fairyhill, Kildare (K.L.D.A.).
250 Doyle to Fanning, 1 May 1820 (K.L.D.A.).
251 Ibid.
252 The resolutions of this lay committee are included in a letter of Patrick Brennan to Doyle,
    15 June 1820 (K.L.D.A.).
253 Patrick Brennan to Doyle, 15 June 1820 (K.L.D.A.).
254 Patrick Brennan to Doyle, 23 June 1820 (K.L.D.A.).
255 John McEvoy, C.C., to Doyle, 7 Feb. 1823 (K.L.D.A.).
256 McEvoy and Cummins to Doyle, 10 Mar. 1823 (K.L.D.A.).
257 Doyle, Diocesan Book.
258 Raheen ceased to be a mensal parish and its administration was annexed to the newly
    erected parish of Mountrath during the lifetime of its first incumbent, Matthew Malone,
    P.P., who died in 1835. Cf. chapter 2.
259 Doyle, *S.O.I. evidence*, p. 185, H.C. 1825 (129), viii, 173.
260 Doyle, *S.O.I. evidence*, p. 231, H.L. 1825 (181), ix, 1.
261 Ibid. For a note on episcopal incomes see K. Theodore Hoppen, *Elections, politics and
    society in Ireland 1832–1885* (Oxford, 1984), p. 226. Bishop Delany's income in 1800 was
    £297. Cf. Castlereagh (ed.), *Memoirs and Correspondence*, iv, 142. In 1835 the president of
    Carlow College informed de Tocqueville that Kildare and Leighlin was one of the poorest
    dioceses in Ireland. Cited in J.A. Murphy, 'The support of the Catholic clergy in Ireland,
    1750–1850' in J.L. McCracken (ed.), *Historical Studies*, v (London, 1965), pp 104–5.
262 Doyle, *S.O.I. evidence*, p. 185, H.C. 1825 (129) viii, 173.
263 Doyle, *S.O.I. evidence*, p. 315, H.L. 1825 (181), ix, 1.
264 Doyle, *S.O.I. evidence*, p. 185, H.C. 1825 (129), viii, 173.
265 Ibid.
266 Castlereagh (ed.), *Memoirs and Correspondence*, iv, 151.
267 A figure based on the details given in this paragraph. A figure of £40 per annum has been
    suggested as an annual farm income of the parish priests. Cf. D.J. Keenan, *The Catholic
    church in nineteenth-century Ireland* (Dublin, 1983), p. 230, In 1822 a Kildare and Leighlin
    priest claimed that the average revenue of the parishes of the diocese was £250 per annum.
    See 'Clericus Leighlinensis' to Doyle, 14 Mar. 1822 (K.L.D.A.). In his Diocesan Book,
    1819–20, Doyle recorded the annual income for thirty-two named parishes. The average
    was £202 (MS in K.L.D.A.).
268 Castlereagh (ed.), *Memoirs and Correspondence*, iv, 149.
269 Corish, *Ir. Cath. Experience*, pp 175, 185.
270 Doyle, *Pastoral, Nov., 1822*, p. 15.
271 L.M. Cullen, The *emergence of modern Ireland, 1600-1900* (Dublin, 1983 reprint), p. 179.
272 Delumeau, *Catholicism between Luther and Voltaire*, p. 188.

273 This was one of the reasons why Doyle was opposed to state payment of the Irish Catholic clergy. This however was pursued in 1825 as one of the wings of the Catholic Emancipation Bill and in his evidence before the house of lord's select committee on 21 March 1825 Doyle was not prepared to withhold his consent from any such arrangement if such opposition on his part was likely to jeopardise the prospects of the bill then before parliament. Cf. Doyle, *S.O.I. evidence*, p. 232, H.L. 1825 (181), ix, 1; ibid., p. 177, H.C. 1825 (129), viii, 173. See also chapter one of Thomas McGrath, *Politics, Interdenominational Relations and Education in the Public Ministry of Bishop James Doyle of Kildare and Leighlin, 1786–1834* (Dublin, 1998).

274 Doyle, *S.O.I. evidence*, p. 231, H.L. 1825 (181), ix, 1; ibid., pp. 185–6, H.C. 1825 (129), viii, 173; the purpose of Doyle's inventory of parochial incomes was to enable him to judge how benefices ought to be distributed 'having in view to give the most valuable, and at the same time the most important parish, to the most worthy person' (Doyle, *Tithe evidence*, p. 34, H.L. 1831–32 (663), xxii, 181). Doyle added 'at that time I found that the different unions throughout the diocese produced, at an average, something, as I recollect, about 300l. a year' (ibid.,). Doyle's recollection was inaccurate.

275 *Stat. dioec. prov. Dublin., 1831*, p. 86. In the parish of Carlow the clergy were supported partly by chapel-gate collections. See Doyle to John Dunne, P.P., Portarlington, 7 Dec. 1827 (K.L.D.A.).

276 I am dependent on Fitzpatrick, *Doyle*, i, 115, for this statement.

277 *Stat. dioec. prov. Dublin., 1831*, p. 86.

278 Castlereagh (ed.), *Memoirs and Correspondence*, iv, 153.

279 Doyle, *S.O.I. evidence*, p. 187, H.C. 1825 (129), viii, 173; ibid., p. 233, H.L. 1825 (181), ix, 1.

280 Doyle, *S.O.I. evidence*, p. 185, H.C. 1825 (129), viii, 173.

281 Ibid., p. 187. Doyle, *S.O.I. evidence*, p. 233, H.L. 1825 (181), ix, 1.

282 Doyle, *S.O.I. evidence*, p. 232, H.L. 1825 (181), ix, 1.

283 'Bishops' Minute Book, 1829–49' (MS, D.D.A.). Doyle, *S.O.I. evidence*, p. 180, H.C. 1825 (129), viii, 173. Doyle, Diocesan Book, 1819–20 (MS in K.L.D.A.). This diocesan book records the case of Higgins, a curate at Caragh: 'this man embezzles dues, drinks, disobeys, etc., etc. [He] does not exhort funerals and marriages. He is not in future to assist at them as he embezzles. He gives no account of those whom he hears and nor [does he] return an account of baptisms.'

284 Doyle, *S.O.I. evidence*, p. 180, H.C. 1825 (129), viii, 173.

285 Report of the hierarchical sub-committee on Irish church discipline, 1829 ('Bishops' Minute Book, 1829–49', MS, D.D.A.).

286 Doyle, *S.O.I. evidence*, p. 231, H.L. 1825 (181), ix, 1.

287 Ibid., p. 230. Ibid., p. 184, H.C. 1825 (129), viii, 173; 'The marriage fee is usually one guinea' ('Bishops' Minute Book, 1829–49' for 1829, MS, D.D.A.).

288 Doyle, *S.O.I. evidence*, p. 185, H.C. 1825 (129), viii, 173.

289 Fitzpatrick, *Doyle*, i, 115.

290 Doyle, *S.O.I. evidence*, p. 231, H.L. 1825 (181), ix, 1.

291 Ibid. Doyle, *S.O.I. evidence*, p. 185, H.C. 1825 (129), viii, 173; Castlereagh (ed.), *Memoirs and Correspondence*, iv, 156.

292 Oral information from V. Rev. Kevin O'Neill, President, Carlow College, a priest of the diocese of Kildare and Leighlin. This practice could possibly be related to controversy over the access of Catholic priests to 'Protestant' graveyards – a focus of interdenominational tension during the New Reformation period and long afterwards.

293 Doyle, *S.O.I. evidence*, p. 185, H.C. 1825 (129), viii, 173.

294 Ibid., p. 231, H.L. 1825 (181), ix, 1. There is no evidence that the Tridentine recommendation that a fourth of the funeral dues be paid to the Cathedral or parish churches was in fact implemented. See *Council of Trent*, Sess. XXV, Decree on Reformation, c.13.

295 *Stat. dioec. prov. Dublin., 1831*, pp 83–6.

296 Maurice Kearney, Adm., Clane to Doyle, 13 Feb. 1827 (K.L.D.A.). Kearney stated that he prevailed on a parishioner to 'pay his marriage dues without specifying any sum'.

297 Doyle, *S.O.I. evidence*, p. 184, H.C. 1825 (129), viii, 173.

298 Doyle to Nicholas Clayton, O.S.A., 14 Dec. 1814, cited in Fitzpatrick, *Doyle*, i, 68; Doyle, *S.O.I. evidence*, p. 180, H.C. 1825 (129), viii, 173.

299 Doyle, *S.O.I. evidence*, p. 180, H.C. 1825 (129), viii, 173; ibid., p. 232, H.L. 1825 (181), ix, 1.

300 Doyle, *S.O.I. evidence*, p. 232, H.L. 1825 (181), ix, 1.

301 *Disturbed Counties' evidence*, p. 279, H.L. 1831–32 (677), xvi, 1.

302 Murphy to Doyle, 20 Feb. 1827 (K.L.D.A.).

303 Doyle to Patrick Murphy, P.P., Monasterevan, 22 Mar. 1830 (K.L.D.A.).

304 M. Hyland, C.C., Monasterevan, to Doyle, 20 Apr. 1833 (K.L.D.A.).

305 Castlereagh (ed.), *Memoirs and Correspondence*, iv, 154–5.

306 *Disturbed Counties' evidence*, p. 197, H.L. 1831–32 (677), xvi, 1. The priests of Kildare and Leighlin supported their bishop's lonely crusade for an Irish poor law and there is much evidence to suggest that in many parishes the clergy were in the 1820s already managing de facto parochial poor law arrangements.

307 Doyle, Diocesan Book.

308 Castlereagh (ed.), *Memoirs and Correspondence*, iv, 152.

309 Fitzpatrick, *Doyle*, ii, 315; see also Corish, *Ir. Cath. Experience*, p. 158, for the same opinion.

310 Kearney to Doyle, 30 Oct. 1823 (K.L.D.A.). For Kearney see 'Discipline' section of this chapter.

311 Bishop Kinsella to Doyle, 29 Aug. 1829 (Carrigan MSS 38, pp 103–4, St Kieran's College, Kilkenny).

312 Doyle, *Tithe evidence*, p. 97, H.L. 1831–32 (663), xxii, 181; Doyle, *Defence of Vindication*, p. 110; Doyle, *S.O.I. evidence*, p. 231, H.L. 1825 (181), ix, 1. An unusual feature of the diocese was the two perpetual curacies founded by Bishop Delany in his mensal parishes of Tullow and Mountrath. The bishop prescribed the duties of these curates. Both were obliged to say four masses each week (with some others on stated days) for Dr Delany's intentions. For this purpose they each received £50 per annum from his trustees. The Mountrath perpetual curacy 'at all times' enjoyed some extra emolument for masses said at the chapel of ease, Clonard. The curate also acted as chaplain to the male and female religious in the town, and was obliged to teach religious knowledge to the school children of the parish. Bishop Delany had also left a small legacy for the distribution of religious books for this purpose. The Mountrath curate was also expected to spend his spare time assisting the parish priest. The perpetual curacy in Tullow did not have any extra source of funding and Dr Doyle was obliged to add £15 to that curate's £50 'that he may be enabled to subsist'. Confer Doyle, Diocesan Book; Bishop Delany's intentions are fully catalogued in Brigidine Annals, pp 26–35 (T.B.A.).

313 Doyle to Gerald Doyle, P.P., Naas, undated, cited in Fitzpatrick, *Doyle*, ii, 435 and Doyle to Martin Doyle, P.P., Graiguenamanagh, 2 Feb. 1827 (K.L.D.A.).

314 *Stat. dioec. prov. Dublin., 1831*, 'De Co-adjutoribus Parochorum', pp 32–3.

315 Corish, *Ir. Cath. Experience*, p. 158.

CHAPTER 4

1 *Council of Trent*, Sess. XXV, On Reformation, c. 1.

2 Strictly speaking lay brothers are not religious.

3 Doyle to Daniel O'Connor, O.S.A., 26 Dec. 1823 (I.A.P.A.). Doyle held that about twenty

years was the ideal age for entry into the ecclesiastical state. See Doyle to Daniel O'Connor, O.S.A., 25 July 1830 (I.A.P.A.).

4   Cited in Fitzpatrick, *Doyle*, ii, 16.

5   Hugh Fenning, *The undoing of the friars in Ireland: a study of the novitiate question in the eighteenth century* (Louvain, 1972), p. 330.

6   Cited in [John P. Lynch], *The life of Brother Paul J. O'Connor* (Dublin, 1867), p. 61.

7   Doyle to Dr John Gibbons, O.S.A., 18 Sept. 1824 (I.A.P.A.).

8   A written communication from James Crane, O.S.A., quoted in Fitzpatrick, *Doyle*, ii, 316. Doyle's successors Nolan and Haly continued 'this extraordinary privilege'. Fitzpatrick makes no mention of whether James Walshe, bishop of Kildare and Leighlin, 1856-88, did so.

9   Butler, *Near Restful Waters*, p. 148.

10   Housebook '1798–1830', entry for 8 Aug. 1817 (MS, O.S.A. priory, New Ross).

11   See chapter 1, note 59.

12   Doyle preached at his month's mind. *D.E.P.*, 2 Sept. 1823.

13   Doyle to Dr John Gibbons, O.S.A., provincial, 17 Oct. 1823 (I.A.P.A.).

14   Fitzpatrick, *Doyle*, ii, 299.

15   Housebook '1825–1838', entry for 22 Sept. 1824 (MS, O.S.A. priory, New Ross).

16   Housebook, '1825–1838', entry for 25 July 1825, signed by Daniel O'Connor, O.S.A., (MS, O.S.A. priory, New Ross). This entire affair finds no mention in John B. Cullen, 'The Augustinians in New Ross' in *I.E.R.*, fifth series, xv (Jan.-June, 1920), pp 302–12, or in Butler, *Near Restful Waters*.

17   He died on 25 May 1826 aged seventy-two years according to a plaque on a wall in the Augustinian church in New Ross.

18   Battersby, *Hist. of the Augustinians in Ire.*, p. 65. When provincial John Gibbons died in early 1827, the first definitor, Augustine McDermott became rector-provincial and remained so until the July 1827 chapter which elected Daniel O'Connor (Cf. 'Acts of the Irish province, 1782–1867', pp 157–64, MS, I.A.P.A.).

19   Doyle to Daniel O'Connor, O.S.A., 25 July 1830 (I.A.P.A.). An advertisement for the New Ross School described it as an Augustinian seminary preparing young men for entrance to Maynooth, Carlow and other ecclesiastical seminaries. Doyle was credited with not only fully approving of the system of education offered in New Ross but with having arranged or suggested all its details. See *Carlow Morning Post*, 25 Jan. 1830.

20   Doyle to Nicholas Clayton, O.S.A., 14 Dec. 1814, cited in Fitzpatrick, *Doyle*, i, 68.

21   Doyle to Daniel O'Connor, O.S.A., undated [Aug.-Sept. 1830], cited in ibid., ii, 151.

22   Doyle to Daniel O'Connor, O.S.A., 3 Aug. 1829 (I.A.P.A.).

23   Doyle to Daniel O'Connor, O.S.A., 30 July 1829 (I.A.P.A.).

24   Doyle to Daniel O'Connor, O.S.A., 3 Aug. 1829 (I.A.P.A.).

25   Doyle to Daniel O'Connor, O.S.A., 20 Oct. 1829 (I.A.P.A.). For British influence at Rome which prevented Foran's appointment as bishop of Waterford and Lismore see Cardinal Albani to Lord Burghersk, 31 Dec. 1829 (copy no. 60102 F.O. 170–24, P.R.O., Kew).

26   Doyle to Charles Stuart, O.S.A., 30 Jan. 1833 (I.A.P.A.).

27   Doyle to Daniel O'Connor, O.S.A., 12 Sept. 1830 (I.A.P.A.).

28   Propaganda to Archbishop Murray, 10 Apr. 1834 (File 31/4 (1834), no. 96, D.D.A.).

29   See Archbishop Curtis to Doyle, 2 Oct. 1825 (K.L.D.A.). Curtis sought Doyle's intervention in a Meath diocesan squabble. Cf. also Bishop O'Shaughnessy (Killaloe) to Doyle, 26 May 1827 (K.L.D.A.). O'Shaughnessy sought Doyle's mediation to end the Birr 'schism'.

30   The authority on this issue is Hugh Fenning, *The undoing of the friars in Ireland: a study of the novitiate question in the eighteenth century* (Louvain, 1972).

31   Castlereagh (ed.), *Memoirs and Correspondence*, iv, 150, 153.

32   Dr Bartholomew Esmonde, S.J., to Doyle, 2 June 1824 (C.S.J.A.).

33   Doyle, Diocesan Book.

34   Doyle to Daniel O'Connor, O.S.A., 24 Oct. 1822 (I.A.P.A.).

35 This is the implication of Doyle to Daniel O'Connor, O.S.A., 25 Jan. 1828 (I.A.P.A.).
36 Ibid. Doyle to O'Connor, 8 Feb. 1828 (I.A.P.A.); Doyle's anxiety was justified by the anti-regular clauses in the Roman Catholic Relief Act, 1829.
37 Doyle, Diocesan Book.
38 Edward Earle, P.P., Carbury to Doyle, 8 Mar. 1824 (K.L.D.A.).
39 Doyle, Diocesan Book. MacSuibhne (ed.), *Knockbeg*, p. 83.
40 Comerford, *Collections*, ii, 197.
41 Doyle to Daniel O'Connor, O.S.A., 8 Feb. 1828 (I.A.P.A.).
42 Fitzpatrick, *Doyle*, ii, 58–9.
43 John Joseph Donovan, O.S.F., to Doyle, 30 Oct. 1821, cited in Comerford, op. cit., ii, 197.
44 Letter to Doyle, dated 15 Nov. 1821 (K.L.D.A.).
45 Castlereagh (ed.), *Memoirs and Correspondence*, iv, 150.
46 Doyle, Relatio Status, 6 Nov. 1820 (Scritture (Irlanda), vol. 23, p. 301).
47 Acts of the Irish Provincial Chapter, 1819. John Spratt's list of the province, 1816–21; Acts of the Irish Provincial Chapter, 1823 (MSS in Irish Carmelite Provincial Archives, Gort Muire, Dundrum, Dublin 16).
48 Doyle to Murray, 2 Dec. 1827 (File 30/10 (1827), no. 7, D.D.A.).
49 *Notices, pursuant to 10 Geo. IV, c. 7 by Jesuits and other religious orders, transmitted to the chief secretary in Ireland, and in Great Britain to the secretary of state*, p. 6, H.C. 1831–32 (66), xxx, 51.
50 Doyle to Cardinal Pedicini, 13 Apr. 1833 (Scritture (Irlanda), vol. 25, p. 679); Murray to Cardinal Pedicini, 29 Apr. 1833 (ibid., vol. 25, p. 690).
51 Doyle, Diocesan Book; while still only bishop-elect Doyle (in accord with the *Council of Trent*, Sess. V, Decree on Reformation, c. 2 'On preachers of the word of God, and on Questors of Alms') sought information on one McCann who was a vagrant Carmelite. He required details of the validity of his profession and ordination. See Doyle to John Rice, O.S.A., (in Rome), 5 June 1819 (Scritture (Irlanda), vol. 22, p. 173).
52 Doyle, Relatio Status, 6 Nov. 1820 (Scritture (Irlanda), vol. 23, p. 301).
53 Doyle to Rev. M. Coleman, convent, Leighlinbridge, 8 June 1820 (K.L.D.A.).
54 Acts of the Irish Provincial Chapter; John Spratt's list of the province, 1816–21 (MSS in Irish Carmelite Provincial Archives, Gort Muire, Dundrum, Dublin 16).
55 Acts of the Irish Provincial Chapter, 1823 (ibid.).
56 There is a reference to an unnamed regular who committed suicide after having been rebuked by Doyle in Fitzpatrick, *Doyle*, i, 464.
57 Thomas Coleman to Doyle, 26 Feb. 1826, K.L.D.A.
58 In 1833 both Bishop Doyle and Dr Andrew Fitzgerald came to Thomas Coleman's aid when he was complained to Rome by some members of his province. Doyle told Coleman that he at all times considered him 'a most excellent clergyman, filled with piety and zeal, and engaged incessantly, not only in the work of the ministry but in the more arduous and ungrateful work of reforming the habits of your brethren and re-establishing, though not with great success, the discipline prescribed by your Rule and constitution'. See Doyle to Coleman, 21 Apr. 1833 (Scritture (Irlanda), vol. 25, pp 686–7). See also (ibid., p. 682) Fitzgerald to Coleman, 15 Apr. 1833: 'The order and religious observance you have introduced, where disorder and scandal had before prevailed, is the real source of those accusations, which are now preferred'.
59 Doyle, *S.O.I. evidence*, pp 203–4, H.C. 1825 (129), vii, 173; and also *S.O.I. evidence*, pp 241–2, H.L. 1825 (181), ix, 1.
60 Dr Bartholomew Esmonde, S.J., to Doyle, 2 June 1824 (C.S.J.A.). Rev. Malachy McMahon to Rev. Peter Kenney, 21 February 1823 (Kenney papers in Irish Jesuit Archives). This letter begins 'I am told the gentlemen of the College would attend the chapels to instruct the people had they my consent, etc.'. McMahon gave the Jesuits full permission: 'you or any of the gentlemen can preach at mass or in the evening at all times; also attend the sick,

hear confessions, same as myself or curate, for which I shall feel thankful'. But see below for McMahon's true attitude.

61 Esmonde to Doyle, 23 Apr. 1824, in response to Doyle to Esmonde, 5 Apr. 1824 (C.S.J.A.). Fitzpatrick, *Doyle*, i, 142-3, 242-5, alludes briefly and in a seriously deficient manner to this controversy. He has, however, a couple of very short but valuable snippets from letters probably no longer extant. He had the benefit of Dr Esmonde's oral recollections of Doyle but he does not appear to have seen (or if he did, he decided not to use) Esmonde's three major letters (one of eight foolscap pages) to Doyle which are still extant in the Clongowes archives.

62 According to Patrick J. Corish, 'Catholic marriage under the Penal code' in Art Cosgrove (ed.), *Marriage in Ireland* (Dublin, 1985), p. 73.

63 Delumeau, *Catholicism between Luther and Voltaire*, p. 208.

64 Joseph P. Chinnici, *The English Catholic Enlightenment: John Lingard and the Cisalpine movement, 1780–1850* (Shepherdstown, U.S.A., 1980), p. 54.

65 Doyle to Martin Doyle, C.C., Clonegal, 14 Nov. 1814 (K.L.D.A.).

66 Doyle, Relatio Status, 6 Nov. 1820 (Scritture (Irlanda), vol. 23, p. 301).

67 This letter of Peter Kenney to Doyle, 6 March 1823, is in K.L.D.A.

68 Doyle, *S.O.I. evidence*, p. 242, H.L. 1825 (181), ix, 1.

69 Doyle, *S.O.I. evidence*, p. 203, H.C. 1825 (129), viii, 173.

70 See Doyle to Miss Gurley, from Allen, 6 May 1823, cited in Fitzpatrick, *Doyle*, i, 239-44.

71 Fitzpatrick, *Doyle*, i, 135.

72 Fitzpatrick, op. cit., i, 245. Fitzpatrick may have received this account from Dr Esmonde.

73 Doyle, *Vindication*, p. 71.

74 J.M. Harty, 'Probabilism' in *Cath. Ency.*, xii, 441-6.

75 See chapter 5.

76 Dr Bartholomew Esmonde, S.J., to Doyle, 2 June 1824 (C.S.J.A.). See also Rev. Thomas Nolan, P.P., Kill, to Rev. John Connor, S.J., 15 March 1824 (C.S.J.A.). This letter makes clear that Nolan was quite happy about any of his parishioners who went from Kill to Clongowes for confession and communion, attributing their absence from his parish to their distance from his chapels.

77 J. Derek Holmes and Bernard W. Bickers, *A short history of the Catholic church* (Tunbridge Wells, 1983), p. 185.

78 Like some of the Irish Jesuits of his time he was a member of an old Anglo-Norman family. The Esmondes owned Huntingdon Castle, Clonegal, County Carlow. Sir Thomas Esmonde, bart., brother of Bartholomew, was active in Catholic politics.

79 Doyle to Esmonde, 5 April 1824 (C.S.J.A.). For Rev. Kennedy see chapter 3 on 'Discipline'.

80 Esmonde to Doyle, 23 April 1824 (C.S.J.A.). See also Esmonde to Doyle, 2 June 1824 (C.S.J.A.).

81 Esmonde to Doyle, 2 June 1824 (C.S.J.A.).

82 Esmonde to Doyle, 23 Apr. 1824 (C.S.J.A.).

83 Quoted in Fitzpatrick, *Doyle*, i, 145.

84 Esmonde to Doyle, 23 Apr. 1824 (C.S.J.A.).

85 T. Slater, S.J., 'Mental Reservation' in *Cath. Ency.*, x, 195-6; according to Slater no Catholic theologian defended the lawfulness of strict mental reservation after this condemnation by the Holy See.

86 Harold Castle, 'Saint Alphonsus Liguori' in ibid., i, 334-41.

87 Esmonde to Doyle (quoting Doyle) undated [mid-1824], (C.S.J.A.).

88 Esmonde to Doyle, undated [mid-1824], (C.S.J.A.).

89 Ibid.

90 Doyle to Esmonde, 28 May 1824 (C.S.J.A.).

91 Esmonde to Doyle, 2 June 1824 (C.S.J.A.).

92 This system is discussed in chapter 5.
93 Esmonde to Doyle, 2 June 1824, C.S.J.A. On this point see Doyle to Esmonde, 28 May 1824 (C.S.J.A.).
94 Esmonde to Doyle, undated [July 1824], (C.S.J.A.).
95 Doyle to Esmonde, 30 July 1824 (C.S.J.A.).
96 Doyle to Esmonde, 7 Aug. 1824; on the same paper P.K. [Peter Kenney] to Esmonde, 12 Aug. 1824 (C.S.J.A.).
97 Doyle to Daniel O'Connor, O.S.A., 30 July 1829 (I.A.P.A.). The Jesuit community's library in Clongowes contains two busts of Doyle by Tournelly.
98 Doyle, *S.O.I. evidence*, p. 241, H.L. 1825 (181), ix, 1; J.H. Pollen, S.J., 'Society of Jesus' in *Cath. Ency.*, xiv, p. 83.
99 Doyle, *S.O.I. evidence*, p. 204, H.C. 1825 (129), viii, 173. For another perspective on this controversy see the work of the Jesuit historian, Dr Thomas Morrissey, *As one sent: Peter Kenney, S.J., 1779–1841. His mission in Ireland and North America* (Dublin, 1996), pp 195–205.
100 See 'The story of the college' in *Newbridge College Magazine* (1900), pp 40–52; 'From cabin to college' in *Newbridge Quarterly*, vol. 5, no. 18 (Easter, 1936) unpaginated, continued in ibid., vol. 5, nos 19, 20, 21 (Summer, Autumn and Winter 1936). See also 'The Dominicans in Newbridge', in *Newbridge College Annual* (1948), pp 4–12.
101 Ibid., p. 51.
102 Ibid., p. 50.
103 'The story of the college' in *Newbridge College Magazine* (1900), p. 52. In his Relatio Status, 6 Nov. 1820, Doyle stated that there were two Dominicans in Newbridge (see Scritture (Irlanda), vol. 23, p. 301).
104 Doyle to Dunne, 30 Aug. 1823 ('Coleman letter-book', p. 109, MS in Dominican Archives, St Mary's, Tallaght, Co. Dublin).
105 Doyle to Dunne, 22 Feb. 1824 ('Coleman letter-book', p. 113, MS in Dominican Archives, St Mary's, Tallaght, Co. Dublin).
106 Doyle to Dunne, 12, 26 July 1826 (in ibid., pp 123, 133).
107 'The story of the college' in *Newbridge College Magazine* (1900), p. 52.
108 See chapter 2.
109 Linus H. Walker, *To build and to plant* (Carlow, n.d.), pp 29–30.
110 *Patrician Rule*, p. 26.
111 Cf. Scritture (Irlanda), vol. 25, p. 161.
112 *Presentation Rule*, p. 69.
113 *Patrician Rule*, pp 1–13 at p. 6.
114 Ibid., p. 9.
115 MS account of Brother Serenus Kelly (compiled *c.*1840–50) in annals (T.P.A.).
116 Annals (T.P.A.). The brothers began reading the office in Latin in 1826.
117 Ibid.
118 Ibid. For this school, which taught Irish among other subjects, see the *Carlow Morning Post*, 29 July 1828, 25 July 1831.
119 Annals (T.P.A.). This letter was almost a literal translation of a letter from Bishop Corcoran to Serenus Kelly, 8 Dec. 1818, giving him leave to make a quest in the west of Ireland (in ibid.).
120 Annals (T.P.A.).
121 Quoted in Bishop Archdeacon to Propaganda, 6 Dec. 1819 (Scritture (Irlanda), vol. 23, p. 141).
122 Annals (T.P.A.).
123 Ibid. See also three letters of Bishop Doyle to Bro. Paul O'Connor, dated 22 Mar., 16 July 1827, 29 May 1829, cited in [John P. Lynch], *The life of Paul J. O'Connor* (Dublin, 1867), pp 60–70.

124 In his letter of 16 July 1827, Bishop Doyle told Bro. Paul O'Connor, that Tullow 'was about forming a new establishment in the diocese of Ossory', cited in ibid., p. 67. See also Annals (T.P.A.).

125 Comerford, *Collections*, iii, 412.

126 D.J. Keenan, The *Catholic church in nineteenth-century Ireland* (Dublin, 1983), p. 146.

127 Cf. William Hutch, *Nano Nagle, her life, her labours, and their fruits* (Dublin, 1875), passim.

128 Quoted in Fitzpatrick, *Doyle*, ii, 380.

129 Doyle to Daniel O'Connor, O.S.A., 8 Feb. 1828 (I.A.P.A.).

130 Ibid. *Brigidine* Rule, p. 11.

131 Doyle to Daniel O'Connor, O.S.A., 8 Feb. 1828 (I.A.P.A.).

132 *Presentation Rule*, p. 14.

133 Annals, p. 76 (T.B.A.).

134 Hannah Gurley who became Mother Superior of Maryborough Presentation convent in 1829 was a convert and a correspondent of Bishop Doyle.

135 Annals, unpaginated (Presentation convent, Carlow).

136 Curtis to Doyle, 27 Feb. 1826 (K.L.D.A.); 'Register', pp 12, 17, and Annals, pp 15, 33 (MSS, Presentation convent, Maryborough); Doyle, Relatio Status, 13 May 1829 (Scritture (Irlanda), vol. 25, p. 161).

137 See inside cover of 'Register of postulants, novices and religious of the Presentation convent established in Carlow, 1811' (MS, Presentation convent, Carlow).

138 Annals, pp 23–4 (Presentation convent, Maryborough). For another similar case of an illegitimate seeking to enter the religious life, see Doyle to Mother Meade, 28 May 1825 (archives of Discalced Carmelite convent, Malahide, Co. Dublin).

139 *Brigidine Rule*, p. 27.

140 Ibid.

141 Ibid.

142 Ibid., p. 17.

143 Ibid., p. 37. Doyle inquired closely into the suitability of postulants for profession. The annals of the Presentation convent, Carlow, record that 'During the retreat for profession – the novices are directed to read the Rule of St Augustine, a copy of which is kept in the archives of the convent – translated by the bishop, Right Revd Doctor Doyle, for this community'.

144 *Brigidine Rule*, p. 35.

145 Annals, pp 4–8 (Presentation convent, Maryborough).

146 Annals, unpaginated (Presentation convent, Carlow). The nun in question was Mother Lyons of the Carmelite convent, Warrenmount, Dublin, the leader of the reform movement within the Discalced Carmelite nuns in Ireland. The annals of the Presentation convent Carlow, record that Mother Lyons was in the convent in 1819 for 'health purposes' but it could well be the case that she was there at Bishop Doyle's invitation to introduce a primitive observance to the house.

147 [Mother] Margaret Mary Dunne, *Gleanings from the Brigidine annals* (Carlow, 1945), p. 22 ('private circulation only').

148 Mother Mary Anne Lalor to Doyle, 12 July 1821 (K.L.D.A.).

149 Annals, pp 46–7 (Presentation convent, Maryborough).

150 O'Riordan, *Delany*, p. 247.

151 Annals, p. 81 (Presentation convent, Maryborough).

152 Annals, unpaginated (Presentation convent, Carlow).

153 Henry Young, *Catholic Directory* (Dublin, 1821), p. 41.

154 Doyle to Sister Mary Nolan, 30 Nov. 1820, quoted in Fitzpatrick, *Doyle*, i, 133.

155 Annals, unpaginated (Presentation convent, Carlow).

156 Ibid.

157 Annals, p. 1 (Presentation convent, Maryborough).

158 Chapter 2, note 91.
159 Annals, p. 3 (Presentation convent, Maryborough).
160 Ibid., p. 10.
161 Ibid., p. 12.
162 Ibid., pp 91–2.
163 MacSuibhne, *Cullen and his contemporaries*, i, 188–9.
164 Annals, unpaginated (Presentation convent, Kildare).
165 Annals, unpaginated (Presentation convent, Kildare); Doyle to Mother Dolan, 24 April 1830 (archives of the Discalced Carmelite convent, Malahide, Co. Dublin).
166 Annals, p. 68 (T.B.A.).
167 Ibid.
168 Annals, pp 69 (16 Jan. 1821); 70 (? Mar. 1824); 75 (22 Mar. 1828); 81 (2 Mar. 1833),(T.B.A.).
169 Ibid., p. 69.
170 Doyle to Sister Mary Joseph, (?) Nov. 1820, cited in Fitzpatrick, *Doyle*, ii, 524. In this letter Doyle referred to 'some addition' to the Brigidine rules which he had made.
171 Annals, p. 75 (T.B.A.).
172 *Directory of the Brigidine Sisters* (Dublin, 1956), p. 8.
173 *Directory of the Brigidine Sisters* (Dublin, 1956), p. 8; Annals, p. 75 (T.B.A.).
174 This statement is based on a comparison of the *Presentation rule* with the *Brigidine rule*.
175 Annals, pp 44–63 (T.B.A.).
176 In the printed rule and constitutions, Doyle's name is given on the title page and on p. 44 (the final page) but pride of place is again (as with the *Patrician rule*) very generously conceded to Dr Delany.
177 *Directory of the Brigidine Sisters* (Dublin, 1956), p. 8, where it is stated that 'instead of giving them a distinctive habit, he gave them that of the Presentation Sisters', which continued to be worn until 1920.
178 Annals, p. 19 (Brigidine convent, Mountrath).
179 *Brigidine rule*, pp 10, 16; *Presentation rule*, p. 44.
180 [Mother] Margaret Mary Dunne, *Gleanings from the Brigidine annals* (Carlow, 1945), p. 22.
181 Annals, p. 18 (Brigidine convent, Mountrath).
182 Annals, p. 70 (T.B.A.).
183 Ibid.
184 *Brigidine rule*, p. 16; *Presentation rule*, p. 28. Gibbons, *Glimpses*, p. 220, is seriously in error when she attributes 'Jansenistic views respecting the reception of the Sacraments' to Bishop Delany.
185 Annals, p. 71 (T.B.A.).
186 Annals, p. 72.
187 Ibid., pp 72–3.
188 Ibid., p. 71.
189 Ibid. In 1837 Bishop Edward Nolan gave permission to the Brigidines to receive boarders because it was the clear intention of Bishop Delany and a useful source of funds (Annals, p. 21, Brigidine convent, Mountrath).
190 For the Brigidines in Roscrea, see Ignatius Murphy, *The diocese of Killaloe, 1800–1850* (Dublin, 1992), pp 135, 149–53. For the Brigidines in Castlecomer see Nicholas Shearman, C.C., to Doyle, 13 June 1829 (K.L.D.A.).
191 Comerford, *Collections*, iii, 415.
192 Doyle to Sister Albert Gosson, 4 August 1827; Doyle to Mother Dolan, 10 September 1831 (archives of St Joseph's Discalced Carmelite convent, Malahide, Co. Dublin). The Ranelagh convent transferred to Malahide in 1975 and Doyle's letters are found in its archives. Unless otherwise stated, all references below are to this source. The letters of the Ranelagh Carmelites to Doyle are not in the Doyle papers in Carlow and do not apparently survive.

193 Doyle to Mother Dolan, 24 January 1829.
194 Doyle to Mother Dolan, 14 February 1830.
195 Doyle to Mother Dolan, 13 December 1829.
196 Doyle to Mother Dolan, 2 July 1829.
197 See Sr Teresa O'Shea, O.D.C., 'Annals of St Joseph's Carmelite Monastery, Ranelagh' p. 61. This is a very useful typescript history (in 119 foolscap pages) of the convent. See pp 64–100, passim, for references to Doyle.
198 Doyle to Mother Meade, 23 December 1823.
199 See Doyle to Mother Dolan, 6 January 1827, 15 January 1828, 27 May 1828, 10 March 1830.
200 Doyle to Mother Dolan, 10 January 1828.
201 Doyle to Mother Meade, 20 April 1829.
202 Doyle to Mother Meade, 26 January 1824.
203 Doyle to Propaganda, 21 February 1824 (in draft in K.L.D.A.).
204 Doyle to Mother Meade, 10 August 1824.
205 Doyle to Mother Meade, 2 January 1825.
206 Propaganda to Doyle, 9 April 1825 (K.L.D.A.).
207 Doyle to Mother Meade, 28 May 1825.
208 Doyle to Mother Meade, 13 June 1825.
209 Doyle to Propaganda, 16 July 1825, in Acta, vol. 189, pp 10–11. Draft of 16 July 1825 (K.L.D.A.).
210 Cardinal Somaglia to Murray, 27 August 1825 (File 30/9 (1825), no. 60, D.D.A.).
211 Murray to Propaganda, 30 October 1825 (Acta, vol. 189, p. 12).
212 Doyle to Mother Meade, 16 July 1825.
213 Doyle to Mother Meade, 21 January 1826.
214 Confer 'Sull' Instanza per la translazione di alcune Monache Carmelitare Scalze dal Monasterio di S. Giuseppe di Ranelagh nella Diocesi di Dublino al Monastero de erigersi nel villagio di Edenderry nella Diocesi di Kildare' (Acta, vol. 189, pp 5–12).
215 Gio Nepho di S. Luiga to Propaganda, 4 December 1825 (Acta, vol. 189, p. 12).
216 Doyle to Mother Dolan, 2 April 1826.
217 Doyle to Mother Dolan, 23 November 1826, 24 November 1826.
218 See Acta, vol. 190, pp 543–52; vol. 194, pp 20–29; Scritture (Irlanda), vol. 25, p. 737.
219 Doyle to Mother Dolan, 19 December 1826.
220 Doyle to Mother Dolan, 26 December 1826.
221 Doyle to Mother Dolan, 19 April 1827.
222 See MS 'Memorandum Book' [1828–1832], pp 15–18 (Archives of St Joseph's Discalced Carmelite convent, Malahide, Co. Dublin).
223 Ibid., p. 38. Bishop McGettigan of Raphoe was also present.
224 See Doyle to Christopher Boylan, 19 November 1830 (Scritture (Irlanda), vol. 25, p. 344).

CHAPTER 5

1 Thomas McGrath, *Politics, Interdenominational Relations and Education in the Public Ministry of Bishop James Doyle of Kildare and Leighlin, 1786–1834* (Dublin, 1998).
2 Doyle, *Education Inquiry*, p. 792, H.C. 1825 (400), xii.
3 William H.W. Fanning, 'Confraternity' in *Cath. Ency.*, iv, 223; M.C. Glancey, 'Christian Doctrine Confraternity' in ibid., iii, 711.
4 Corish, *Cath. Comm.*, pp 85, 93.
5 Doyle, *Pastoral, Lent 1821*, p. 52; Connolly, *Priests and people*, p. 92, states that Butler founded his confraternity in 1788 but Brenan, *Schools*, p. 25 states that Delany established his confraternity in Tullow in 1785.
6 Doyle, *Pastoral, Lent 1821*, p. 52.
7 Fitzpatrick, *Doyle*, i, 117–18.

8 Doyle, *Pastoral, Lent 1821*, p. 54.
9 Doyle, *Pastoral, Lent 1821*, pp 53–6.
10 Ibid., p. 56; see also *Stat. dioec. prov. Dublin., 1831*, pp 75–7.
11 M. C. Glancey, 'Christian Doctrine Confraternity' in *Cath. Ency.*, iii, 711. At the time of Borromeo's death there were 40,000 pupils in his diocese under instruction in 740 Christian Doctrine schools, taught by 3,000 teachers (Brenan, *Schools*, p. 15).
12 Glancey, loc. cit. Brenan, *Schools*, p. 14.
13 Connolly, *Priests and people*, p. 84.
14 Doyle, *Pastoral, Lent 1821*, pp 54–5.
15 See appendix I, 'Rules of the Society of the Christian Doctrine' in *Stat. dioec. prov. Dublin., 1831*, pp 95–7.
16 Ibid., p. 96.
17 Ibid., p. 97. Doyle, *Pastoral, Lent 1821*, p. 55.
18 For such efforts in Carlow and Clonegal parishes see parish reports on education, 1824 (MSS, K.L.D.A.).
19 Brenan, *Schools*, p. 24.
20 Doyle, Diocesan Book. Grange chapel had yet to be built.
21 Doyle, Diocesan Book.
22 Doyle, Relatio Status, 6 Nov. 1820 (Scritture (Irlanda), vol. 23, p. 300).
23 Doyle, *S.O.I. evidence*, p. 198. H.C. 1825 (129), viii, 173.
24 Doyle, *Pastoral, Lent 1821*, pp 56–7.
25 'Kildare and Leighlin in 1829' copied from a MS in the hand-writing of Bishop Doyle, in Comerford, *Collections*, i, 324–9.
26 Gerald Doyle to Doyle, 9 Mar. 1829 (K.L.D.A.).
27 Carlow parish report on education, 1824 (MS in K.L.D.A.). Fitzpatrick, *Doyle*, i, 493, has a reference to mass being celebrated for 1,000 children in Carlow chapel. How widespread these children's masses were is not known, but Fitzpatrick suggests they were said in 'many other parts of the diocese'.
28 See parish reports on education, 1824 (MSS in K.L.D.A.).
29 See Appendix 3 of this work. In Dublin city centre there was a Sunday school attendance of considerably more than a thousand in all the parish chapels. See Archbishop Murray's evidence in *Education Inquiry*, p. 792, H.C. 1825 (400), xii.
30 Doyle, *Education Inquiry*, p. 793, H.C. 1825 (400), xii.
31 Corish, *Ir. Cath. Experience*, p. 170.
32 Doyle, circular letter to his clergy, undated [1821], (K.L.D.A.).
33 Clonbullogue parish report on education, 1824 (MS in K.L.D.A.). See also similar comments from the parish clergy of Ballon and Hacketstown in parish reports on education, 1824 (MSS in K.L.D.A.).
34 Kildare parish report on education, 1824 (MS in K.L.D.A.).
35 See parish reports on education, 1824 (MSS in K.L.D.A.); M.V. Ronan, *An apostle of Catholic Dublin – Father Henry Young* (Dublin, 1945), p. 165.
36 Clonbullogue parish report on education, 1824 (MS in K.L.D.A.).
37 *Education Inquiry*, p. 792, H.C. 1825 (400), xii.
38 Doyle, Diocesan Book.
39 Carbury parish report on education, 1824 (MS in K.L.D.A.).
40 Clane parish report on education, 1824 (MS in K.L.D.A.).
41 Monasterevan parish report on education, 1824 (MS in K.L.D.A.).
42 See parish reports on education, 1824 (MSS in K.L.D.A.).
43 Ibid.
44 Abbeyleix parish report on education, 1824 (MS in K.L.D.A.).
45 Edenderry parish report on education, 1824 (MS in K.L.D.A.).
46 Doyle, Diocesan Book.

47 Clane parish report on education, 1824 (MS in K.L.D.A.).
48 Clonegal parish report on education, 1824 (MS in K.L.D.A.).
49 Brenan, *Schools*, p. 37 fn. 1.
50 This average is computed from the times given in seven parishes – Bagenalstown, Paulstown, Hacketstown, Kill, Mountmellick, Rosenallis and Tullow. Cf. Parish reports on education, 1824 (MS in K.L.D.A.).
51 *D.E.P.*, 30 Dec. 1826.
52 Edenderry parish report on education, 1824 (MS in K.L.D.A.).
53 Parish reports on education, 1824 (MS in K.L.D.A.).
54 *D.E.P.*, 17 Mar. 1827; Battersby, *Life of Doyle*, p. 242.
55 Connolly, *Priests and people*, p. 85.
56 Abbeyleix parish report on education, 1824 (MS in K.L.D.A.).
57 Carlow parish report on education, 1824 (MS in K.L.D.A.).
58 Suncroft parish report on education, 1824 (MS in K.L.D.A.).
59 Bagenalstown parish report on education, 1824 (MS in K.L.D.A.).
60 Ibid.
61 Evidence of Archbishop Kelly, *Education Inquiry*, p. 792, H.C. 1825 (400), xii.
62 Portarlington, Paulstown, Allen, Rosenallis and Clonaslee parish reports on education, 1824 (MSS in K.L.D.A.).
63 Hacketstown, Kildare and Portarlington parish reports on education, 1824 (MSS in K.L.D.A.).
64 Corish, *Ir. Cath. Experience*, p. 170.
65 In Bagenalstown and Edenderry the *General Catechism* is mentioned as the only class-book in 1824 but in Abbeyleix and Kildare both it and the *Abridgement of the Christian Doctrine* were taught. Cf. Bagenalstown, Edenderry, Abbeyleix, Kildare, parish reports on education, 1824 (MSS in K.L.D.A.).
66 *Cath. Ency.*, v. 80.
67 Doyle, *S.O.I. evidence*, p. 235, H.L. 1825 (181), ix, 1.
68 Ibid.
69 Doyle, printed circular letter to his clergy, undated [1821], (K.L.D.A.).
70 See Doyle's edition of the *General Catechism* (Dublin, 1823), p. 2.
71 Ibid.
72 Ibid., pp 4–5.
73 Corish, *Ir. Cath. Experience*, p. 169.
74 *D.E.P.*, 27 Oct. 1827.
75 Cf. Michael Tynan, *Catholic Instruction in Ireland 1720–1950. The O'Reilly/Donlevy catechetical tradition* (Dublin, 1985).
76 Curtis to Doyle, 3 Dec. 1824 (K.D.L.A.)
77 M.V. Ronan, *An apostle of Catholic Dublin – Father Henry Young* (Dublin, 1944), p. 50.
78 Doyle (ed.), *Abridgement of the Christian Doctrine*, p. iii.
79 Doyle, *Strictures on the charge of Dr Elrington to his clergy* (Dublin, 1827), p. 4; *D.E.P.* 30 Oct. 1827. For the Doyle-Elrington controversy see chapter three of Thomas McGrath, *Politics, Interdenominational Relations and Education in the Public Ministry of Bishop James Doyle of Kildare and Leighlin, 1786–1834* (Dublin, 1998).
80 Doyle (ed.), *Abridgement of the Christian Doctrine*, pp iii–iv.
81 *The Defence of the Seven Sacraments expounded by the Rt Revd Doctor Doyle, Catholic Bishop of Kildare and Leighlin* (London, n.d.), 16th edition. Printed by James Mason. Bound in R.I.A., Halliday pamphlets, vol. 1296 (1824).
82 Ibid., pp 5–6.
83 See his advertisement in *D.E.P.*, 30 Nov. 1830.
84 The full title of the work was *Sermons and Moral Discourses for all the Sundays and Principal festivals of the year on the most important truths and maxims of the Gospel* (Dublin, 1825), 3rd edition, revised and corrected in two volumes.

85 Ibid., vol. 1, pp iii–iv.
86 Doyle to Thomas Spring Rice, 25 Dec. 1822 (Monteagle papers, MS 13345, N.L.I.); there are several copies of this edition of Gahan in the Museum room of the Brigidine convent in Tullow.
87 His preface was approximately 5,000 words in length.
88 Alban Butler, *Lives of the* Saints (Dublin, 1833 ed.), 2 vols, i, pp i, x.
89 Doyle (ed.), *Abridgement of the Christian Doctrine*, p. iv.
90 *Stat. dioec. Prov. Dublin., 1831*, p. 96.
91 Doyle, Diocesan Book.
92 Doyle (ed.), *Abridgement of the Christian Doctrine*, p. v.
93 Doyle, *Education Inquiry*, p. 799, H.C. 1825 (400), xii.
94 M.V. Ronan, *An apostle of Catholic Dublin –Father Henry Young* (Dublin, 1944), p. 50.
95 Ibid., p. 175.
96 Ibid., p. 50.
97 Doyle, Relatio Status, 13 May 1829 (Scritture (Irlanda), vol. 25, p. 160).
98 Doyle, *Pastoral, Lent 1820*, p. 3.
99 Doyle, *Pastoral, Lent 1821*, p. 55.
100 Tullow parish report on education, 1824 (MS in K.L.D.A.).
101 Doyle, *Pastoral, Lent 1821*, pp 57–9.
102 See appendix II: 'Rules of the Religious Book Society' in *Stat. dioec. prov. Dublin., 1831*, pp 98–100.
103 Doyle, *S.P.I. evidence*, p. 428, H.C. 1830 (654), vii, 1.
104 See Carlow, Clonegal, Hacketstown parish reports on education, 1824 (MSS in K.L.D.A.).
105 Tullow parish report on education, 1824 (MS in K.L.D.A.).
106 Clonbullogue parish report on education, 1824 (MS in K.L.D.A.).
107 Portarlington parish report on education, 1824 (MS in K.L.D.A.).
108 *Stat. dioec. prov. Dublin., 1831*, p. 99.
109 See Appendix 4.
110 See chapter 6.
111 Doyle, *Pastoral, Nov. 1822*, p. 20.
112 Doyle to Mrs G. Burdett, 24 Dec. 1823 (K.L.D.A.).
113 Doyle, *Pastoral, Lent 1825*, pp 19–20.
114 Doyle, *S.O.I. evidence*, p. 198, H.C. 1825 (129), vii, 173.
115 Thomas Spring Rice to Doyle, 14 Dec. 1822 (Monteagle papers, MS 13345, N.L.I.).
116 Doyle to Thomas Spring Rice, 25 Dec. 1822 (Monteagle papers, MS 13345, N.L.I.).
117 Suncroft parish report on education, 1824 (MS in K.L.D.A.).
118 Doyle, *S.O.I. evidence*, p. 198, H.C. 1825 (129), viii, 173.
119 Doyle to Thomas Spring Rice, 25 Dec. 1822 (Monteagle papers, MS 13345, N.L.I.).
120 A computation based on the data in Appendix 4: 'Parochial Chapel Libraries in 1829'.
121 Doyle, *S.P.I. evidence*, p. 428, H.C. 1830 (654), vii, 1.
122 Doyle, *Pastoral, Lent 1834*, p. 4.
123 See episcopal letters to Archbishop Murray on the foundation of the Society in File 214/1, D.D.A. For the New Reformation, see chapter three of Thomas McGrath, *Politics, Interdenominational Relations and Education in the Public Ministry of Bishop James Doyle of Kildare and Leighlin, 1786–1834* (Dublin, 1998).
124 Battersby, *Life of Doyle*, p. 246.
125 Thomas Wall, 'Catholic Periodicals of the Past – 1. The Catholic Penny Magazine, 1834-1835' in *I.E.R*, fifth series, 101 (Jan.-June 1964), p. 234.
126 Doyle to Yore, 13 July 1824, quoted in Fitzpatrick, *Doyle*, i, 358–60.
127 Battersby, *Life of Doyle*, p. 246.
128 Ibid.
129 Corish, *Ir. Cath. Experience*, p. 172.
130 *First report of the Catholic Book Society* (Dublin, [1828]), pp 5, 9, 12.

131 Ibid., p. 36. Battersby, *Life of Doyle*, p. 246.
132 See statement of accounts of the Catholic Book Society by the committee to Archbishop Murray, 4 Feb. 1830, File 31/2 (1830), no. 91, D.D.A.
133 Kelly to Murray, 27 Feb. 1827 (File 214/1, D.D.A.).
134 Egan to Murray, 23 Feb. 1827 (File 214/1, D.D.A.)
135 Ffrench to Murray, 27 Feb. 1827 (File 214/1, D.D.A.).
136 O'Shaughnessy to Murray, 25 Feb. 1827 (File 214/1, D.D.A.).
137 Keating to Murray, 28 Feb. 1827 (File 214/1, D.D.A.).
138 Coen to Murray, 2 Mar. 1827 (File 214/1, D.D.A.).
139 Flanagan to Doyle, 18 Apr. 1827, quoted in Patrick Wallace, 'Irish Catechesis – The heritage from James Butler II, Archbishop of Cashel 1774-1791' (unpub. Ph.D. thesis, Catholic Univ. of America, 1975), p. 110.
140 *First Report of the Catholic Book Society* (Dublin, [1828]), pp 11, 7, 23–34.
141 Battersby, *Life of Doyle*, p. 247.
142 Ibid., pp 247–52.
143 Flanagan to Marum, 19 Sept. 1827, quoted in Wallace, op. cit., p. 110.
144 Battersby, *Life of Doyle*, p. 251.
145 See printed statement, 4 Feb 1830, of affairs of the Catholic Book Society in File 31/2 (1830), no. 91, D.D.A.
146 'Bishops' Minute Book, 1829–49' for 1829 (MS, D.D.A.).
147 See File 31/2 (1830), no. 91, D.D.A.
148 'Bishops' Minute Book, 1829–49' for 1830 (MS, D.D.A.).
149 *First report of the Catholic Book Society* (Dublin, [1828]), pp 19, 18, 21.
150 File 31/2 (1830), no. 91, D.D.A.
151 Corish, *Ir. Cath. Experience*, p. 172.
152 Doyle, *Pastoral, Lent 1821*, pp 5–31.
153 Ibid., pp 9, 11, 13, 17, 18, 22, 24, 26.
154 Ibid., p. 10.
155 Ibid., pp 22, 32.
156 Sorrow should be in proportion to guilt but 'greater indeed than sorrow of any other kind' (ibid., p. 15). Fitzpatrick, *Doyle*, i, 146, held that Doyle 'expressed himself too strongly' in this passage.
157 Doyle, *Pastoral, Lent 1821*, pp 20, 21, 25, 27.
158 Ibid., pp 23–4.
159 Fitzpatrick, *Doyle*, i, 480–1.
160 Doyle, *Pastoral, Lent 1821*, pp 29–30.
161 Doyle, *S.O.I. evidence*, p. 196, H.C. 1825 (129), viii, 173. Wakefield also drew attention to this point: 'On the 9th of January, 1809, while I was on a visit to Lord de Vesci, the parish priest brought his lordship a sum of money which he said belonged to him, asserting, that he had been robbed by one of his parishioners, and he had obliged him to return it. When I was at the house of the Right Hon. George Ogle, the coadjutor bishop of Ferns [Dr Patrick Ryan] sent him money under similar circumstances' (*An account of Ireland, statistical and political* (London, 1812), 2 vols, i, 555).
162 Letter in *D.E.P.*, 14 Feb. 1828. For another example of restitution of money through the confessional, in the parish of Tinryland, see *Carlow Morning Post*, 9 July 1832.
163 Doyle, *S.O.I. evidence*, pp 245, 209, H.L. 1825 (181), ix, 1.
164 Ibid., p. 308; ibid., p. 197, H.C. 1825 (129), viii, 173.
165 Fitzpatrick, *Doyle*, i, 396, 470.
166 Doyle, *Pastoral, Lent 1821*, p. 26.
167 Doyle to Martin Doyle, 14 Nov. 1814 (K.L.D.A.). Doyle was glad that Bishop Delany had expressed his disapprobation of the abuse before his death.
168 See *Council of Trent*, Sess. XXIV, on Reformation, c. 18. From the parochial clergy alone parishioners 'may receive the sacraments'.

169 Doyle to Gerald Doyle, 16 May 1823, cited in Fitzpatrick, *Doyle*, ii, 435; see also Doyle (ed.), *General Cathecism*, p. 34, which, following Trent, decreed that the eucharist was to be received in one's own parish from one's own pastor.
170 Doyle (ed.), *General Catechism*, p. 21.
171 Doyle, *Education Inquiry* pp 784-5, H.C. 1825 (400), xii.
172 Doyle (ed.), *General Catechism*, p. 34.
173 Doyle, circular letter to his clergy, undated [1821], (printed copy in K.L.D.A.).
174 Butler, *Near Restful Waters*, p. 97.
175 M.V. Ronan, *An apostle of Catholic Dublin – Father Henry Young* (Dublin, 1944), p. 235.
176 Fitzpatrick, *Doyle*, i, 74.
177 Annals, unpaginated, Presentation convent, Carlow.
178 Broughall to Doyle, 22 June 1821 (K.D.L.A.).
179 For an instance of this, see D.G. Marnane, *Land and violence: A history of West Tipperary from 1660* (Tipperary, 1985), p. 168.
180 Doyle, *S.O.I. evidence*, p. 197, H.C. 1825 (129), viii, 173.
181 John Dunne, P.P., to Doyle, 4 May 1832 (K.L.D.A.).
182 See chapter 4.
183 It seems significant that when Doyle excommunicated some people in Staplestown chapel in Clane parish, the parishioners made haste to Clongowes to seek the Jesuits' intervention with Doyle on their behalf. (Fitzpatrick, *Doyle*, i, 513).
184 Dr Bartholomew Esmonde to Doyle, 2 June 1824 (C.S.J.A.).
185 Ibid.
186 Ibid.
187 Ibid. Esmonde recommended that the general practice of the church requiring the penitent to bring to the parochial clergy at Easter a ticket (as was usual in Italy), subscribed by the confessor, would be by far the most satisfactory method of securing all points. Esmonde's system would have given dispensation of the tickets to the confessors and not the parish clergy and so afforded the faithful an unhindered choice in the determination of their confessor.
188 'Kildare and Leighlin diocesan statutes, 1821' (MS, K.L.D.A.); Doyle, *Pastoral, Lent 1821*, p. 33. For the less severe punishment decreed by the Synod of Dublin (1685) for the same offence, see Comerford, *Collections*, i, 255.
189 'Kildare and Leighlin diocesan statutes, 1821' (MS, K.L.D.A.).
190 'Kildare and Leighlin diocesan statutes, 1820', p. 3 (printed copy in K.L.D.A.).
191 Ibid.
192 'Kildare and Leighlin diocesan statutes, 1821' (MS, K.L.D.A.). On application from the parish priest a vicar forane (rural dean) could dispense with the 'obligation of personal attendance prescribed for those absent from their Easter duty in favour of an individual or individuals but not of entire classes of persons' (ibid.).
193 Corish, *Ir. Cath. Experience*, pp 134, 178.
194 Castlereagh (ed.), *Memoirs and Correspondence*, iv, 154.
195 Ibid., p. 156.
196 Desmond J. Keenan, *The Catholic church in nineteenth-century Ireland* (Dublin, 1983), p. 222.
197 Fitzpatrick, *Doyle*, i, 461.
198 Doyle, Diocesan Book.
199 'Kildare and Leighlin diocesan statutes, 1820', p. 2 (printed copy in K.L.D.A.).
200 Fitzpatrick, *Doyle*, i, 106 and 291, also erred when he stated that station dinners were one of the 'first abuses' which Doyle resolved to suppress with a firm hand.
201 'Clericus Leighlinensis' to Doyle, 22 Mar. 1822 (K.L.D.A.).
202 Troy to Doyle, 3 Apr. 1822 (File 30/7 (1822), no. 21, D.D.A.); Doyle to Troy, undated, same sheet.
203 Marum to Doyle, 7 Apr. 1822 (K.L.D.A.).

204 Brennan to Doyle, 3 Nov. 1822 (K.L.D.A.). The parish priest of Bagenalstown, Dr Michael Prendergast, V.G., liked to bring a bottle of his favourite wine to stations (Fitzpatrick, *Doyle*, i, 112 fn.).

205 Corish, *Ir. Cath. Experience*, pp 178–9. K. Theodore Hoppen has stated that 'the Dublin province eventually adopted strict legislation, but substantial loopholes long allowed a flexible interpretation' *(Elections, politics and society in Ireland 1832–1885* (Oxford, 1984), p. 209). It may have been that these loopholes were intentional.

206 *First report of the commissioners of Public Instruction, Ireland*, H.C. 1835 (45) (46), xxxiii, 1. 892.

207 Corish, *Ir. Cath. Experience*, p. 187.

208 *First report of the commissioners of Public Instruction, Ireland*, p. 6, H.C. 1835 (45) (46), xxxiii, 1. 892.

209 Ibid., p. 1. There are 2,445 civil parishes in Ireland (William Nolan, *Tracing the Past* (Dublin, 1982), p.17). James Reynolds, *The Catholic emancipation crisis in Ireland, 1823–1829* (Westport, Connecticut, 1970 reprint), p. 28 and Fergus O'Ferrall, *Catholic Emancipation; Daniel O'Connell and the birth of Irish democracy 1820–30* (Dublin, 1985), p. 176 both imply that there were 2,500 Catholic parishes in Ireland. This figure is far too high. In Kildare and Leighlin Catholic clergymen had some in-put into the statistics for twenty-five parishes or parts thereof.

210 Ibid.

211 *First report of the commissioners of Public Instruction, Ireland*, pp 7b, 25b, 33b, 39b, H.C. 1835 (45) (46), xxxiii, 1. 892.

212 David W. Miller, 'Irish Catholicism and the Great Famine' in *Journal of Social History*, ix, no. 1 (Sept. 1975), pp 81–98.

213 Ibid., p. 86.

214 Ibid.

215 Ibid.

216 Ibid., p. 84. Corish, *Ir. Cath. Experience*, p. 167.

217 Corish, *Ir. Cath. Experience*, p. 167.

218 Ibid.

219 Ignatius Murphy, *The diocese of Killaloe, 1800–1850* (Dublin, 1992), pp 342–7 passim. For relevant argument see also Ambrose Macaulay, *William Crolly. Archbishop of Armagh, 1835–49* (Dublin, 1994), pp 114–20, 237–9.

220 The parishes for which no information capable of statistical analysis is extant are Balyna, Caragh, Doonane, Leighlin and Portarlington. These parishes would possibly tend to decrease rather than increase the average Sunday diocesan mass attendance figure.

221 See *First report of the commissioners of Public Instruction, Ireland*, H.C. 1835 (45) (46), xxxiii, i. 892, passim.

222 Ibid., pp 33b, 39b, 37b, 27b, 11b, 17b, 53b.

223 *First report of the commissioners of Public Instruction, Ireland*, pp 11b, 13b, 17b, 27b, 31b, 33b, 37b, 41b, 49b, 51b, 55b, 57b, H.C. 1835 (45) (46), xxxiii, 1. 892.

224 Corish, *Cath. Comm.*, p. 89.

225 Doyle, Diocesan Book.

226 Ibid.

227 Cited in Comerford, *Collections*, i. 82.

228 Doyle, Diocesan Book, 1819–20 (MS in K.L.D.A.); Parish visitation returns (MSS in K.L.D.A.).

229 Ibid.

230 Ibid.

231 Parish visitation returns (MSS in K.L.D.A.).

232 Ibid.; Doyle, Diocesan Book, 1819–20 (MS in K.L.D.A.).

233 Ibid.

234 Ibid.
235 Ibid.
236 Doyle, *Pastoral, Lent 1821*, p. 33.
237 *Irish Catholic Directory*, 1836, p. 140.
238 Figure based on data in Appendix 5.
239 Doyle, circular letter to his clergy, undated [1821], (printed copy in K.L.D.A.).
240 K. Theodore Hoppen, *Elections politics and society in Ireland 1832-1885* (Oxford, 1984), p. 201; Corish, *Ir. Cath. Experience*, p. 174; Bishop Plunkett of Meath recorded several instances of neglect of Paschal duty on his visitation round in 1822. Cf. A. Cogan, *The diocese of Meath, ancient and modern*, 3 vols (Dublin, 1862-1870), iii, 442–4.
241 Doyle, Diocesan Book; Comerford, *Collections*, i, 324–9.
242 See Appendix 5.
243 Ibid. These were Abbeyleix, Ballinakill, Ballyadams, Baltinglass, Borris, Clonaslee, Graiguenamanagh, Leighlinbridge, Raheen and St Mullin's.
244 Doyle, *S.P.I. evidence*, p. 422, H.C. 1830 (654), vii, 1; Doyle, *S.O.I. evidence*, p. 207, H.C. 1825 (129), viii, 173 ('early and improvident marriages ... are a cause why we are oppressed with this starving population'); Doyle, *Letters on the state of Ire.*, pp 108–9; for a general survey see S.J. Connolly, 'Marriage in pre-famine Ireland' in Art Cosgrove (ed.), *Marriage in Ireland* (Dublin, 1985), pp 78–98.
245 Doyle, *S.O.I. evidence*, p. 208, H.C. 1825 (129), vii, 173.
246 Ibid.
247 Parish visitation returns (MSS in K.L.D.A.); Doyle, *S.O.I. evidence*, p. 422, H.C. 1830 (654), vii, 1; see also Doyle to Gerald Doyle, P.P., Naas, 7 Jan. 1828, cited in Fitzpatrick, *Doyle*, ii, 438.
248 D.G. Marnane, *Land and violence: A history of West Tipperary from 1660* (Tipperary, 1985), p. 51.
249 Corcoran to Doyle, 28 Feb. 1816 (K.L.D.A.).
250 Doyle, *S.P.I. evidence*, p. 423, H.C. 1830 (654), vii, 1.
251 Ibid.
252 Connolly, *Priests and people*, pp 182, 190.
253 Cited in Fitzpatrick, *Doyle*, ii, 261.
254 Ibid.
255 'Bishops' Minute Book, 1829–49' for 1829 (MS, D.D.A.).
256 Letter from Maher, in *D.E.P.*, 1 Feb. 1827.
257 'Bishops' Minute Book, 1829–49', for 1829 (MS, D.D.A.).
258 This was in line with the *Council of Trent*, Sess. XXIV, Decree on the Reformation of Marriage, c. 6. For an abduction case see *Carlow Morning Post*, 23 January 1832. On 3 January 1832 a party of 50 to 100 men, most with firearms, attacked and broke into the dwelling of Mrs Bridget Fox at Millick, near Rosenallis. They beat Mrs Fox 'in a most savage manner' and demanded her daughter Catherine against her will. They brought the twenty-year-old daughter to the house of Martin Delany at Red Castle near Mountrath where she was rescued by the police. Martin Delany and James Delany, principals in the abduction, were committed to the county jail.
259 'Kildare and Leighlin diocesan statutes, 1821' (MS, K.L.D.A.).
260 Doyle, *S.O.I. evidence*, p. 215, H.C. 1825 (129), viii, 173.
261 Petition of Dowling and Prendergast to Archbishop Troy, 20 Mar. 1820 (K.L.D.A.).
262 Troy to Doyle, 23 Mar. 1820 (on same paper as petition). Dominick O'Reilly of Kildangan Castle and Archbishop Murray were interested in the case.
263 Doyle to Murrray, 24 Mar. 1832 (File 31/3 (1831-32), no. 134, D.D.A.). Incest here may mean marriage within the forbidden degrees of consanguinity.
264 Ibid.
265 Ibid. For further evidence of Doyle reluctantly granting a dispensation see Doyle to Rev.

Francis Haly, 1 June 1832 (C.S.J.A.). This was the case of 'P. Lynch and his reputed wife'. He authorised Haly to marry them privately and without witnesses. Doyle stated he had an 'abhorrence' of Lynch and wished he could be prevailed on to leave the diocese. 'I would this morning as soon set out on a pilgrimage to Lough Derg as grant him a dispensation'.

266 Doyle to Murray, 3 Feb. 1832 (File 31/3 (1831–32), no. 130, D.D.A.).
267 Curtis to Dr. McCann, P.P., Dundalk, 19 May 1824 (File 30/8 (1824), no. 13, D.D.A.).
268 *Council of Trent*, Sess. xxiv, Decree on the reformation of marriage, c. 1.
269 This is the main theme of Art Cosgrove, 'Marriage in medieval Ireland' in Art Cosgrove (ed.), *Marriage in Ireland* (Dublin, 1985), pp 25–50.
270 Corish, *Ir. Cath. Experience*, p. 220; see also the same author's 'Catholic marriage under the penal code' in Art Cosgrove (ed.), op. cit., pp 67–77.
271 Connolly, *Priests and people*, p. 197.
272 Corish, *Ir. Cath. Experience*, p. 220.
273 Connolly, op. cit., p. 197.
274 Patrick J. Corish, 'Catholic marriage under the penal code' in Art Cosgrove (ed.), op. cit., p. 70.
275 Ibid., updating Connolly, op. cit., p. 220.
276 Corish, *Ir. Cath. Experience*, p. 135. For the main outline of the 1753 Act, which was directed against clandestine marriages, see John Bossy, 'Challoner and the Marriage act' in Eamon Duffy (ed.), *Challoner and his church* (London, 1981), p. 126.
277 Doyle, *S.O.I. evidence*, p. 309, H.L. 1825 (181), ix, 1. For Catholic recourse to Protestant ministers for marriage, see Doyle, *S.O.I. evidence*, p. 423, H.C. 1830 (654), vii, 1.
278 Bossy, *Eng. Cath. Comm.*, p. 139 fn.
279 William H.W. Fanning, 'Mixed Marriages' in *Cath. Ency.*, ix, 698–9.
280 Patrick J. Corish, 'Catholic marriage under the penal code' in Art Cosgrove (ed.), *Marriage in Ireland* (Dublin, 1985), p. 74.
281 Connolly, *Priests and people*, p. 197.
282 Corish, loc. cit., p. 73.
283 Cardinal Antonellus to Troy, 19 Mar. 1785, printed in *Stat. dioec. prov. Dublin., 1831*, pp 66–7.
284 *Stat. dioec. prov. Dublin., 1831*, p. 66.
285 'Laws and constitutions' adopted for the diocese of Leighlin in 1748 by Bishop Gallagher, printed in Comerford, *Collections*, i, 79–80.
286 Ibid., p. 80.
287 Comerford, *Collections*, i, 8.
288 Connolly, *Priests and people*, p. 201.
289 Doyle, *S.O.I. evidence*, p. 314, H.L. 1825 (181), ix, 1.
290 See *An account of the number of persons in Holy Orders in the Church of Rome, otherwise Popish priests, or reputed Popish priests, or persons pretending to be Popish priests who under certain acts passed in the parliament of Ireland, have during the last twelve years been convicted of celebrating any marriage, between two Protestants, or reputed Protestants or between a Protestant or a reputed Protestant and a papist: stating the sentence and, if fine, whether paid or remitted; and if imprisonment, in what places and for what period respectively*, pp 3–6, H.C. 1831–32 (589), xxx, 65.
291 O'Hanlon and O'Leary, *Queen's County*, ii, 683 fn. 3.
292 'Kildare and Leighlin diocesan statutes, 1821' (MS, K.L.D.A.). In an undated visitation return for Clonmore parish, under the heading 'public sinners', the parish priest drew Doyle's attention to the case of John Connors of Ballyrahan who 'attempted a clandestine marriage with Bridget Byrne, was denounced, separated for a time from her, but received her back and has neglected to do public penance'. A visitation return for Baltinglass parish, dated 25 Sept. 1832, notices clandestine marriage as a public abuse for the bishop's attention (MSS in K.L.D.A).

293 I have been unable to find this letter in the archives but Desmond J. Keenan, *The Catholic church in nineteenth-century Ireland* (Dublin, 1983), pp 212–13 has the reference, though the date of the letter is more likely to be late in 1823 than 1824 as given by Keenan.

294 Consalvi to Murray, 17 Jan. 1824 (File 30/8 (1824), no. 88, D.D.A.).

295 Keating to Murray, 1 Mar. 1824 (File 30/8 (1824), no. 10, D.D.A.).

296 Connolly, *Priests and people*, p. 202.

297 Keating to Murray, 1 Mar. 1824 (File 30/8 (1824), no. 10, D.D.A.).

298 Marum to Murray, 1 Mar. 1824 (File 30/8 (1824), no. 11, D.D.A.).

299 Plunkett to Murray, 16 Feb. 1821 (File 30/5 (1821), no. 83, D.D.A.).

300 Through A.R. Blake, Dr Murray inquired from the attorney general, W.C. Plunket, 'would government be displeased if we were to enforce among our Catholics here the same discipline respecting marriages which prevails in Waterford, Cork, Limerick, Derry, Drogheda, etc.?' (Murray to A.R. Blake, 1 Mar. 1824, Fitzpatrick papers, MS 15495, N.L.I.).

301 Murray to Propaganda, 20 Mar. 1824 (File 30/8 (1824), no. 80, D.D.A.).

302 Doyle, Diocesan Book.

303 See Doyle's printed circular letter to his clergy, 14 Nov. 1827 (K.L.D.A.).

304 Doyle, *S.O.I. evidence*, p. 423, H.C. 1830 (654), vii, 1.

305 Doyle, *S.O.I. evidence*, p. 231, H.L. 1825 (181), ix, 1.

306 Marum to Murray, 3 Mar. 1824 (File 30/8 (1824), no. 11, D.D.A.).

307 Connolly, *Priests and people*, p. 199; Corish, *Ir. Cath. Experience*, p. 198.

308 Doyle to his clergy, printed circular letter, 14 Nov. 1827 (K.L.D.A.).

309 Murray to Doyle, 1 Nov. 1827 (File 214/1, D.D.A.).

310 Murray to Doyle, 10 Nov. 1827 (K.L.D.A.); for the long-running saga of divisions within the Catholic wardenship of Galway see Martin Coen, *The wardenship of Galway* (Galway, 1984), passim.

311 'Bishops' Minute Book, 1829–49' for 1829 (MS, K.L.D.A.).

312 Connolly, *Priests and people*, p. 129 gives the year as 1826 and on p. 181 as 1829; it was in fact 1828.

313 Fitzpatrick, *Doyle*, ii, 522, omits '... and all who were present with them when they attempted to get married in Dublin ...'.

314 Doyle to Martin Doyle, P.P., Graiguenamanagh, 27 Feb. 1828 (K.L.D.A.).

315 Doyle to Peter Doyle, 30 Nov. 1827 (K.L.D.A.).

316 Doyle, Diocesan Book.

317 Connolly, *Priests and people*, p. 213.

318 Ibid., p. 204.

319 Comerford, *Collections*, iii, 313–14; see also Máire MacNeill, *The festival of Lughnasa – a study of the survival of the Celtic festival of the beginning of the harvest* (Oxford, 1962), pp 233, 263–8.

320 Comerford, op. cit., ii, 102.

321 Ibid., iii, 163.

322 Comerford, *Collections*, iii, 389; ii, 70; Edward O'Toole, 'The holy wells of County Carlow' in *Bealoideas* 4 (1936), p. 12. In the case of Myshall the pattern day sheep fair may have been of later origin.

323 See Appendix 6, 'Holy wells and Patterns'; the sources used were the Ordnance Survey Name and Letter Books in N.L.I. The letter books are the most comprehensive source: especially the volumes for *Kildare* (2 vols); *King's County* (2 vols – vol.1 only relevant); *Queen's County* (2 vols); *Wicklow* (1 vol.); *Kilkenny* (vol. 1–2); and *Carlow* (1 vol.). Also useful are Comerford, *Collections*, vols 2 and 3, passim; Edward O'Toole, 'The holy wells of County Carlow' in *Bealoideas* 4 (1936), pp 3–23, 107–30; Patricia Jackson, 'The holy wells of County Kildare' in *Journal of the Co. Kildare Archaeological Society* xvi, no. 2 (1978–80), pp 133–61. The latter article is based on folklore sources in the Department of Irish Folklore, University College, Dublin.

324 Comerford, *Collections*, iii, 326.
325 Connolly, *Priests and people*, pp 138–9; see also Máire MacNeill, *The festival of Lughnasa* (Oxford, 1962), p. 271.
326 Arnold Van Gennep, *Manuel de folklore français contemporain* (Paris, 1943-58), 12 vols, iv, 1734, quoted in Delumeau, *Catholicism between Luther and Voltaire*, p. 166.
327 See *D.E.P.*, 26 June 1832 for Archbishop Murray's injunction against drunkenness at the festival of St John at St John's Well, Kilmainham, which his predecessor Archbishop Carpenter had tried to prohibit in 1786-7 (Connolly, *Priests and people*, p. 144).
328 See the final section of this chapter.
329 See Appendix 6 on 'Holy wells and Patterns'.
330 Ordnance Survey Letter Book (hereafter O.S.L.B.), *Queen's County*, i, 238.
331 O.S.L.B., *Queen's County*, ii, 16.
332 O.S.L.B., *Wicklow*, p. 150.
333 O.S.L.B., *King's County*, i, 69.
334 O.S.L.B., *King's County*, i, 114.
335 Certainly Martin Doyle who was only five years older, and born in the next townland to Doyle, spoke Irish. Garret FitzGerald has estimated that Irish was spoken by between three and nine per cent of the population in Doyle's native barony in the decade 1781–91 (cf. 'Estimates for baronies of minimum levels of Irish-speaking among successive decennial cohorts 1771–1781 to 1861–1871' in *R.I.A. Proc.*, Sect. C. lxxxiv (1984), Map 2).
336 In the parish of St Mullin's the stations of confession were conducted at least partly through Irish. See Doyle to Thomas Dowling, P.P., St. Mullin's, 19 July 1826 (K.L.D.A.).
337 O.S.L.B., *Queen's County*, i, 1.
338 Ibid., p. 83.
339 O.S.L.B., *Kilkenny*, i–ii, 4.
340 Doyle, *S.O.I. evidence*, pp 245–6, H.L. 1825 (181), ix, 1. Doyle was probably not well informed on Lough Derg which attracted an annual attendance of 60,000 in the 1820s (figure quoted in K. Theodore Hoppen, *Elections, politics and society in Ireland 1832–1885* (Oxford, 1984), p. 219).
341 Comerford, *Collections*, iii, 6, and Connolly, *Priests and people*, p. 145; Edward O'Toole, 'The holy wells of County Carlow' in *Bealoideas* 4 (1936), p. 21 has an oral tradition that a Baltinglass pattern was suppressed for a similar reason.
342 Comerford, op. cit., iii, 197.
343 Ibid, iii, 239.
344 O.S.L.B., *King's County*, i, 55.
345 Comerford, *Collections*, iii, 343.
346 Ibid., iii, 330.
347 Ibid., iii, 389.
348 Cited in Comerford, *Collections*, i, 81–2; on this topic see Séan Ó Súilleabháin, *Irish wake amusements* (Cork, 1967), especially pp 130–65.
349 Comerford, op. cit.
350 Fitzpatrick, *Doyle*, i, 291.
351 Ibid. In 1825 Doyle allowed that though the attendance at wakes and funerals was 'still considerable' it was declining 'for at present the people are throwing aside some of their ancient usages' (Doyle, *S.O.I. evidence*, p. 182, H.C. 1825 (129), viii, 173). Under Bishop Delany the Patrician Brothers in Tullow 'attended at all wakes in the parish, introducing the rosary, prayers for the dead and spiritual reading in place of games and excessive drinking which had previously marked these occasions ... Each wake continued over two or three nights, and the remains were removed directly from the house to the cemetery' (Linus H. Walker, *To build and to plant* (Carlow, n.d.), p. 2).
352 'Extracts from the statutes of the united diocese of Kildare and Leighlin' [1824], p. 11 (printed copy in K.L.D.A.); visitation returns (MSS in K.L.D.A.); *Stat. dioec. prov. Dublin, 1831*, pp 89–91; Connolly, *Priests and people*, p. 161; Corish, *Ir. Cath. Experience*, p. 181.

353 Doyle and Carr had been on the board of Houghton Fever Hospital together. See chapter 1.
354 Doyle to Rev. G.W. Carr on Temperance Societies, dated Carlow, 20 Dec. 1829, printed in *D.E.P.*, 2 Jan. 1830. There are errors in Elizabeth Malcolm's treatment of Doyle's attitude to drunkenness in her book *'Ireland sober, Ireland free.' Drink and Temperance in nineteenth-century Ireland* (Dublin, 1986).
355 *D.E.P.*, 2 Jan 1830.
356 Ibid. An uncle of Doyle's, Martin Doyle, was a publican in Mullinderry and subsequently in New Ross *(The People*, 3 May 1913).
357 Henry's letter is in the *D.E.P.*, 16 Jan. 1830.
358 Ibid.
359 *D.E.P.*, 29 Mar. 1830, for Doyle's letter to Dr. Harvey.
360 Ibid. Despite this Malcolm in *'Ireland sober, Ireland free.' Drink and Temperance in nineteenth-century Ireland* (Dublin, 1986), p. 84, has written that Doyle 'regarded even moderation as "too perfect for the generality of men"; had he lived (he died in 1834), he certainly would have opposed the even more perfectionistic view of the teetotallers'.
361 *D.E.P.*, 12 Apr. 1830; also in early April, John Browne, M.D., expressed himself anxious to establish a temperance society in Carlow along with anti-gambling, anti-duelling and anti-slavery societies and an auxiliary association for the deaf and dumb. Doyle replied 'when you have formed a Temperance Society ... you may calculate upon my best exertions to promote the object of it' (*D.E.P.*, 15 Apr. 1830).
362 Malcolm, op. cit., p. 76.
363 Connolly, *Priests and people*, p. 169.
364 *Disturbed Counties' evidence*, pp 89, 91 (appendix), H.L. 1831–32 (677) xvi, 1.
365 Ibid., p. 182.
366 Doyle, *Pastoral, Lent 1834*, p. 11.
367 *D.E.P.*, 2 Jan. 1830.
368 Doyle, *Pastoral, Lent 1834*, p. 11.
369 Doyle, *Pastoral, Lent 1834*, p. 11. The extant parochial visitation returns for thirty-three parishes refer to drinking as a problem for Doyle's attention in only three parishes: Baltinglass, Clonmore and Hacketstown. In a letter from Denis Lawlor, P.P., Hacketstown to Doyle of 11 August 1830 (in K.L.D.A.), it was stated: 'There were some persons addicted to drunkenness and quarrelling, particularly at funerals last winter, about Kilamoate. It was owing in a great measure to the excessive hospitality of the friends of the deceased – and also to women bringing whiskey for sale to the graveyard. I hope the evil habit has ceased'.
370 *Stat. dioec. prov. Dublin., 1831*, p. 79.
371 Doyle, *Pastoral, Lent 1834*, pp 11–12.
372 Ibid., p. 12.
373 Ibid., p. 13.
374 Doyle, *S.P.I. evidence*, p. 452, H.C. 1830 (654), vii, 1; Herbert Thurston 'Calendar' in *Cath. Ency.*, iii, 158–66; F.G. Holweck, 'Feasts' in *Cath. Ency.*, vi, 21–3.
375 Thurston, loc. cit., p. 165.
376 Ibid.
377 Ibid. Holweck, 'Feasts', loc. cit., p. 22.
378 F.G. Holweck, 'Feasts' in *Cath. Ency.*, vi, p. 23.
379 Bossy, *Eng. Cath. Comm.*, p. 120.
380 Corish, *Cath. Comm.*, pp 92–3; and the same author's *Ir. Cath. Experience*, pp 132–3. For a full list of the holy days applying in seventeenth century Ireland see Comerford, *Collections*, i, 249–50.
381 Ibid.
382 Doyle, *S.O.I. evidence*, p. 315, H.L. 1825 (181), ix, 1.
383 Doyle to Cardinal Capellari, prefect of Propaganda, 21 Aug. 1828 (File 30/11 (1828), no.

64, D.D.A.).
384 Doyle to Pope Pius VIII, undated [1830], draft letter of eight foolscap pages (MS in K.L.D.A. henceforth referred to as Doyle, 'MS on holy days, 1830').
385 Ibid., p. 8.
386 This problem is noted in the present writer's 'Interdenominational relations in pre-famine Tipperary' in William Nolan and Thomas McGrath (ed.), *Tipperary: History and Society* (Dublin, 1985), p. 277.
387 William F. Burton to Doyle, 29 May 1827 (K.L.D.A.).
388 Doyle to Lord Cloncurry, 11 Dec 1829, cited in Cloncurry, *Personal Recollections*, p. 310. See *D.E.P.*, 12, 17 Dec. 1829 for Cloncurry/Doyle correspondence on holy days. Cf. also Cloncurry to Doyle, undated, cited in Fitzpatrick, *Doyle*, ii, 175 where Cloncurry sought the elimination of holy days on 18, 24, 29 June, 15 August and 8 September. The holy days in question, which fell at the height of the agricultural season, were respectively: Saint Mark's day, St John the Baptist's day, SS Peter and Paul, Assumption and the Nativity of the Blessed Virgin Mary.
389 Doyle, 'MS on holy days, 1830', p. 7 (K.L.D.A.).
390 Doyle to prefect of Propaganda, 21 Aug. 1828 (File 30/11 (1828), no. 64. D.D.A.; this letter is also in Acta, vol. 192, pp 320–1.).
391 Cardinal Capellari (prefect of Propaganda) to Murray, 30 Sept. 1828 (Acta, vol. 192, p. 321).
392 For Easter Monday as a notable day of celebration and festivity, see Connolly, *Priests and people*, p. 167.
393 The fair of Ballingarry, South-Tipperary, on Whit Monday, 1828, was described by Amhlaoibh Ó Súilleabháin as 'an aonaigh is coirphte i gCúige Mumhan ná i gcúige Laighean' (T.de Bháldraithe (ed.), *Cine lae Amhlaoibh* (Dublin, 1970), p. 34).
394 'Bishops' Minute Book, 1829–49' for 1829 (MS, D.D.A.).
395 Letter in Acta, vol. 192, p. 318.
396 See Acta, vol. 192, pp 313–22.
397 Curtis to Murray, 24 Sept. 1829 (File 31/2 (1829–30), no.10, D.D.A.). This letter encloses the letter received by Curtis from Propaganda. The decree was granted on 23 August and dated 29 August 1829.
398 Doyle 'MS on holy days 1830', p. 3 (K.L.D.A.); Corish, *Cath. Comm.*, p. 108.
399 'Bishops' Minute Book, 1829–49' for 1830 (MS, D.D.A.).
400 Doyle, 'MS on holy days, 1830', p. 3 (K.L.D.A.).
401 Propaganda Fide to Curtis, 3 Apr. 1830 (File 31/2 (1829–30), no. 140, D.D.A.).
402 Murray to Curtis, 3 May 1830 (K.L.D.A.).
403 'Bishops' Minute Book, 1829–49' for 1831 (MS, D.D.A.).
404 Connolly, *Priests and people*, p. 169; in the parish of Callan in the diocese of Ossory the abolition of the feast-day of St John the Baptist did not take place until 1834. On 24 June 1834 Humphrey O'Sullivan noted: 'This day was always a holiday of obligation till today, but it has been suppressed by the church; for it was a great day for drinking, after bonfire night' (Michael McGrath (ed.), *The diary of Humphrey O'Sullivan*, 4 vols (London, 1928–31), iv, 41).
405 Doyle, 'MS on holy days, 1830', p. 4 (K.L.D.A.).
406 Ibid.
407 Ibid.

CHAPTER 6

1 Doyle to Duanne (K.L.D.A.).
2 Dowling to Doyle, 25 Jan. 1820 (K.L.D.A.).
3 *Pastoral, Lent 1820*, p. 2.

4 Doyle, *Pastoral, Nov. 1822*, p. 5.

5 Doyle to Peter Doyle, 30 Jan. 1821 (K.L.D.A.).

6 For the Delany report see *Disturbed Counties' evidence*, p. 256, H.L. 1831–32 (677), xvi, 1. For the Baltinglass episode see David and Jill Berman, 'Journal of an officer stationed in Naas and Baltinglass, 1832–3' in *Journal of the County Kildare Archaeological Society*, vol. xv, no. 3 (1973–4), pp. 268–78 at p. 276.

7 Captain Whelan, Rathglass to Major James Tandy, 30 Jan. 1822 (State of the Country papers, carton 138, no. 2368/11, National Archives).

8 *Disturbed Counties' evidence*, pp 251, 274, H.L. 1831-32 (677), xvi, 1.

9 Ibid., pp 179, 192.

10 Ibid., p. 251.

11 *Disturbed Counties' evidence*, p. 253, H.L. 1831–32 (677), xvi, 1.

12 Ibid., p. 43 (appendix).

13 Ibid., p. 270.

14 Doyle, *Tithe evidence*, p. 96, H.L. 1831–32 (663), xxii, 181.

15 *Disturbed Counties' evidence*, p. 179, H.L. 1831-32 (677), xvi, 1. For the Finnegans see the *Carlow Morning Post*, 2 May, 25 July, 29 July, 5 Aug., 8 Aug. 1822. See also the report on Rev. Martin Doyle, 18 October 1833, in H.O. 100/244, pp 557–60. The Protestant parishioners of Clonegal offered thanks to Rev. Martin Doyle for his 'unceasing exertions' to promote peace and good order. See Peadar MacSuibhne, *Clonegal parish* (Ballon, 1975), p. 58.

16 *Disturbed Counties' evidence*, p. 251, H.L. 1831–32 (663), xxii, 181.

17 Doyle, *S.O.I. evidence*, p. 179, H.C. 1825 (129), viii, 173.

18 Doyle to Rev. Martin Doyle, 28 May 1832 (K.L.D.A.). For Maher see note 106 below.

19 Doyle, *Pastoral, Lent 1821*, pp 36, 38–9. For evidence of outrages in the barony of Rathvilly see *Carlow Morning Post*, 19 April, 10 Dec. 1821, 4 and 14 Nov. 1822.

20 Ibid., p. 40.

21 Ibid., p. 41.

22 Fitzpatrick, *Doyle*, i, 148.

23 Doyle, *Pastoral, Lent 1821*, pp 41–2.

24 Ibid., pp 43–4.

25 Duke of Leinster to Marquis Wellesley, 3 Nov. 1822 (State of the Country papers, carton 138, no. 2368/69, National Archives).

26 Doyle, *Pastoral, Nov. 1822*, p. 7.

27 See chapter one of Thomas McGrath, *Politics, Interdenominational Relations and Education in the Public Ministry of Bishop James Doyle of Kildare and Leighlin, 1786–1834* (Dublin, 1998).

28 Doyle, *Pastoral, Nov. 1822*, pp 7–8.

29 Ibid., p. 9.

30 Doyle's draft address to King George IV, undated, is in K.L.D.A. On this point, see chapter one of Thomas McGrath, *Politics, Interdenominational Relations and Education in the Public Ministry of Bishop James Doyle of Kildare and Leighlin, 1786–1834* (Dublin, 1998).

31 Doyle, *Pastoral, Nov. 1822*, p. 9.

32 *Letters on the state of Ire.*, p. 83.

33 Doyle, *Pastoral, Nov. 1822*, p. 9.

34 Ibid.

35 Ibid., pp 10–11.

36 Doyle, *Pastoral, Nov. 1822*, pp 11–12.

37 Examination of J.S. Rochfort, magistrate in Counties Carlow, Kilkenny and Queen's in *S.O.I. evidence*, p. 440, H.C. 1825 (129), viii, 293. For further discussion of Pastorini see Thomas McGrath, *Politics, Interdenominational Relations and Education in the Public Ministry of Bishop James Doyle of Kildare and Leighlin, 1786–1834* (Dublin, 1998).

38 Doyle, *S.O.I. evidence*, p. 247, H.L. 1825 (181), ix, 1.
39 Doyle, *Pastoral, Lent 1825*, p. 17.
40 Doyle, *S.O.I. evidence*, p. 247, H.L. 1825 (181), ix, 1.
41 Doyle, *Pastoral, Lent 1825*, p. 19.
42 Doyle, *S.O.I. evidence*, p. 248, H.L. 1825 (181), ix, 1.
43 Doyle, *Pastoral, Nov. 1822*, p. 20.
44 Doyle, *Pastoral, Nov. 1822*, pp 20–1.
45 Doyle, *Pastoral, Lent 1821*, p. 60.
46 Copy of Doyle to Plunket, 22 Nov. 1822 (File 30/6 (1822), no. 13, D.D.A.); Plunket to Doyle, 30 Nov. 1822 (K.L.D.A.).
47 Murray to Doyle, 3 Dec. 1822 (K.L.D.A.).
48 *D.E.P.*, 17 Dec. 1822.
49 Spring Rice to Doyle, 14 Dec. 1822 (Monteagle papers, MS 13345, N.L.I.).
50 *D.E.P.*, 26 Nov. 1822.
51 Doyle, *S.O.I. evidence*, p 197, H.C. 1825 (129), viii, 173.
52 *D.E.P.*, 23 Nov. 1822.
53 Doyle, *S.O.I. evidence*, p. 197, H.C. 1825 (129), viii, 173. For the duke of Leinster, see Charles Stuart, O.S.A., to Doyle, 11 Dec. 1822 (K.L.D.A.).
54 *D.E.P.*, 15 June 1824.
55 Fitzpatrick, *Doyle*, i, 205.
56 Doyle, *S.O.I. evidence*, p. 197, H.C. 1825 (129), viii, 173.
57 State of the Country papers, carton 138, no. 2368/84, National Archives.
58 Doyle, *S.O.I. evidence*, p. 197, H.C. 1825 (129), viii, 173.
59 Doyle to Haly, 17 Mar. 1823 (K.L.D.A.).
60 Doyle, *Pastoral, June 1823*, pp 7–8.
61 Doyle, *Pastoral, Lent 1825*, pp 16–17.
62 See statement of Rev. Nicholas O'Connor, P.P., Maryborough, in *Disturbed Counties' evidence*, p. 187, H.L. 1831–32 (677), xvi, 1.
63 See Thomas Joseph Browne, O.S.B., to Doyle, 11 Oct. 1831; Doyle to Browne, 19 Oct. 1831 (K.L.D.A.). Browne was president of Downside Abbey.
64 *D.E.P.*, 7 Nov. 1829. This pastoral was printed in full in *The Times*, 12 Nov. 1829.
65 *Disturbed Counties' evidence*, pp 180-181, 185, 274, H.L. 1831–32 (677), xvi, 1; for this evidence disputed see ibid., pp 113–14 (appendix). Evictions on the Cassan and Cosby estates were referred to in parliament on 8 March 1833. See *Hansard*, 3rd ser., xvi, 495. See also *Carlow Morning Post*, 26 Oct. 1829 for an article on the state of the Queen's County which argued that there was one law for Catholics and another for Protestants.
66 *Disturbed Counties' evidence*, pp 187–8, H.L. 1831–32 (677), xvi, 1.
67 Ibid., pp 180, 253.
68 Ibid., p. 181.
69 Ibid., pp 181–2.
70 Ibid., p. 274.
71 Ibid., pp 253, 251–2.
72 Ibid., p. 182; *Carlow Morning Post*, 3 Aug. 1829.
73 *Disturbed Counties' evidence*, p. 181, H.L. 1831–32 (677), xvi, 1.
74 Ibid., pp 180–1.
75 MS draft of November 1829 pastoral (in K.L.D.A.). 'The law of self-preservation is a primary duty of man, and anterior to that which created property and rendered it inviolable' (Doyle, *Letters on the state of Ire.*, p. 87).
76 *Carlow Morning Post*, 29 Oct., 12 Nov., 10 Dec. 1829. Doyle to Mother Dolan, 24 Apr. 1830 (archives of the Discalced Carmelite convent, Malahide, Co. Dublin).
77 Walter Blackney to Thomas Wyse, 12 Oct. 1830 (Wyse papers, MS 15024 (13), N.L.I.).
78 Doyle to Rev. J. Maher, 15 Oct. 1830 (File 31/2 (1829-30), nos 121–2, D.D.A.). Viscount Beresford was illegitimate.

79 See chapter three of Thomas McGrath, *Politics, Interdenominational Relations and Education in the Public Ministry of Bishop James Doyle of Kildare and Leighlin, 1786–1834* (Dublin, 1998).
80 *Disturbed Counties' evidence*, pp 64–74, 72 (appendix), H.L. 1831-32 (677), xvi, 1. [Doyle], *Church of Ireland, Tithes!!! A most important dialogue between a bishop and a judge* (Dublin, 1831), 14 pp. O'Connell subsequently accused Baron Smith of political partisanship in his judgements. See debate on conduct of Baron Smith on 13 and 21 Feb. 1834 in *Hansard*, 3rd ser., xxi, 271–352, 695–753.
81 *Disturbed Counties' evidence*, pp 60-3 (appendix), H.L. 1831–32 (677), xvi, 1.
82 See *Hansard*, 3rd ser., xi, 1158 (Stanley); ibid., xii, 1420–1421 (Grattan), 1417 (Parnell), 1418 (Coote), 1419–1420 (Stanley); ibid., xiii, 1192 (Roden).
83 *Disturbed Counties' evidence*, p. 233, H.L. 1831–32 (677), xvi, 1.
84 Pastoral published in *D.E.P.*, 1 Dec. 1831.
85 *Disturbed Counties' evidence*, p. 180, H.L. 1831–32 (677), xvi, 1.
86 *Tithe evidence*, p. 26, H.L. 1831–32 (271), xxii, 1.
87 Ibid.
88 *Disturbed Counties' evidence*, p. 179, H.L. 1831–32 (677), xvi, 1.
89 Pastoral published in *D.E.P.*, 28 May 1829; MS in K.L.D.A.; *Carlow Morning Post*, 9 Aug. 1830, 2 May 1831.
90 *Tithe evidence*, pp 22, 24–5, H.L. 1831–32 (271), xxii, 1; see *Carlow Morning Post*, 28 Nov. 1831, for a good account of the attempted rescue and Captain Mathew's statement.
91 *D.E.P.*, 1 Dec. 1831.
92 Ibid.
93 *Disturbed Counties' evidence*, p. 191, H.L. 1831–32 (677), xvi, 1.
94 *Tithe evidence*, p. 95, H.L. 1831–32 (663), xxii, 181.
95 *Carlow Morning Post*, 5 Dec. 1831; *Disturbed Counties' evidence*, p. 87 (appendix), H.L. 1831–32 (677), xvi, 1.
96 Ibid., p. 43 (appendix); *Carlow Morning Post*, 16 Apr. 1832. Letter of Patrick Lalor dated 12 Apr. 1832.
97 Doyle to Mother Dolan, 30 April 1832 (archives of the Discalced Carmelite convent, Malahide, Co. Dublin); *Disturbed Counties' evidence*, p. 195, H.L. 1831–32 (677), xvi, 1.
98 There is a printed copy of the pastoral in K.L.D.A.
99 This indicates that this devotion was in the chapels.
100 Bishop Kinsella of Ossory followed suit with an almost identical pastoral (see *D.E.P.*, 31 May 1832).
101 As we have seen, absence from the confessional though not from the chapel was a known sign of the activity of illegal societies. Cf. chapter 5. The cholera plague did not reach Maryborough until the beginning of September 1832 when, according to the Presentation convent annals, 'it increased hourly here, and with devastating effect and swept numbers away'. At the P.P.'s desire the schools were closed for about three weeks – 'indeed it would be nearly useless to keep them open as the greater part of the inhabitants of the town retired to the country and the people of the vicinity dreaded the contagion too much to venture in, so that in a few days the place seemed almost depopulated, the solitary foot of the priest or physician was alone heard in the street or the dismal noise of the cart destined to convey the devoted victims of disease to the hospital was heard roll along. Terror so universally prevailed that those who closed their career in this world were instantly enclosed in coffins until they could be secretly conveyed to the grave to prevent the survivors from greater alarm ... On the 9th inst. a deputation of the pious inhabitants waited on V. Rev. N. O'Connor to request there would be a solemn High Mass on the following day in order to supplicate the divine mercy, and obtain a cessation of the universal calamity, mass took place in the parish chapel attended by a numerous congregation who by sighs and tears sought to appease the wrath of heaven and stop the arm of divine justice – God listened propitiously to the cry and prayers of his people! and by a most visible interposi-

tion of his divine mercy arrested the violence of this visitation from that hour in consequence of which another solemn High Mass was offered in thanksgiving for so wonderful a mark of his infinite goodness' (Annals, pp 83–7).

102 Dunne to Doyle, 4 May 1832 (K.L.D.A.).

103 The idea of self-defence associations was not in the original MS of the 5 May 1832 pastoral in K.L.D.A.

104 *Disturbed Counties' evidence*, p. 372, H.L. 1831–32 (677), xvi, 1. Doyle's letter is cited in the evidence of Robert Cassidy of Monasterevan.

105 *Carlow Sentinel*, 12 May 1832.

106 *Disturbed Counties' evidence*, p. 190, H.L. 1831–32 (677), xvi, 1. As related by Cardinal Moran, Rev. James Maher, as parish priest of Paulstown, failed to secure the approval of his local magistrate to arm his parishioners to combat the depredations of the Whitefeet. 'Father Maher, without delay proceeded to Kilkenny, and having obtained an order for the police to unite with the parishioners in pursuit of the plunderers, he put himself at their head, and after a few days the bands of Whitefeet were completely dispersed, and security was fully restored to that district. On another occasion a body of Whitefeet appeared in arms on a Sunday morning, in the neighbourhood of Paulstown. Father Maher addressed the congregation at last Mass, on the necessity of putting an end to this wicked organization; the result was that immediately after Mass the whole body of the parishioners went in pursuit of the Whitefeet, and having apprehended a considerable number of them, handed them over to the police.' See Patrick F. Moran (ed.), *The letters of Rev. James Maher, D.D., late P.P. of Carlow-Graigue, on religious subjects; with a memoir* (Dublin, 1877), pp xxxv–xxxvi.

107 *Disturbed Counties' evidence*, p. 373, H.L. 1831–32 (677), xvi, 1. Doyle's letter is cited in the evidence of Robert Cassidy.

108 Ibid., pp 258, 269, 270.

109 See letters from Maryborough priests in *D.E.P.*, 14 June 1832.

110 *Disturbed Counties' evidence*, p. 185, H.L. 1831–32 (677), xvi, 1.

111 See remarks of Myles O'Reilly, magistrate, in ibid., pp 359–60.

112 The same was also true of County Carlow. The Carlow county M.P.s Walter Blackney and Sir John Milley Doyle informed the chief secretary, E.G. Stanley on 14 May 1831 that 'the people as well as we ourselves have not the slightest confidence in the local Magistracy of this County - generally speaking and that we do not expect to receive a particle of justice at their hands including the clerical as well as the lay magistrates' (State of the Country papers, general, carton 153, no. 2995/4 (copy), National Archives).

113 *Disturbed Counties' evidence*, p. 169, H.L. 1831–32 (677), xvi, 1.

114 'Bishops' Minute Book, 1829–49' for 1829 (MS, D.D.A.).

115 *Disturbed Counties' evidence*, p. 117, H.L. 1831–32 (677), xvi, 1.

116 Doyle, *S.O.I. evidence*, p. 248, H.L. 1825 (181), ix, 1.

CHAPTER 7

1 See Propaganda to Doyle, 17 March 1833, and Paul Cullen, Irish College, Rome, to Doyle, 27 March 1833 (K.L.D.A.).

2 Doyle to Mother Dolan, Discalced Carmelite convent, Ranelagh, 1 July 1833 (archives of the Discalced Carmelite convent, Malahide, County Dublin.).

3 *Carlow Morning Post*, 30 November 1833.

4 Ibid., 7 December 1833.

5 Doyle to Mother Dolan, Discalced Carmelite convent, Ranelagh, Dublin, 13 January 1834 (archives of Discalced Carmelite convent, Malahide, County Dublin.).

6 Ibid., 4 January 1834.

7 As reported in *Carlow Morning Post*, 1 March 1834.
8 As reported in ibid., 5 April 1834.
9 *Carlow Morning Post*, 26 April 1834; *Dublin Evening Post*, 24 April 1834.
10 Doyle to Martin Doyle, P.P., Graiguenamanagh, 10 April 1834 (K.L.D.A.).
11 *Carlow Morning Post*, 31 May 1834.
12 *Carlow Morning Post*, 21 June 1834; see also reports of Doyle's death in *D.E.P.*, 17, 19, 21, 24 June 1834; *The Courier*, 18 June (following *Dublin Mercantile Advertiser*) and 23 June 1834 (following *Dublin Register*); *Dublin Evening Mail*, 16 June 1834. *The Times*, 19 June 1834 (following *Dublin Evening Mail*) and 26 June 1834.
13 *Carlow Morning Post*, 24 Jan. 1831 quoting *Morning Chronicle*.
14 Even before Doyle died the *D.E.P.*, of 12 May 1834 was reporting that evangelicals were circulating the notion that Doyle had apostasised on his sick bed and embraced Protestantism. The *D.E.P.*, of 19 and 21 June 1834 defended Doyle from charges of apostasy made in *Dublin Evening Mail and Saunders' Newsletter*. See also *Carlow Morning Post*, 28 June 1834.
15 Kinsella's panegyric is given in *Carlow Morning Post*, 19 July 1834.
16 *Carlow Morning Post*, 26 July 1834 has a full report of this meeting.
17 See John Turpin, *John Hogan, Irish neoclassical sculptor in Rome, 1800–1858* (Dublin, 1982), pp 65–8.
18 Doyle, *Pastoral, June 1823*; *Pastoral, Jan. 1831*.
19 Doyle, *Pastoral, Jan. 1831*.
20 Scritture (Irlanda), 13 May 1829, vol. 25, p. 161.
21 Ibid.
22 Ibid.
23 In the second half of the nineteenth century both Tullow foundations became motherhouses for filiations, especially in Australia and India. The Patricians received papal approval for their institute in 1893. See *Cath. Ency.*, xi, 553. Similarly the Brigidines ceased to be a diocesan congregation and became a Catholic Institute in 1907. See *Cath. Ency.*, xvi, 14.
24 Doyle, *Pastoral, June 1823*, p. 8.
25 Doyle, *Pastoral, Lent 1821*, pp 36, 3.
26 Doyle, *Pastoral, Lent 1823*, p. 9.
27 Doyle, *Pastoral, June 1823*, p. 6.
28 Doyle, *Pastoral, Lent 1821*, p. 34.
29 Doyle, *Defence of Vindication*, p. 75.
30 *Stat. dioec. prov. Dublin.*, 1831, pp 73–4.
31 Doyle, *Pastoral, June 1823*, p. 8.
32 Scritture (Irlanda), vol. 25, p. 161.
33 Connolly, *Priests and people*, p. 219.
34 See Thomas McGrath, *Politics, Interdenominational Relations and Education in the Public Ministry of Bishop James Doyle of Kildare and Leighlin, 1786–1834* (Dublin, 1998).
35 Emmet Larkin, 'The Devotional Revolution in Ireland, 1850–1875 'in *American Historical Review*, lxxxxvii, no. 3 (June, 1972), pp 625–52 at p. 651.
36 Thomas McGrath, 'The Tridentine evolution of modern Irish Catholicism, 1563–1962: a re-examination of the "Devotional Revolution" thesis' in *Recusant History*, vol. 20, no. 4 (October, 1991), pp 512–23.

APPENDIX 1

1 The Catholic parish registers of the diocese of Kildare and Leighlin are on microfilm, p. 4189–4209, in N.L.I.

APPENDIX 2

1 This appendix is based upon 'Kildare and Leighlin in 1829' copied from a manuscript in the handwriting of Doyle and printed in Comerford, *Collections*, i, 324–9.

APPENDIX 3

1 This appendix is based partly upon 'Kildare and Leighlin in 1829' copied from a manuscript in the handwriting of Doyle and printed in Comerford, *Collections*, i, 324–9.

APPENDIX 4

1 This appendix is based upon 'Kildare and Leighlin in 1829' copied from a manuscript in the handwriting of Doyle and printed in Comerford, *Collections*, i, 324–9.

APPENDIX 5

1 The sources for this appendix are Doyle's Diocesan Book for the 1820/23 figures and Comerford, *Collections*, i, 324–9, for the 1829 data which is based on a Doyle manuscript.

APPENDIX 6

1 Comerford, *Collections*, iii, 60. Not mentioned in Ordnance Survey Letters.
2 Ibid., ii, 63–4; see also Patricia Jackson 'The holy wells of Co. Kildare' in *Journal of the Co. Kildare Archaeological Society* xvi, no. 2 (1979–80), pp 142–3 for an account based on folklore sources.
3 O.S.L.B., *Kildare*, i, 200.
4 O.S.L.B., *Queen's Co.*, ii, 41.
5 Comerford, op. cit., iii, 88.
6 Ibid., iii, 89.
7 Ibid., iii, 91–2.
8 Edward O'Toole, 'The holy wells of County Carlow' in *Bealoideas* 4 (1936), p. 121.
9 Ibid., p. 18.
10 Comerford, *Collections*, iii, 111.
11 Ibid., iii, 112.
12 Ibid., iii, 117.
13 Ibid., iii, 118.
14 O'Toole, loc. cit., p. 21.
15 Comerford, op. cit., iii, 156.
16 O'Toole, loc. cit., p. 20.
17 O.S.L.B., *Wicklow*, i, 93, 99.
18 Comerford, op. cit., ii, 70.
19 O.S.L.B., *Kildare*, ii, 42.
20 Comerford, *Collections*, ii, 72.

21 Ibid.
22 Ibid.
23 Ibid., may be the same as Tober-a-la well, see O.S.L.B., *Kildare*, i, 101.
24 Comerford, op. cit., iii, 162.
25 Ibid., iii, 163.
26 Ibid., iii, 164.
27 Ibid., iii, 168.
28 O.S.L.B., *Kildare*, i, 115.
29 Comerford, op. cit., iii, 162.
30 O.S.L.B., *Kildare*, i, 72.
31 O.S.L.B., *Queen's Co.*, i, 208.
32 Edward O'Toole, 'The holy wells of County Carlow' in *Bealoideas* 4 (1936), p. 9; Comerford, *Collections*, iii, 173.
33 O.S.L.B., *Wicklow*, p. 242.
34 O'Toole, loc. cit., p. 125; Comerford, op. cit., iii, 174.
35 O'Toole, p. 125.
36 Comerford, op. cit., iii, 173.
37 O'Toole, loc. cit., p. 113.
38 Comerford, op. cit., iii, 191.
39 O.S.L.B., *Wicklow*, p. 107.
40 Comerford, *Collections*, iii, 197.
41 Ibid., iii, 321.
42 Ibid.
43 Comerford, op. cit., iii, 226–7. John O'Donovan's account of Graiguenamanagh in the O.S.L.B., *Kilkenny*, gives no account of this parish's holy wells.
44 Ibid., iii, 224.
45 Ibid., iii, 227–8.
46 Comerford, *Collections*, iii, 335.
47 Ibid., iii, 237.
48 Ibid., iii, 239.
49 O.S.L.B., *Wicklow*, p. 130.
50 O.S.L.B., *Kildare*, iii, 157.
51 Ibid., i, 65.
52 Ibid., i, 142.
53 Ibid.
54 O.S.L.B., *King's Co.*, i, 3.
55 O.S.L.B., *King's Co.*, i, 53.
56 Ibid., i, 55, 69; Comerford, *Collections*, lacks the detail of John O'Donovan in the O.S.L.B. for *King's Co.*
57 Peadar MacSuibhne, *Killeshin/Graiguecullen* (Portlaoise, 1972), pp 35, 45, 73 (includes photograph of well).
58 O.S.L.B., *Queen's Co.*, i, 39.
59 Comerford, op. cit., iii, 6; Connolly, *Priests and people*, p. 145.
60 O.S.L.B., *Queen's Co.*, i, 165; Comerford, op. cit., iii, 274.
61 Comerford, *Collections*, ii, 235.
62 Ibid., ii, 241.
63 Ibid.
64 Ibid., ii, 243.
65 O.S.L.B., *Kildare*, ii, 160.
66 O.S.L.B., *Queen's Co.*, i, 193–4.
67 Comerford, op. cit., iii, 291, 298.

68 Ibid., iii, 319; Edward O'Toole, 'The holy wells of County Carlow' in *Bealoideas* 4 (1936), p. 12.
69 O.S.L.B., *Kildare*, i, 163.
70 Comerford, *Collections*, ii, 204, 293.
71 Ibid., iii, 330.
72 Ibid., ii, 305.
73 Ibid., iii, 337.
74 Ibid., iii, 343.
75 Ibid., iii, 349.
76 Comerford, *Collections*, iii, 351.
77 Ibid., iii, 353.
78 Ibid., ii, 326.
79 O.S.L.B., *Queen's Co.*, i, 204.
80 O.S.L.B., *Carlow*, p. 443; Comerford, op. cit., iii, 313-4.
81 Comerford, op. cit., iii, 379.
82 Ibid., iii, 387.
83 Ibid.
84 Ibid., iii, 389.

BIBLIOGRAPHY

For an examination of Doyle historiography see 'Doyle scholarship to date: a bibliographical essay' in Thomas McGrath, *Politics, Interdenominational Relations and Education in the Public Ministry of Bishop James Doyle of Kildare and Leighlin, 1786–1834.*

This Bibliography is arranged as follows

Manuscript collections
Parliamentary papers
Contemporary newspapers and journals
Contemporary works, pamphlets, etc.
Collections of printed correspondence, memoirs, diaries and biographies
Secondary sources
Works of reference

MANUSCRIPT COLLECTIONS

Ballyboden, County Dublin
Irish Augustinian Provincial Archives
    'Grantstown A/C Book 1804–42'
    'Acta of the Irish Province, 1782–1867'
    'MS Book no. 70'
    'Doyle letters file'

Carlow
Kildare and Leighlin Diocesan Archives in Bishop's house
    Doyle papers
Carlow College Archives
    'Account Bk no. 41'
    'J.K.L. – Account book 1817–1833' (N.L.I. microfilm, p. 7113)
Presentation Convent
    Annals (1842 copy)
    'Register of the Postulants, Novices and Religious of the Presentation Convent established in Carlow, 1811 ...'

Clongowes Wood, Clane, County Kildare
Archives of the Society of Jesus
    Drafts of Rev. Dr Bartholomew Esmonde's letters to Doyle in 1824

Coimbra, Portugal
Archives of the University of Coimbra
    Register (1807) Bk 37
    'Relaçao dos Estudantes Matriculados na Universidade de Coimbra no anno lectivo de 1807 para 1808'

Dublin
Dublin Diocesan Archives
    Files 30/3 (1819) – 31/4 (1833–5); File 214/1; 'Bishop's Minute Book, 1829–49'; 'Letters of J.K.L. and Edward Hay' in Section 60/2, file xvi. Proceedings of the Catholic Association
Irish Jesuit Archives, Leeson Street
    Papers relating to Clongowes Wood College
National Archives
    State of the Country papers, 1819–34
    Registered Papers, 1819–34
National Library of Ireland
    Catholic Registers
    Cushenstown and New Ross parishes, County Wexford, microfilm p. 4259
    Parishes of the diocese of Kildare and Leighlin, p. 4189–p. 4209
    Fitzpatrick Papers
        MS 15499(3) – 'Life of J.K.L.'
        MS 15495 – 'Notes, etc. on the life of Archbishop Murray of Dublin'
        MS 1562 – 'Letters, documents, Dr Troy, Dr Doyle, A.H. Rowan, etc.'
    Monteagle Papers MS 13345
    Ordnance Survey Letter Books
        Carlow (1 vol.: 1839)
        Kildare (2 vols: 1837)
        Kilkenny (vols 1–2: 1839)
        King's County (2 vols: 1837–8)
        Queen's County (2 vols: 1838)
        Wexford (1 vol.: 1840)
        Wicklow (1 vol.: 1840)
    Ordnance Survey Name Books
        County Carlow
        King's County
        County Wicklow
    Wyse Papers MS 15024 (13)
Trinity College
    Fitzpatrick papers
        Miscellaneous MS IV

Gort Muire, County Dublin
Irish Calced Carmelite Provincial Archives
 'John Spratt's list of the province, 1816–21'
 'Acts of Irish Provincial Chapter, 1823'

Kew, England
P.R.O. F.O. 170–23

Kildare
Presentation Convent
 Annals

Killiney, County Dublin
Irish Franciscan Archives
 O'Meara papers

Kilkenny
St Kieran's College
 Carrigan MSS 38

Malahide, County Dublin
St Joseph's Carmelite Monastery
 Letters of Bishop Doyle to Ranelagh Carmelites; Memorandum Book

Maynooth, County Kildare
Maynooth College, President's Office
 'Minutes of the Trustees of Maynooth'
 Bound MS volume

Mountrath, County Laois
Brigidine Convent
 Annals

Mullinderry, Foulksmill, County Wexford
'Notes on the Ryan family' by Rev. Nicholas Ryan
 Typescript in possession of Ryan family, Mullinderry

New Ross, County Wexford
Augustinian priory
 Manuscript house books
 'Missale no. 31'; '1798–1830'
 '1809–1879'; '1823–1830'; '1825–1838'

Paris
Archives de St Sulpice
    Letter from Rev. Andrew Fitzgerald, O.P., president
    Carlow College to Rev. Antoine Garnier, 22 May 1824

Paulstown, County Kilkenny
Brigidine Convent
    Mary O'Riordan, 'Life of Dr Delany: Bishop of Kildare and Leighlin' bound type-
    script, written *c.*1972

Portlaoise, County Laois
Presentation Convent
    Annals and Register

Rome
Archives of the Congregation of Propaganda Fide
    Acta Congregationum generalium anni, 1819–34, vols 182–97 on microfilm in N.L.I.,
    p. 5207–15
    Scritture riferite nei congressi, Irlanda, 1819–34, vols 22–5 on microfilm in N.L.I., p.
    5415–21

Salisbury, Wiltshire, England
Ebbesbourne Wake, Congleton Papers in possession of Lord Congleton
    Letter from Bishop Michael Corcoran to Sir Henry Parnell, 17 Dec. 1816

Tallaght, County Dublin
St Mary's, Irish Dominican Archives
    'Coleman letter-book 1' bound MS volume

Thurles, County Tipperary
Cashel Diocesan Archives
    'Notes' compiled by Rev. Thomas O'Carroll (mid-nineteenth century)

Tullow, County Carlow
Brigidine Convent
    Annals
Patrician Generalate
    Annals

PARLIAMENTARY PAPERS

*Second report from the select committee appointed to inquire into the state of Ireland more
    particularly with reference to the circumstances which may have led to disturbances in that
    part of the United Kingdom*, H.C. 1825 (129), viii, 173.

Minutes of evidence taken before the lords' select committee appointed to inquire into the state of Ireland, more particularly with reference to the circumstances which may have led to disturbances in that part of the United Kingdom, H.L. 1825 (181), ix, 1.

First report of the commissioners of Irish education inquiry, H.C. 1825 (400), xii, 1.

Second report of the commissioners of Irish education inquiry, H.C. 1826–7 (12), xii, 1.

Third report of the commissioners of Irish education inquiry, H.C. 1826–27 (13), xiii, 1.

Eighth report of the commissioners of Irish education inquiry, H.C. 1826–7 (509), xiii, 537.

Ninth report of the commissioners of Irish education inquiry, H.C. 1826–7 (516), xiii, 999.

Minutes of evidence taken before the select committee on the state of the poor in Ireland, H.C. 1830 (654), vii, 1.

Second report from the select committee appointed to inquire into the collection and payment of tithes in Ireland and the state of the laws relating thereto, H.C. 1831–2 (508), xxi, 245.

Second report from the select committee of the house of lords appointed to inquire into the collection and payment of tithes in Ireland and the state of the laws relating thereto with minutes of evidence and an appendix, and index, H.L. 1831–2 (663), xxii, 181.

Minutes of evidence taken before the lords' select committee appointed to inquire into the state of the disturbed counties in Ireland, with the immediate causes which have produced the same, and with the efficiency of the laws for the suppression of outrages against the public peace, H.L. 1831–2 (677), xvi, 1.

Notices, pursuant to 10 Geo. IV, c. 7 by Jesuits and other religious orders, transmitted to the chief secretary in Ireland, and in Great Britain to the secretary of state, H.C. 1831–2 (66), xxx, 51.

An account of the number of persons in Holy Orders in the church of Rome, otherwise Popish priests, or reputed Popish priests, or persons pretending to be Popish priests, who under certain acts passed in the parliament of Ireland, have during the last twelve years been convicted of celebrating any marriage, between two Protestants or reputed Protestants or between a Protestant or a reputed Protestant and a papist, stating the sentence and, if fine, whether paid or remitted and if imprisoned, in what places and for what period respectively, H.C. 1831–2 (589), xxx, 65.

First report of the commissioners of Public Instruction, Ireland, H.C. 1835 (45) (46), xxxiii, 1.892.

CONTEMPORARY NEWSPAPERS AND JOURNALS

Carlow Morning Post
Dublin Correspondent
Dublin Evening Post
Irish Catholic Magazine
Catholic Penny Magazine
The Times

Carlow Sentinel
Dublin Evening Mail
Freeman's Journal
Morning Chronicle
The People (Wexford)

CONTEMPORARY WORKS, PAMPHLETS, ETC.

Battersby, W.J., *A history of the abbeys, convents, etc., of the order of St Augustine in Ireland* (Dublin, 1856).

——, *The Catholic priesthood of Ireland vindicated* (Dublin, n.d.).

Bowden, Charles Topham, *A tour through Ireland* (Dublin, 1791).

Catechism of the Council of Trent translated by Rev. Jeremiah O'Donovan (Dublin, 1829).

Clowry, William, *Controversial letters in reply to the Rev. Mr Daly, Rev Dr Singer, etc, etc; to which are added the letters signed B.E.* [James Doyle] (Dublin, London, 1827).

Constitutiones Provinciales et Synodales Ecclesiae Metropolitanae et Primitalis Dublinensis (n.p., 1770).

Coote, Charles, *General view of the agriculture and manufacturers of the Queen's County* (Dublin, 1801).

Decreta Synodi Plenariae Episcoporum Hiberniae apud Thurles habitae anno MDCCCL (Dublin, 1851).

Dens, P., *Theologica Moralis* (Dublin, 1832, reprint).

Doyle, James / J.K.L., *Thoughts on the education of the Irish poor, as contained in the letters of the Right Rev. Dr Doyle, R.C.B., the Rev. Mr Caldwell and a layman lately published in the Carlow Morning Post. Also the pastoral letter of the Right Rev. Doctor Doyle on Lent* (Carlow, [1820]).

——, *Pastoral instructions for the Lent of 1821, addressed to the Roman Catholic laity of the diocese of Kildare and Leighlin being a brief explanation of the sacrament of penance and the laws of the church, relating to Paschal Communion, with observations on the nature and tendency of illegal associations to which is subjoined on appendix* (Carlow, [1821]).

——, *A letter to His Grace, the Protestant Archbishop of Dublin, in consequence of unjust animadversions against the Roman Catholic religion, delivered by him in a charge to the clergy of his Archdiocese, on the 24th of October 1822 in St Patrick's Cathedral* (Dublin, 1822).

——, *Pastoral letter addressed to the Roman Catholic clergy of the Deanery of Kilcock to be read to their respective flocks* (1822; corrected ed., Dublin, 1823).

——, *Second letter of J.K.L. a Roman Catholic bishop in reply to the charge with notes of the Protestant Archbishop of Dublin* (Dublin, 1822).

——, *The General Catechism edited by Dr Doyle* (Dublin, 1823).

——, *A second excellent pastoral letter from the Rt Rev. Dr Doyle, Catholic Bishop of Kildare and Leighlin* (Dublin, 1823).

——, *Miracle wrought by Prince Hohenlohe in the person of Miss Maria Lalor, of Rosskelton, Queen's County, who recovered the use of speech after more than six years' privation of that faculty through the intercession of James Doyle, D.D., Roman Catholic Bishop of Kildare and Leighlin – from the original MSS in English, Latin and French* (Dublin, [1823]).

——, *A Vindication of the religious and civil principles of the Irish Catholics in a letter addressed to his Excellency, the Marquis Wellesley, K.G. Lord Lieutenant General, and General Governor of Ireland, etc., etc., by J.K.L.* (Dublin, 1823).

——, *A Defence by J.K.L. of his Vindication of the religious and civil principles of the Irish Catholics* (Dublin, 1824).

——, *A letter from the Right Reverend Doctor Doyle, Bishop of Kildare and Leighlin to the Catholic Association, in reply to the mis-statements reported to the House of Commons by Mr North on the Education of the Poor of Ireland* (Dublin, 1824).

——, *Letters on a re-union of the churches of England and Rome from an to the Rt Rev. Dr Doyle, R.C. Bishop of Kildare, John O'Driscoll, Alexander Knox and Thomas Newenham* (Gloucester, [1824]).

——, *Letters on the state of Education in Ireland, and on Bible Societies, addressed to a friend in England* (Dublin, 1824).

——, *Pastoral instructions for the Lent of 1825 addressed to the Catholic clergy and laity of the diocese of Kildare and Leighlin* (Carlow, [1825]).

——, *Letters on the state of Ireland addressed by J.K.L. to a friend in England* (Dublin, 1825).

——, Preface to William Gahan, *Sermons and moral discourses for all the Sundays and principal festivals of the year on most important truths and maxims of the Gospel*, 2 vols. (3rd ed., Dublin, 1825).

——, *An essay on the Catholic Claims addressed to the Right Honourable the Earl of Liverpool K.G., etc. etc.* (Dublin, London, 1826).

——, *Pastoral address to the Catholic clergy and laity of the diocese of Kildare and Leighlin* (Dublin, 1826).

——, *Pastoral address on the education of the Catholic poor* (Dublin, 1827).

——, *J.K.L.'s letter to Lord Farnham* (Dublin, 1827).

——, *A reply by J.K.L. to the late Charge of the Most Rev Doctor Magee, Protestant Archbishop of Dublin; submitted most respectfully, to those to whom the above charge was addressed* (Dublin, 1827).

——, *Strictures on the Charge of Dr Elrington to his clergy, as delivered by him in 1827* (Dublin, 1827).

——, *A reply by the Right Rev James Doyle to the Appendix, etc., by the Right Rev. Father in God, Thomas Elrington, D.D., M.R.I.A., Lord Bishop of Leighlin and Ferns* (Dublin, 1827).

——, *An abridgement of the Christian Doctrine with proofs of scripture in points controverted by way of question and answer composed in 1649 by H.T. of the English College at Douay, now revised by the Right Rev. James Doyle, D.D. and prescribed by him to be used in the united dioceses of Kildare and Leighlin* (Dublin, 1828).

——, *A letter to the Duke of Wellington on the Catholic claims* (Liverpool, 1828).

——, *Observations addressed to the Rev. Henry Philpotts, D.D., Rector of Stanhope, on his letter to an English layman, respecting the Coronation oath* (Dublin, London, 1828).

——, *Letter to Daniel O'Connell, Esq., on the formation of a National Literary Institute for the extension of science to all classes of Irish youth* (Dublin, 1829).

——, *A letter from Bishop Doyle to the secretary of the New Ross Temperance Society* (Dublin, 1830).

——, *Dr Doyle on drunkenness. Letter to Dr Harvey, Secretary of the Dublin Temperance Society* (Dublin, 1830).

——, *Letter to Thomas Spring Rice, Esq., M.P., etc., etc., on the establishment of a legal provision for the poor and on the nature and destination of church property* (Dublin, London, 1831).

——, *The Rt Rev Dr Doyle's Reply to Lord Farnham, relative to the observations made on him by his Lordship, in the House of Lords* (Dublin, 1831).

——, *Dr Doyle on poor laws in reply to Mr Senior of London* (Dublin, 1831).

——, *Church of Ireland, Tithes!!! A most important dialogue between a bishop and a judge* (Dublin, 1831). [Published anonymously].

——, *Letter from Dr Doyle to the Marquis of Anglesey on the Tithe Meetings* (Dublin, 1832).

——, Preface to Alban Butler, *Lives of the Saints* (Dublin, 1833 ed.).

——, *Pastoral letter* (Dublin, 1834).

——, *A dissertation on popery or an analysis of Divine Faith. Addressed to the Protestants of England, more particularly the men of Kent. A posthumous work. By the late Right Rev. James Doyle of Kildare and Leighlin. To which is added an appendix containing invaluable papers on Tithes, Poor laws and elections, written under the signature B.E. and several important letters addressed to distinguished individuals* (Dublin, 1835).

——, *An essay on education and the state of Ireland* [1825]. By an Irish Catholic. W.J. Fitzpatrick (ed.) (Dublin, 1880).

First report of the Catholic Book Society (Dublin, [1828]).

General Rules for the governing of the New Ross Houghton fever hospital and dispensary (Waterford, 1829).

Inglis, H.D., *Ireland in 1834*, 2 vols (London, 1834).

J.K.L.: see under James Doyle.

Kinsella, William, *Controversial letters, in reply to Rev. Mr Pope, Rev. Mr Daly, Rev. Dr Singer and others. Also remarks on the canons of scriptures* (Dublin, 1826).

Lewis, G.C., *On local disturbances in Ireland* (London, 1836).

McGhee, Robert J., *The bible, the rights of conscience and the Established Church vindicated* (Dublin, 1818).

Massillon, Jean Baptiste, *The ecclesiastical conferences, the synodal discourses and episcopal mandates of Massillon, bishop of Clermont on the principal duties of the clergy*, 2 vols translated by Rev. Christopher H. Boylan (Dublin and London, 1825).

Mongan, James, *A report of the trials before the Right Hon. the Lord Chief Justice and the Hon. Baron Sir William C. Smith, Bart., at the Special Commission at Maryborough commencing on the 23rd May and ending on the 6th June* [1832] (Dublin, 1832).

Parnell, Henry, *A history of the penal laws against Irish Catholics* (Dublin, 1808).

Pastoral instructions of the archbishop and bishops of the R.C. Church in Ireland on the subject of the General Jubilee (Dublin, 1826).

'Pastorini, Signor' [Charles Walmesley], *The general history of the Christian Church, from her birth to her final triumphant state in heaven* [1771] (3rd ed., Dublin 1800).

Ranson, T.J., *Statistical survey of the County of Kildare* (Dublin, 1807).

Rules and Constitutions of the institute of the religious Sisterhood of the Presentation of the ever blessed Virgin Mary established in the city of Cork, for the charitable instruction of poor girls, conformably to the Rules of the late Pope Pius VI (Dublin, 1809).

Rules and Constitutions of the religious congregation of the Sisters of St Brigid ... established in the town of Tullow, conformably to the rules and constitutions prescribed by the founder ... Dr Delany, Bishop of Kildare and Leighlin, and by his Lordship's successor in the above Sees ... James Doyle, D.D. (Dublin, 1850).

Ryan, John, *The history and antiquities of the county of Carlow* (Dublin, 1833).

Statuta Diocesana, per provinciam Dubliniensem observanda, et a R.R. mis DD. Daniele Murray, Archiepiscopo Dubliniensi; Jacobo Keating, Episcopo Fernensi; Jacobo Doyle, Episcopo Kildarensi et Leighlinensi; et Guilielmo Kinsella, Episcopo Ossoriensi, in suis respective Synodis Dioecesanis edita et promulgata, Hebdomada quarta mensis Julii, A.D. 1831 (Dublin, 1831).

The Bull of His Holiness, Leo XII, extending the Universal Jubilee to the whole Catholic world (Dublin, 1826).

The Rules and Constitutions of the Congregation of St Patrick, written by the Rt Rev. Dr Delany, Bishop of Kildare and Leighlin, who founded this congregation at Tullow, February 2, 1807 [*sic*] *Revised, approved and augmented by his successor, the Rt Rev Dr Doyle* (Manchester, 1826).

Wakefield, Richard, *An account of Ireland, statistical and political*, 2 vols (London, 1812).

Wyse, Thomas, *Historical sketch of the late Catholic Association of Ireland*, 2 vols (London, 1829).

COLLECTIONS OF PRINTED CORRESPONDENCE, MEMOIRS, DIARIES AND BIOGRAPHIES

[Battersby, W.J.], *The life of the Rt Rev. Dr Doyle, compiled from authentic documents by the author of the 'Priesthood vindicated'* (Dublin, 1834, 3rd ed., improved and enlarged, Dublin, 1850).

Bolster, Evelyn, 'The Moylan correspondence in Bishop's House, Killarney: Part 1' *Collect. Hib.*, no. 14 (1971), pp 83–142.

——, 'The Moylan correspondence in Bishop's house, Killarney: Part 2' *Collect. Hib.*, no. 15 (1972), pp 56–109.

Brenan, Martin, *Schools of Kildare and Leighlin, A.D. 1775–1835* (Dublin, 1935).

Butler, Charles, *Historical Memoirs of the English, Irish and Scottish Catholics*, 4 vols (London, 1822).

Carroll, W.G., *A memoir of the Right Rev. James Thomas O'Brien, D.D.* (Dublin, 1875).

Castlereagh (ed.), *Memoirs and Correspondence of Viscount Castlereagh*, 4 vols (London, 1848–9).

Cloncurry, *Personal recollections of the life and times with extracts from the correspondence of Valentine, Lord Cloncurry* (Dublin, 1849).

Comerford, Michael, *Collections relations to the dioceses of Kildare and Leighlin*, 3 vols (Dublin, [1883–6]).

De Bhaldraithe, Tomás (ed.), *Cin lae Amhlaoibh* (Dublin, 1970).

Fitzpatrick, William John, *The life and times of Lord Cloncurry* (Dublin, 1855).

——, *The life, times and correspondence of the Right Rev. Dr Doyle, Bishop of Kildare and Leighlin*, 2 vols (1st ed., Dublin, 1861; revised ed., Dublin 1861 (reprinted, Boston, 1862); 2nd ed., Dublin, 1880, reprinted 1890).

——, *Memoirs of Richard Whately, Archbishop of Dublin, with a glance at his contemporaries and times*, 2 vols (London, 1864).

—— ed., *Correspondence of Daniel O'Connell*, 2 vols (London, 1888).

Guilday, Peter, *The life and times of John England, first bishop of Charleston (1786–1842)*, 2 vols (New York, 1927).

[Lynch, John P.], *The life of Brother Paul J. O'Connor* (Dublin, 1867).

MacDonagh, Michael, *Bishop Doyle* (Dublin, 1896).

McGrath, Michael (ed.), *The diary of Humphrey O'Sullivan*, 4 vols (London, 1928–31).

McHugh, Roger (ed.), *Carlow in '98: The autobiography of William Farrell of Carlow* (Dublin, 1949).

MacHale, John, *The Letters of the Most Reverend John MacHale D.D.* (Dublin, 1847).

MacSuibhne, Peadar (ed.), *Paul Cullen and his contemporaries*, 5 vols (Naas, 1961–77).

Mason, William Shaw, *A statistical account, or parochial survey of Ireland, drawn up from communications of the clergy*, 3 vols (Dublin, 1814–19).

Mayer, J.P. (ed.), *Alexis de Tocqueville, Journeys to England and Ireland* (London, 1958 ed.).

Meagher, William, *Notices of the life and character of his Grace Most Reverend Daniel Murray, late Archbishop of Dublin ... with historical and biographical notes* (Dublin, 1853).

Messmer, Sebastian G., *The works of ... J. England*, 7 vols (Ohio, 1908).

Moran, P.F., *Spicilegium Ossoriense, being a collection of original letters and papers illustrative of the history of the Irish church from the Reformation to the year 1800*, 3 vols (Dublin 1874–84).

——, (ed.), *The letters of Rev James Maher, D.D., late P.P. of Carlow-Graigue, on religious subjects; with a memoir* (Dublin, 1877).

——, *The Catholics of Ireland under the penal laws in the eighteenth century* (Dublin, 1900).

O'Connell, Maurice R. (ed.), *The correspondence of Daniel O'Connell*, 8 vols (Dublin, 1972–81).

Renehan, L.F., *Collections on Irish church history*, 2 vols (Dublin, 1861–74).

Wellington (ed.), *Despatches, correspondence and memoranda of Field Marshal Arthur Duke of Wellington K.G.*, 8 vols (London, 1867–80).

SECONDARY SOURCES

Unpublished Theses

Keenan, Desmond J. 'The Catholic church in Ireland *c.*1800–*c.*1860: a social and socio-logical study' (Queen's University, Belfast, Ph.D. thesis, 1979, Faculty of Economic and Social Sciences).

Power, Conleth J., 'James Doyle, Bishop of Kildare and Leighlin, and the Roman Catholic Relief Movement, 1822–25' (University College Dublin, M.A. thesis, 1968).

Power, John, 'Doyle and Education' (University College Dublin, M.Ed. minor thesis, 1951).

Wallace, Patrick, 'Irish Catechesis – the heritage from James Butler II, Archbishop of Cashel 1774–1791' (Catholic University of America, Ph.D. thesis, 1975).

Published works

Ahern, John, 'The plenary synod of Thurles' in *Irish Ecclesiastical Record*, lxxv (May, 1951), pp 385–403; lxxviii (July, 1952), pp 1–20.

Barry, P.C., 'The legislation of the synod of Thurles, 1850' *Irish Theological Quarterly*, new series, xxvi no. 2 (Apr., 1959), pp 131–66.

Berman, David and Jill, 'Journal of an officer stationed in Naas and Baltinglass,1832–3' in *Journal of the Co. Kildare Archaeological Society*, xv, no. 3 (1973–4), pp 268–78.

Birch, Peter, *St Kieran's College, Kilkenny* (Dublin, 1951).

Bolster, Evelyn, *A history of the diocese of Cork from the penal era to the famine* (Cork, 1989).

Bossy, John, 'The Counter-Reformation and the people of Catholic Ireland, 1596–1641' in T.D. Williams (ed.), *Historical Studies*, viii (1971), pp 155–69.

——, *The English Catholic Community* (London, 1977 pbk).

——, 'Challoner and the Marriage Act' in Eamon Duffy (ed.), *Challoner and his Church* (London, 1981), pp 126–36.

——, *Christianity in the West 1400–1700* (Oxford, 1985).

Bourke, Ulick, *Sermons in Irish-Gaelic by Most Rev. James O'Gallagher* (Dublin, 1881).

Bowen, Desmond J., *The Protestant crusade in Ireland, 1800–70: a study of Catholic-Protestant relations between the act of union and disestablishment* (Dublin, 1978).

——, *Paul Cardinal Cullen and the shaping of modern Irish Catholicism* (Dublin, 1983).

Boyle, Patrick, *The Irish college in Paris (1578–1905) with a brief sketch of the other Irish colleges in France* (London and Dublin, 1905).

——, 'Irish colleges on the continent' *Catholic Encyclopaedia* (New York, 1910) viii, 162–3.

Brady, John and Corish, Patrick J., *The Church under the penal code* in P.J. Corish (ed.), *A History of Irish Catholicism*, vol. iv, no. 2 (Dublin, 1971).

Brady, John, 'Funeral customs of the past' in *Irish Ecclesiastical Record*, fifth series, lxxviii (Nov. 1952), pp 330–9.

Brenan, Martin, *The confraternities of Christian doctrine in Ireland: A.D. 1775–1835* (Dublin, 1934).

——, 'Bishop Keefe of Kildare and Leighlin, A.D. 1702–1787' *Irish Ecclesiastical Record*, fifth series, l (July–Dec. 1937), pp 113–26.

Brenan, M.J., *An ecclesiastical history of Ireland to the year mdcccxxxix* (Dublin, 1864 ed).

Broderick, J.F., *The Holy See and the Irish movement for the repeal of the union with England, 1829–47* (Rome, 1951).

Broeker, Galen, *Rural disorder and police reform in Ireland, 1812–36* (London, 1970).

Brophy, P.J., 'The parish of Killeshin in the 19th century' in *Carloviana*, vol. 1, no. 1 (Jan., 1947), pp 7–11.

——, 'A pioneer Irish educationist' in *Carlovian* (1949), pp 19–30.

Burke, William, P., *The Irish priests in the penal times 1660–1760* (Shannon, 1968 reprint of 1914 1st edition).

Burns, R.E., 'The Irish penal code and some of its historians', *Review of Politics*, xxi (Jan., 1959), pp 276–99.

——, 'The Irish popery laws: a study of eighteenth century legislation and behaviour', *Review of Politics*, xxiv (Oct., 1962), pp 485–508.

——, 'Parsons, priests and people: the rise of Irish anti-clericalism, 1785–89', *Church History*, xxxi (1962), pp 151–63.

Butler, Thomas C., *Journey of an abbey, History of the Augustinians in Dungarvan 1292–1972* (Ballyboden, [1973]).

——, *Near Restful Waters – The Augustinians in County Wexford* (Ballyboden, 1975).

——, *The friars of Fethard* (Ballyboden, 1976).

——, *The Augustinians in Callan, 1467–1977* (Callan, 1977).

——, *John's Lane, History of the Augustinian friars in Dublin 1280–1980* (Dublin, 1983).

——, *A parish and its people: History of Carrig-on-Barrow parish* (Grantstown, Co. Wexford, 1985).

——, *The Augustinians in Cork 1280–1985* (Cork, 1986).

Cannon, Sean, *Irish episcopal meetings, 1788–1882: a juridico-historical study* (Rome, 1979).

Carey, Patrick, *An immigrant bishop: John England's adaptation of Irish Catholicism to American Republicanism* (New York, 1982).

Carrigan, William, *History and antiquities of the diocese of Ossory*, 4 vols (Dublin, 1905).

Castle, Harold, 'Saint Alphonsus Liguori', *Catholic Encyclopaedia* (New York, 1907), i, 334–41.

Chadwick, Owen, *The popes and European revolution* (Oxford, 1981).

Chart, D.A., *Ireland from the Union to Catholic Emancipation 1800–1829* (London, 1910).

Chinnici, Joseph P., *The English Catholic enlightenment: John Lingard and the Cisalpine Movement 1780–1850* (Shepherdstown, U.S.A., 1980).

Clark, Paul, *A free Church in a free society. The ecclesiology of John England, Bishop of Charleston, 1820–1842* (Hartsville, South Carolina, 1982).

Clear, Caitriona, *Nuns in nineteenth century Ireland* (Dublin, 1987).

Coadley, R., *J.K.L. – A great Irish bishop* (Dublin, 1930) [C.T.S. Pamphlet].

Coen, Martin, *The wardenship of Galway* (Galway, 1984).

Cogan, A., *The diocese of Meath, ancient and modern*, 3 vols (Dublin, 1862–70).

Coleman, Ambrose, 'Armagh' *Catholic Encyclopaedia* (New York, 1907), i, 732.

Connell, K.H., *The population of Ireland, 1750–1845* (Oxford, 1950).

——, *Irish peasant society: four historical essays* (Oxford, 1968).

Conrolly, S.J., 'Catholicism in Ulster, 1800–1850', in Peter Roebuck (ed.), *Plantation to partition: Essays in Ulster history in honour of J.L. McCracken* (Belfast, 1981), pp 157–71.

——, *Priests and people in pre-famine Ireland 1780–1845* (Dublin, 1982).

——, 'Religion, Work Discipline and Economic Attitudes: The case of Ireland', in T.M. Devine and David Dickson (ed.), *Ireland and Scotland 1600–1850* (Edinburgh, 1983), pp 235–45.

——, 'The "Blessed Turf"; Cholera and popular panic in Ireland, June 1832', *Irish Historical Studies*, xxxiii, 91 (1983), pp 214–32.

——, 'Religion and history', *Irish Economic and Social History*, x (1983), pp 66–80.

——, *Religion and society in nineteenth-century Ireland* (Dundalk, 1985).

——, 'Marriage in pre-famine Ireland' in Art Cosgrove (ed.), *Marriage in Ireland* (Dublin, 1985), pp 78–98.

Corish Patrick J. (ed.), *A History of Irish Catholicism*, v, fascicules vi-x (Dublin, 1970–1).

——, (ed.), 'Bishop Caulfield's Relatio Status, 1796', *Archivium Hibernicum*, xxviii, (1966), pp 101–13.

——, (ed.), 'Irish College, Rome: Kirby papers', *Archivium Hibernicum*, xxx (1972), pp 29–115; xxxi (1973), pp 1–94; xxxii (1974), pp 1–62.

——, 'Gallicanism at Maynooth: Archbishop Cullen and the Royal Visitation of 1853' in Art Cosgrove and Donal McCartney (ed.), *Studies in Irish history presented to R. Dudley Edwards* (Dublin, 1979), pp 176–89.

——, *The Catholic community in the seventeenth and eighteenth centuries* (Dublin, 1981).

——, 'The Catholic community in the nineteenth-century', *Archivium Hibernicum*, xxxviii, pp 26–33.

——, *The Irish Catholic experience. A historical survey* (Dublin, 1985).

——, 'Catholic marriage under the penal code' in Art Cosgrove (ed.), *Marriage in Ireland* (Dublin, 1985), pp 67–77.

——, *Maynooth College, 1795–1995* (Dublin, 1995).

Cosgrove Art, 'Marriage in Medieval Ireland' in Art Cosgrove (ed.), *Marriage in Ireland* (Dublin, 1985), pp 25–50.

Cragg, Gerald, *The church and the age of reason 1648–1789* (London, 1983 pbk ed.).

Cullen, E.J., *The origin and development of the Irish Vincentian foundations 1833–1933* (Dublin, [1933]).

Cullen, J.B., 'The Augustinians in New Ross', *Irish Ecclesiastical Record*, fifth series, xv (Jan.-June, 1920), pp 302–12.

Cullen, L.M., *The emergence of modern Ireland 1600–1900* (Dublin, 1983 pbk ed.).

Curran, M.J., 'Dr Michael Blake and the re-establishment of the Irish College, Rome', *Reportorium Novum*, 1, no. 2 (1956), pp 434–42.

D'Alton, E.A., 'Penal laws in Ireland' in *Catholic Encyclopaedia* (New York, 1911), xi, 614–16.

Danaher, Kevin, *The year in Ireland* (Cork, 1972).

De Blacam, Aodh, *Gaelic literature surveyed* (Dublin, 1973 ed.).

Degert, Antoine, 'Honore Tournely', *Catholic Encyclopaedia* (New York, 1912), xiv, 800.

De Ghellinck, Joseph, 'Denis Petau (Dionysius Petavius)', *Catholic Encyclopaedia* (New York, 1911), xi, 743–4.

Delamarre, Louis N., 'Jacques-Benigne Bossuet', *Catholic Encyclopaedia* (New York, 1907), ii, 698–702.

Delumeau, Jean, *Catholicism between Luther and Voltaire: a new view of the Counter-Reformation* (English ed., London, 1977).

Directory of the Brigidine Sisters (Dublin, 1956).

Donnelly, J.S., *The land and people of nineteenth-century Cork* (London, 1975).

——, 'Pastorini and Captain Rock: millenarianism and sectarianism in the Rockite movement of 1821–4' in Samuel Clark and J.S. Donnelly, Jr., (ed.), *Irish peasants: violence and political unrest 1780–1914* (Madison, Wisconsin, 1983).

Dowling, E., 'Irish seminaries in the eighteenth century', *Irish Ecclesiastical Record*, fifth series, lviii (July-Dec. 1941), pp 424–42.

Dunford, David 'Dean', *Catholic Encyclopaedia* (New York, 1908), iv, 659–60.

Dunne, Margaret Mary, *Gleanings from the Brigidine Annals* (Carlow, 1945 – 'Private circulation only').

Dunny, Patrick and O'Leary, Michael, *The village of the monks – Duiske Abbey, Graiguenamanagh* (Freshford, 1980).

Evans, E.E., *Irish folk ways* (London, 1957).

Fanning, W.H.W., 'Chapter', *Catholic Encyclopaedia* (New York, 1908), iii, 582–4.

——, 'Conferences, Ecclesiastical', *Catholic Encyclopaedia* (New York, 1908), iv, 213–14.

——, 'Confraternity', *Catholic Encyclopaedia* (New York, 1908), iv, 223.

——, 'Mixed Marriages', *Catholic Encyclopaedia* (New York, 1910), ix, 698–9.

——, 'Vicar General', *Catholic Encyclopaedia* (New York, 1912), xv, 402–3.

Fenning, Hugh, *The undoing of the friars in Ireland: a study of the novitiate question in the eighteenth century* (Louvain, 1972).

——, 'Cork imprints of Catholic historical interest 1805–1830: a provisional check list (part 2)' in *Jnl of the Cork historical and archaeological society*, 101 (1996), pp 115–42.

FitzGerald, Garret, 'Estimates for baronies of minimum levels of Irish speaking among successive decennial cohorts, 1771–1781 to 1861–1871', *Royal Irish Academy Proceedings*, Section C, lxxxiv (1984), pp 117–55.

Fitzpatrick, J.D., 'The beginnings of the Christian Brothers – their relations with various ecclesiastical authorities' in *Proceedings of the Irish Catholic Historical Committee* (1961), pp 23–7.

Flood, W.H. Grattan, *History of the diocese of Ferns* (Waterford, 1916).

Ford, Franklin L., *Europe 1780–1830* (London, 1970).

Freeman, T.W., *Post-famine Ireland* (Manchester, 1957).

'From cabin to college' *Newbridge Quarterly*, 5, no. 18 (Easter, 1936), unpaginated; 5, no. 19 (Summer, 1936); 5, no. 20 (Autumn, 1936); and 5, no. 21 (Winter, 1936).

Fullerton, Georgiana, *A sketch of the life of the late Father Henry Young of Dublin* (London, 1874).

Garner, William, *Carlow architectural heritage* (Dublin, 1980).

Gash, Norman, *Lord Liverpool* (London, 1984).

——, *Mr Secretary Peel* (2nd ed., London, 1985).

Gibbons, Margaret, *Glimpses of Catholic Ireland in the eighteenth century: restoration of the daughters of St Brigid by Most Rev. Dr Delany* (Dublin, 1932).

Gladstone, W.E., *The Vatican decrees in their bearing on civil allegiance: a political expostulation* (London, 1874).

Glancey, M.C., 'Christian Doctrine Confraternity', *Catholic Encyclopaedia* (New York, 1908), iii, 711.

Glynn, Jarlath, 'The Catholic Church in Wexford Town, 1800–1858', *The Past*, no. 15 (1984), pp 5–53.

Griffith, Arthur (ed.), *Meagher of the sword* (Dublin, 1916).

Gwynn Denis, 'Bishop Doyle and Catholic Emancipation', *Studies*, xvii (Sept. 1928), pp 353–68.

J.M. Harty, 'Probabilism', *Catholic Encyclopaedia* (New York, 1911), pp 441–6.

Healy, John, *Maynooth College: its centenary history 1795–1895* (Dublin, 1895).

Holmes, J. Derek and Bickers, Bernard, *A short history of the Catholic Church* (London, 1983).

Holweck, F.G., 'Feasts', *Catholic Encyclopaedia* (New York, 1909), vi, 21–3.

Hoppen, K. Theodore, *Elections, politics and society in Ireland 1832–1885* (Oxford, 1984).

Hore, P.H., *History of the town and county of Wexford*, 5 vols (London, 1900–1906).

Hughes, E.W., 'On penal day sites in the Barrow Valley', *Old Kilkenny Review*, 2 no. 2 (1980), pp 44–8.

Hutch William, *Nano Nagle, her life, her labour and their fruits* (Dublin, 1875).

Jackson, Patricia 'The holy wells of County Kildare', *Journal of the Co. Kildare Archaeological Society*, xvi, no. 2 (1979–80), pp 133–61.

Johnson, Christine, *Developments in the Roman Catholic Church in Scotland 1789–1829* (Edinburgh, 1983).

Keenan, Desmond J., *The Catholic Church in nineteenth-century Ireland* (Dublin, 1983).

Kennedy, Liam, 'The Roman Catholic Church and economic growth in nineteenth-century Ireland', *Economic and Social Review*, x, 1 (1978), pp 45–60.

Kennedy, T.P., *Church building* in Patrick J. Corish (ed.), *A History of Irish Catholicism*, v, fascicule 8 (Dublin, 1970).

Kerr, Donal A., *Peel, priests and politics. Sir Robert Peel's administration and the Roman Catholic Church in Ireland 1841–1846* (Oxford, 1982).

——, 'James Browne, bishop of Kilmore, 1829–65', *Breifne*, vi, no. 22 (1983–4), pp 109–54.

——, *'A nation of beggars'? Priests, people and politics in Famine Ireland, 1846–1852* (Oxford, 1994).

Killen, W.D., *The ecclesiastical history of Ireland* (London, 1875).

Kingston, John, 'The Carmelite nuns in Dublin, 1644–1829', *Reportorium Novum*, iii, no. 2 (1964), pp 331–60.

Larkin, Emmet, 'Church and state in Ireland in the nineteenth century', *Church History* (1962), pp 294–306.

——, 'Economic growth, capital investment and the Roman Catholic Church in nineteenth-century Ireland', *American Historical Review*, lxxii (1967), pp 852–84.

——, 'The devotional revolution in Ireland, 1850–75', *American Historical Review*, lxxvii (1972), pp 625–52.

——, 'Church, state and nation in modern Ireland' *American Historical Review*, lxxx (1975), pp 1244–76.

——, *The historical dimension of Irish Catholicism* (New York, 1976).

Lee, Joseph, 'The Ribbonmen' in T.D. Williams (ed.), *Secret societies in Ireland* (Dublin, 1973), pp 26–35.

Macaulay, Ambrose, *Dr Russell of Maynooth* (London, 1983).

——, *William Crolly. Archbishop of Armagh, 1835–49* (Dublin, 1994).

McCaffrey, J., *History of the Catholic Church in the nineteenth century*, 2 vols (London, 1909).

MacCurtain, Margaret, 'Pre-famine peasantry in Ireland: definition and theme', *Irish University Review*, iv, 2 (1974), pp 188–98.

MacDonagh, Oliver 'The politicization of the Irish Catholic bishops, 1800–1850', *Historical Journal*, xviii (1975), pp 37–53.

McDowell, R.B., *Public opinion and government policy in Ireland 1801–1846* (London, 1952).

McGrath, Thomas, 'Archbishop Slattery and the episcopal controversy on Irish national education, 1838–1841', in *Archivium Hibernicum*, xxxix (1984), pp 13–31.

——, 'Interdenominational relations in pre-famine Tipperary' in William Nolan and Thomas McGrath (ed.), *Tipperary: history and society* (Dublin. 1985), pp 256–87.

——, 'Bishops of Kildare and Leighlin, 1752–1819' unpublished paper delivered to Carlow College seminar, 25 April 1986.

——, 'The historiography of the papers of Bishop James Doyle, O.S.A. (1786–1834) in the Kildare and Leighlin diocesan archives' in *Archivium Hibernicum*, xliii (1988), pp 88–94.

——, 'The Tridentine evolution of modern Irish Catholicism, 1563–1962: a re-examination of the "Devotional Revolution" thesis' in *Recusant History*, vol. 20, no. 4 (October, 1991), pp 512–23.

——, *Politics, interdenominational relations and education in the public ministry of Bishop James Doyle of Kildare and Leighlin, 1786–1834* (Dublin, 1998).

Machin, G.I.T., *The Catholic question in English politics, 1820–1830* (Oxford, 1964).

MacLysaght, Edward, *Irish life in the seventeenth century* (Dublin, 1979 ed.).

McNamee, Brian, 'The "Second Reformation" in Ireland', *Irish Theological Quarterly*, xxxiii (1966), pp 39–64.

——, 'J.K.L.'s letter on the union of churches', *Irish Theological Quarterly*, xxxix (1969), pp 46–69.

MacNeill, Máire, *The festival of Lughnasa: a study of the survival of the Celtic festival of the beginning of the harvest* (Oxford, 1962).

MacSuibhne, Peadar 'The early history of Carlow College', *Irish Ecclesiastical Record*, fifth series, lxiii (July-Dec., 1943), pp 230–48.

——, (ed.), *Knockbeg Centenary Book* (Carlow, [1948]).

——, 'The beginnings of Carlow College', *Capuchin Annual* (1960), pp 290–9.

——, *Saint Brigid and the shrines of Kildare* (Naas, [1972]).

——, *Parish of Killeshin/Graiguecullen* (Portlaoise, 1972).

——, *'98 in Carlow* (Carlow, 1974).

——, *Clonegal Parish* (Carlow, 1975).

——, *Rathangan* (n.p., 1975).

——, *Carlovia* 1 (Carlow, 1976).

——, *Carlovia* 2 (Carlow, 1977).

——, *Carlovia* 3 (Carlow, 1977).

——, *Kildare in '98* (Naas, 1978).

——, *Ballon and Rathoe* ([Carlow], 1980).

Malcolm, Elizabeth, *'Ireland sober, Ireland free': drink and temperance in nineteenth century Ireland* (Dublin, 1986).

Marnane, Denis G., *Land and violence: a history of West Tipperary from 1660* (Tipperary, 1985).

Martin, F.X., 'The Rossiters of Rathmacknee Castle I, 1169–1627' in *The Past*, no. 5 (1949), pp 103–16.

——, 'The Rossiters of Rathmacknee Castle II' in *The Past*, no. 6 (1950), pp 13–25; 'II John Baptist Rossiter, O.S.A.', pp 26–44.

——, 'The Irish Augustinians in Rome, 1656-1956' in J.F. Madden (ed.), *The Irish Augustinians in Rome* (Rome, 1956), pp 16–74.

Meehan, James J., *The patriot Bishop Doyle, 1786–1834 – 'J.K.L.'* (Dublin, 1967) [C.T.S. Pamphlet].

Meigs S.A., *The Reformations in Ireland. Tradition and confessionalism, 1400–1690* (Dublin, 1997).

Miller, David W., 'Irish Catholicism and the Great Famine', *Journal of Social History*, ix, no. 1 (Sept., 1975), pp 81–98.

Miller, Samuel J., *Portugal and Rome c.1748–1830. An aspect of the Catholic enlightenment* (Rome, 1978).

Morris W.B., 'James Doyle, bishop of Kildare and Leighlin' in *Irish Ecclesiastical Record*, fourth series (Jan.-June, 1897), pp 22–38.

——, 'Bishop Doyle and his biographers', *Irish Ecclesiastical Record*, fourth series (Jan.-June, 1897), pp 289–304.

Morrissey, Thomas, *As one sent. Peter Kenney SJ 1779–1841. His mission in Ireland and North America* (Dublin, 1996).

Murphy, Ignatius, 'Some attitudes to religious freedom and ecumenism in pre-emancipation Ireland', *Irish Ecclesiastical Record*, fifth series, cv (Feb., 1966), pp 93–104.

——, *The diocese of Killaloe in the eighteenth century* (Dublin, 1991).

——, *The diocese of Killaloe 1800–1850* (Dublin, 1992).

Murphy, John A., 'The support of the Catholic clergy in Ireland, 1750–1850' *Historical Studies*, v (1965), pp 103–21.

——, 'Priests and people in modern Irish history', *Christus Rex,* xxiii (1969), pp 235–59.

Nolan, William, *Fassadinin: land, settlement and society in south-east Ireland 1600–1850* (Dublin, 1979).

Norman, E.R., *The Catholic Church and Ireland in the age of rebellion, 1859–1873* (London, 1965).

Normoyle, M.C., *A tree is planted – the life and times of Edmund Rice* (2nd ed., n.p., 1976, 'private circulation').

——, *A companion to 'A tree is planted'* (n.p., 1977, 'private circulation').

——, *The Roman correspondence* (n.p., 1978, 'private circulation').

O'Donoghue, Patrick, 'Causes of the opposition to tithes, 1830–38', *Studia Hibernica,* no. 5 (1965), pp 7–28.

——, 'Opposition to tithe payment in 1830–31', *Studia Hibernica,* no. 6 (1966), pp 69–98.

——, 'Opposition to tithe payment in 1832–3', *Studia Hibernica,* no. 12 (1972), pp 77–108.

O'Dwyer, Peter, *The Irish Carmelites (of the ancient observance)* (Dublin, 1988).

O'Farrell, Patrick, 'Millenialism, messianism and utopianism in Irish history', *Anglo-Irish Studies,* ii (1976), pp 45–68.

Ó Fearghail, Fearghus, 'The Catholic Church in County Kilkenny 1600–1800' in W. Nolan, K. Whelan (ed.), *Kilkenny: history and society* (Dublin, 1990), pp 197–249.

O'Fearghail, Liam, 'Fr John Gahan, P.P. Rathvilly' in Peadar MacSuibhne (ed.), *Knockbeg Centenary Book* (Carlow, [1948]), pp 103–4.

O'Ferrall, Fergus, '"The only lever ...": the Catholic priest in Irish politics, 1823–29', *Studies,* lxx, 280 (1981), pp 308–24.

——, *Catholic Emancipation, Daniel O'Connell and the birth of Irish democracy 1820–30* (Dublin, 1985).

O'Hanlon, John and O'Leary, Edward, *History of the Queen's County,* 2 vols (Kilkenny, 1981 reprint).

'Omurethi', 'Customs peculiar to certain days, formerly observed in County Kildare', *Kildare Archaeological Society Journal,* v (1906–8), pp 439–55.

O'Riordan, Michael, 'The Irish College in Rome', *Catholic Encyclopaedia* (New York, 1910), viii, 158.

O'Shea, James, *Priest, politics and society in post-famine Ireland – a study of County Tipperary 1850–1891* (Dublin, 1983).

Ó Súilleabháin, Seán, *Irish wake amusements* (Cork, 1967).

O'Toole, Edward, 'The holy wells of County Carlow', *Bealoideas,* 4 (1936), pp 3–23; 107–30.

Ó Tuathaigh, Gearóid, *Ireland before the famine, 1798–1848* (Dublin, 1972).

Pakenham, Thomas, *The year of liberty* (London, 1972 pbk).

Peres, Damiao (ed.), *Historia da Igreja de Portugal,* 4 vols (Barcelos and Porto, 1967–1971).

Phillips, W.A. (ed.), *History of the Church of Ireland from the earliest times to the present day,* 3 vols (London, 1933–4).

Pollen, J.H., 'Society of Jesus', *Catholic Encyclopaedia* (New York, 1912), xiv, 81–110.

Reynolds, James, A., *The Catholic Emancipation crisis in Ireland 1823–1829* (Westport, Connecticut, 1970 reprint).

Renan, Myles V., *An apostle of Catholic Dublin – Father Henry Young* (Dublin, 1944).
——, 'Archbishop Murray 1768–1852' in *Irish Ecclesiastical Record*, fifth series, lxxvii (Apr., 1952), pp 241–9.
Ryan, Eileen, *Monasterevan parish, Co. Kildare* (Naas, 1958).
Rude, George, *Revolutionary Europe 1783–1815* (London, 1964).
Scott, Geoffrey, '"The times are fast approaching" Bishop Charles Walmesley, O.S.B. (1722–1797) as prophet', *Journal of Ecclesiastical History*, 36 (Oct., 1985), pp 590–604.
Shearman, J.F. , *Loca Patriciana* (Dublin, 1879).
Slater, T., 'Mental Reservation', *Catholic Encyclopaedia* (New York, 1910), ix, 334–41.
Swords, Liam, *A hidden Church. The diocese of Achonry 1689–1818* (Dublin, 1997).
'The Dominicans in Newbridge', *Newbridge College Annual* (1908), pp 4–12.
'The story of the college', *Newbridge College Magazine* (1900), pp 40–52.
Thomas, Keith, *Religion and the decline of magic* (London, 1973, reprint).
Thompson, E.P., *The making of the English working class* (London, 1968 ed.).
Thurston, Herbert, 'Calendar', *Catholic Encyclopaedia* (New York, 1908), iii, 158–66.
Tierney, Mark, *Murroe and Boher – The history of an Irish country parish* (Dublin, 1966).
'Two unpublished MSS of J.K.L.', in *Carlovian* (1914), pp 216–21.
Tynan, Michael, *Catholic instruction in Ireland, 1720–1950. The O'Reilly/Donlevy catechetical tradition* (Dublin, 1985).
Walker, Linus H., *The purpose of his will* [Bishop Daniel Delany] (Galway, 1981).
Wall, Maureen, 'Catholic loyalty to king and pope in eighteenth century Ireland', *Irish Catholic Historical Committee Proceedings* (1960), pp 17–24.
——, *The penal laws, 1691–1760* (Dundalk, 1976 reprint).
Wall, Thomas, *The sign of Dr Hay's Head* (Dublin, 1958).
——, 'Catholic Periodicals of the Past' *Irish Ecclesiastical Record*, fifth series, 101 (Jan.-June, 1964), pp 234–44; 289–303; 375–88; 102 (July-Dec., 1964), pp 17–27.
Walsh, T.J., *Nano Nagle and the Presentation Sisters* (Dublin, 1959).
Walsh, William, 'The alleged Gallicanism of Maynooth, and of the Irish clergy', *Dublin Review*, third series (Jan.-Apr., 1880), pp 210–53.
Whelan, Kevin, 'The Catholic parish, the Catholic chapel and village development in Ireland', *Irish Geography* 16 (1983), pp 1–15.
——, 'The Catholic Church in County Tipperary, 1700–1900' in William Nolan and Thomas McGrath (ed.), *Tipperary: history and society* (Dublin, 1985), pp 215–55.
Whyte, J.H., 'The appointment of Catholic bishops in nineteenth-century Ireland', *Catholic Historical Review*, xlviii (1962), pp 12–32.
Wright, A.D., *The Counter-Reformation* (London, 1982).

WORKS OF REFERENCE

Boylan, Henry, *Dictionary of Irish biography* (Dublin, 1978).
Brady, John, *Catholics and Catholicism in the eighteenth century press* (Maynooth, 1965).
Brady, William M., *The episcopal succession in England, Scotland and Ireland. A.D. 1400–1875*, 3 vols (Rome, 1877).
Burtchaell, G.D. and Sadleir, T.U. (ed.), *Alumni Dublinenses* (Dublin, 1935 ed.).

Carlen, Claudia, *The Papal encyclicals (1740–1981)*, 5 vols (n.p. [McGrath Publishing Co., U.S.A.], 1981).

Catholic Directory, Almanac and Registry (Dublin, 1836–), under various titles.

Catholic Encyclopaedia, 16 vols (New York, 1907–1914); *Supplement*, vol. xvii (New York, 1922).

Dictionary of National Biography, Leslie Stephen and S. Lee (ed.), (London, 1910–).

Keane, Edward, Phair, P.B., and Sadleir, T.U. (ed.), *King's Inns admission papers 1607–1867* (Dublin, 1982).

Lewis, Samuel, *Topographical dictionary of Ireland*, 2 vols (London, 1837).

Moody, T.W., Martin, F.X., Byrne, F.J., *A new history of Ireland*, ix (Oxford, 1984).

Young, Henry, *Catholic Directory* (Dublin, 1821).

Index